LIBRARY MANAGEMENT 101

ALA Editions purchases fund advocacy, awareness, and accreditation programs for library professionals worldwide.

LIBRARY MANAGEMENT 101

A PRACTICAL GUIDE

EDITED BY Diane L. Velasquez

An imprint of the American Library Association | Chicago • 2013

Diane L. Velasquez is program director of the Library and Information Management and Business Information Management programs and lecturer at the University of South Australia. She teaches information governance, readers' advisory, and management and supervises the placement into industry of her students and the capstone project course. She was previously an assistant professor at a university in the Midwest. Her research interests include management and e-government in public libraries, readers' advisory, and librarians' perception of readers of genre fiction, especially the romance genre. Dr. Velasquez has a PhD in LIS from the University of Missouri, an MBA in management from Golden Gate University in San Francisco, an MLS from the University of Arizona, and a BA from San Jose State University. She spent 20 years in corporate America before switching careers to librarianship and academe.

Printed in the United States of America

17 16 15 14 13 5 4 3 2 1

ISBNs: 978-0-8389-1148-8 (paper); 978-0-8389-9502-0 (PDF)

Library of Congress Cataloging-in-Publication Data

Library management 101: a practical guide / edited by Diane L. Velasquez.
pages cm
Includes bibliographical references and index.
ISBN 978-0-8389-1148-8 (alk. paper)
1. Library administration—United States. 2. Library administration—Canada. I. Velasquez, Diane, editor of compilation.
Z678.L4725 2013
025.1—dc23 2012044514

Cover design by Karen Sheets de Gracia. Image ©oriontrail/Shutterstock.
Text design by Adrianna Sutton in Stemple Schneidler and Futura.

∞ This paper meets the requirements of ANSI/NISO Z39.48–1992 (Permanence of Paper).

For Rich and Lisa—both of you have kept me sane during a very difficult time. Thanks.

—Diane

CONTENTS

Supplemental materials, including a companion bibliography of references and further readings are available online at www.alaeditions.org/webextras.

PREFACE

Library and information science (LIS) schools accredited by the American Library Association (ALA) don't all consider a management course to be a requirement. Many of the schools view a specialty course on academic libraries, public libraries, and so forth to be enough of an introduction to the topic of management for LIS students. I disagree wholeheartedly, but then I am not an unbiased viewer on this subject. I have taught the overview management course every semester for the past five years at an ALA-accredited LIS school in the Midwest.

The sad fact is that the majority of students in LIS programs don't believe they will be managers of anything, at any time or in any type of library, in the United States or Canada. I beg to differ. Even if only professional librarians or paraprofessionals, the majority of us manage something—a section of books, a budget, students, volunteers, our time, acquisitions, reference collections, children and youth materials, technology, facilities . . . I could go on and on. All of us are managing something all of the time. Just because what we do isn't formally called management doesn't mean that it isn't management.

HOW THIS BOOK CAME ABOUT

This book originated with my realization, as an LIS professor teaching management, that no adequate textbooks in this field existed. Regardless of the textbook I would choose, either from within or outside of the LIS field, students would complain about it. Other professors in LIS departments faced a similar dilemma; they would use only parts of the books available, choose books from outside of the LIS field, or use articles from all over the LIS, management, and public administration literature, essentially creating homegrown course packs. What we all needed, and wanted, was a straightforward treatment of the basics of management specific to the LIS field. I decided to fill this void, and the result is this management textbook.

This textbook pulls together best practices from people who teach management at ALA-accredited LIS schools, both throughout the

United States and in Canada, as well as from people who have experience working in academic and public libraries. Many of us also have practical management experience. The outline for the book started from a 15-week course syllabus that grew to include topics and elements from our students' information "wish lists." Students expressed interest in learning about grant writing, diversity, outsourcing, and managing facilities, and these topics are included in this book. The chapters together offer a solid general overview of management within academic, public, and special library settings.

This book does not address school libraries, because school libraries or library media centers tend to be specialized management situations due to their location—within schools—and their audience—children and young adults. Many excellent books on school libraries and media centers have been written over the past few years. Some examples are Jean Donham's (2008) *Enhancing Teaching and Learning*, Betty J. Morris's (2010) *Administering the School Library Media Center*, Barbara Stein Martin and Marco Zannier's (2009) *Fundamentals of School Library Media Management*, and Blanche Woolls's (2008) *The School Library Media Manager*. Additionally, the American Association of School Librarians (AASL) has come out with new standards for the 21st-century learner as well as workbooks, guidebooks, and online resources that incorporate these new standards:

Empowering Learners: Guidelines for School Library Programs (AASL, 2009a)
Standards for the 21st-Century Learner in Action (AASL, 2009b)
A Planning Guide for Empowering Learners (AASL, 2012a)
A 21st-Century Approach to School Librarian Evaluation (AASL, 2012b)

PEOPLE AND MANAGEMENT

Managing any people is like herding cats.
—Warren Bennis (1999, p. 7)

Management is complicated because the majority of the time it involves managing people, and all of the different aspects of those people. This book discusses different types of management, but the one aspect they all have in common is people. People are the basis of the organizations that we call libraries and information centers, and if you treat (i.e., manage) your people well, they will serve the organization well. I recently presented a case as part of a management course I am teaching; in it, the CEO comments that he wants his people to be excited to come to work every day. This is a sentiment that we, as managers, should share because happy employees make for happy patrons.

References

American Association of School Librarians. (2009a). *Empowering learners: Guidelines for school library programs.* Chicago, IL: Author.

American Association of School Librarians. (2009b). *Standards for the 21st-century learner in action.* Chicago, IL: Author.

American Association of School Librarians. (2012a). *A planning guide for empowering learners* (online program assessment and planning module). Chicago, IL: Author and Britannica Digital Learning.

American Association of School Librarians. (2012b). *A 21st-century approach to school librarian evaluation.* Chicago, IL: Author.

Bennis, W. (1999). *Managing people is like herding cats.* Provo, UT: Executive Excellence Publishing.

Donham, J. (2008). *Enhancing teaching and learning* (2nd ed.). New York, NY: Neal-Schuman.

Martin, B. S., & Zannier, M. (2009). *Fundamentals of school library media management: A how-to-do-it manual.* New York, NY: Neal-Schuman.

Morris, B. J. (2010). *Administering the school library media center.* Santa Barbara, CA: Libraries Unlimited.

Woolls, B. (2008). *The school library media manager.* Westport, CT: Libraries Unlimited.

ACKNOWLEDGMENTS

The collaborators for this book were brave souls who agreed to go on a journey with someone who, as usual, bit off a bit more than I could chew by agreeing to edit and then write half the chapters when some folks pulled out due to other commitments. The person who should be my coeditor—and if there's a second edition will be—is Lisa K. Hussey from Simmons College, who wrote both theory chapters as well as those on organizational communication, conflict negotiation and mediation, and diversity, and who also cowrote the future trends chapter with me. She has on this and other occasions saved me. We work well together.

The other collaborators deserve mention as well: Mary Wilkins Jordan from Simmons College, who wrote the strategic planning and leadership chapters; Jennifer Campbell-Meier from the University of Alabama, who wrote the assessment and evaluation chapter; Lenora Berendt from the Berkeley (IL) Public Library, who wrote the facility management chapter; Cathy Hakala-Ausperk from Kent State University, who wrote the grants chapter; and Heather Hill from the University of Western Ontario, who wrote the outsourcing chapter. They have all been patient with the editing process and contributed wonderful insights through their chapters.

The folks at ALA Editions have been great as well. At one point over the summer I thought this puppy wouldn't get completed due to some personal issues, and Michael Jeffers and Amy Knauer, my editors, were patient and wonderful.

1
INTRODUCTION TO MANAGEMENT

Diane L. Velasquez

Management is about managing people as well as the places where they work and the activities they undertake. Management is an art, not a science. Why? Well, management is mainly about managing people, and people, when being managed, tend to react emotionally, not rationally, because they are emotional beings. Many theories of management are written based upon the idea that people will react rationally, but because management involves people who, thanks to emotions, cannot be counted on to behave rationally in all situations at all times, it will never be a wholly rational science.

PROFESSIONAL ACCREDITATION AND DEVELOPMENT

Most professional librarians will have a master's degree in library and information science called an MLIS or MLS. Other staff members are considered paraprofessional because they don't have an MLIS but they may have a bachelor's of arts or science degree (BA or BS), an associate's degree, or some technical library degree. Other paraprofessionals have no degree beyond a high school diploma and have received mostly on-the-job training, a combination that can be just as viable as an advanced degree. Some directors, deans, and senior management may have a doctorate, or doctor of philosophy (PhD), a research degree that is received after writing a dissertation thesis (i.e., a book-length research paper). The PhD can come before or after the MLIS. If in a law library, some directors or deans will have a juris doctorate (JD), which is a law degree. Still others will have a master's of business administration (MBA) or a master's of public administration (MPA). Again, it all depends. Many of us have a combination of degrees.

Those people who want to work in an academic library may find that there is a requirement for a second master's degree in any subject of interest—English, history, economics, physics, and so forth—so it could conceivably be a master's of science or arts (MS or MA). Those with the MLIS/MLS and a second master's degree are considered subject specialists in academic libraries. Are you confused yet? The number and variety of degrees available are staggering. Some people appear to enjoy collecting degrees, while others will pursue just what they need to do their jobs. The specific degree really doesn't matter as long as it meets the qualifications for the job at hand.

The idea of professional development will be brought up as you wind your way through library school and look at finishing. I can already hear those of you at the end of your program: "What, I need more school?" Yes. As professional librarians, all of us need to keep up with what is going on in the field, and this can be accomplished through a number of different ways: reading journals offered through professional memberships in the American Library Association (ALA), Public Library Association (PLA, a division of ALA), Association of College and Research Libraries (ACRL, a division of ALA), and so on; going to conferences and attending sessions; signing up for webinars; and taking continuing education sessions available through national, regional, state, and local associations.

If you are thinking of a career in administration, you will need more than the typical overview course in management offered at your library school, as this will not be enough to prepare you for being a department head or director of a library. This book is a good start toward that end, but be prepared to take many more courses.

If a directorship or dean position is an ultimate goal, there is a definite set of courses that you should consider; if you are up for it, perhaps seek an MPA or MBA. A core course list would include accounting, finance, marketing, human resources management, labor relations (especially if the library system being considered has unions), economics, advocacy, research methods (quantitative and qualitative), strategic planning, public speaking, facilities management, and project management. Most of these courses are available through professional development, but with the number of courses involved, pursuing a master's degree would be another way to formally take the courses.

HOW THIS BOOK IS ORGANIZED

The theoretical models of management underpin how departments and organizations are run, so this book starts off with an examination of the classical and modern theories of management in Chapters 2 and 3. Max Weber and Frederick Taylor are, in many ways, the fathers of the modern management movements of today. Weber's theories of bureaucracy should be familiar material to those working in libraries and other information-based organizations, as many such organizations have their roots in bureaucracy and hierarchical models. Frederick Taylor's scientific management is what Melvil Dewey used when he started working in library management in the late 1800s and early 1900s. Dewey viewed library work as task based and used scientific management as a basis for his ideas. He thought many of the tasks could be performed by the lesser-paid female staff who made up the bulk of the staff for libraries in his day (Wiegand, 1996). When Dewey began managing libraries in the late 1800s, men ran the show for the most part, and women were the labor force. Today, employment environments are much more evolved with, hopefully, better-paid staff who are managed well by both males and females.

The most important people in any organization are those who do the work—the library's human resources. Thus, Chapter 4 discusses human resources management, focusing on the nuts and bolts as well as the laws behind what it takes to manage people, including a brief look at the role of unions, their contracts, and member relationships.

Once the people are in place, the management structures need to be detailed for the rest of the organization. This is where strategic planning, the subject of Chapter 5, comes into play. Everything in the organization should be considered from the viewpoints expressed in the organization's mission and vision. If an organization doesn't have a sound mission and vision, it will be difficult to build a road map for where the organization is headed. Once the mission and vision are established, the rest of the elements—goals, objectives, and so forth—can be developed from them.

Implementing a strategic plan takes strong leadership and excellent decision-making skills, the subjects of Chapter 6. Bad leadership seems easy enough to recognize, but what defines good leadership? Why are some people better at leading than others? Can leadership be taught? I believe it can be by, first, learning to "know yourself" (Bennis, 1999, p. 103). The other ingredients leaders share, according to Bennis (2009), are a guiding vision, passion, and integrity. Once you know yourself, you will be able to discover the type of leader you are and learn to become a better one (Bennis, 2003). Creative leaders make sure their people understand that everyone is in this together, thus creating an environment in which leadership can grow and the people feel nurtured. Toward this end are these six things that a good leader creates:

1. A compelling vision
2. A climate of trust
3. Meaning
4. Success
5. A healthy, empowering environment
6. Flat, flexible, adaptive, decentralized systems and organizations (Bennis, 1999, pp. 95–98)

Once you have a great leader, a fantastic strategic plan, and fabulous people, the next step is to learn how to communicate well within your organization, the subject of Chapter 7. The cornerstone here is always to communicate what is going on in the organization. Avoid keeping secrets and discourage gossiping, both of which will lead to a negative work environment. Encouraging communication is key, and the transfer should go both ways—up and down (vertical) and back and forth (horizontal)—so that all lines of communication are open.

The organizational culture also plays a role in creating a comfortable working environment, especially in times of change—a constant in today's employment sector. Chapter 8 takes a look at both change management and organizational culture. The ability to get things done well in cooperation with one another should not be undervalued. After all, who wants to work in a place that has an atmosphere so thick you could cut it with a knife? The group dynamics of an organization often originate with the leaders at the top and are the result of a combination of factors that together define how members of the organization interact. As Schein (2003) discusses, the artifacts of the organization are the visible, tangible structures and processes that every group collects and organizes; the espoused values and beliefs of the group are embodied in the organization's strategies, goals, and philosophies; and the underlying assumptions, often taken for granted, come from the beliefs, perceptions, thoughts, and feelings shared by everyone in the group.

Once the organization "knows itself," it's time to let others know about it. If no one knows the library is there, after all, who will use the services and programs? Most of us like to believe that everyone realizes that our libraries are out there, but do they know what our libraries offer? Marketing, the topic of Chapter 9, is the strategy to employ to get the word out, and all types of libraries should market their services. Marketing efforts can be as simple as word of mouth, posting flyers, or sending e-mails or more far-reaching, such as advertisements in the newspaper or on the radio—anything that lets the community know what is going on at the library.

Marketing takes money, as do many other aspects of library operations. Financially managing a library is something all library directors, deans, and department heads need to know how to do, and librarians will sometimes be tasked with managing portions of the budget, so they, too, need to be aware of how the numbers work. Chapter 10 offers an overview of financial management basics, with an examination of the different types of funding and the rules associated with receiving and spending funds. Where does the money come from to finance the library? This often depends on the type of library. Public libraries are funded primarily through property taxes. Academic libraries come in many different types—public, private, nonprofit private, for-profit private, and so on—and thus their funding sources vary; for example, publically funded academic libraries receive funds from two sources—income taxes that are allocated through state legislatures and student tuitions and fees that are paid every semester. Special libraries are funded in many different ways as well.

Responsible financial management allows libraries to pursue their mission of providing services and developing programs that will benefit their target audiences. When a library undertakes a project, the management team or director will want the project to be assessed and evaluated to find out how well it did. If the particular project is going to be repeated, assessment and evaluation can show where problems exist and which aspects went well. Chapter 11 discusses both assessment, determining the good and the bad in a program, and evaluation, assigning numbers to the assessment so it can be quantified or, if the evaluation is qualitative, measuring through observations, focus groups, or interviews. No matter the method, the bottom line is to find out how well the program went and how to improve it for the next time.

Chapter 12 turns its attention to the internal and external stakeholders of the organization. When looking at internal and external stakeholders for a library or information center, the idea is to discover how well these stakeholders are served. Internal stakeholders include employees, the parent organization, and department, and external stakeholders can be people who donate money, employees, city workers . . . the list can go on and on.

Ethics and confidentiality, the subject of Chapter 13, are at the heart of library service. Guidelines such as those offered by the ALA—for example, the ALA Code of Ethics and the Library Bill of Rights—are valuable tools for library service. How well we provide information to patrons and keep this information confidential reflects on organizational integrity. Many times our personal viewpoints need to be parked at the door when we walk into work because we may or may not agree with someone, but this does not give us, as librarians, the right to censor a book choice. Other professional organizations, such as the American Association of Law Libraries (AALL), Medical Library Association (MLA), and Special Library Association (SLA), also have codes of ethics similar to ALA's but with guidelines specific to their particular focus, such as law, health sciences, or special librarianship. The full text of the ALA, AALL, and MLA codes and the Library Bill of Rights is included at the end of the chapter.

Strong library services result from cooperative working relationships in an effective work environment—aspects of which, because people are involved, may require routine maintenance. Chapter 14 explains the nature of conflict and how to resolve it in the workplace through such techniques as negotiation and mediation. Conflict happens all the time, and addressing conflict when it happens, instead of letting it fester, is always best. Negotiations between two people in conflict may respond better to mediation.

Chapter 15 examines diversity, another critical aspect of a strong work environment. Diverse workplaces usually allow for richer environments and experiences for the people working there and those patrons who interact in the library. Defining what exactly diversity is can be difficult, but every organization has to determine for itself how to define and promote diversity in its workplace. ALA does so through its Spectrum Scholarship Program (www.ala.org/offices/diversity/spectrum), an effort designed to address the underrepresentation of minorities in the library workforce.

Facilities management, the subject of Chapter 16, shifts the focus from working with people to managing buildings and dealing with any problems that arise with their physical aspects, both interior and exterior, such as replacing worn carpeting or painting exterior walls. Energy management is another important part of physical buildings that focuses on maintaining a comfortable and energy-efficient environment through regulation of temperature and monitoring electrical sources and online services. The final piece of the facility has to do with safety and security. Today's buildings can be secured in many different ways, from old-fashioned keys to high-tech swipe cards and punch-in pass codes.

Information technology (IT) management, Chapter 17's topic, generally involves troubleshooting and repair for the technological infrastructure, such as computers and electrical panels. Such tasks are not always the director's or dean's responsibility, but in medium and small libraries they might be. IT management has become a large part of the library today, something no one could have foreseen years ago. In libraries of all kinds there are Internet-connected public access computers, staff computers, online public access computers (OPACs) that connect to the catalog, e-readers, playaways, printers, scanners, copiers, servers, hubs . . . the list goes on. All of those items need to be managed and in many ways connected to one another through either a server or Wi-Fi connection to enable interactivity, both within and outside of the library. Making sure the hardware works with the software is a type of management. Then add to that the troubleshooting that goes along with all of this and IT management can become a huge undertaking for any library administrator to handle. The proper management of all the technology in a library is critical because patrons depend upon the computers to be working so they can access and use the software for their needs. The technological and information age we are in today has changed the role the library plays for our patrons, a role that will continue to change over time as content and our uses of that content continue to evolve.

A library needs money to purchase a new collection of books or wants to invite a group of authors to do a series of book discussions but doesn't have the money in the budget—a familiar scenario in these tough economic times. Where can the library get the money it needs? One possibility is through a publicly or privately funded grant. How does the library find out about and apply for such a grant? Chapter 18, written by someone with experience writing grants and obtaining them for a public or academic library, has the answers.

Outsourcing as a means to achieve cost savings is not a new concept in librarianship. Previously, it meant to outsource a portion of our work, like cataloging or processing books, but now some public libraries in the United States are outsourcing the entire management of the library. Chapter 19 approaches this topic from a researcher's perspective, examining U.S., U.K., and Australian libraries engaged in outsourcing. This approach to library management is becoming more popular with local U.S. governments as a cost-saving measure.

Finally, Chapter 20 examines future trends in librarianship. What will the future bring, and how will it affect the management of libraries? As funding of libraries is cut even further, how will the idea that "everything is on the Internet" continue to have a negative impact, particularly on public libraries? Electronic sources are tools, as are computers, and they should not be seen as the be-all and end-all in the library. Academic libraries face new and different trends as well. What are today's trends, and are libraries ready for the changes that are coming?

Most chapters include either a case study or discussion questions, along with lists for further readings on the chapter topics. This textbook ends with a glossary gleaned from all of the chapters to provide readers with a convenient resource for clarifying their comprehension of particular terms. As a bonus, a bibliography that combines the reference and further reading lists from all 20 chapters is offered as a Web Extra, accessible at www.alaeditions.org/webextras.

References

Bennis, W. (1999). *Managing people is like herding cats.* Provo, UT: Executive Excellence Publishing.

Bennis, W. (2003). *On becoming a leader* (Rev. ed.). New York, NY: Basic Books.

Bennis, W. (2009). *The essential Bennis.* San Francisco, CA: Jossey-Bass.

Schein, E. H. (2003). *Organizational culture and leadership* (3rd ed.). San Francisco, CA: Jossey-Bass.

Wiegand, W. A. (1996). *A biography of Melvil Dewey: Irrepressible reformer.* Chicago, IL: American Library Association.

2
CLASSICAL THEORY

Lisa K. Hussey

Theories about management are plentiful and varied. It seems as if there is a theory for every type of organization, leader, and situation, yet there are always new situations and new ideas. There are as many ideas and theories about management are there are regarding the meaning of life. Some might say the two aren't mutually exclusive concepts, as one needs to manage in order to survive and be successful in life, but that's not a road we need to go down at this time. Suffice it to say, management theories are abundant, and new ones are introduced all the time. To function effectively in modern times, managers need to understand the concepts, the history, and the application (or lack thereof) of theory in organizations.

With this in mind, theory begins with managers' responsibilities. Essentially, a manager's job consists of planning, organizing, directing, and controlling the resources of an organization, which include people. As management emerged as part of modern organizations, theories as to how best supervise, motivate, direct, plan, and control also came about. As organizations grew and evolved, so did how people viewed them. Many illustrations and images describe organizations, but two of the most common descriptions are as a machine and as an organism. Both are reflected in management theories.

However, before we address the theories directly, there are a couple of important points to highlight. To begin with, the theories presented in Chapters 2 and 3 are primarily focused on Western culture and business. Modern management, as we know and will discuss in this book, developed in Western societies, such as the United States, Great Britain, Canada, and Europe. Although principles of management are practiced all over the world, the formal discipline of management tends to be heavily influenced by Western culture and ideas. Even the theories that have grown out of the Japanese business culture (Theory Z, Kaizen, total quality management, etc.) are still influenced by the Western point of view, at least when they are applied to business, especially in the United States and Canada.

As the various theories are introduced, it is also important to remember that the individual theories tend to be reflective of their time periods. The ideas and concepts presented may seem archaic or out of date but were often revolutionary in their time. Additionally, social norms and behaviors also influenced the portrayal of workers and the expectations of management. It is very easy to criticize theories from a century ago for simplistic ideas or patronizing views, but these developed in a much different society and business environment. Remember, we might not have our modern ideals and theories if we did not have the original theories from which to build on, expand, and evolve.

One final thing to consider before we dive into the theories is that all management theories, regardless of the school of thought, tend to have two basic tenets: motivation and control. The underlying concepts of management theory is to present an ideal of what an organization can be or can accomplish and then try to answer two questions: How do you motivate employees to complete their work? How do you make sure the work is carried out and completed as it should be?

With all this in mind, let's now turn to actual theories. In this chapter, we focus on some of the earliest management theories, which are often referred to as the classical theories. These include scientific management, bureaucracy, and administrative management.

SCIENTIFIC MANAGEMENT

Scientific management is often considered to be the first management theory. This school of thought focuses on the organization as a machine. The underlying concept is that organizations are rational enterprises designed and structured to achieve predetermined ends (having given goals and objectives, a rational structure of jobs and activities, and the beliefs that the organizational chart is a blueprint and that people are instruments of organizational action). The emphasis is on the means to ends. Terms often connected with scientific management include efficiency, One Best Way, and increasing productivity. Scientific management theory looks at the organization through workers and tasks. Each task is broken down to the smallest components possible, and each step of the process is analyzed to eliminate wasted time and effort and to develop standards in order to create the One Best Way to complete the work. To introduce scientific management, we concentrate on four influential theorists: Frederick Taylor, Frank and Lillian Gilbreth, and Henry Gantt.

Frederick Taylor (1856–1915)

Although there are other theorists who contributed greatly to the theory, Taylor is considered the father of scientific management. His seminal work, published in 1911, *The Principles of Scientific Management,* laid out the theoretical ideas and steps.

The problem, as Taylor saw it, was that workers were inefficient because they tended to ration their workload or to work less than they could for fear of running out of work, a practice Taylor (1911) referred to as "soldiering." Taylor, however, did not see this as a fault of the workers but rather placed blame for the lack of efficiency on management for failing to structure work effectively. "[I]f a man falls down, the presumption is that it is [management's] fault first, that [management] probably have not taught the man right, have not given him a fair show, have not spent enough time showing him how to do his work" (Taylor, 1916, p. 20). Taylor also believed that management needed to provide sufficient incentives to motivate workers, such as increased pay for higher productivity. He felt that pay for performance rather than hourly pay would better motivate individual workers to increase their efforts in order to earn more money.

Taylor's theory has four main elements:

1. Management is a true science. Taylor believed that management could be analyzed like most scientific work. Through observation and study, managers could detect the individual contribution to the overall work process and use this knowledge to improve on it and to increase productivity.
2. The selection of workers is a science. This idea focuses on making sure the right employee is assigned the right job. After determining what is needed to complete the work effectively and efficiently, managers should look for those characteristics in potential employees. This is an extension of the idea of management as a science.

3. Workers are to be developed and trained. The purpose of developing a One Best Way is to institute one practice for all workers. If there is One Best Way to complete the work, then all employees can benefit from learning it. However, it is up to management to ensure that employees are developed and trained.
4. Scientific management is a collaboration of workers and managers. Taylor viewed the principles of scientific management to be beneficial to both workers and managers. It required management to develop the One Best Way, or the best practices, and workers to implement them. Also, if employees had better knowledge of how to best complete their work, managers would be able to spend less time forcing efforts from employees. Taylor (1911) saw this as a preferable alternative to the practice of intimidation and coercion carried out by many factory floor supervisors.

Each of Taylor's elements is based in rational thought and behavior. Taylor believed management, like any other science, could be rationally dissected and analyzed to find well-defined and universally defined principles, which when applied to an organization would result in efficient processes and increased productivity. Workers would be selected based on the analysis and resulting expectations, and these workers were to be trained in the One Best Way of completing the tasks. If the right workers are hired and they are properly trained, supervisors can spend more time overseeing the process rather than having to put pressure on workers to get the job done. It is only with the willing cooperation of both management and workers that these goals can be accomplished.

Taylor's ideas tend to be patronizing. The relationship between management and workers is presented in a parent/child framework. Managers are seen as the mature and knowledgeable partner, while workers need to be directed and supervised. This point of view was probably influenced by Taylor's own background. Taylor came from a wealthy family. Although he began his work on the factory floor, he looked at organizing factories from the owner's point of view. Taylor's views of workers are also simplistic, reducing them to mindless tools or cogs rather than seeing them as individuals. His theory of scientific management depends heavily on workers being motivated by money and only money.

As most literature will mention, his ideas were criticized even during his time. Unions opposed the idea of pay-per-piece, as they saw it as an opportunity for management to set high quotas for low costs. Taylor was also criticized for his comments regarding workers, including one reference to a worker being "dumb as an ox" (Rainey, 2003, p. 26) and intending it to be complimentary. However, Taylor saw his work as beneficial for both workers and management, as it provided the means for workers to increase their pay through efficient work practices, which in turn provided better results for management. His practice of pay-per-piece was eventually outlawed, and a standard basic wage was instituted.

Frank Gilbreth (1868–1924) and Lillian Gilbreth (1878–1972)

The Gilbreths were a married couple who collaborated on scientific management. Frank was a bricklayer, a building contractor, and a management engineer. Lillian was a psychologist. Using their combined skills, they developed time and motion studies to learn how to improve the productivity of workers. Like Taylor, they looked at the motions involved in work, the way these motions were combined to form methods of operation, and the basic time each motion took. The Gilbreths connected the concepts of motion and fatigue — every motion that was eliminated reduced fatigue. By reducing fatigue, workers would be able to improve performance. They developed a tool, named Therblig (more or less *Gilbreth* spelled backwards), to help break down the work process and determine where improvements could be made. The Therblig was made up of a mixture of 18 actions by workers to be reviewed and analyzed (Ferguson, 2000):

1. Search
2. Find
3. Select
4. Grasp
5. Hold
6. Position
7. Assemble
8. Use
9. Disassemble
10. Inspect
11. Transport loaded
12. Transport unloaded
13. Preposition for next operation
14. Release load
15. Unavoidable delay
16. Avoidable delay

17. Plan
18. Rest to overcome fatigue

As seen in the Therblig, the Gilbreths advocated the importance of rest times (breaks) in order to allow workers to further combat fatigue. They believed, as did Taylor, in a One Best Way of doing work, but they also acknowledged that a new best way was possible and that the old one could be eliminated when the new was discovered. (A bit of trivia: the book *Cheaper by the Dozen* is based on the Gilbreths and their 12 children.)

Henry Gantt (1861–1919)

Gantt initially worked with Taylor but began to rethink many of Taylor's management ideas after working as a consultant. He came up with the idea of bonus incentives based on finishing the day's assigned workload. Supervisors received a bonus based on how many of their workers reached the daily quota. This practice created a stronger tie between management and worker productivity. Gantt recorded performance on a chart using black on days that workers met standards and red on days when they didn't.

Gantt also originated a charting system for production and scheduling, which is still used today. The Gantt chart is constructed with a horizontal axis representing the total time span of the project, broken down into increments (days, weeks, or months), and a vertical axis representing the tasks that make up the project. The interior graph area contains horizontal bars for each task connecting the period start and period ending symbols. This chart is mainly used as part of project management for scheduling projects.

BUREAUCRACY

Bureaucracy is far and away the best known of the classical theories, as well as being the most used.

Max Weber (1864–1920)

Weber developed a theory of bureaucratic management that stressed the need for a strictly defined hierarchy governed by clearly defined regulations and lines of authority. He considered the ideal organization to be a bureaucracy. It was ideal because the activities and objectives were rationally thought out and the divisions of labor were explicitly spelled out. Weber also believed that technical competence should be emphasized and the performance evaluations should be made entirely on the basis of merit. Weber sought to improve the performance of socially important organizations by making their operations predictable and productive. Like scientific management and the other classical theories, efficiency is a big part of bureaucracy. The goal of bureaucracy is a predictable, systematic, impersonal organization where control is based on authority and expertise. Again, like the other classical theories, bureaucracy focuses on control, but unlike the others, bureaucracy looks at the entire organization, not just production and management. Bureaucracy depends on a rational–legal authority in which all functions and offices are governed by well-defined and codified rules. The organization is broken down into clearly differentiated spheres of competency and control, all of which are organized into a well-established hierarchy.

Some key characteristics of bureaucracy include the following (Weber, 1946):

1. A body of laws consisting of a set of abstract rules is intentionally established. These laws demand obedience from members of a corporate group.
2. The typical person in authority occupies an office position, issues commands to subordinates, and is subject to impersonal orders from higher levels in the organizational hierarchy.
3. People owe obedience to the authority of the office a person holds, not to the person who holds the office.
4. The bureaucracy is a functioning organization of official activities bound by rules.
5. The division of labor provides for specialized training and specific spheres of competence.
6. The organization of offices follows the principle of hierarchy, with each lower office being under the control of a higher office.
7. Rules concerning the conduct of an office must be specifically associated with the performance of that office; in other words, they must be used for the good of the organization, not for personal gain.
8. Administrative acts, decisions, and rules are recorded in writing, even when they evolve from oral discussion.
9. Bureaucratic officials are subject to authority only with respect to their impersonal official obligations.
10. Bureaucratic officials are appointed, not elected, on the basis of their technical and specialized qualifications.

11. The "office" is treated as the sole occupation of the incumbent, and it constitutes a "career." Promotion is awarded by superiors and is influenced strongly by seniority.
12. A bureaucratic official's work does not carry the privilege of ownership. Bureaucrats do not use the office for their own measures in the conduct of official business.

The guiding principle in bureaucracy is the idea of top-down management. However, Weber didn't see this as the top being independent of the rest of the organization. Rather, the idea is that each level is dependent on the one below it because the lower levels provide the reasons for the higher levels. Think of the organizational chart and you can see the logic in this idea—each level is built on and supported by the departments below it on the chart. The top-down approach was also seen as a way to appeal to a higher office. There are different levels of authority, which can be used at different times. Authority resides with the office, not with the individual. Weber stressed the idea of codification of policy and procedures, which should be available to all within the organization. Records are to be kept of all communication and decisions. The process for advancement is clearly defined, including the expectations of skills, education, and seniority within the organization needed in order to occupy any office.

One thing that should be glaringly obvious here is that bureaucracy is meant to be quite impersonal, objective, and removed from the biases that come from favoritism and personal feelings. This is what Weber saw as being the ideal. Weber saw bureaucracy as a great equalizer. To Weber, bureaucracy was the polar opposite of patrimonialism, which dealt with privileges based on who you knew and the power of your family or connections. Instead, all who sought assistance from the bureaucracy would be treated equally. The prince would have to deal with the same rules as the serf.

There has been quite a bit of criticism of bureaucracy. Terms such as *impersonal* do a lot to make bureaucracy seem very mechanistic and inhuman, but that wasn't Weber's intention. Weber did readily admit that bureaucracy could turn into something like how we see it today, but that was not his overall purpose. In fact, Weber saw bureaucracy as a way to level the playing field, to provide a fair way to deal with each individual within the organization and with those who use the organization.

Much of the criticism of bureaucracy focuses on the rigid rules and impersonal nature of the theory. The strict rules and procedures can easily limit original thinking and creativity. If everything is proscribed, employees and managers do not need to think about what they do. It has already been decided. This focus on established rules and procedures can produce tunnel vision in employees and managers, an inability to look beyond the goals and expectations of a department or a specific job description. In a bureaucracy, there is very little impetus to understand the organization beyond an employee's department and its reporting structure. The rigid hierarchy and well-delineated departments have the strong potential to create silos and competition for materials and funding. A bureaucratic structure and governance do not encourage collaboration. The nature of the theory can lead to such issues as management controls being too discreet, impersonal, and secretive. Adhering strictly to bureaucratic principles reduces the personalized qualities of relationship. The relationship is between offices, not individuals, and this allows managers and employees to remove anything personal from their actions. While it is important to be objective in one's work, not recognizing people as people can have disastrous results. This impersonal approach can also simplify promotions and evaluations by focusing too much on rote details—seniority, skills—and not considering intangibles.

ADMINISTRATIVE MANAGEMENT

Administrative management is a set of theories that emphasizes the manager and the functions of modern management. Unlike scientific management, administrative management focuses on the role and responsibilities of the manager, not just the direction and control of workers. As with other classical theories, set characteristics and/or rules govern management and workers. While there are some key differences from scientific management and bureaucracy, administrative management is still rather rigid. The theorists of administrative management, like those of scientific management, tend to focus on the best way to define work and responsibilities. The concepts included are often taken from scientific management.

Henri Fayol (1841–1925)

Fayol was a French industrialist and a contemporary of Frederick Taylor. Fayol worked in the mining industry, starting out as a mining engineer and working his way up to managing director. Under his guidance, Commentry Fourchambault et Décazeville went from the edge of bankruptcy to being one of France's largest firms in terms of financial capitalization. However, as he was focused on France and its mining industry, Fayol's works were not widely available outside of France. It was not until the 1940s that Fayol's writings were translated and his ideas found widespread recognition.

Fayol broke down management into two categories: the functions of management and the principles of management. He is one of the first to identify and clearly define the specific functions of management: *planning, organizing, commanding, coordinating,* and *controlling* (Lamond, 2003). Managers, to be effective and successful, need to understand these functions and be able to balance the responsibilities of each one. Iterations of this breakdown are still used widely today, usually replacing *commanding* with *leadership* and combining *coordinating* and *controlling* into one function. Although this idea has been influential, Fayol is best known for his 14 principles of management that must be adhered to for a successful organization (Fayol, 1949; Rodrigues, 2001):

1. Division of work—Work and tasks should be performed by people specialized in the work, and similar tasks should be organized as a unit or department.
2. Authority—Delegated persons (managers, supervisors) ought to have the right to give orders and expect that they be followed.
3. Discipline—Workers should be obedient and respectful of the organization. If they do not follow this principle, workers should be disciplined.
4. Unity of command—Employees should receive orders from only one person with authority.
5. Unity of direction—The organization and employees are dedicated to one plan of action or set of objectives (i.e., the mission and vision).
6. Subordination of individual interests to the general interest—Organizational conflict should be limited by the dominance of one objective. If everyone is working toward the same goals, there should be little conflict regarding what needs to be done.
7. Remuneration—Although Fayol provides no guidance on pay, the organization must recognize the economic value of employees and that their economic interests are important.
8. Centralization—Whether an organization should be centralized or decentralized depends on such factors as communications and the importance of who should make the decisions.
9. Scalar chain—Authority in an organization moves in a continuous chain of command from top to bottom.

10. Order—Everything, people and resources, has a place where it belongs.
11. Equity—Fairness is important in management–employee relations.
12. Stability of tenured personnel—Turnover is disruptive; shared experience is important.
13. Initiative—Workers are exhorted to be productive and motivated.
14. Esprit de corps—There is a need for harmony and unity within the organization.

Fayol took many of the basic ideas of scientific management—such as the division of work, remuneration, and order—and expanded them beyond just the superior/subordinate roles to a much broader view of the organization. The value of workers, beyond just the results of productivity, is introduced, and motivation is expanded beyond just money, although money is still seen as significant. Fayol recognized that organizations are more likely to have success if everyone involved understands their role, the organizational expectations and goals, and how these work together to create an effective and efficient organization.

Fayol's functions of management have undergone many transformations since he introduced them into the management discipline. One of the better-known iterations is administrative theorist Luther Gulick's (1937) POSDCORB. You would be hard pressed to find any management textbook that does not discuss this theory. POSDCORB is an acronym that stands for *planning, organizing, staffing, directing, coordinating, reporting,* and *budgeting.* Gulick expanded on Fayol's ideas by further breaking down the functions of management. The underlying concept is that managers who learn and develop the skills to master the functions of management can create a well-functioning organization. In addition to his expansion on the functions of management, Gulick (1937) also developed some universal principles of organization:

1. Unity of authority—As did Fayol, Gulick believed it was important that each person in the organization answer to only one person, that the lines of authority in the organization are clearly defined.
2. Scalar chain of authority—This concept is needed in order to ensure the unity of authority. The chain of command should be clear, from top to bottom, so that there is no question who is giving orders and who is required to obey.
3. Limited span of control—Gulick felt that one individual could

effectively supervise only a limited number of subordinates. The fewer the subordinates, the easier to provide individual assessment and feedback and to effectively direct the work toward the organizational goals.

4. Distinction between line and staff—Management must recognize the difference between those who do the work (line) and those who provide support (staff). Each group requires different approaches to supervision.
5. Division of labor and specialization—The work within an organization must be broken down into logical divisions in order to best organize the work flow. One of the most effective ways, according to Gulick, is to group like processes together. This is often referred to as the principle of homogeneity.

Other theorists also supported administrative management, but the essential principles tend to be the same throughout: span of control, one master, and technical efficiency through the principle of homogeneity. The concepts and presentation of management are rational, and the focus is on efficiency. While these concepts help create a framework for management, they are also the basis for criticism of the theory. The criticisms of administrative management are similar to those of scientific management; namely, that they are too limited and too rigid. They rely on an expectation that workers and managers will be rational in making decisions about their jobs and livelihood. Administrative management relies heavily on a hierarchical structure, one that becomes much taller as the span of control shrinks. Taller hierarchies often lose efficiencies as it takes much longer to push orders and information through the many layers of management and workers. The principle of homogeneity, while logical, does not allow for much innovation and, as with bureaucracy, creates departmental silos.

One notable characteristic of the classical theories is that they all focus on the formal organization, which is defined by the organizational chart and job definitions. There is no consideration of relationships among departments, except in terms of the hierarchy. However, as anyone who has ever had a job understands, there is also an informal organization that is just as influential on the functioning of an organization. With the introduction of the behavioral school of management, the scope of the theoretical constructs changes.

However, before we get into the next school of theories, I want to include two other influential thinkers who don't entirely fit in with the classical theories, who built off of many of the principles but went in a different direction. Both Mary Parker Follett and Charles Barnard brought the role of the worker in management into focus. Whereas the previous theorists tended to view organizations from management down, both Follett and Barnard recognized the importance of also considering them from the bottom up. Workers are more than tools that serve just one function; rather, they contribute to the overall functioning of the organization. This concept also leads to a new way to view organizations. Rather than being seen as machines, organizations are more like organisms. The idea is that the organization is a living being. The goals of the organization are adaptation and survival. There are roles for individuals and groups and their needs in the organization. The importance of the organizational environment and its demands is recognized. And, rather than presenting a theory able to define everything, the concept of contingency plays a role in how to work within and manage an organization.

Mary Parker Follett (1868–1933)

Follett was a contemporary of the scientific management theorists. Her work laid the foundation for later management thinkers to develop concepts regarding organizational behavior, conflict mediation, and contingency theory. Follett was a social worker. Her experience working in underprivileged neighborhoods led her to develop her concepts of management regarding the importance of the situation, the role and power of employees, and the significance of the relationships among workers and management.

According to Follett, business is a cooperative undertaking in which both owners and laborers have an interest in the continued success of the organization. This common interest in ongoing success is undermined when management and labor engage in conflict that advances narrow objectives. In other words, organizations cannot function effectively if management and workers are focused on their individual goals rather than on the goals of the organization. Conflict leads to domination or compromise in which one or both sides lose. Follett considered the best approach to conflict resolution to be integration of interests. Rather than each side having to give something up through compromise, conflict should be resolved by beginning with a common interest and both sides building a common solution from that point.

Follett's theory is based on the concept of circular behavior, in which people are interdependent. Managers need workers in order to manage, and workers need managers to provide structure and procedures. This idea forms the basis for her law of the situation, which stresses that there is not one best way to do something; rather, it all depends on the situation (Follett, 1973). Follett posits that managers should not just give orders but also allow the situation to determine what needs to be done. According to the theory, managers and workers should not rely on a rigid set of rules but instead work within a flexible framework of expectations and goals and allow what is currently happening to determine the next step. This determination should be arrived at jointly by managers and workers, as the managers know the goals and expectations and the workers know how to do the work.

Chester Barnard (1886–1991)

Barnard was a CEO of New Jersey Bell Telephone. Based on his experience, he wrote *The Functions of the Executive,* in which he discussed how organizations should be managed. He described the legitimacy of supervisors' directives and the supervisors' dependence on the extent of the subordinates' acceptance of the directives. One of management's roles is strategic planning, which has three factors: establish and maintain an effective communication system; hire and retain effective personnel; and motivate those personnel. His main emphasis is on the role of the employee. Barnard postulated the acceptance theory of authority, which states that managers have only as much authority as employees allow them to have. The acceptance of authority depends on four characteristics (Barnard, 1971):

1. Employees must understand what the manager wants them to do.
2. Employees must be able to comply with the directive.
3. Employees must think that the directive is in keeping with organizational objectives.
4. Employees must think that the directive is not contradictory to personal goals.

To put it simply, managers cannot expect the blind obedience of workers. Before carrying out an order, an employee must first understand it and be able to do it. Once these have been established, the employees must also believe the order is within the rules and expectations of the organization and that it will not lead to any career or personal repercussions.

In conjunction with the acceptance theory of authority, Barnard believed that each person has a zone of indifference, or a range within which each individual would willingly accept orders without consciously questioning authority. The larger the zone, the more that will be done without questioning. This introduced the concept of trust of management, particularly an employee's trust in management, something that hadn't been addressed by previous theorists. Barnard also saw value in informal groups or cliques as a way for employees to meet individual goals, and he felt an organization needed to use these informal groups effectively, even if they sometimes work counter to the organization.

Both Follett and Barnard introduced the idea of human relations into management and recognized how social forces influence organizational functioning. While not always grouped with them, both theorists' ideas are reflected in the behavioral/human relations schools of thinking.

BEHAVIORAL SCHOOL OF MANAGEMENT

Over time, it became clear that the classical theories did not address all aspects of management. The strong focus on efficiency and an impersonal approach was not as effective as expected. This led to questioning these approaches to managing and developing new ideas. Theorists began looking at the employees and considering how they contributed to the organization, not just as a nameless group but as individuals who influenced the overall functioning of the organization. A significant part of this movement is the human relations movement. *Human relations* was often used to describe the ways in which managers interact with their employees.

Hawthorne Experiments (1924–1933)

The Hawthorne experiments are perhaps some of the best-known examinations of motivations in the workplace. Elton Mayo, Fritz Roethlisberger, W. J. Dickson, and W. Lloyd Warner conducted experiments at the Hawthorne Works electric company in Cicero, Illinois. The experiments were designed to study the impacts of environmental conditions, rest periods, and other factors on the productivity of employees. What they learned the most about, however, was the importance of the role of the social in the workplace and its influence on workers.

There were several experiments, but the most famous is the one that looked at the impact of lighting on the productivity of workers. The expectation was that better lighting would lead to higher productivity. However, the results showed an increase in productivity for both the test group and the control group. The change factor was the attention given by the observers, not the lighting. In another experiment, which looked at the use of rest periods, the researchers discovered the influence of peer groups. In groups, the individuals were socialized to maintain a certain level of work. If a worker's productivity was too low, he or she could be ostracized for pulling other group members down. This influence and pressure worked the other way as well. Workers who were too productive were pressured to slow down their work so that the rest of the group did not look bad in comparison.

In addition to observing the Hawthorne workers, the researchers interviewed them to learn what was important to them. The most significant finding was that work was not always the most significant thing to them. At work employees are influenced by both the workplace and their personal lives.

These studies recognized the role of the social in the work environment at both the individual and the group levels. Three important ideas emerged from the experiments. First, in order to understand the behavior of workers, you also have to understand their feelings or sentiments or at least acknowledge that these are part of work behaviors. Second, sentiments or feelings are not easy to identify. Individuals can choose not to overtly show their feelings, but their feelings often come across in their actions and deeds. The challenge is that the same actions can represent different feelings for different workers. Finally, feelings and sentiments are not independent; they both rely on the situation of the individual. Hence, even if it possible to identify the feeling or sentiment, it does not guarantee that it will be the same in the next situation (Roethlisberger, 1941).

Although the results of the study have been questioned, including the validity of the subject groups and the fact that incentives play a larger role than the Hawthorne studies concluded, the important result was that researchers began to consider the role of interaction with employees and how it affects productivity. It was a definitive break from scientific management in that the needs or expectations of the employee played a larger role than was previously realized. Managers need to recognize the impact of the social environment on the workplace.

Abraham Maslow's (1908–1970) Hierarchy of Needs

Maslow was not a management theorist but rather a professor of psychology. He was interested in what motivates people, what drives individuals to work toward self-actualization or being the best they can be. He developed a theory of human motivation that consists of a hierarchy of needs, which he defined as physiological needs, safety needs, love needs, esteem needs, and self-actualization needs (Maslow, 1943):

1. Physiological needs—These are the basic needs for survival: food, water, air, and so forth. According to Maslow, this set is what drives our basic functioning.

2. Safety needs—These include having a safe place to be, wanting some level of security in one's job or home, and having good health and available resources.
3. Love needs—These needs involve love, affection, and belonging. They are not just about being loved but also about finding a place to belong. Workers want to find a job where they feel comfortable, a place where others are familiar or at least open to accepting a new worker.
4 Esteem needs—These refer to needs such as self-respect and respect of others. Once an individual belongs somewhere, it becomes important to start building up esteem, to prove one's worth.
5. Self-actualization needs—Self-actualization is one need that Maslow felt was rarely, if ever, met. It is kind of an "ultimate" happiness, of acceptance of self. This is the need that humans are always striving to fulfill.

The needs are usually modeled as a pyramid, with the most basic needs (physiological) on the bottom and self-actualization on the top. The theory posits that once one need is met or close to being met, an individual begins to be motivated by the next level of needs. Maslow didn't see these as completely separate steps but rather as overlapping. It is possible to be motivated by more than one level of need, but a single level still tends to be a priority.

Maslow's work, while still popular today, was not without criticism. Maslow himself recognized that his hierarchy did not fit everyone and that the needs were not universal, and he acknowledged the fact that a need may seem unimportant (a person who has always had it might not understand that it's a need). In his later writing, Maslow freely admitted that he had little empirical evidence—and there still is little evidence, yet this theory is generally taken at face value. There are a few reasons for this, including the fact that much of what he said is common sense. Yet, not all of it is the same for everyone. Culture and gender can have major influences on motivation, and Maslow thought these should be considered (Dye, Mills, & Weatherbee, 2005).

The behavioral school of management had as many critics as the classical theories. To begin with, there is too much focus on one dimension, in this case the human dimension. While it is important to include the role of workers, it is as important to include procedures and rules in order to provide a framework for organizational functioning. In the end, despite the Hawthorne experiments, there was no real evidence of increased production. Maslow had nothing beyond his own ideas and observations, and the results of the Hawthorne experiments have not been repeated. Finally, while the human element is very important, so is money. Compensation may not be the primary motivation, but it can still have an important influence on work behaviors.

CONCLUSION

The theories discussed in this chapter create the foundation for modern theories and views of management. In the second half of the 21st century, management theories tend to incorporate many of the principles of these earlier theories while also trying to provide a new way to view management and worker responsibilities. Scientific management has influenced every management theory that has followed it, either by building on the principles or rejecting the ideas. Administrative management is still used as the basis for defining the functions of management, and bureaucracy is evident in almost every governmental organization in existence. The behavioral school of management introduced many of the ideas now incorporated into human resources, quality theories, and organizational behavioral theories. Follett's and Barnard's ideas can be seen in modern strategies for conflict resolution and mediation, as well as in many of the management theories that focus on quality control. The concept of management has evolved and expanded over time, yet these early theories continue to influence management theory. In the next chapter we will discuss the modern view of management theory. At the end of Chapter 3 are discussion questions that together cover the concepts discussed in both theory chapters.

References

Barnard, C. I. (1971). *The functions of the executive: 30th anniversary edition.* Cambridge, MA: Harvard University Press.

Dye, K., Mills, A. J., & Weatherbee, T. (2005). Maslow: Man interrupted: Reading management theory in context. *Management Decision, 43,* 1375–1395.

Fayol, H. (1949). *General and industrial management.* New York, NY: Pitman.

Ferguson, D. (2000). Therbligs: The keys to simplifying work. Retrieved from http://gilbrethnetwork.tripod.com/therbligs.html

Follett, M. F. (1973). *Dynamic administration: The collected papers of Mary Parker Follett.* New York, NY: Hippocrene Books.

Gulick, L. (1937). Notes on the theory of organization. In L. Gulick & L. Urwick (Eds.), *Papers on the science of administration* (pp. 1–49). New York, NY: Routledge.

Lamond, D. (2003). Henry Mintzberg vs. Henri Fayol: Of lighthouses, cubists and the emperor's new clothes. *Journal of Applied Management and Entrepreneurship, 8,* 5–23.

Maslow, A. H. (1943, July 1). A theory of human motivation. *Psychological Review, 50*(4), 370–396.

Rainey, H. (2003). *Understanding and managing public organizations* (3rd ed.). San Francisco, CA: Jossey-Bass.

Rodrigues, C. A. (2001). Fayol's 14 principles of management then and now: A framework for managing today's organizations effectively. *Management Decision, 39,* 880–889.

Roethlisberger, F. J. (1941). *Management and morale.* Cambridge, MA: Harvard University Press.

Taylor. F. W. (1911). *The principles of scientific management.* New York, NY: Harper & Row.

Taylor, F. W. (1916, December). The principles of scientific management. *The Bulletin of the Taylor Society, 2*(5), 13–23.

Weber, M. (1946). *From Max Weber: Essays in sociology.* New York, NY: Oxford University Press.

Further Readings on Classical Theory

Boddewyn, J. (1961, August). Frederick Winslow Taylor revisited. *The Journal of the Academy of Management, 4*(2), 100–107.

Dye, K. (2005). Maslow: Man interrupted: Reading management theory in context. *Management Decision, 43*(10), 1375–1394.

Farquhar, H. H. (1919, May). Positive contributions of scientific management. *The Quarterly Journal of Economics, 33*(3), 466–503.

Gilbreth, F. B. (1913, July). Units, methods, and devices of measurement under scientific management. *The Journal of Political Economy, 21*(7), 618–629.

Parker, L. D., & Ritson, P. (2005). Fads, stereotypes and management gurus. *Management Decision, 43*(10), 1335–1357.

Simon, H. (1952). Comments on the theory of organizations. *The American Political Science Review, 46*(4), 1130–1139.

Wrege, C. D., & Hodgetts, R. M. (2000, December). Frederick Taylor's 1899 pig iron observations. *The Academy of Management Journal, 43*(6), 1283–1291.

Wren, D. A., Bedelan, A. G., & Breeze, J. D. (2002). The foundations of Henri Fayol's administrative theory. *Management Decision, 40*(9), 906–918.

3
MODERN THEORY

Lisa K. Hussey

The previous chapter focused on the earliest management theories. These theories—scientific management, administrative management, bureaucracy, and the behavioral school of management—are a strong base for the more modern views of management. Yet, as influential as these theories are, they are also limited and somewhat incomplete. The classical theories focus too much on process and rules, with little consideration for employees. The behavioral school tried to address this failing but tended to focus too much on the people and not enough on organizational functioning. The modern theories tend to recognize the complexity of management, the fact that effective management involves a diversity of skills and abilities. Managing is not limited to just rules and procedure, but both are necessary. Effective managers must understand the social aspect and how it influences the workplace, as well as being able to apply and work within the rules and procedures required for organizational functioning.

As we move forward, many management theories begin to parse out specific aspects of management rather than try to provide a broad, all-encompassing view of management. Leadership and organizational development begin to evolve as their own topics rather than simply as parts of management. A focus on quality measures and the role of organizational culture also become more significant to the study of management. Communication, conflict, and diversity are included as part of management and as important aspects of management theory. In other words, from this point forward, management theorists began to acknowledge the complexity of management and the diversity of skills needed to effectively manage.

EARLY INFLUENTIAL MODERN MANAGEMENT THEORISTS

With this in mind, I'd like to begin with two management theorists who tend to be in a class by themselves, Douglas McGregor and Peter Drucker. Both have been incredibly influential over the past 60 years because their ideas and theories have remained relevant and applicable regardless of the time period. McGregor's book *The Human Side of Enterprise*, originally published in 1960, has never gone out of print. A 25th anniversary edition was published in 1985 and an annotated version was published in 2006, but his work has remained as it was originally published—and you are unlikely to find a management textbook that doesn't mention theory X/theory Y. Drucker's work spans from his first book (in German) in 1933 to his death in 2005. He has been called the creator and father of modern management.

Douglas McGregor (1906–1964)

McGregor is known for the seminal work *The Human Side of Enterprise,* in which he introduced a humanistic approach to management, a fact that often groups him with the behavioral school of management. However, McGregor was quite critical of the school and built his ideas based on a balance between the needs of the organization and the motivations of the employee. He recognized the importance of social groups but also acknowledged that social groups could not replace effective management.

As with many other theorists, McGregor's ideas are often distilled down to a simple concept, in his case theory X and theory Y. These theories look at two different approaches to management. McGregor thought that every managerial action rests on a theory. In other words, everything that management does is driven by assumptions and expectations. In McGregor's concept, the attitude and approach of managers is what creates the basis for either effective or incompetent management. McGregor spends less time on providing actual steps or spelling out what to do. Instead, *The Human Side of Enterprise* and theory X/ theory Y are more about how to look at management and the organization and how a manager's attitude can contribute to or work against organizational functioning.

He saw traditional approaches to management as what he termed *theory X*:

1. The average human being has an inherent dislike of work and will avoid it if he can.
2. Because of this human characteristic of dislike of work, most people must be coerced, controlled, directed, or threatened with punishment to get them to put forth adequate effort toward the achievement of organizational objectives.
3. The average human being prefers to be directed, wishes to avoid responsibility, has relatively little ambition, and wants security overall. (McGregor, 2006)

When McGregor describes and analyzes theory X, he brings up a couple of interesting points. First, he puts a lot of the responsibility on the manager, not to make the worker work, but rather not to create a situation in which people won't work or won't put in a good effort. According to McGregor, when employees don't want to work, it is more likely a symptom of a bad situation rather than automatically a bad worker. "Theory X explains the consequences of a particular managerial strategy; it neither explains nor describes human nature although it purports to" (McGregor, 2006, p. 55). He also highlights the fact that in theory X, the rewards connected to work are significant only outside of work—that is, what can be purchased with money. In a very insightful observation, McGregor notes that "work is perceived as a form of punishment which is the price to be paid for various kinds of satisfaction away from the job" (McGregor, 2006, p. 53).

Theory Y, on the other hand, saw employees as contributors to the organization, a way to integrate individual and organizational goals:

1. The expenditure of physical and mental effort in work is as natural as play or rest.
2. External control and the threat of punishment are not the only means for bringing about effort toward organizational objectives. Humans will exercise self-direction and self-control in the service of objectives to which they are committed.
3. Commitment to objectives is a function of the rewards associated with their achievement.
4. The average human being learns, under proper conditions, not only to accept but also to seek responsibility.

5. The capacity to exercise a relatively high degree of imagination, ingenuity, and creativity in the solution of organizational problems is widely, not narrowly, distributed in the population.
6. Under the conditions of modern industrial life, the intellectual potentialities of the average human being are only partially utilized. (McGregor, 2006)

"The principle of integration demands that both the organization's and individual's needs be recognized" (McGregor, 2006, p. 71). In other words, success depends on both sides. This is where he disagrees with human relations—that it is not just the worker but the organization as well that matters. He sees this as a need to change attitudes and perceptions on the part of management; managers will have to revise their ideas about satisfying needs. It's not satisfying needs that management *thinks* exists; it's actually collaborating to discover the common ground for both sets of needs. "If employees are lazy, indifferent, unwilling to take responsibility, intransigent, uncreative, uncooperative, Theory Y implies that the causes lie in the management's methods of organization and control" (McGregor, 2006, p. 66).

One thing that is often ignored when people discuss McGregor and theory X/theory Y is that he never claims that some of the actions connected to theory X are always inappropriate. He states that "assumptions of Theory Y do not deny the appropriateness of authority, but they do deny that it is appropriate for all purposes and under all circumstances" (McGregor, 2006, p. 76). Basically, McGregor wanted managers to question their assumptions about employees and see where a different set of assumptions might take them in better achieving worker commitment and effort: people will contribute more to the organization if they are treated as responsible and valued employees.

It is important to note that McGregor is a realist in regard to his ideas. He admits that management by integration and self-control takes time. It's a messy process, which he illustrates with examples throughout his book. The process requires a lot of dialogue, continual back-and-forth between management and employees. In addition, managers must have faith while relinquishing control. McGregor stressed the need to examine assumptions and asks managers to think about how they think. He's not telling them to change, but he is asking them to consider how they think and what that means to the organization.

Peter Drucker (1910–2005)

Drucker was truly a management guru. He wrote 39 books have been translated into over 30 languages. His work and his ideas were relevant for over 60 years, an amazing feat for anyone, never mind for someone in such a dynamic field as management. Drucker is often credited with coining the term *information worker* and with recognizing the evolution of industry in the United States from factories to service. He built his ideas and theories around the core concepts of service. Additionally, unlike many other theorists, Drucker looked at management in both the for-profit and the nonprofit domains. Rather than just gush over his accomplishments, I want to highlight some of his key ideas, all of which are relevant to management, regardless of the setting. However, before I do, it is important to note that Drucker, like McGregor, rarely provides simple steps for managers to follow. Instead, he often presents broad concepts that can be shaped to work within different organizations and environments. It is this flexibility of ideas that contributes to Drucker's longevity of contribution to management.

Central to all of Drucker's work is the concept of respect: respect for the worker, respect for the organization, and respect for the customer/user/constituency. Managers and leaders have to begin with respect and build from there. For example, Drucker viewed employees as the most important assets of any organization. Managers should approach employees with respect for their contributions and work. This does not mean, however, that managers don't discipline, identify problems, or terminate bad employees. It simply means that managers and leaders need to respect the workers enough to trust them to do their jobs and to evaluate how well that work is done. Drucker puts a lot of emphasis on identifying strengths, pointing out that employees can build only on strengths, not weaknesses. He understood that employees are adults and tend to be rather set in their outlook, attitudes, and values, and, as a result, "one has to use people's personalities the way they are, not the way we should like them to be" (Drucker, 1990, p. 147). Managers must respect the skills and abilities employees have to offer and find ways to develop these to benefit both the employee and the organization. Drucker puts responsibility of self-development onto the individual. Managers and leaders are responsible for their self-development and also for the development of their subordinates. However, subordinates are also responsible for their own development as well as developing the leader. It's a very symbiotic relationship.

One of Drucker's better-known management theories is the idea of management by objectives (MBO), in which managers and employees work together to set up goals and objectives for the employees to reach. The process further reinforces the importance of respect. The objectives need to be challenging but reachable, a balance that respects both an employee's abilities and potential. The objectives, while unique to each employee, are built within the framework of the mission and value of the organization. "The objectives should always derive from the goals of the business" and include how the contributions fit with the overall organization and how other employees are supported by other goals and objectives (Drucker, 2001, p. 115). After setting the goals, managers must follow up and make sure these objectives are met. This is not micromanaging but rather a tool for self-management by providing constructive feedback and recognizing the work that is done. In other words, each manager is respecting the employees and their contributions. However, effective management is not limited to just respecting and developing employees. It also relies on understanding the organization's constituency and its ability to deliver services. As mentioned earlier, service is central to many of Drucker's tenets. It is essential for any organization to recognize whom they serve. Within that service pool, managers need to identify the most important groups—the key constituencies—and recognize how they are each unique. Services need to be tailored to fit these groups, but this has to be done within the context of the mission and values of the organization. Drucker viewed this as a particular challenge in the nonprofit sector, where helping and assisting communities is the goal rather than profit. The way to respect and serve the organization's constituency is to provide the highest level of service based on what is possible for the organization. No organization can be everything to everyone. Instead, organizations must identify what they can do and do well based upon what is needed by those it serves.

All of these ideas should happen within the context of planning for the organization. Drucker stressed again and again the importance of continually looking forward and the need to innovate and evolve as the needs and expectations of an organization's community and environment change over time. The biggest mistake an organization can make, according to Drucker, is to rely on past successes. This allows an organization to become complacent and miss opportunities for innovation and growth. The guiding principle in all of this should be the mission of the organization. The mission, according to Drucker, should focus on how the organization wants to be remembered.

As influential as Drucker and McGregor are, there are many other important modern theories and theorists. These theories evolved from the classical theories and the behavioral school, even if in reaction to rather than collaboration with the ideas. As the business world began to expand well beyond national borders, management ideas from other cultures began to influence the practice and approach to management.

ORGANIZATIONAL BEHAVIOR

Although the behavioral school of management was incomplete, it still had significant contributions to the perception of modern management. Modern theories and research tend to focus on certain influences or characteristics of organizational behaviors, such as organizational culture, organizational development, and group dynamics. As with the earlier theories, organizational behavior is often viewed as unreliable for determining or predicting future outcomes, yet these theories do not focus on prediction but rather try to determine patterns and identify trends within organizational functioning. The overall intent is to provide some way to determine how the people within the organization are going to act and react, but it is not meant to be used as a predictor as much as it is to help identify trends. Trends can help you predict some outcomes, but they are better used to understand what is currently happening and how that will influence what you may try to accomplish.

Edgar Schein (1928–)

One of the best-known scholars in organizational development is Edgar Schein. With a PhD in psychology, Schein approaches management from the aspect of relationships and the influence of groups. The organizational culture or atmosphere is created through the relationships within and among groups in organizations. These are manifested in three levels of organizational culture (Schein, 2003):

1. Artifacts—These are anything tangible or verbally identifiable. Artifacts include such things as office furniture, stories and jokes about the organization or its members, logos or official identifying materials, and even the dress code.
2. Espoused values—These are the very public goals and objectives of an organization. These include the mission and vision, as well as any planning statements or public declarations about expectations and services of an organization. Espoused values are the public presentation of what is deemed of value to an organization.
3. Assumptions—These are the actual, unconscious values that drive the everyday behaviors and expectations of individuals within an organization. Assumptions are never clearly stated, acknowledged, or even recognized; rather, they are the values that individuals simply "know" because they represent how things are done. In a healthy organization, assumptions and espoused val-

> ues are very similar; however, this is not always the case. In a dysfunctional organization, the espoused values and assumptions have very little in common.

Schein used these ideas to develop process consultation, which is a psychodynamic analysis of an organization. He developed this approach from his background in psychology. Psychodynamic analysis focuses on the "dynamic interplay of the psychological process" (Coleman, 2009). It is a process that looks beyond just the policy, structure, and artifacts of an organization and considers the motivations of leadership and employees and how these work together to form the organization.

The process—and Schein stresses that it is a process, not a simple list of steps or activities—involves an in-depth analysis of the organization, looking at artifacts and their presentation, considering the espoused values, and uncovering the attitudes that drive the organization. To be successful, it is strongly encouraged to have the consultant be an outsider, someone who is not invested in the current organization's culture or values. This provides a fresh view of the organization and helps expose the conflicting values that may stymie any organizational development and innovation. Process consultation is not without its challenges. The process requires an outsider to have access to every aspect of the organization, from the frontline workers to the top administration. Administrators, while often happy to allow an outsider to review and analyze workers, tend to balk at the idea of allowing this same outsider to attend their meetings or review their notes. However, without buy-in and participation from administration, the process is useless.

Schein's analysis of organization development also considered the role of groups in organizations and how they influenced and shaped the organization's values and culture. As with process consultation, groups are defined and analyzed through psychology. According to Schein, a group is "any number of people who (1) interact with each other, (2) are psychologically aware of one another, and (3) perceive themselves to be a group" (Schein, 1980, p. 145). The awareness and perception makes the definition of groups very narrow. For a group to be defined as a group there must be a sense of "we" rather than a sense of "me and others." A department where individuals do not interact much or an organization with rigid boundaries between functions is not a group, as there is little perception of "we" in either situation. Groups can be formal, such as departments or project teams, or informal, such as cliques or lunch groups. Formal groups are set by the organization and administration. Informal groups can happen within or among departments or include different individuals from different hierarchical levels:

> How this tendency works itself out in actual creation of groups, however, depends very much on the physical location of people, the nature of their work, their time schedules, and so on. Informal groups therefore arise out of the particular combination of formal factors and human needs. (Schein, 1980, p. 146)

Each type of group fulfills a different function. Formal groups work toward organizational goals. Informal groups, however, fulfill personal and psychological needs, such as a sense of belonging, a feeling of security, and a way to get things done, usually outside the context of official channels or processes.

While he spends time discussing both types of groups, Schein gives much more importance to informal groups. What Schein addresses is the fact that groups may have a formal component, but it's the informal ones that create the strong sense of loyalty and commitment—how the group advances the goals and needs of the individual, all of which depends on such things as environmental factors, membership factors, and dynamic factors—how the group is formed, the manner of leadership, training and skills, and so on. To have a strong understanding of organizational functioning, one must analyze more than just the formal groupings and structure, as that will provide only a superficial view of the organization. It is the informal groups that will help identify the assumptions and values that drive the organizational culture and strongly influence innovation and growth.

Schein's study of groups leads to another aspect of organizational development: the study of group dynamics. The theories and research related to group dynamics focus on the mutual relationships and the reciprocal actions or emotions related to close interaction. Group dynamics is not looking at how individuals behave in groups but rather how groups act, both as a group and in relation or reaction to other groups. The concept of group dynamics is as complex as it is a concept that is hard to describe, quantify, explain, or identify. It is interesting to note that the discussion of how groups act, not how individuals in groups act, did not really enter management theory until the modern era. It is also an odd concept to consider, the actions of groups rather than the actions of individuals.

Alvin Gouldner (1920–1980)

At the center of group dynamics are the concepts of perception and expectations. Where Schein looked at formal and informal groups,

Gouldner looked at the social roles of groups. The social role is a "shared set of expectations directed towards people who are assigned a given social identity" (Gouldner, 1957, p. 283). In this context, groups in organizations are divided into Cosmopolitans, those employees who focus on specialized skill sets rather than on loyalty to the organizations, and Locals, who are more focused on loyalty to the organization than on developing specialized skill sets. These group roles are often latent, manifesting only when there is a cause for identification with one side or another, such as promotion based on skills (Cosmopolitan) or on seniority (Locals). The salient point is that individuals are judged and sometimes act based on images or identities imposed by such groups as social groups, organizations, departments, and so forth. These judgments are based on both explicit and implicit roles more or less "relevant" to the situation. Gouldner looked at how organizations and the people within them judge the contribution and expectations related to workers based on their loyalty to the organization, commitment to skills, and reference group orientation. These represent some of the assumptions discussed by Schein.

Groupthink and the Abilene Paradox

A more active example of group dynamics is the concept of group decision making. Teams or groups must often make decisions on many different issues; some may be simple, such as setting up a meeting time, or more complicated, such as deciding on the goals and expectations of the group. While there is a plethora of literature about group decision making, there are two particular phenomena that are important to consider: groupthink and the Abilene paradox. These concepts are two sides of the same issue—domination by an idea. Groupthink is a much more overt and conscious action—working against contrary ideas. Groupthink happens in a situation where the group or team is dominated by an idea or expectation. The members of the group end up agreeing with plans or policies, even once these are shown to be ineffective. Any contrary view is dismissed, often disparagingly, and the focus is firmly on the group's agreed choice. The main commonality in groupthink is "that of remaining loyal to the group by sticking with the policies to which the group has already committed itself, even when those policies are obviously working out badly and have unintended consequences that disturb the conscience of each member" (Janis, 1971, p. 44). A notable historical example is the Johnson Administration's decision to escalate involvement in the Vietnam War. Any view contrary to this decision was kept away from President Johnson, dissenting voices were quickly removed from positions of authority, and the United States continued to commit resources and troops to a war that was clearly not successful.

In contrast to groupthink is the Abilene paradox. This concept deals more with working off of the fear of expectations and the fear of being contradictory. In the Abilene paradox, groups are unable to make a solid decision, or the one that is made is weak and ineffective. This results from individuals understanding the situation and potential solutions, but failing to communicate their desires and beliefs for fear of appearing contrary. A solution is suggested, usually a weak or ineffective solution, and, rather than present a different idea, members will agree simply to be part of the group. The end result is a bad decision, one that is often counterproductive, and the group members end up frustrated and dissatisfied by the process. One of the more interesting aspects of the Abilene paradox is the idea that rather than avoid the fears of exclusion or repercussions, the paradox actually results in exactly what one was afraid of in the first place—that is, losing respect, losing a job, losing social standing, and so forth—because of the poor decisions and results. Not surprisingly, the solution for both groupthink and the Abilene paradox is to question, to make sure that someone is being critical in a constructive way, and that everyone feels safe in contributing, even when it may be against the prevailing mind-set.

Organizational development is characterized by views of the overall organization and how the functioning of groups and individuals contribute to effectiveness, growth, and development. The next theory builds on the holistic view of the organization and identifies the relationships, interactions, and functions that create the system that is the organization.

SYSTEMS THEORY

Systems theory grew out of the sciences, particularly biology, physics, and thermodynamics, although it is used in many others. Theorists realized that there was a relationship between how nature functions and how organizations function, that there are more than just simple, linear lines of work and clearly visible relationships within an organization. The underlying concept of this theory is a big picture or holistic way of looking at the overall organization. This involves both the overall working of an organization and how the different departments interact and work to achieve a common goal. An important concept in systems theory is the idea of synergy, or how the whole is more than just the sum of its parts.

Systems theory grew out of a response to scientific reductionism. Think back to scientific management and the idea that the best way to run an organization (think factory) is to break down each task to its basic functions and find the best way to complete it and the best worker (in the case of the factory, the strongest) to do the job. Basically, the classical theories all tended to focus on the idea of differentiation, of breaking down organizations into parts, which when put together will create a well-functioning organization. There is very little in the early theories about relationships and interaction. Systems theory, on the other hand, focuses more on the relationships and interactions than on just the parts.

Systems theorists believe that it is not the individual part but the whole that is important. This is not to discount the individual but rather to focus on the contribution to the larger picture. Knowledge lies in discovering the nature of the whole, not in analyzing the parts. The focus is on the wholes and interdependent relationships. The relationship among the parts is as important as the parts themselves; this is why the whole is greater than the sum of its parts. The systems paradigm is based on the conceptual orientation that replaces traditional linear, analytical, and reductionist thinking with an organismic, dynamic, synthetic, and expansionist view of the world.

Systems thinking (or systems theory) has two main objectives, both of which are aimed at enabling the thinker to manage dynamic complexity, as one might find in an organization. First, it aims at discovering the patterns that lie behind events (see not only the obvious but also what is underneath). Second, it helps to empower the individual to manage those patterns of events. That is, systems theory is a way of looking at an organization (or a department) so that you can figure out who works together, which functions are symbiotic and which are parasitic, and what is and isn't being done.

Another important characteristic of systems theory is the relationship with the environment. Organizations as systems do not exist in a vacuum but rather as part of a larger organization or social entity. The idea is that smaller systems work within larger systems, which helps the functioning of the overall system. Within this context, systems can be split into two categories: closed and open systems.

Closed systems are separate from their environment. There are strong boundaries between the organization and the environment. Most closed systems do not rely on their environment for functioning; they can be picked up and moved to any spot. However, closed organizations tend to stagnate and die, as there is little opportunity for innovation or change. The strong boundaries of a closed system discourage the introduction of new ideas or any recognition of changes to the larger environment.

Open systems, on the other hand, interact with the environment with both inputs and outputs. Open systems are able to evolve and change with changes in the environment. They can be both proactive and reactive, but, either way, an open system has limited, permeable boundaries with the environment in order interact with the environment. The boundaries in open systems allow for direct innovation with environment, which in turn provides opportunities for feedback and the potential for innovation and growth.

THE LEARNING ORGANIZATION

The concept of the learning organization developed out of the need for organizations to be able to adapt and evolve within a dynamic environment.

Peter Senge (1947–)

Although many theorists have introduced and analyzed the learning organization, few have been as successful or as well known as Peter Senge and his book *The Fifth Discipline.* The main thrust of the theory is that organizations need to be able to learn in order to adapt. The way to do this, according to Senge, is to develop the five disciplines, which when used together will allow an organization to grow into a learning organization. The five disciplines are as follows:

1. Systems thinking—Members of an organization need to view the organization as a whole, not as individual pieces. The whole system includes the organization, the individuals within the organization, and the environment of the organization. By not limiting the view to a department or a specific focus, one can identify relationships, correct mistakes, rethink assumptions, and learn how to evolve and change as needed. Systems thinking results from the application of the other four disciplines.
2. Personal mastery—Senge states that individuals must first be willing to learn before an organization can learn. This process involves "continually clarifying and deepening our personal vision, of focusing our energies, of developing patience, and of seeing reality objectively" (Senge, 1990, p. 7). In other words, it is

the continual willingness to question one's own approach to the organization and to be open to learning.

3. Mental models—To be open to learning, individuals need to be able to alter their own mental models, which Senge (1990) defines as "deeply ingrained assumptions, generalizations, or even pictures or images that influence how we understand the world and how we take action" (p. 8). To change, we have to be aware of our mental models and understand how they influence what we see and do.
4. Building a shared vision—For individuals to effectively work together, there needs to be a shared understanding or goal, "to hold a shared picture of the future [they] seek to create" (Senge, 1990, p. 9). People who are inspired by a "true vision" as opposed to a generic vision statement will work to excel because they want to excel.
5. Team learning—In the learning organization, it is not enough for individuals to learn; the organization must also be able to learn and adapt. This is done by setting aside assumptions and working together to discover new ideas and insights. As Senge (1990) points out, "Team learning is vital because teams, not individuals, are the fundamental learning unit in the modern organization" (p. 10).

Senge doesn't present the five disciplines as steps or goals to be achieved. Instead, he saw the disciplines as ideals to constantly strive toward. It's not that it is impossible to achieve the disciplines, it's simply that the dynamic nature of organizations and their environment make it that there is always more to learn. "To practice a discipline is to be a lifelong learner . . . you spend your life mastering the disciplines" (Senge, 1990, p. 11). Senge further explains the idea of the learning organization through his laws (pp. 58–67). These are somewhat pithy sayings that could be easily discounted, but they have a solid grounding in reality and common sense:

1. Today's problems come from yesterday's solutions.
2. The harder you push, the harder the system pushes back.
3. Behavior grows better before it grows worse.
4. The easy way out usually leads back in.
5. The cure can be worse than the disease.
6. Faster is slower.
7. Cause and effect are not closely related in time and space.

8. Small changes can produce big results—but the highest levels of leverage are often the least obvious.
9. You can have your cake and eat it too—but not at once.
10. Dividing the elephant in half does not produce two small elephants.
11. There is no blame.

A common thread through Senge's "laws" is that we tend to take action or make decisions based on the immediate past, and our past may lead us down the wrong path. We may create problems for ourselves and have our actions reinforced because the immediate aftermath may indeed be positive, but eventually the lack of foresight leads to further problems that weren't foreseen (success leading to failure). Think about your own experiences and how often a "solved" problem comes back again (perhaps in a different department or in a slightly different form, but it still comes back to bite you). Then, think about how hard it is not to try to use your own experience as a way to figure something out. It's not entirely realistic, but he does have a point in that just because it worked before doesn't mean it will work again, especially if the problem is eerily familiar. Perhaps it didn't work in the first place.

One of Senge's most interesting "laws" is "faster is slower." This tends to run counter to the advice of many pundits, who claim that we have to respond very quickly or we'll be swept away by more nimble organizations. Yet, it is important to consider that there are many interrelated forces that affect the ultimate outcome. The more complex an environment is, the more factors need to be considered to make the right decision. The learning organization seeks to examine all the factors so as to make the most effective decision (and this should not be confused with inaction). The learning organization also realizes that something needs to be done; delaying action because of extended study or examination is itself a decision.

QUALITY THEORIES

The quality theories share many principles with the learning organization, such as constant learning and improvement. These theories focus on the quality of work and the participation of all employees in the improvement of the organization. Not surprisingly, teamwork and group decision making are central to these theories.

The quality theories evolved out of a Japanese management model, and the principles reflect many characteristics of Japanese culture. Perhaps the most significant characteristic is the importance of the group (the organization) over the individual. This is counter to Western, particularly American, culture. Any attempt to implement the quality theories requires a long-term commitment to organizational development and buy-in at every level of the organization, particularly in administration.

W. Edward Deming (1900–1993)

One of the earliest theorists to introduce Japanese business models to American industry is W. Edward Deming. His contribution to management is significant. Early in his career, Deming advocated moving away from traditional management models and using a statistical quality control process. Deming felt this process provided managers with a reliable way to determine the best course of action, to intervene to make corrections or to be hands-off and allow the work to continue as is. While his ideas had some success in the United States, it wasn't until after World War II that his theories of using statistical controls to maintain quality processes were widely recognized and used. Deming's contribution to Japan's industrial recovery cannot be underestimated. He is often credited with making a significant contribution to the overall resurgence of Japan's industries.

In his theory, Deming posits 14 points for quality management. These are central to the implementation of his statistical quality control process (1986, pp. 23–24):

1. Create constancy of purpose for improvement of product and service. The focus of the organization should be on the constant improvement of quality, not profit. It is a radical rethinking of the purpose of for-profit organizations.
2. Adopt the new philosophy. Acceptance of subpar or just acceptable work must stop. The new focus must be the continual improvement; negativity and mistakes are no longer part of the overall culture.
3. Cease dependence on mass inspection. Deming saw the practice of inspecting items as they came off the assembly line and making corrections as a waste of time. Instead, organizations should focus on improving quality so that inspections are not needed. This process, to be effective, should include all employees, especially those involved in the manufacturing process.

4. End the practice of awarding business on the price tag alone. Basically, the idea here is that just because a supplier is cheaper doesn't mean it will help improve your process. Rather than focus on price, management should work with organizations that provide quality items and build a long-term relationship. This will allow an organization to begin with quality tools and resources to build quality products.
5. Improve constantly and forever the system of production and service. Quality is an ongoing process. Improvement is not a one-time step, but a continual effort. There is always something to improve on, and organizations need to be working toward higher quality at all times.
6. Institute effective job training. Employees are not going to automatically know how to do everything. As new processes or new employees are introduced to an organization, there needs to be complete and effective training to ensure a high level of quality work. If employees are not trained, they will not know or understand the expectation of quality.
7. Institute leadership. Rather than focus on the negative and highlight mistakes, supervisors need to act as leader to their employees, modeling the expected behaviors, providing constructive feedback, and working with employees to develop their skills and abilities.
8. Drive out fear. For Deming's ideas to work, employees need to be able to ask questions, to be honest about mistakes, and to get clarification and feedback without fear of reprisal or loss of status. Security, not fear, will help facilitate quality work.
9. Break down barriers between departments. For an organization to implement quality measures there needs to be a common goal, one that is understood at both the micro level—how the individual department contributes—and the macro level—how each department contributes to the overall quality of the organization. To build this understanding and agree on goals, departments need to be able to communicate and work with each other.
10. Eliminate management-imposed slogans, exhortations, and targets for the workforce. Management may think it understands what is important to workers, but it is the workers themselves who know what motivates them. Rather than impose them, allow the workers to actually create their own slogans and targets, ones that support their expectations within the context of the organization.

11. Eliminate numerical quotas. These types of quotas create a pressure to focus on quantity rather than quality, resulting in lower quality and costly mistakes. Focusing instead on quality provides the opportunity for better end results and fewer mistakes.
12. Remove barriers to pride of workmanship. In order to do quality work, employees must have quality tools and the freedom to actually do the work. Faulty equipment, subpar materials, and overbearing supervisors should be removed or replaced so that workers can focus on the work, not the impediments.
13. Institute a vigorous program of education and retraining. To adopt statistical quality control measures, management and employees need to understand the process and the intended outcomes. Time spent on education and training is an investment in the process and in the employees in the organization.
14. Take action to accomplish the transformation. Deming recognized that his ideas could not be instituted overnight. It is a process, one that takes time and requires a commitment at every level of the organization. The initial costs may seem high, but they will be balanced by the eventual savings from higher quality and fewer mistakes.

William Ouchi (1943–)

Deming's ideas and his work with Japan provided a strong base and influence on the later quality theories. One such theory is theory Z, developed by Ouchi. Ouchi introduced theory Z as an attempt to westernize the Japanese organizational theories. The name, theory Z, is in recognition of McGregor's theory X/theory Y. He wanted to illustrate the expansion of management theory beyond McGregor's two models.

Ouchi recognized, correctly, that it is not possible to simply transfer the same managerial practices from Japan to the United States. There had to be some adjustment for the different cultures and mind-sets. The focus of theory Z is more on organizational philosophy, focusing on the best way to manage rather than focusing on the technology or methods of production. Ouchi viewed the organizational philosophy as "primarily a mechanism for integrating an individual into an organization . . . a mechanism for integrating an organization into society . . . an elegant informational device" (Ouchi & Price, 1993, pp. 68–69). In other words, the organizational philosophy acts as the basis for socialization and the setting of goals and expectations, and because all members of an organization are thus socialized, "a philosophy of management provides a form of control at once all pervasive and effective because it consists of a basic theory of how the firm should be managed" (Ouchi & Price, 1993, pp. 68–69).

Theory Z advocates something similar to a clan model (Ouchi & Price, 1993) where there is homogeneity of values and expectations. Socialization into the clan usually results in individual goals being aligned with clan or organizational goals. The organizational goals should also be aligned with those of the larger society. This relationship among goals helps to counter any potential conflict between individual and organizational goals. Ouchi is trying to provide a framework for organizations to look beyond just profit and be able to focus on goals such as quality of employees and of product. Organizations that align with societal goals tend to be more productive and stable because they are working toward common goals with employees. The process also helps to better integrate individuals into the organization because it isn't necessary to socialize individuals into an organization and try to focus on goals if they are already in line with the larger societal goals.

Perhaps one of the more contrary characteristics of theory Z for Western organizations is the policy of promotion and evaluation. In a theory Z organization, promotion and advancement are limited in an employee's early career. Evaluations, beyond the normal feedback, are not conducted in an employee's early years. Rather than stress a narrow specialization of skills, Ouchi suggests that a slower process of evaluation and promotion while rotating employees through different functions will ensure that employees are in fact prepared in both skills and attitude to take advantage of opportunities and successfully accept high levels of responsibility. Theory Z stressed the development of a strong overall worker rather than a specialized skill set aimed at a particular promotion and advance track. Although this idea contradicts the traditional management model of specialization and expectation of promotion, theory Z organizations provide a security of employment, which helps counter the slower pace of promotion and advancement.

As with Deming's ideas, theory Z requires a large commitment of time and resources, a point that Ouchi acknowledges. While a bit idealistic in his view, he does recognize that to be successful a philosophy has to begin at the top—those with power—and it has to be tested through practicality and then be taught. It's not an automatic process.

Kaizen and Six Sigma

Two other significant quality theories are Kaizen and Six Sigma. Both focus strongly on continued improvement throughout the organization. Kaizen is an all-encompassing theory, one in which workers are as responsible for contributing to continued improvement as administration. Frontline workers are expected to provide suggestions for improvement on processes; their input is viewed as more valuable because they actually continually participate in the process. Decision making is a group process. It is a very different model from the more traditional management styles of command and control.

Six Sigma also focuses on quality, and it was developed in the United States at Motorola. The principles of Six Sigma are based on Deming's ideas. The underlying principle is that the goal of the organization is to lower the number of defects in the manufacturing process. The term *Six Sigma* comes from statistical modeling and represents a 99.99966% quality of production, with only 3.4 defects per million items produced. Six Sigma is achieved through a process of constant improvement, including the contributions of all employees. This is done within a framework of strong leadership, guidance from mentors and champions (who are rated in terms of belts—green belt, black belt, master black belt), and a commitment to decision making based on verifiable information rather than intuition or guesses. As with the other quality theories, Six Sigma requires commitment and training, including off-site training for advancement to different stages of belts.

Although the quality theories are more applicable to the manufacturing industries, service and nonprofit organizations can adapt principles to help improve the quality of service. For example, the practice of soliciting input from frontline workers is useful when making decisions about introducing new services, making changes to policies, or adding to existing collections. Socializing individuals into an organization can encourage loyalty, especially when organizational goals and individual goals align. Finally, although service cannot be measured in the same way as manufacturing, minimizing mistakes and missteps as much as possible can only benefit an organization.

CONCLUSION

At best, this chapter and the previous one have provided a basic overview of management theories. There are many popular theories that I haven't discussed, and there are new theories and ideas of management being introduced all the time. Books such as *The One Minute Manager* (Blanchard & Johnson, 1981) and *Who Moved My Cheese?* (Johnson, 1998) provide commonsense suggestions and practices for effective managers. In the 1960s, there was a resurgence of the principles of scientific management with the introduction of management science, a theory focused on the use of inventory control, probability models, and other scientific methods to solve management problems. Management scholars have continually introduced ideas about management, decision making, motivation, and leadership, and it won't stop any time soon. There's always going to be a new idea, a new approach to management, but regardless of what is introduced or presented, the new ideas will also be influenced to some degree by at least one of the theories or concepts introduced here and in the previous chapter.

However, before you move on to the next chapter, I want to bring up a couple of points. First, in the review of these theories, you might have noticed a few things that haven't been mentioned in the theories, such as diversity and gender difference. In all of them, Follett is one of the few examples of the differences between men and women. Without sounding too stereotypical, she does present a more nurturing point of view in regard to management. This is related somewhat to her own background, as she spent time working with social and charitable organizations. The discussion of diversity in management is also limited. What is available generally focuses on the importance of a diverse workforce and little discussion of the potential tension that can arise out of inherent differences. It is important to recognize that these omissions are not automatically intentional but rather more of a reflection of social norms. Before the civil rights movement, the prevailing mind-set was one of a homogenous workforce (i.e., a white, male workforce), but this perception has changed over time. As with any discipline, it takes time for management theories to catch up with the current perceptions of society. As more women take on leadership roles and diversity in society and in organizations becomes commonplace, theories of management will develop to incorporate these characteristics into the management mind-set and discipline.

DISCUSSION QUESTIONS

1. Consider all the theories covered in both Chapters 2 and 3. What theory makes the most sense to you? Why? How would you use or apply this theory?
2. What is still missing in management theory? What ideas or concepts still need to be addressed? Why are these concepts important or relevant to management?

3. Is it possible for one theory to apply to many settings or any setting? Why or why not?
4. What have you experienced in your own work history? Have you been introduced to any of these theories? Did a previous manager seem to favor a particular theory? How well did it work? What was done successfully? What challenges or problems resulted?
5. What differences exist between for-profit and nonprofit organizations? What does this mean in terms of management theory?

References

Coleman, A. M. (2009). *A dictionary of psychology* (3rd ed.). New York, NY: Oxford University Press.

Deming, W. E. (1986). *Out of the crisis.* Boston, MA: MIT Press.

Drucker, P. (1990). *Managing the non-profit organization: Principles and practices.* New York, NY: Harper Business.

Drucker, P. (2001). *The essential Drucker.* New York, NY: Harper Business.

Gouldner, A. W. (1957). Cosmopolitans and locals: Toward an analysis of latent social roles. *Administrative Science Quarterly, 2*(3), 281–282.

Janis, I. L. (1971, November). Groupthink. *Psychology Today, 5*(6), 43–46, 74–76.

McGregor, D. (2006). *The human side of enterprise: Annotated edition.* New York, NY: McGraw Hill.

Ouchi, W. G., & Price, R. L. (1993). Hierarchies, clans and theory Z. *Organizational Dynamics, 21*(4), 62–70.

Schein, E. H. (1980). *Organizational psychology* (3rd ed.). Englewood Cliffs, NJ: Prentice Hall.

Schein, E. H. (2003). *Organizational culture and leadership* (3rd ed.). San Francisco, CA: Jossey-Bass.

Senge, P. (1990). *The fifth discipline: The art & practice of the learning organization.* New York, NY: Doubleday.

Further Readings on Modern Theory

Alire, C. (2004, Winter). Two intriguing practices to library management theory: Common sense and humanistic approaches. *Library Administration & Management, 18*(1), 39–41.

Blanchard, K., & Johnson, S. (1982). *The one minute manager: The quickest way to increase your own prosperity.* New York, NY: Berkley Books.

Burnes, B. (2007, June). Kurt Lewin and the Harwood studies: The foundations of OD. *The Journal of Applied Behavioral Science, 43*(2), 213–231.

Collins, J. (2001). *Good to be great: Why some companies make the leap and others don't.* New York, NY: Harper Collins.

Drucker, P. (1998, October). Management's new paradigms. *Forbes, 162*(7), 152–170.

Hammer, M., & Champy, J. (2003). *Reengineering the corporation: A manifesto for business revolution.* New York, NY: Harper Collins.

Johnson, S. (1998). *Who moved my cheese? An amazing way to deal with change in your work and your life.* New York, NY: G.P. Putnam & Sons.

Kanter, R. M. (1993). *Men and women of the corporation.* New York, NY: Basic Books.

Kruger, V. (2001). Main schools of TQM: "The big five." *The TQM Magazine, 3*(1), 146–155.

Mintzberg, H. (2007). *Mintzberg on management: Inside our strange world of organizations.* New York, NY: Free Press.

Natemeyer, W. E., & McMahon, J. T. (2001). *Classics of organizational behavior* (3rd ed.). Prospect Heights, IL: Waveland Press.

Rainey, H. (2009). *Understanding and managing public organizations* (4th ed.). San Francisco, CA: Jossey-Bass.

Scarnati, J. T. (2002). The godfather theory of management: An exercise in power and control. *Management Decision, 40*(9), 834–841.

Schein, E. H. (1998). *Process consultation revisited.* Reading, MA: Addison-Wesley.

4
HUMAN RESOURCES MANAGEMENT

Diane L. Velasquez

The most important resources in a library are the people who work there. Without the people who perform the different functions in the library, the organization cannot run efficiently and productively. Making sure that all librarians and staff members come to work and give the best that they can to serve their patrons is a responsibility of the management team that runs the library. Human resources management (HRM) is the most important responsibility of being the director, dean, or manager of a department. Everything that a director or manager does on the job is tied to HRM or personnel issues that occur on a day-to-day basis in the library with staff.

The management of the people and paperwork associated with the staff can be enormous depending on the size of the staff. There are federal and state legal requirements that come into play that must be taken into account. Every staff person's records are confidential, and no one has the right to see them except the HR department, the employee, and the supervisor of that employee. The ability to manage everything and keep up to date on all the state and federal laws can, at times, be daunting. Some states have more complex laws than others.

The management team in a large or medium-sized public or academic library would consist of a director and the heads of the different departments. In a small academic, special, or public library, most of the professionals (librarians) would report to the director or dean. The paraprofessionals, students, or volunteer staff could be supervised by the librarians. In a solo or very small rural library there may be just a librarian and one or two other staff members.

HIRING

Hiring a staff member for a library is where the cycle of bringing employees into the organization begins. Everyone who is considered for a position typically runs through the same gauntlet of starting by answering a job ad with a cover letter, résumé, and three professional references. How does this cycle begin on the library's side? Let's see.

There is an opening in the library for a page or shelver for 20 hours a week. Human resources management—whether there is a person or persons who handle it for the library or the director's assistant handles the administrative piece—starts with the circulation manager or department head telling the director that there is an opening for a page. What happens next? Follow these steps:

1. Make sure there is a solid job description in place.
2. Place an ad in the community at the local high school, community college, and job board; on the library website and local organization (city, university/college) websites; and so forth.
3. Once the résumés start coming in, screen them.
4. Give the résumés to the hiring manager or search committee.
5. The hiring manager
    a. further screens the résumés;
    b. calls the top 10 candidates to further screen for salary demands, hours, and so forth;
    c. does background checks;
    d. brings in the top three candidates for interviews; and
    e. offers the job to the top candidate.

All the steps in hiring someone appear easy, right? Depending on the position, the salary level, how many résumés are sent in, and the screening, it can be easy or difficult. There are no hard-and-fast rules when screening résumés. Everyone who screens cover letters and résumés usually has ideas about the quality. Are there typos or misspelled words? That is usually a clue that the person rushed through the process of submitting the letter and résumé. This lack of proofreading can give some insight regarding how well someone will do on the little stuff of his or her job.

Job Description

The job description is very important. A job description gives the candidate a snapshot of what the job will entail. A page is someone who:

- Primarily shelves books
- Puts them in Library of Congress (LC) or Dewey Decimal Classification (DDC) order
- Empties the book collection bins
- Helps process books with technical services when shelving is slow
- Helps at circulation
- Is able to bend, stoop, lift 40 pounds (book boxes can be heavy), sit, and stand
- Reads and speaks English fluently
- Is able to use computers
- Performs all other duties as assigned
- Works 20 hours per week as scheduled by circulation manager
- Receives minimum wage or just above that level

This job description is incredibly simple, but it is for explanation and discussion purposes. Every position in the library from the dean or director down should have a written job description that is updated every three to five years at the minimum. Yearly updates are even better at the time when the annual reviews are done.

While the previous example job description is very simple, a formal job description should have the following items in it:

- Job title
- Pay grade or schedule
- Identification of job
- Educational requirements
- Summary of job duties
- Activities and procedures
- Relationship of job to the institution
- Job requirements
- To whom the position reports

None of these items is difficult to come by, and all should be included.

Interviews

The top three candidates are scheduled for an interview with the hiring manager and HR department. In some organizations, the person to be interviewed goes through three or four interviews before being offered the job. What kind of questions should or should not be asked of someone looking for a job? Or, in other words, is anything off limits?

According to Title VII of the Civil Rights Act of 1964 the candidate cannot be asked specific questions about national origin, race, color, religion, and sex. Under the Age Discrimination in Employment Act (ADEA) candidates cannot be asked their age. No candidate being interviewed can be asked about national origin or citizenship under the Immigration Reform and Control Act (ICRA). The American Disabilities Act (ADA) doesn't allow hiring managers to ask about disabilities. The National Labor Relations Act (NLRA) does not allow questions about union members. If the candidate is a former member of the uniformed services (military), the questions are limited under the Uniformed Services Employment and Reemployment Rights Act (USERRA). Financial questions are limited under the Bankruptcy Act. Questions regarding children are not allowed under the Child Support Enforcement Amendments. The laws mentioned here are just the federal laws that need to concern hiring managers. Each state also has laws that could come into play. Some states are stricter than others.

Unless the candidate makes a comment regarding any of these items, no one can ask a question about them. There are questions referring to these items that can be asked, but the person asking the question must be very careful about how they are phrased. Here is a list of example questions that are allowed and follow the guidelines set out in the laws:

- What's your name?
- Are you a citizen of the United States?
- Are you old enough to do this type of work?
- Can you supply transcripts of your education?
- If hired, can you prove eligibility to work in the United States?
- What professional associations are you a member of?
- Are you available to travel frequently?
- Can you work overtime with no notice?
- Can you work evenings and weekends?
- When we check references or run a background check, are there other names we should look under?
- Have you ever been convicted of a crime?
- If hired, will you be able to prove you are at least 18 years old?
- Are you capable of performing the essential functions of this position with or without reasonable accommodation?
- Will you sign a form authorizing us to perform a credit check?

- What experience did you gain in the uniformed service (military) that is relevant to the job you would be doing?

The question about reasonable accommodation alludes to the ADA and is asking indirectly if the prospective employee will need some sort of change to the work environment. It can be as simple as an ergonomic keyboard or as difficult as a specific desk or chair. The employer must provide reasonable accommodations for employees who have disabilities.

If there is a candidate who knows the law and is aware of what can and cannot be asked, interviewers who have not been trained can be tripped up if they ask the wrong type of questions. Asking questions about pregnancy—whether the candidate is pregnant or plans to have children—is off limits as well. It is none of the employer's business. Every now and then a story is told about someone who asked inappropriate questions. The lawsuit payouts for these types of offenses if someone chooses to sue can be big and, if the jury determines the employer is out of line, can make management look stupid for not training their hiring managers.

The Society for Human Resource Management (www.shrm.org) has some good resources available for nonmembers on its website regarding interview questions and human resources in general. If the library or its parent organization has a human resources professional, becoming a member of SHRM is never a bad idea.

Background Checks

Background checks are typically performed prior to offering a job to someone. Depending on the position, several types of background checks may be applicable. Criminal and educational background checks are two of the most common.

The criminal background check will reveal whether there are felonies in the candidate's background. If the person will be working around children, this check is imperative. Educational background checks will verify a person's degrees. If someone says he or she has a master's degree in anthropology from Utopia University and an MLS from there as well but cannot come up with the transcripts, there's likely a problem with the claim, and someone should call or take a trip to the university to verify the person attended. People are not always truthful on résumés or curricula vitae, and checking to verify attendance is sometimes the only way to find out. If the candidate provides transcripts in sealed envelopes from all of the college institutions, then your organization is home free. Many times informal transcripts provided as a scanned PDF file are acceptable to the hiring manager with the provision that formal transcripts will be provided if the candidate is hired.

Some organizations, especially if the person is going to be bonded because he or she will be handling money, run a financial background check. The financial background check looks to make sure the person has never embezzled or had major problems with money.

All background checks need the prospective employee's approval to move forward. The prospective employee will need to sign a document giving permission for every type of background check that will be made. When verifying previous employment without a prospective employee's approval, all the previous employer can divulge is (1) confirmation the person worked there, (2) when the person worked there, and (3) the title the person held. That's it. If more is given and the person is the top candidate and loses the job because of something said by a former employer and the candidate finds out, the candidate can sue the former employer. So be very careful about what you say about somebody who has worked for you. Libraryland is a very small place, and word gets around eventually.

If the prospective employee will be driving a company car or a personal one on business, the organization is within its rights to request a driving record. Anyone can obtain a printout of someone's driving record as long as they pay the fee and have the person's driver's license number. The report will state whether or not the person's license is valid to drive on currently, is suspended, or has been revoked. The report will also list any violations and points that are on the person's record. All accidents and violations (tickets) that have been reported will be listed.

Job Offer

Depending on the type of organization, once the candidate is chosen the job offer may be verbal, written, or both. The verbal job offer allows an opportunity for the prospective employee and the new manager to negotiate the terms of the agreement. Many employees when being offered a salary lower than what they expected may decide to negotiate their pay. Why? Prospective employees may believe they are worth more than the offer and may already have a number in mind of what they are worth. The negotiating is a way for both employers and employees to get what they want—happy and satisfied employees who will want to stay with their employers for the long term. All positions have a high, middle, and low range. For instance, for the position of librarian I, the high point may be $55,000, the low point $37,000, and the midpoint $45,500. For a new hire, the hiring manager probably does not want to pay more than $41,000. How is this figured? It is the median between the low point and the middle point. There is usually some wiggle room if the person who retired was a librarian V who was making $75,000. It is always cheaper to bring in a librarian I making $41,000 plus benefits at entry level. What is the point here? Negotiate. What's the worst that can happen? The answer will be no, or maybe some additional perks will need to be negotiated, as is discussed later in the chapter. An employee who just says okay may become unhappy with the salary later, leading to morale issues and unhappiness with the whole situation in a couple of years. The hiring manager would rather have a happy employee than one who is not.

Once the negotiation is completed, a letter should go out putting the terms in writing. This enables the HR department to know exactly what was agreed to between the employee and the hiring manager. The letter will set out the negotiated start date and any other perks that may have been negotiated that are different from the norm.

Pay

Everybody likes a paycheck, and one is needed to live. The ability to survive is crucial, and it is included in Maslow's hierarchy of needs. Although finances are covered in a later chapter, note here that the majority of the budget for a library (academic, public, and special) or information center, typically 45% to 55%, is for personnel pay and benefits. When a line item in a budget takes up that much of the overall total it is important to understand what goes into the numbers. For the example illustrated in Table 4.1, the number used is $50,000 being paid biweekly or with 26 pay periods.

As Table 4.1 demonstrates, the employer is responsible for Social Security (FICA) taxes, Medicare, federal unemployment tax (FUTA), and the employer's portion of any medical, dental, or vision plans if offered. The employee is responsible for Social Security taxes, Medicare, the employee portion of medical and dental, and any 401k or other pension plans that employees can contribute to. The state tax liability can vary by state, and some states (Alaska, Florida, Nevada, New Hampshire, South Dakota, Tennessee, Texas, Washington, and Wyoming) do not collect any state income taxes.

Table 4.1 Salary Deduction Example

	Employee's Biweekly Deductions	Employee's Full Year Deduction	Employer's Part	Employer's Full Year
Salary	0	0	1,923.08	50,000
Federal taxes	126.51	3,289	0	0
State taxes	67.31	1,750	0	0
FICA (Social Security)	124.04	3,225	124.04	3,225
Medicare	27.88	725	27.88	725
Medical/dental	125.00	3,250	213.46	5,500
Unemployment tax	0	0	115.38	3,000
TOTAL	470.74	12,239	2,403.84	62,450

From *Publication 15: Circular E, Employers Tax Guide*, by the Internal Revenue Service, 2011, retrieved from www.irs.gov/pub/irs-pdf/p15.pdf

Libraries have traditionally paid poorly. The discussion of this situation is a philosophical one and does not belong here. The comment to be made is that paying your employees appropriately for the location will result in happy employees who will want to stay with the library.

Benefits

Some libraries give benefits only to full-time employees, while others will prorate benefits to part-time employees. One of the benefits to libraries that use part-time employees is not having to pay medical and other optional benefits. The decision is usually made at the governmental agency level if it is a public agency such as a state university or a city public library. If it is a true nonprofit that is run with no tax dollars, it is up to the funding nonprofit.

Another benefit that many in management do not often consider is vacation, sick, and paid time off. This is a benefit that all employees should get whether they are full or part time. The determination of whether or not part-time employees get prorated vacation, sick, or paid time off is typically at the policy level of the library or parent organization. Depending on how the time is accrued, it can be a perk that is a good negotiating tool if someone wants more salary and the organization cannot afford it. For instance, professional development can be a touchstone for many professionals. Going to conferences to present papers or to just attend can be meaningful professional development. Many times it is difficult to get the time off. If the librarian is involved in the American Library Association (ALA) or one of its divisions or roundtables, this can be an important negotiating point. Giving the person paid time off that is not vacation time along with a minimal amount of travel money to defray part of the expenses instead of an extra amount of pay can sometimes be valuable to potential employees. The key point is not going back on management's word and for the new hire to get this in writing.

FEDERAL LEGAL PROTECTIONS

Civil Rights Act of 1964

The Civil Rights Act of 1964, Title VII—Equal Employment Opportunities protects an employee from discrimination based on national origin, race, color, religion, and sex (gender). The protections are tied to the Civil Rights Act of 1964, and enhancements and improvements have been made following congressional and federal court actions. All rights under this act are regulated by the Equal Employment Opportunity Commission (EEOC).

Fair Labor Standards Act (FLSA)

FLSA determines whether or not a particular position is considered exempt or nonexempt. Many positions that are "professional," such as librarians and managers who supervise two or more employees, are exempt, are paid a salaried wage, and are not eligible for overtime or minimum wage (Department of Labor, Wage and Hour Division, n.d.). Employees who do not supervise employees, have no bearing on policies or procedures, and are not considered professional employees are nonexempt and are paid overtime (Department of Labor, Wage and Hour Division, n.d.). A good example of a nonexempt employee is an administrative assistant, clerk, or page. Many employers feel that if the employee is deemed "hourly" this is the only test needed and the employee is nonexempt. See Table 4.2 for further tests to distinguish between exempt and nonexempt status.

Age Discrimination Act of 1967

The Age Discrimination Act of 1967 prohibits employers from discriminating against persons over the age of 40 in decisions about hiring,

TABLE 4.2 FEDERAL LABOR STANDARD ACT DEFINITIONS

Executive Employee Exemption

Exempt executive employees generally are responsible for the success or failure of business operations under their management. Other critical elements are (1) whether management is the employee's primary duty, (2) whether the employee directs the work of two or more full-time-equivalent employees, and (3) whether the employee has the authority to hire/fire other employees or, alternatively, whether the employee's suggestions and recommendations as to the hiring, firing, advancement, promotion, or other change of status of other employees are given particular weight.

	YES	NO
1. Is the employee compensated on a *salary basis* at a rate not less than $455 per week?	☐	If no, stop. The employee is not exempt.
2. Does the employee's primary duty consist of managing the enterprise or a customarily recognized department or division thereof? If yes, please describe:	☐	If no, the employee is not exempt under this test.
3. Does the incumbent regularly and customarily supervise two or more employees who are employed in the department or subdivision that the employee manages?	☐	☐
Interview, select, and train employees? Coach employees in proper job performance techniques and procedures?	☐	☐
Direct the work of employees and set/adjust their rates of pay and hours of work?	☐	☐
Maintain records on employee productivity for use in supervision or control?	☐	☐
Appraise employees' productivity and efficiency to recommend promotions or other changes in status?	☐	☐
Handle employee complaints and grievances and discipline employees when necessary?	☐	☐
Plan other employees' work and determine the techniques used in their work?	☐	☐

	YES	NO
Apportion work among different employees?	☐	☐
Determine the types of materials, supplies, or tools to be used by other employees?	☐	☐
Control the flow and distribution of materials and supplies?	☐	☐
Provide for the safety of employees and the property of the employer?	☐	☐
Control the budget? If yes, please explain:	☐	☐
Monitor or implement legal compliance measures?	☐	☐
4. Does the incumbent have shared responsibility for the supervision of the same employees in the same department? If yes, please describe:	☐	☐
5. Does the incumbent have the authority to hire or fire other employees?	☐	☐
If no, is it part of the incumbent's job to make recommendations on hiring, firing, advancement, promotion, or other change of status?	☐	☐
Are the incumbent's recommendations frequently relied upon?	☐	☐
6. What percentage of working time does the incumbent spend providing the leadership duties and responsibilities described above?	_____%	
7. List the employees whose work is customarily and regularly directed by the incumbent:		

Administrative Employee Exemption

The duties portion of the administrative exemption test establishes a two-part inquiry for determining whether an employee performs exempt administrative duties. First, what type of work is performed by the employee? Is the primary duty the performance of work directly related to management or general business operations? Second, what is the level or nature of the work performed? Does the employee's primary duty include the exercise of discretion and independent judgment with respect to matters of significance? All of the relevant factors must be considered when determining whether an employee in an administrative position is exempt.

	YES	NO
1. Is the employee compensated on a *salary basis* at a rate not less than $455 per week?	☐	If no, stop. The employee is not exempt.
2. Please describe the incumbent's primary duty: Is this primary duty directly related to the management or general business operations of the organization or its customers?	☐	If no, the employee is not exempt under this test.
3. Does the incumbent's *primary duty* require the exercise of discretion and *independent* judgment with respect to matters of significance? If yes, does the employee:	☐	If no, the employee is not exempt under this test.
Have the authority to formulate, affect, interpret, or implement management policies or operating practices? If yes, please provide an example:	☐	☐
Carry out major assignments in conducting the operations of the university?	☐	☐
Perform work that affects business operations to a substantial degree?	☐	☐
Have the authority to commit the organization in matters that have significant financial impact? If yes, please provide an example:	☐	☐

	YES	NO
Have the authority to waive or deviate from established policies and procedures without prior approval? If yes, please provide an example:	☐	☐
Provide consultation or expert advice to management?	☐	☐
Have the authority to negotiate and bind the organization on significant matters? If yes, please provide an example:	☐	☐
Have involvement in planning long- or short-term business objectives?	☐	☐
Investigate and resolve matters of significance on behalf of management? If yes, please provide an example:	☐	☐
Represent the organization in handling complaints, arbitrating disputes, or resolving grievances? If yes, please provide an example:	☐	☐

TABLE 4.2 FEDERAL LABOR STANDARD ACT DEFINITIONS (continued)

Computer Employee Exemption

The duties portion of the administrative exemption test establishes a two-part inquiry. An employee who meets the consolidated duties test for computer professionals will be exempt if he or she meets either the salary or fee basis test or is paid at least $27.63 hourly. To qualify as an exempt computer employee, a worker must have a primary duty that consists of the four duties described under #3. The primary duty requirement applies to both salaried and hourly computer employees.

	YES	NO
1. Is the employee compensated on either a *salary* or *fee basis* at a rate not less than $455 per week or, if compensated on an *hourly basis,* at a rate not less than $27.63 per hour?	☐	If no, stop. The employee is not exempt.
2. Is the incumbent employed as a computer systems analyst, computer programmer, software engineer, or other similarly skilled worker in the computer field? If yes, please describe the incumbent's *primary duty:*	☐	If no, the employee is not exempt under this test.
3. Does the incumbent's primary duty consist of:		
(a) The application of systems analysis techniques and procedures, including consulting with users to determine hardware, software, or system functional specifications? If yes, please give an example:	☐	☐
(b) The design, development, documentation, analysis, creation, testing, or modification of computer systems or programs, including prototypes, based on and related to user or systems design specifications? If yes, please give an example:	☐	☐
(c) The design, documentation, testing, creation, or modification of computer programs related to machine operating systems? If yes, please give an example:	☐	☐
(d) A combination of the aforementioned duties, the performance of which requires the same level of skills? If yes, please give an example:	☐	☐

Professional Employee Exemption

The professional exemption actually encompasses two exemptions, one for learned professionals and one for creative professionals. To be an exempt learned professional an employee must have a primary duty that is the performance of work requiring knowledge of an advanced type, including the consistent exercise of discretion and judgment in a field of science or learning where the advanced knowledge is acquired by a prolonged course of specialized intellectual instruction (examples include lawyers, doctors, architects, teachers, etc.). To meet the test for the creative professional exemption, an employee must have a primary duty that involves the performance of work requiring invention, imagination, originality, or talent in a recognized field of artistic or creative endeavor (examples include actors, musicians, novelists, etc.).

Learned Professional Employee

	YES	NO
1. Is the employee compensated on either a *salary* or *fee basis* at a rate not less than \$455 per week?	☐	If no, stop. The employee is not exempt.
2. Please describe the incumbent's primary duty:	☐	☐
3. Does the incumbent's primary duty involve the performance of work requiring advanced knowledge in a field of science or learning that is customarily acquired by a prolonged course of specialized intellectual instruction?	☐	☐
4. Is the incumbent's primary duty predominantly intellectual in character? If yes, please describe:	☐	☐
5. Does the incumbent's primary duty require that his or her advanced knowledge be used to analyze, interpret, or make deductions from varying facts or circumstances? If yes, please give an example:	☐	☐
6. Does the incumbent's primary duty include the consistent exercise of discretion and judgment?	☐	☐

TABLE 4.2 FEDERAL LABOR STANDARD ACT DEFINITIONS (continued)

Creative Professional Employee

	YES	NO
1. Is the employee compensated on either a *salary* or *fee basis* at a rate not less than $455 per week?	☐	If no, stop. The employee is not exempt.
2. Please describe the incumbent's primary duty:	☐	☐
3. Does the incumbent's primary duty involve the performance of work requiring invention, imagination, originality, or talent in a recognized field of artistic or creative endeavor?	☐	☐

Note. *Primary duty* means the main tasks related to the job the incumbent in the position is assigned to do. From "Federal Labor Standard Act Definitions," by the Society for Human Resource Management, n.d., retrieved from http://www.shrm.org

promotion, termination, compensation of terms, conditions, or privileges of employment (Department of Labor, Wage and Hour Division, n.d.). Age discrimination is also regulated by the EEOC.

Continuation of Health Coverage (COBRA)

The Consolidated Omnibus Budget Reconciliation Act (COBRA) gives workers and their families who lose their health benefits the right to choose to continue their group health coverage by their group provider for 18 months under certain circumstances such as voluntary or involuntary job loss, reduction in the hours worked, transition between jobs, death, divorce, and other life events. Qualified individuals are required to pay the entire premium for coverage up to 102% of the cost of the plan.

Occupational Safety and Health Act (OSHA)

OSHA regulations took over seven years to write. All employees are entitled to safe work environments free from workplace hazards. All workplaces have potential hazards. All employees have a right to file anonymous complaints with OSHA. Employers cannot or should not retaliate. If they do, the employee should file another complaint within 30 days under the OSHA Act. Repetitive motion injuries can be hazardous to the health of employees in libraries and information centers, so employees should take breaks often. They should also take care to lift objects correctly.

Worker's compensation injuries are expensive to employers, and no one wants to be injured on the job. Caution employees to be careful and take their time to do things correctly.

Americans with Disabilities Act of 1990 (ADA)

ADA prohibits employers with more than 15 employees to discriminate against qualified individuals based on a disability. Employers must make "reasonable accommodations" for employees. The presence of a disability is sometimes readily apparent, such as those that require a wheelchair. Other disabilities are not, such as acute asthma and fibromyalgia. All three situations are considered disabilities under ADA and need to have some accommodations. The amount of the accommodations can vary, and some are not as noticeable as others. Unseen disabilities like asthma or fibromyalgia tend to be misunderstood because the individual appears able-bodied. Walking up steps when there is no elevator or not having a disability parking placard in the case of the asthmatic can be problematic. The employer should be just as empathetic with unseen disabilities as with seen disabilities and allow for accommodations under ADA.

The Family and Medical Leave Act (FMLA)

According to FMLA, all employees with one year or more of service with an employer are entitled to 12 weeks of unpaid leave for certain medical and family situations (e.g., adoption, caring for a parent) for either the employee or a member of the covered and eligible employee's immediate family; however, in many instances paid leave may be substituted for unpaid FMLA leave. In the FMLA language the 12 weeks can be given all at once or cut up as days or hours at a time. The way in which the 12 weeks (480 hours) are used is up to the agreement of the employee and employer. In most cases, it is to the employer's benefit to be generous and flexible with the employee in negotiating the hours used in FMLA benefits. In many cases, employees with a sick parent or terminally ill family member will use up all vacation and sick time first before using FMLA time.

Health Insurance Portability and Accountability Act (HIPAA)

HIPAA provides rights and protections for participants and beneficiaries in group health plans. HIPAA includes protections for coverage under group health plans for limit exclusions for preexisting conditions, prohibits discrimination against employees and their dependents based on their health status, and allows a special opportunity to enroll in a new plan to individuals under certain circumstances.

Genetic Information Nondiscrimination Act of 2008 (GINA)

GINA is a federal law that prohibits discrimination in health coverage and employment based on genetic information (National Institute of Health, National Human Genome Research Institute, 2009). GINA provides a baseline level of protection against genetic discrimination for all Americans. Some states already have laws that protect against genetic discrimination in health insurance and employment situations. The degrees of protection provided vary widely; some states have less coverage and others more. All entities that are subject to GINA must, at a minimum, comply with all applicable GINA requirements and may also need to comply with more restrictive state laws.

DISCIPLINE

The downside of managing employees is dealing with those who push the limits of behavior, show up late all the time, treat patrons with poor customer service, treat other employees poorly, or otherwise do not do their job. What should a manager do to make sure that the employee and the employer are covered in this instance? Document everything. Everything should be written down so that if it is a performance issue, examples exist of what it is. If the employee or staff member sends out a letter to a patron full of misspellings and the manager finds a copy of it in the file, keep a copy in your office file under the employee's name. Every manager should have a file for every staff member they supervise. All excellent and poor things done should make their way into the file. How can someone remember at evaluation time everything that needs to be covered? The file documenting what has occurred can assist.

Every time the employee is late or absent should be written down. Attendance charts should be kept for every employee so that if someone takes a vacation day or FMLA time off, is tardy, or is ill, it is easy to keep track of the time off. This way if someone is abusing the system it is easy to tell. For computerized documentation, Microsoft Excel is easy to set up to track attendance, as is a database in Access.

The best system of discipline is progressive discipline. This sets up a schedule so that everyone knows what happens. There are steps, and they follow a set pattern. The only thing that can change from organization to organization is the length of time it takes between the steps. Unless there is a union contract that sets out the time frames, err on the side of generous time frames. It costs money to replace employees. Second chances are much cheaper.

Verbal warnings occur once a pattern appears to have been set. Let's say that an employee has begun to be late every Monday or Friday. It has happened every Monday for a month in our example. On the fifth Monday, the employee should be brought into a meeting with the supervisor to discuss the problem. If the meeting is done in a positive way, as the manager wants to help the employee fix the problem, this may be the only warning that need occur. The verbal warning is between the employee and supervisor. It is documented by the supervisor, dated, and put in the employee's file with a 45- to 60-day limit to fix the problem. Many things could occur in the meeting. The supervisor may discover a child care issue, with the provider not ready to take the children at a certain time. Maybe changing the employee's start time by 15 minutes would solve the problem, or maybe there is something else going on. Whatever it is, stay flexible, keep it confidential, and try to assist the employee. Sometimes just listening is all that is needed. Once more, keep it confidential—no one else but you and the employee need to know what is going. If this warning solves the problem, great; it's all done. If not, take the next step in the formal discipline process.

The next step is to give a written warning. The employee is brought in and given a written warning that has been completed and typically signed by the supervisor's boss. Again, the issue is discussed, and ideas are floated on how to solve the problem. At this point, the time frame is again generous—60 to 90 days to give the employee a chance to solve it. The employee is also told that a final warning will be given if necessary at the end of the 60 or 90 days. The final warning means that he or she could lose the job.

If the employee has not solved the disciplinary issue by the end of the prescribed time frame (60 or 90 days), the employee is given a final warning of 30 days. At this point the staff member is told that if the problem is not solved within 30 days, extreme consequences will occur, up to and including termination. A smart employee will understand quickly that if the problem isn't fixed in 30 days he or she will be fired. If the problem still isn't fixed by 30 days, the employee is terminated.

When an employee is terminated, there are a few steps to take the day before the employee leaves for the last time. Erase the employee's log-in and password from all computer systems that the employee had access to. Some people get testy when they are fired and may do all kinds of damage to the integrated library system, electronic databases, and anything else they can think of, including e-mail. Servers can be vulnerable during this time. I have seen hard drives and servers reformatted before. Change any office security pass codes there may be. The morning of the termination, make sure you are the first one in the library along with your IT and security people.

After letting the person go and handling the final check issues according to state law, have the person walked out of the building after packing up all personal items. People do get upset and will do stupid things at this point, and you want to make sure you, your staff, patrons, and library stay safe. Make sure to get all key cards, keys, and any security items back.

TRAINING AND RETAINING

New Hires

Once a shelver or page is hired, this person is now termed a *new hire*. Each new hire has to go through a plethora of paperwork and begins the indoctrination into the ways of the library. Typically the new hire will fill out the W4 federal tax withholding form and the federal I-9 form to prove citizenship, which requires showing two forms of ID, and read the library handbook of the policies and procedures. The employer will explain how the pay system works and where time cards are turned in (electronic or paper). Once all the paperwork is signed, the new shelver is turned over to the hiring manager for training.

Existing Employees

Hiring and training new employees is expensive. Once employees are on board and trained, most organizations want to keep them employed unless there is a performance problem (as discussed earlier). If the person hired is a great hire, works hard for the organization, and contributes to the library, everyone should be happy with the people at the library. How do we keep them? Good morale in the workplace is the most important thing, and many organizations do a really poor job of keeping this up. Good communication with all employees is one aspect. Make sure everyone knows what is going on so they do not hear things through the grapevine or read them in the newspaper after the fact.

Sharing in the good and bad times at the library will also help the staff. When there are good and bad decisions to make, ask the staff's opinions on what they would do. Managers may be surprised that those on the line on a day-to-day basis have a good idea of what is going on and have effective ideas about how to save money.

CLASS EXERCISE

Hiring library personnel is often done through a search committee of four to ten people. Depending on the position to be filled, the institution will have criteria for what type of hiring procedure will be used. For this exercise, the group will go through each step together to determine what would be best for the department and library.

1. Prepare a job description for a part-time clerk.
2. Determine what the hourly wage should be.
3. In the job description, make sure to set out what this person would do and to whom he or she will report.
4. Determine in which department the person will work.
5. Describe your dream person for this position.
6. Put together an ad for this position.

The group can choose from the following three résumés. Take a look at each one and determine which of the three applicants you would hire. Make the assumption that this person was interviewed. Hire one of them for the position you have open. Discuss in class why the choice is the best for the library and the department.

NATHAN TRUCK **4505 25TH AVENUE**
MELROSE PARK, IL 60164
708-555-4958

Work Experience

Produce Assistant, Jewel, Melrose Park, IL, 2009 to Present

- Get produce ready to be put out on display for customers
- Clean the back room of boxes and other garbage
- Help customers find produce as needed
- Assist produce manager as needed

Bagger, Jewel, Melrose Park, IL, 2007–2009

- Bag groceries at checkout stands
- Collect carts in the parking lot
- Take groceries to cars for customers
- Restock grocery bags at checkout stands

Education

- West Leyden High School, Northlake, IL, 2005–2009
- Triton College, River Grove, IL, 2009 to Present

CARMEN GARCIA **507 W. 75TH AVE.**
CHICAGO, IL 60601
312-555-5678

Work Experience

Hairstylist, For Appearances Sake, River Forest, IL, 2008 to Present

- Cuts and styles clients hair
- Colors and perms hair
- Customer service

Education

- Cosmetology, ABC Beauty School, Chicago, IL, 2007

CARRIE TWIGGY **1234 MAIN ST.**
CHICAGO, IL 60601
312-555-1234

Education

• Hickman High School, Columbia, MO, 2004–2008

Work Experience

Juice Barista, Juice Bar R Us, Chicago, IL, 2008 to Present

• Preparing juice based drinks for customers as requested
• Running a cash register and giving back appropriate change

Cashier, Granola Bar & Twigs Health Food Store, Columbia, MO, 2007–2008

• Ran cash register
• Balanced at end of shift
• Gave appropriate change to customers

Hobbies

• Basket Weaving
• Knitting
• Reading

References

Available upon request

References

Department of Labor, Wage and Hour Division. (n.d.). *Federal Labor Standard Act.* Retrieved from www.dol.gov/whd/regs/compliance/hrg.htm

National Institute of Health, National Human Genome Research Institute. (2009, April 6). *The Genetic Information Nondiscrimination Act of 2008, "GINA."* Retrieved from www.genome.gov/24519851

Further Reading on Human Resources Management

Mathis, R. L., & Jackson, J. H. (2008). *Human resource management* (12th ed.). Mason, OH: Thomson-Southwestern.

5
STRATEGIC PLANNING

Mary Wilkins Jordan

Strategic planning is a concept that too often strikes fear into the heart of even the bravest librarian. A good strategic plan can help libraries in so many ways! It allows libraries to anticipate problems and handle them effectively (when, not if, they arise) rather than being overwhelmed. A strategic plan gives libraries the opportunity to take full advantage of every opportunity that comes along and to be as successful as possible in any situation. It provides a roadmap toward goals the library wants to achieve. Rather than just being buffeted by events or reacting to every changing circumstance, the library will know how to proceed.

So, what is strategic planning? Why does this misplaced fear exist?

Strategic planning is the process of looking into the future, figuring out where to go, and deciding how to get there. In the past, this kind of planning has looked about five years into the future and that is fine. As the pace of societal and technological changes has increased, however, strategic time lines have often become more like two- to three-year plans for the future. The time period can be adjusted to suit the needs of the library. Librarians wishing to engage in strategic planning should create plans on a time line that is reasonable for them, considering their own individual environments and needs.

The fear has likely come about because of the difficulty of looking too far into the future with any kind of accuracy. Guessing about the future and being wrong can be an expensive mistake to make—not something any manager wants to do or any library can easily afford.

A good strategic planning process takes into account the impossibility of looking at the future and being omniscient. You do not have to be entirely accurate with predictions and plans, just ready to react to changing circumstances. With a good plan, which provides a good understanding of where you are and what resources you have at hand, reacting to either good or bad changes is much easier and potentially less costly when things do go wrong.

In this chapter we will walk through the basic process of creating a strategic plan and offer suggestions on making the process easier and more effective. At the end is a case study that illustrates a situation in which strategic planning is important, along with some questions to help guide you in figuring out your approach before you begin your own strategic planning process.

SETTING UP A STRATEGIC PLAN

As with any kind of planning process, just talking about it or thinking about it is a nice start—but you need to follow through and get things done to be successful. This follow-through, from ideas to action, is the difference between a real strategic plan and just aimless chatting about ideas. We will be talking about strategic planning in libraries, but these ideas can be transferred to any aspect of long-range planning—career planning, plans for outside agencies, and collaboration with community partners or university departments. The main thing to remember about planning is this: Do it. Do not hesitate and wonder and daydream about it—get it done. Your library will thank you.

If you are in a small library, or an unmotivated one, you may be working on this process alone. That is not a bad thing (and streamlines the discussion, certainly), but you will want to at least bounce ideas off other people. Planning is always better accomplished with a group of people. Involve the staff as much as possible. Why bother bringing in the ideas of other people who may not agree with your visions of the future? The answer is very simple, but one that constantly surprises me with its effectiveness: other people know things and see things that you do not. When you involve them in the strategic planning process, they will be able to contribute pieces to the puzzle that would otherwise be missing. The final plan will be stronger for any vigorous debate that occurs during the process.

Do not forget to write all of this down. It is fine to have conferences and brainstorming sessions with your committee or others (great even!), but if you do not start with an agenda and end with some written documentation of the process, it is nothing but a big waste of time for anyone involved. After you finish meeting, no two people will remember the plan the same way, so you want to be sure ideas are recorded. Sharing plans, and edits to plans, will help keep things moving—and keeps everyone on topic.

One of the guiding constructs to any kind of planning purposes should be the library's mission or vision statement. This should be a positive, aspirational statement, letting everyone know what the library does and what its service focus is for the community. The strategic plan should all be tied back to this vision of what the library can do and what it can provide. In any library, the entire mission is always to serve the community; defining that community and its needs will be a starting point and provide a constant touchstone for the development of a good strategic plan.

Step 1: Gather Data

The first step in any planning process is to start scurrying around the library and figuring out where all kinds of documents are located. If the library already has a strategic plan, or any sort of plan, that is great! Grab that first, along with any copies going back a few years. No plans already existing? You can take a moment to be disappointed (but not surprised), then move on to the other documents you will need. Collect the budget for this year, two or three years in the past, and any plans for upcoming budgets. Budget documents are plans with dollar signs attached to them, so they will be very useful in the strategic planning process. Any annual reports your library files would be good to have, and again pick up a few prior years if they are available. Does your library have a marketing plan? Go ahead and include that. You may want to look wider in this process, beyond your own walls. Does your city include the library in its strategic planning process? Grab a copy of that. (If they do not mention you—why not?) If you are in an academic or school library, look to see what kind of planning documents your school district or college or university has, particularly anything that mentions your library or is relevant to your work. Likewise in a special library, see what kinds of planning documents exist, and figure out how you can insert yourself into them if you are not already there.

Take a final look around the file cabinet or the website. Are there other important-looking pieces of paper or documents? Collect those too. Anything you can find that gives you information about the state of the library now, where it has been lately, and where it may be headed will be helpful to you. The more information you start with as you plan, the easier it will be to make a good plan without as much wasted time and effort.

Step 2: Assess the Current Situation

Now you probably have a physical and virtual pile of documents and some sense of the tasks ahead of you. Why bother picking up all these items from past years (which may or may not have been positive ones for your library)? It is valuable to know what you have been doing—and sometimes very illuminating to see what has been going on in the past that you either did not know about or were not present for when it occurred.

This is where you may be working with a committee or group, assigning different piles of documents to different people to review. If you are alone in the process, then spend some quality time planning out how you will conduct your review. In this step, you want to gain an understanding of the places your library has been and what kind of resources you have now. This will give you the foundation of your plan to determine where you have been and what will be good and bad for your library.

Maybe you have worked with the traditional favorite of planners everywhere: the SWOT analysis. If not, this is a perfect time to try it out. SWOT, which stands for *strengths, weaknesses, opportunities,* and *threats,* is a structured way for you to assess the current state of your library:

1. Strengths—These are the things your library already does well. Do you have a great programming selection? This is something to record in your analysis. Does your library have an endowment for some of your collection development purchasing? Mention it here. Dedicated group of volunteers? Strong community support? Devoted storytime attendees? All of these are good, and your library probably has a lot more of these good things than you realize. This is a fun place to start the evaluation process, as you can bask in the glow of the successes the library has attained.
2. Weaknesses—Keep hold of the positive things you learned in the first part to buoy your spirits here. This does not need to be depressing; no library can be as practically perfect in every way as Mary Poppins was in her profession. A common area of weakness for libraries is the budget. Too often, no one really knows how the library's budget is created or even what is in it. While the pro-

cess of creation and approval may be fiendishly difficult in some libraries, the actual budget itself is not terribly difficult to work with: money comes in and money goes out, and it is best to keep track of both. The problem of a shrinking budget, or a stable budget with increased demand, is becoming too common in libraries. Other potential weaknesses may include a volatile host agency—the city or school district or company your library serves may be in chaos. It may fail to see the value of your library (you will need to address that forcefully!). A staffing shortage may exist in your library, temporary or long term. There may not be anyone who is managing and caring for your website (your electronic branch), making your library look shabby. Be brave and just write them all down. Improvements can happen only when you have some ideas about what you need to improve!

3. Opportunities—Look around your library and your community and patron population. What kind of opportunities do you see here? Would an increase in your social media presence help educate patrons about your resources and increase usage of both electronic and in-house materials? Would some outreach to a department of your host business or university help it realize the services your library provides? Do you have an enthusiastic group of teens in the library who could be formed into a Teen Board, helping develop some programming and training focused on helping youth members of your library learn about and take advantage of resources? Are Library Services and Technology Act (LSTA) grants or other potentially useful grants coming up soon? Could a staff member create an online newsletter, helping connect your library to a host of potential users in your community? Could there be Friday Movie Night in the library complete with popcorn? Or Wii Wednesday in the meeting room, bringing in kids and adults to battle it out in virtual skateboarding combat? There are a lot of possibilities for things that you could do, and maybe you and your committee have seen the possibilities for a few different ideas but have not had the time or money or initiative to get there. Put those ideas into this section.
4. Threats—What problems do you see looming ahead? Do you know a factory or business in town that is going to close down, taking jobs and property values with it? Do you know that one of your two librarians will be out on maternity leave for a while, and you will have to scramble to fill those hours? Is there a bookstore in town with competing programming on the same night or

nights the library has programming? Threats can be big or small, but they should be fairly realistic. It is possible that a threat to the library could include an asteroid from space destroying the building, and maybe you should be sure the insurance is up to date, but otherwise leave fanciful threats out of this discussion. Is there an election coming up, with a potentially (or definitely) antilibrary candidate in the race? That would certainly be a threat, and one that libraries seem to increasingly face. Likewise budget decreases, layoffs, floods of patrons needing job-hunting experience, and more may be affecting your library. Put them all down here, and then they can be dealt with more effectively.

Using the SWOT analysis to determine your library's current situation will help you to move on to the next step in the strategic planning process.

Step 3: Set Goals
This is another fun part—what do you want to do? This is where you and your group can get together and brainstorm and dream and look ahead to your future. After you have gathered all your information and analyzed your current situation, you will be in good shape to move forward. In the early stages of dreaming about the future, go ahead and dream big—write down all the wild things you would like to do in the library and outside the walls. Figuring out how to get there is a later step. Even if you are not able to include your possible goals into this strategic plan, hang onto them because you never know when something unexpected will happen and you can be ready with some goals.

Another common acronym (management is full of them!) that pertains to goal setting can help you to keep on track with your crazy dreams by guiding you to set and meet certain standards. Goals should be SMART, which stands for *specific, measurable, achievable, realistic,* and *timely:*

1. Specific—You may want to circulate more books in your library, but what does this really mean? A specific goal would include the detail of wanting to increase circulation 3% each year for the next three years, for example, or that you want to double the circulation of Spanish language materials in your library, or that you want to increase the homebound population you serve to 50 participants this year. Adding in a number or a percentage helps you make the goal specific; once you have a specific goal, you can see

how to achieve it. Without specificity, goals are flabby and just hang around the strategic plan looking vaguely like good ideas that no one ever followed up on accomplishing.

2. Measurable—Now that you have those fancy numbers included to make the goal specific, you can easily tell where you are now and where you need to be in the future. You may have a goal of "increased participation in information literacy classes," but you need to have some numbers in there to know when an increase occurs. Likewise, if your goal is "to make contact with all third-grade teachers in the district," you want to know how many people that will entail. You can achieve what you can measure, so figuring out how to measure your goals will give you the tools you need to get to those goals.
3. Achievable—You may need more money for your library and plan to engage in fundraising to meet necessary budget goals. A goal like "I will call 50 alumni a day to raise money for the new university library bookshelves" sounds nice, but how likely is it that you have time to do this? Likewise, a goal of raising one million dollars may be out of the reach of most libraries without professional fundraisers to assist them. (Maybe figuring out how to get a professional fundraiser could be a goal for your library?)
4. Realistic—Making goals achievable and realistic does not mean they should be puny ideas. They can be as grand and exciting as you can dream them! But you should be able to accomplish them within your strategic planning period. So a long-term goal may be to build a new building for your library, but the realistic goals you can set during this time may include things like hiring a general contractor, writing an Institute of Museum and Library Science (IMLS) grant, finding land for expansion, and drafting plans for the new building. These may be realistic for your library to accomplish in two years. Or your realistic goal may be to add in two more special programs a year—something that would stretch your current offerings but would still give you the chance to realistically achieve the goal. *Realistic* is defined only from the perspective of your library, so work with what you have and what you can dream—together.
5. Timely—This means the goals should be able to be completed within the time period of your strategic plan. Setting your plan for a specific time frame means that you understand the scope of your goals and how to plan for them to best ensure the plan's success. It also means you work to accomplish your goals within

this time period. It would not be a timely goal to plan for a construction grant for a new building if these grants are offered only every few years and the next one is five years away. If your goals have been fitting into the other criteria for SMART goals, this part may come easily. Giving goals a definite time line lets you think through the things that need to be accomplished sooner rather than put them off, and deadlines focus everyone to work on the goal. Letting goals be amorphous, "someday we will get to that," may be easier but does not get anything done.

Step 4: Establish Evaluation Standards

At this point, you have completed the hard part of the planning process, so you want to be sure it does not all go to waste! The best way to do that is to set up some standards for measuring your progress toward the goals you have created. This does not have to be a complicated process, but you need to think about the right way to get things done. What are you trying to accomplish? Maybe you have a SMART goal of doubling the number of outreach programs you offer to incoming freshmen over the next three years. How will you measure success? You need to start off by knowing how many programs you are currently offering, identifying those programs you want to offer (new ones or repeats of current ones), and then figuring out how to get it done. Then you can set some intermediate goals to move you toward the big goals: 50% more programs this year and 50% the next, focus groups with patrons to discover what kind of programs they want, the number of people attending each program, evaluation of the success of each program through surveys, and so forth. At this point, whatever you want to accomplish will be the things you want to measure to see whether you are achieving them. Defining these measurements will let you see where the plan is succeeding and where it needs to be improved or adjusted along the way.

Step 5: Implement the Plan

There is nothing more frustrating to staff (and to you!) than a lot of work that comes to nothing. After you have invested all this time and effort in the plan, be sure you *do* something with it!

Too many libraries put together plans or spend a lot of time collecting data for things that mean nothing and are never used. Do you know a library where everyone collects reference statistics or circulation statistics—but nothing is ever done with these data? This pointless busywork takes away time that could be spent doing exciting or valuable things to advance the library's goals.

Of course this can be difficult; as everyone who has made the leap from "good plan on paper" to "good plan in action" knows, there will be bumps and changes along the way. That is fine! Progress is never easy and straightforward; it always requires some work and some struggle. Without this process—without naming and chasing down goals—libraries stagnate. We have all seen the issues with stagnating libraries—from bored, burned-out staff who preside over ever-decreasing patron counts, to libraries out of touch being irrelevant to their communities and finally being closed. Who wants to work in a place like that, when instead you can work in a library that is intent on improving services and materials for the community? Working toward a positive goal will help keep librarians and staff motivated and help them continue to build their professional skills to keep them interested in helping the library.

Take action! Get that plan going!

Step 6: Assess the Plan

As you continually check on the evaluation standards you set up, it is likely that not all the goals will be met, and those that are met may need to be modified. This is not a problem; this is how plans work. You look into the future and make your best possible guesses about the ways you and your library will be able to take action. The guesses made are never 100% correct, so keep modifying the plan to reflect those changes. This should not mean you give up on your goals—it could mean that you increase them! But even if some of the goals are difficult for you, that is fine. You respond as well as possible and keep moving forward.

As you move forward in time to reach the end of your strategic planning period, looking back over the plan to see what has and has not been accomplished is crucial for setting up the next plan. Not everything will be finished or done as planned, but if regular checks were done on the plan's progress, those revised goals can become part of the overall plan. You will want to have the next plan in place before this one expires, if possible. This will help you to stay on your forward-moving course.

Final Step: Celebrate!

This is my favorite part of any plan: the celebration! It is important to acknowledge the work and effort that went into a plan and the effort made to achieve the goals. Whether or not your plan was a total success, it is good to have an end period—a time to mark that these particular work goals are over and that new things are ahead on the horizon.

Hopefully, this is a celebration of successful completion of one plan and a look ahead to the next plan, which is built on the foundations of this one. If the celebration is more aptly described as "so glad that's over," this is still worthy of notice. Take the time to celebrate the end of the plan, and staff will appreciate your appreciation of their work.

POTENTIAL PROBLEMS

Now that we have walked through the process of setting up the plan, let's note a few potential problems that can arise with every strategic plan. They usually come from two familiar sources: staff and patrons.

Bringing changes to people's work routines and responsibilities almost inevitably means they are going to be upset or disturbed or refuse to go along with the plan. At worst, they may actively try to sabotage the plan's chance for success. So what can you do in advance to help your staff respond in a more positive way to changes? Or to make your patrons feel more comfortable with new things in the library?

Maintaining transparency is often the best and easiest solution when working with any kind of plan. As we discussed previously, involving staff in the process from the very beginning to help brainstorm, or bring in their own ideas and suggestions, not only acknowledges their involvement but also shows them you are committed to their participation and assistance. Not every idea or suggestion will be implemented in a plan, and being up front about that will be helpful to the process; then they won't feel like their input was ignored and that they aren't valuable members of the team. Working with a committee of people from across the library, or from across the department if you are working with only part of the library, will be helpful to the plan by making it stronger and to the staff by getting them involved before it is finalized. They will not only be able to provide ideas to the committee and report on the committee's progress to other staff, but they can also serve as ambassadors in explaining the process of the planning and the ideas that are being raised. Staff should be committed volunteers, if at all possible, not people dragged into the process against their will. Without some positive energy from people committed to success in this group, the plan will be troubled from the start.

Patrons can also resist changes in the library as strategic plans are implemented. New catalog interfaces can throw them off their usual routine of searching. Elimination of some programs, even with the addition of others, can leave them feeling slighted or threatened. As with staff members, being as transparent as possible with patrons will help to overcome their resistance to changes. Also similar to dealing with staff, a manager needs to refuse to become overwhelmed by voices of negativity. Someone needs to be responsible for pushing forward with a plan, even when other people are nervous or upset—and that person is the manager. Working with patrons to give them a forum to share ideas can be helpful in breaking down resistance. Open meetings, online surveys, usability testing, focus groups, or even just asking people how they are doing and what they are thinking as you share details of the plan can all help to reduce opposition and bring people over to supporting the plan.

CONCLUSION

Change is not easy for most people, and a strategic plan can represent a lot of change over time and look overwhelming in the beginning to everyone. But with persistence, communication, and a good strategy for success, strategic planning can play an important positive role in every library. In this chapter, we looked at the process of strategic planning and have walked through the basics of creating a strategic plan while avoiding some of the obstacles. Fear of the strategic plan is not necessary; a good plan and a good planning process are both useful and helpful tools to help a library be successful.

Although the basic process of strategic planning is not complicated, as outlined in this chapter, a richer understanding of it may give you more confidence or help make your plan easier. Many people have written about strategic planning, and we encourage you to read some of the resources included in the Further Readings section. It is always helpful to see how other libraries handle issues, including planning. It is also good to look outside the profession, to see how problems and issues are addressed by others. This may bring new ideas to your plan or help you consider problems you did not think of by learning about how they were solved elsewhere.

CASE STUDY AND DISCUSSION QUESTIONS

Jane recently started her new job as head of the Children's Department at the Harding Public Library. The position had been vacant for a little while, since the previous head retired after 25 years, to save some money in the budget. The collection is well stocked but could probably use some more weeding. The staff seems pretty good, with two degreed librarians, five part-time paraprofessionals, and a small group of volunteers. The library does not make use of any social media, and the website has not been updated in a while. The previous head had organized school outreach visits in the past, but this had faded away as she was getting ready to retire.

Jane has heard there are training opportunities available through the city's training department, which may be of use to the staff. She knows the next round of LSTA grants will be announced in about three months; as the library has been impacted by budget cuts, she definitely wants to be ready to apply for a grant. She has noticed there seems to be a large number of homeschooled families in the library. Her staff tells her this is due partly to the poor reputation of the local schools; many parents from the military base nearby prefer to homeschool their children, as do other families in the community. They all make frequent use of the library. Jane wants to be active in the professional world also, to keep her skills sharp, so she wants to find some useful children's librarians groups to join but has not had time to look for them yet. She would like to do more outreach to the community, particularly to the growing Hispanic population who have not traditionally used the library very much.

1. How should Jane start putting together a strategic plan for her department?
2. What goals should she include?
3. What things would be assigned to year one?
   a. Year two?
   b. Beyond that?
   c. And how do you decided what goes in each and what comes first?
4. What resources will she need?
   a. What people?
   b. What information that she does not yet have?
5. How will she evaluate progress along the way?
6. How can the plan be assessed at the end to see whether it was successful?

Further Readings on Strategic Planning

Allison, M. (2003). *Strategic planning for nonprofit organizations* (2nd ed.). Hoboken, NJ: Wiley.

Billings, M. (2005). Web-based strategic planning. *Community College Journal of Research & Practice, 29*(8), 609–610.

Bryson, J. M. (2004). *Strategic planning for public and nonprofit organizations: A guide to strengthening and sustaining organizational achievement* (3rd ed.). Hoboken, NJ: Jossey-Bass.

Crowley, J. (2004). *Developing a vision: Strategic planning and the library media specialist.* Santa Barbara, CA: Libraries Unlimited.

Haberaecker, H. J. (2004). Strategic planning and budgeting to achieve core missions. *New Directions for Institutional Research, 2004*(123), 71–87.

Haricombe, L. J., & Boettcher, B. J. (2004). Using LibQUAL+™ data in strategic planning: Bowling Green State University. *Journal of Library Administration, 40*(3/4), 181–195.

Kronenfeld, M. R. (2008). Using strategic goals to guide the development of library resources, services, and web sites. *Journal of Electronic Resources in Medical Libraries, 5*(4), 325–337.

Lampert, C., & Vaughan, J. (2009). Success factors and strategic planning: Rebuilding an academic library digitization program. *Information Technology & Libraries, 28*(3), 116–136.

Matthews, J. (2005). *Strategic planning and management for library managers.* Santa Barbara, CA: Libraries Unlimited.

Nelson, S. S. (2008). *Strategic planning for results.* Chicago, IL: ALA Editions.

Paris, K. A. (2004). Moving the strategic plan off the shelf and into action at the University of Wisconsin–Madison. *New Directions for Institutional Research, 2004*(123), 121–127.

Redlinger, L. J., & Valcik, N. A. (2008). Using return on investment models of programs and faculty for strategic planning. *New Directions for Institutional Research, 2008*(140), 93–108.

Shorb, S. R., & Driscoll, L. (2004). LibQUAL+ ™ meets strategic planning at the University of Florida. *Journal of Library Administration, 40*(3/4), 173–180.

Smith, J., & Love, P. D. (2004). Stakeholder management during project inception: Strategic needs analysis. *Journal of Architectural Engineering, 10*(1), 22–33.

Takhar, J., & Tipping, J. (2008). Using focus groups for strategic planning in a CME unit. *Journal of Continuing Education in the Health Professions, 28*(2), 113–114.

Thompson, K. (2011). If you build it, will they come? *American Music Teacher, 60*(4), 10–14.

Trainer, J. F. (2004). Models and tools for strategic planning. *New Directions for Institutional Research, 2004*(123), 129–138.

Welsh, J. F., Nunez, W. J., & Petrosko, J. (2006). Assessing and cultivating support for strategic planning: Searching for best practices in a reform environment. *Assessment & Evaluation in Higher Education, 31*(6), 693–708.

6
LEADERSHIP AND DECISION MAKING

Mary Wilkins Jordan and Lisa K. Hussey

What is leadership? At first glance, it seems like an easy concept to describe. You can probably think of several people right now who you would consider good leaders; conversely, a few people you would consider to be poor leaders may pop into your mind. So you have some ideas already about the definition of a leader; but, do you really know how to identify a leader? Figure out who will be a good leader? Do you know how you can train people to be leaders? Gaining a fuller understanding of what makes a good leader will help you to identify good leadership attributes in yourself and others.

As with any complex idea, breaking the big overarching concept of leadership into smaller pieces for consideration will make all the difference in helping you to be a better leader for yourself and your organization. Good leadership is a concept people have been thinking about for a long time, probably as long as human beings have existed. So while it may not be possible to understand every aspect of leadership fully in every way, the ideas we will review in this chapter will help you to understand more about the background of leadership, to identify some of the competencies you may want to develop for yourself and encourage in others, and to give you some practical strategies for making decisions—the hallmark of a good leader. Distilling this knowledge for yourself will help you to understand what leadership means to you and in your organization, and it will help you begin the lifelong learning necessary to be a leader, particularly in a fast-changing profession like library and information science (LIS).

Let's begin by looking at some examples of leaders to see what leadership means to different people and in different contexts.

1. Bill Gates—Gates is known for his leadership of Microsoft, for starting the Bill and Melinda Gates Foundation, and for providing leadership in expanding libraries' technological resources and in global health issues such as malaria, polio, and AIDS (Bill & Melinda Gates Foundation, 2012).
2. Ernest Shackleton—Shackleton led an amazing voyage to explore Antarctica, only to see his ship destroyed; he worked with his team to keep them going for the two years it took to be rescued, with every single man coming back alive (NOVA Online, 2002).
3. Martin Luther King Jr.—King won the Nobel Peace Prize in 1964. His words helped to change a nation's views on segregation, and his nonviolent protests shaped the dialogue for social change (The Nobel Foundation, 2012).
4. Neil Armstrong—Armstrong had a long and distinguished career with NASA after he became the first man to walk on the moon. He has been honored by organizations and countries all over the world, but part of his strategy for handling his great influence was to step out of the public eye as much as possible to avoid overshadowing issues (NASA, 2012).

None of these people are librarians, yet all stand as examples of leaders who can be models for the LIS profession. Understanding what is valued in different leaders, as well as different ideas about leaders and the skills they need, will help you develop your own leadership style. Leadership is essentially an individual skill in that everyone has his or her own way of leading; but other people need to understand your leadership style so they know whether to follow.

How is leadership different from management? Warren Bennis (1991) has said the difference between leaders and managers is that managers do things right and leaders do the right thing. While there is merit in looking at these as different concepts, by helping you to focus in on the ideas of leadership and some strategies for leading from any position in an organization, looking at leadership and management separately is really just an academic exercise. To be a good leader in most LIS organizations you will need those skills classified as management, and to be a good manager you need leadership abilities. The best manager is one who understands when to be a manager and when to be a leader. The combination of these is what will help you to not only get hired and promoted but also to be successful in your job.

It may also be helpful to view leadership as both a property and a process (Griffin, 2008). Essentially, leadership can be seen as a combination of who a person is (property) and what that person actually does (process). This is part of what makes the idea of leadership so complex. Some leaders don't have the obvious characteristics of a leader, but their actions are what inspire others, whereas other leaders may not always seem to act accordingly, but who they are can be enough to motivate followers.

Most librarians do not seek out a leadership position. As with greatness, sometimes it is just thrust upon you, and it will be important that you are able to meet the challenge. So, let's start off with some background ideas other people have developed on leadership and go from there.

LEADERSHIP THEORIES

People have spent a great deal of effort thinking about what makes a leader. Although many of these ideas were probably lost or discarded as not helpful, several were formalized into theories, written down, and discussed, and their usefulness is evident to this day. (Note: These are theories generally studied in the United States. Other areas of the world have developed their own theories of leadership that also contribute to the understanding of leadership, and you may wish to explore some of them more broadly after reading this chapter.) While none of these is the One True Description of All Leaders, looking at ideas people have held to be important can give you a sense of the things you would want to focus on in your own leadership development.

Theory of Divine Right and the Power Theory

One of the original theories of leadership is the concept of divine right. This goes back to the days of monarchies and hereditary power structures. The main idea of divine right is that people are born into leadership; their position of power in society is ordained. For this theory to work, society must be a rigidly hierarchical arrangement whereby certain members, by birthright and some kind of divine mandate, are ordained with the right and the responsibility to lead the rest of society. As we look through history, this theory has created both good leaders, such as Queen Elizabeth I, the Virgin Queen, and horrible tyrants, like King Louis XVI, whose reign was ended with the French Revolution.

A similar concept is the power theory, which defines leadership as the successful utilization of power from any power base. The use of power not only will propel the person into a position as a leader, but it will also serve to sustain the person in that position. Machiavelli (1985) wrote about this leadership style in *The Prince.* In Machiavelli's view, the prince's primary responsibility is first to become a prince and then to remain one. The prince is not bound by others' moral codes or laws because he is the prince and whatever he does is right, regardless of laws or moral codes. The use of power by the prince is intended not only to maintain the prince's leadership but to also maintain the stability of the state. Machiavelli saw the role of the prince as both leader and representative of the state. As long as the prince maintains his power, the state or principality remains stable.

Neither the theory of divine right nor the power theory addresses leadership as much as it defines absolute rulers. Although the rulers may have a strong control over their "followers," they do not lead as much as they force compliance. Having power does not automatically make an individual a leader. It is how that power is used that is significant in leadership. This is an important distinction to remember.

Trait Theory

Another attempt to understand and define leadership and identify leaders is the trait theory. Traits are things about a person that generally cannot be changed. Some examples of traits deemed important for being a good leader include being male or being tall. While you cannot learn to be taller or a different gender (surgical options exist, but the traits still defy an ability to be learned), there are other traits that are amenable to a training process. Generally, this theory focuses on finding the relevant traits assigned as good for leaders to know and declaring people with those traits to be the leader (Biggart & Hamilton, 1987). This theory has the advantage of making the leadership selection process easier than if all people are considered as possible leader candidates. However, as is true in so many things, easier is not always the best way to go. Taking the more cumbersome route of really looking at individuals and their particular aptitude for leadership roles should result in better leaders than just identifying traits.

Administrative Management

The administrative school of management and leadership theories was the next to develop to help managers to be successful. Frenchman Henri Fayol developed six primary functions of management, disseminating them in 1918. These are still used by many today in understanding the role and function of managers. Mary Parker Follett was a Boston-based theoretician in this school in the 1910s and 1920s. She focused on the holistic aspect of an organization and on the need to build reciprocal relationships between managers and staff. Her additions to management theory bridged the ideas of administrative and human relations, and her ideas are still valued today. In the 1920s and 1930s, the human relations school of thought rose to prominence. Chester Barnard was one of the most prominent thinkers in this area. He wrote *The Functions of the Executive* in 1938, in which he outlined his ideas on organization and the functions that managers and leaders should carry out in the workplace. His top three functions are to establish and maintain an effective communication system; to hire and retain effective personnel; and to motivate those personnel.

SITUATIONAL THEORIES

Some theorists believe it is the situation that creates the leader. In these theories, the emergence of a leader is the result of time, place, and circumstance. These theories are related to the contingency theories in general management. In his 1967 book *A Theory of Leadership Effectiveness,* Fred Fiedler theorized there was not one best way to manage and that, instead, leaders need to look at each situation individually and fit their leadership style to suit the circumstances. This is the contingency theory, and the emphasis on flexibility makes this a useful skill for leaders. In total quality management (TQM), the focus is on building quality in the workplace by understanding and defining quality and then building up procedures and assessments to ensure it is achieved. This model encourages managers/leaders to have their employees develop the skills necessary to meet the quality standards (Oakland, 2003).

Related to these concepts is the idea of situational leadership, where different circumstances require different types of leadership (Evans, 1970; Graeff, 1983; Hersey & Blanchard, 1969; House & Mitchell, 1974). The idea behind these theories is that the level of leadership provided depends on the task at hand and the maturity of the follower. Maturity in this case refers to the experience, not the age, of the follower. As followers gain more experience at a task, they mature. The task performed also greatly influences the process, as the more ambiguous a job, the more direction and support a subordinate may need. The leader will measure a subordinate's readiness to do a job and then provide the appropriate leadership style for the situation. Examples of leadership styles include telling or directing, persuading or coaching, participative management, and delegation. In the early stages, leaders must devote time to help followers learn and develop. As the followers progress, leaders will give them more responsibility and autonomy until the followers are able to function with minimal input from the leader.

The situational theories focus on developing the follower or the worker. This view recognized the role of followers, as well as the attitude of leaders as part of the overall leadership process. Douglas McGregor (1960), in his book *The Human Side of Enterprise,* also focused on the role of the worker and the attitude of the leader or manager. McGregor's work laid out two different kinds of workers. Theory X says that employees need to be closely monitored, as they are naturally lazy and need to be constantly prodded to work. In theory Y, the managers take a hands-off approach, as the employees are presumed to want to work; managers need only to help bring out the inner self-motivation of their employees. Theory Y managers can be seen as leaders as they work to develop and grow their employees. Managers inspire motivation by allowing employees to do their best work and to develop rather than micromanaging every step.

William Ouchi wrote the book *Theory Z: How American Business Can Meet the Japanese Challenge* in 1981, when Japanese businesses were booming and American industry was declining. His ideas were based on the practices he observed in Japanese corporations, in particular that workers want to have close relationships with people at work, that social/family-style aspects of an organization are as important (or more so) than the work people are doing, and that managers need to be responsible for the well-being of staff. In the application of this theory, managers would function both as facilitators of work and as pseudo heads of a family. However, theory Z does not easily translate to the American workplace. The central focus on improving the group over the individual is not always possible to implement, as individualism is a strong part of the work culture of the United States.

TRANSFORMATIONAL AND TRANSACTIONAL THEORIES

Transformational leadership theory is "a motivational leadership style which involves presenting a clear organizational vision and inspiring employees to work towards this vision through establishing connections with employees, understanding employees' needs, and helping employees reach their potential" (Fitzgerald & Schutte, 2010, p. 495). Working this theory into your own leadership practice would inspire a different type of externalized leadership than would more authoritarian theories. The development of connections with people—staff, patrons—would be necessary to achieve this leadership style; people uncomfortable with this kind of professional intimacy may be more adept at incorporating other theoretical bases into their leadership practice and style.

Related to this theory is that of transactional leadership. Under this theory, leadership is more of a give-and-take situation between leaders and followers; followers give their obedience to leaders and follow directions, or they do not; they achieve goals or they do not (Laohavichien, Fredendall, & Cantrell, 2009, pp. 8–9). Based on this, leaders issue rewards for good behavior or punishments for poor performance in the furtherance of the organization's objectives. It may be less personal, but it is a rational methodology of providing leadership in an organizational structure.

In transformational leadership, the power of the leader comes from the relationship between the leader and follower. Transformational leaders work to improve the situation and work of followers. On the other hand, transactional leaders depend on reward power to motivate their followers. Transactional leaders have power only if the rewards to be given or withheld have value to the follower or worker. It is a much more limited scope of influence and inspiration.

Charismatic Leadership

Another theory of leadership is charismatic leadership. In this theory, the entire system of leadership revolves around the person in the position of leadership and her personal characteristics, which may help drive staff, patrons, and others to want to follow her and her goals for the organization (Hayibor, Agle, Sears, Sonnenfeld, & Ward, 2011). In this theory it may be difficult to learn to be charismatic, but harnessing the personal qualities that make people want to follow a leader may help you hone leadership skills. The downside of this theory is that it is difficult to share power with other people or to delegate powers to others; when power and respect are given to a leader on the basis of personal skills, it may be a challenge for leaders to spread those skills to other managers or leaders who may also need to gather respect from staff. However, it may be valuable for leaders who can use this theory to exercise it in their own work, as it can be a powerful strategy for encouraging others to follow their direction and goals.

While this is nowhere near a complete list, these theories can help you to understand some of the thinking that has gone into developing ideas about leaders and leadership. They go only so far and further serve to emphasize what a slippery concept leadership is to define. All this thinking over all these years about leadership, and there is still not one right way to define or describe leadership. So let's turn to a more practical way of understanding what leaders are and how to become one: competencies.

LEADERSHIP COMPETENCIES

What is a competency? This is yet another fairly slippery idea that has resisted a single definition being placed on it. Competencies are generally understood to be knowledge, skills, and/or abilities—things that can be learned or developed with training and practice. I, and others, have expanded this definition to include other things that are less easily measured but that still could be developed or improved with training. Birdir and Pearson (2000), looking at research chefs to see what made them good leaders, defined competency for the purposes of their study "as skills, ability, knowledge, and other attributes that make a successful research chef" (p. 205).

This definition can come dangerously close to the trait theory but should be distinguished: in this understanding of leadership, competencies can be learned or improved, whereas traits are present or not. There can be some close cases, and they may come down to individual decisions on which side of the line they fall; but that focus on trainability should be the defining factor. If someone can improve—not necessarily become perfect, just improve—then the idea can be considered a competency.

So where are the leadership competencies for the LIS profession found? Some have been developed through research, using different methods and strategies to develop lists; these are the most trustworthy and would be the best place to spend your time in study. Other competency lists were developed by authors from their own experience or from anecdotal experiences of librarians and other professionals. Still others (a significant number of them) are presented in the literature with no discussion of their method of creation, just suggested as important. Although this last group may describe useful competencies, a lack of explanation about their development is troubling and might not result in the most trustworthy group. Again, it will be necessary for you to decide what competencies will be the most necessary and relevant to you in your own development and for your individual organization.

Helmick and Swigger (2006) carried out a study of leadership competencies for librarians, looking at those working in the western part of the United States. Their competencies included building positive staff–patron relationships; responding to customer needs and demands; applying creative thinking and problem-solving skills; and articulating the value of positive attitude (Helmick & Swigger, 2006). Murphy (1988) looked at the leadership competencies of 12 corporate librarians. After considering several different viewpoints from these leaders, she concluded with a list of competencies observed by these leaders to be important for successful library leadership. They include communication, persistence, empowering others, and vision. Schreiber and Shannon assembled a list of competencies (which they refer to as leadership traits) based on ideas they have gathered over many years of training and consulting with leaders. The competencies they identify as important include self-awareness, customer focus, and embracing change (Schreiber & Shannon, 2001, p. 46).

Maureen Sullivan (1999) brings forward her leadership competency list in a discussion about leadership on a national level in the profession. Competencies she believes important include collaboration, persistence, and investment of time and energy (Sullivan, 1999, p. 141). In their discussion of the urban library council training program, Nicely and Dempsey (2005) discuss the effects the program has had on the mentee sponsored in their own library. Competencies they see as developing as a result of this program include confidence, decisiveness, and being savvy at building networks (Nicely & Dempsey, 2005, p. 297).

When looking at competencies, remember to consider whether they can be improved with training or whether they are things that can be learned. It is not unrealistic to assume people will achieve perfection on all identified competencies, but not all competencies are necessarily helpful (delegation is always available). Being aware of the important leadership competencies and improving on each of them is important for good leaders. When you are looking at training programs, look at the goals listed for participants; these are the competencies the program directors believe are most important for leaders to know. If a program has no goals, are there no competencies to be learned? Sadly, this situation is all too common, and it is probably a sign that the training will not be helpful. Any leadership or managerial training that does nothing more than provide a network of other new and aspiring managers for you to meet is probably a waste of your time.

Of all the competencies important for leaders, one stands apart and may be the defining criterion separating leaders from followers: decision making. Without the ability to make decisions—good decisions—a person cannot be a leader. She may have the title, but a leader must be able to make a decision that will affect herself and her organization and then to deal with the consequences of that decision. In the next section, we will walk through some strategies for making good decisions.

DECISION MAKING

Making good decisions is important, but if it were as easy doing it as just saying it, everyone would already be doing it. Decision making can be tough, but having a plan and some experience at it will help you to make decisions that, if not always perfect (which is impossible), will be better than having no plan and no goals. Throughout your career you will want to focus on getting more practice in making good decisions so that when an important one comes along you are ready for it.

How do you start? There are several different ways to make decisions. The director or dean can flip a coin. The manager can go from the gut—making a decision based on instincts. The management team can do the same thing that has always been done in this situation (or a similar one). The library director can ask someone else what to do. The dean can even put off making a decision for so long that the situation resolves itself one way or another. If putting off a decision doesn't resolve the situation, it may fester into an even bigger problem than before. These strategies may work out to provide good decisions, but there is no way to really know whether it was the best decision. To ensure the management team ends up making the best decision in a situation, this procedure can be followed:

Step 1: Define the issue. What are you really trying to decide? What is the issue under consideration? This may be obvious, but sometimes just laying out these details can help you to see the full picture of decisions in a new way that makes the situation clear to you.

Step 2: Develop alternatives. What possible choices are there to make? If this is a new area for the library, it may take a while just to figure out all of the potential options. This may be a wide-ranging choice with lots of options and suboptions. Go ahead and list them all; this way all of the potential options are captured.

Step 3: Compare alternatives. What are the problems with each of them?

What are the positives? A few can probably be easily knocked out of contention right here as impractical—requiring a spare million dollars, or a staff of 20 devoted professionals, or something similar. At least a couple of them will be pretty equally weighed; if not, then the management team probably has already made the decision here! How to choose between two or three pretty good (or less-bad) options? Keep reading. . . .

Step 4: Select the best choice. Now the management team is really looking at them. Are there any that will appeal more to the library's stakeholders: patrons, board, and staff? Are there any that may be more fun for everyone to do than others? These are ones I would choose. Sometimes the library's management team is choosing between options that are all not good or positive; in this case try to go for the one that will result in the least amount of bad PR and bad feelings among people important to the director or dean and to the library.

Step 5: Get in there and do something! Once the decision has been made, do not let it sit on the shelf or in committee while the director fumbles around trying to figure out how to do it or what to do next. Get in there and take action! Start things happening on this decision without worrying about whether it is the perfect decision. Making no decision and waiting for the perfect set of circumstances to present themselves will almost always be the wrong way to go; taking action at least gets the library staff moving toward the desired goal.

Step 6: Assess the decision. Try out the decision, and then look carefully at what is going on as a result. Did it work out the way the management team and board wanted it to? If not, then make some adjustments. Any decision is going to be made at least partially blind: the director or dean cannot know the consequences of every action, so you cannot predict everything that will occur after you make the decision. It's okay. Problems can be fixed, and adjustments can be made to take into account great results.

Step 7: Celebrate! If things go well, then share the good times with staff, patrons, community, or anyone else who may want to join in the happiness! If things go wrong, then it is good to acknowledge the contributions everyone made and the effort put forward.

FOLLOWERS

The last concept to touch on is the role of followers in leadership. Leaders must have followers; otherwise, they are not really leaders. Becoming a follower is a choice. By following a leader, an individual has decided that this person may speak and act on his or her behalf, at least to some degree. This decision to follow comes with responsibilities. To begin with, a follower agrees to support a leader's decisions and to act on a leader's orders. At the same time, followers should never do either of these things blindly. Followers also have a responsibility to question a leader's statements, actions, and goals. Rather than being disrespectful, a follower who is willing to question is demonstrating the willingness to learn. Leaders should always be willing to teach and to support their ideas and decisions. When followers do not question and accept blindly, there is a scary potential for abuse of power, such as occurred in Nazi Germany; Jonestown, Guyana; and Waco, Texas. In all three cases, followers did not question leadership actions or decisions.

In the workplace, workers cannot always choose who they answer to, who is "seen" as the leader of the organization. However, workers can ask questions, especially if actions or orders seem to be working against policy or may result in harming an individual's work or career. If a "leader" in an organization is not willing to answer questions and expects blind obedience, that person is neither a leader nor an effective manager.

CONCLUSION

Although leadership can be difficult to definitively pin down, it is clearly an important skill. After walking through some of the theories people have developed over the years, you should have some strategies to apply as you develop your own leadership style. Looking at some of the competencies identified as important for leaders will help you to focus on specific knowledge, skills, and abilities and other trainable ideas you can use in your own professional development. Librarians and staff may want to use some of these competencies to help identify new leaders in the organization, providing them with training opportunities to develop these competencies themselves. Finally, understanding the formal decision-making process will help you to make better decisions. Although it may be somewhat cumbersome for making everyday decisions or easier ones, the framework described here can be applied to any decision to help you focus on the most relevant details to make the best decision.

Developing your own leadership style and strategy is a career-long process. There will always be something else to know and to improve as you become a better leader and as you spend more time honing your skills. Training programs and self-education can be useful throughout your career. Some suggested readings are presented in the Further Readings section of this chapter to help you get started.

CASE STUDY AND DISCUSSION QUESTIONS

Dan is the head of the Support Services department for the Kingston Public Library. He has been on the job for just over 15 years. He likes his job overall but has the usual problems encountered in this type of department: staff, technology issues, budgets, and so forth.

He has been feeling a little restless lately at work and wants to do some new things to make the department better. He is also starting to think about his own retirement, which is coming up in about five years. He has not discussed this with anyone else at the library yet, but he wants the department to be in good shape for his successor.

Dan wants to identify the people in his department who can move into leadership roles, but he is not sure how to do this. He is also not sure how to help them develop their own leadership skills. There are about 45 people in his department; currently three managers work under Dan's direction: Cataloging, Technology, and Serials. He feels confident in the skills of two of them but is not sure of the third. He is not sure any of them have the competencies—or the drive to develop the competencies—to move up into his job when he leaves.

1. How will Dan help his managers develop their leadership competencies?
2. How will he go about identifying other people in the department, the library, or the larger professional world who might be able to become the next Support Services manager?

For his other goal of putting together some good ideas to improve the department, Dan wants to think of ways to come up with these ideas. He knows some people in the department have strong feelings about changes and does not want to cause them any unnecessary stress at work. He wants to push people to move outside their comfort zones in coming up with innovations and goals that will make the department, and the library, more successful. So he wants to decide whether to involve the department, the library, and other stakeholders (board members, patrons, etc.) in spending the next year brainstorming, surveying, dreaming, and researching new and interesting and useful directions the Support Services department might take. He might decide to just craft a smaller-scale plan himself that can help the department make some important and necessary changes he knows will help it move in a good direction over the next couple of years. Then he can work with someone, or a small team, to develop a plan to move the department forward into his successor's hiring.

1. How can Dan figure out which of these plans to follow?
2. What kind of information does he need to make the best decision?
3. How will he know whether he has made a good decision?

References

Barnard, C. I. (1971). *The functions of the executive: 30th anniversary edition.* Cambridge, MA: Harvard University Press.

Bennis, W. (1991). Learning some basic truths about leadership. *National Forum, 71*(1), 12–15.

Biggart, N. W., & Hamilton, G. G. (1987). An institutional theory of leadership. *The Journal of Applied Behavioral Science, 23*, 429–441.

Bill & Melinda Gates Foundation. (2012). Retrieved from www.gatesfoundation.org

Birdir, B., & Pearson, K. (2000). Research chefs' competencies: A Delphi approach. *International Journal of Contemporary Hospitality Management, 12*(3), 205–209.

Evans, M. G. (1970, May). The effect of supervisory behavior on the path–goal relationship. *Organizational Behavior and Human Performance,* 277–298.

Fiedler, F. (1967). *A theory of leadership effectiveness.* New York, NY: McGraw-Hill.

Fitzgerald, S., & Schutte, N. S. (2010). Increasing transformational leadership through enhancing self-efficacy. *The Journal of Management Development, 29*(5), 495–505.

Graeff, C. L. (1983). The situational leadership theory: A critical view. *Academy of Management, 8*(2), 285–291.

Griffin, R. (2008). *Fundamentals of management* (5th ed.). Mason, OH: South-Western, Cengage Learning.

Hayibor, S., Agle, B., Sears, G., Sonnenfeld, J., & Ward, A. (2011). Value congruence and charismatic leadership in CEO–top manager relationships: An empirical investigation. *Journal of Business Ethics, 102*(2), 237–254.

Helmick, C., & Swigger, K. (2006). Core competencies of library practitioners. *Public Libraries, 45*(2), 54–69.

Hersey, P., & Blanchard, K. H. (1969). Life cycle theory of leadership. *Training and Development Journal, 28*(2), 26–34.

House, R. J., & Mitchell, T. R. (1974). Path–goal theory of leadership. *Journal of Contemporary Business,* 81–98.

Laohavichien, T., Fredendall, L., & Cantrell, R. (2009). The effects of transformational and transactional leadership on quality improvement. *The Quality Management Journal, 16*(2), 7–24.

Machiavelli, N. (1985). *The prince.* Chicago, IL: University of Chicago Press.

McGregor, D. (1960). *The human side of enterprise.* New York, NY: McGraw-Hill.

Murphy, M. (1988). *The managerial competencies of twelve corporate librarians.* Washington, DC: Special Libraries Association.

NASA. (2012, August). Biography of Neil Armstrong. Retrieved from www.nasa.gov/centers/glenn/about/bios/neilabio.html

Nicely, D., & Dempsey, B. (2005). Building a culture of leadership: ULC's executive leadership institute fills libraries' biggest training void. *Public Libraries, 44*(5), 297–300.

The Nobel Foundation. (2012, October 2). Martin Luther King: Biography. Retrieved from www.nobelprize.org/nobel_prizes/peace/laureates/1964/king-bio.html

NOVA Online. (2002, February). Shackleton's voyage of endurance. Retrieved from www.pbs.org/wgbh/nova/shackleton

Oakland, J. S. (2003). *Total quality management: Text with cases.* Burlington, MA: Butterworth-Heinemann.

Ouchi, W. G. (1981). *Theory Z: How American business can meet the Japanese challenge.* Reading, MA: Addison-Wesley.

Schreiber, B., & Shannon, J. (2001). Developing library leaders for the 21st century. *Journal of Library Administration, 32*(3/4), 35–57.

Sullivan, M. (1999). Leadership in the national arena. *Texas Library Journal, 7*(4), 140–141.

Further Readings on Leadership and Decision Making

Adkins, D., & Esser, L. (2004). Literature and technology skills for entry-level children's librarians: What employers want. *Children and Libraries, 2*(3), 14–21.

Ameen, K. (2006). Challenges of preparing LIS professionals for leadership roles in Pakistan. *Journal of Education for Library and Information Science, 47*(3), 200–217.

Auster, E., & Chan, D. (2004). Reference librarians and keeping up-to-date: A question of priorities. *Reference & User Services Quarterly, 44*(1), 57–66.

Barnard, C. (1971). *The functions of the executive: 30th anniversary edition.* Cambridge, MA: Harvard University Press.

Brodie, M. B. (1967). *Fayol on administration.* London, UK: Lyon, Grant and Green.

Covey, S. R. (1991). *Principle-centered leadership.* New York, NY: First Free Press.

Covey, S. R. (2004). *The 7 habits of highly effective people.* New York, NY: Free Press.

Cross, J. (2005). Opportunities for internships in library administration: Results of a survey commissioned by the LAMA education committee. *Library Administration & Management, 19*(4), 193–196.

Tonn, J. C. (2003). *Mary P. Follett: Creating democracy, transforming management.* New Haven, CT: Yale University Press.

Twehous, J., Groves, D. L., & Lengfelder J. R. (1991). Leadership training—The key to an effective program. *Social Behavior and Personality, 19*(2), 109–120.

Unaeze, F. (2003). Leadership or management: Expectations for head of reference services in academic libraries. *The Reference Librarian, 81*, 105–117.

von Dran, G. (2005). Human resources and leadership strategies for libraries in transition. *Library Administration and Management, 19*(4), 177–184.

Wedgeworth, R. (1989). Robert Wedgeworth. In Gertzog, A. (Ed.). *Leadership in the library/information profession.* Jefferson, NC: McFarland & Company.

Weiner, S. (2003). Leadership of academic libraries: A literature review. *Education Libraries, 26*(2), 5–18.

7
ORGANIZATIONAL COMMUNICATION

Lisa K. Hussey

Communication is an essential concept in management. No manager can be successful if she or he does not know how to communicate, as it is tightly tied to many of the basic concepts in management, such as structure and culture. Communication is central to any good relationship, regardless of context. In an organization, communication is complicated by things like diversity of backgrounds, levels of education and understanding, modes of communication, and organizational structure. Communication is probably one of the most complicated concepts in management but one of the ones that most people try hard to simplify. I'm not saying it can't be streamlined, but I don't think anyone who is successful with communication ever sees it as simple.

Before we dive into the definition of communication, I want to introduce a concept that is an important part of understanding communication, the idea of "constructing a shared reality" (Searle, 1994). The process of constructing a shared reality, or a shared understanding, is how we as individuals come to understand one another, how we build a common understanding of word use, presentation of ideas, and all the nonverbal and unwritten aspects of communication. It is a process that takes time and a willingness to learn about new and different ways of communicating ideas. Constructing a shared reality allows for individuals to build understanding between them; they need to build a shared understanding of terminology, context, worldview—basically of reality as they both know it. Now, keep this in mind as we discuss communication.

Again, communication is the process of constructing shared realities—creating shared meanings. It involves our attempts to have others understand our world as we do and our efforts to appreciate the world of those around us. The process is culturally and contextually influenced with success or failure in individual communication competencies—knowledge, sensitivity, skills, and values. As a process for the construction of shared realities, communication is dynamic and ever changing. Communication can be considered a transfer of information, but it is more than that. When two entities are communicating, they are engaged in a social interaction in which they use symbols (words, body language) to attempt to create a shared meaning (mutual understanding) that will result in an effect on both parties.

Organizational communication takes this concept a bit further in that it is more than the daily interactions of individuals within organizations. It is the process through which organizations create and shape events. All organizational communication shares certain characteristics. It occurs within a complex system that is shaped by and influences its environment; it is composed of messages and their flow, purpose, direction, and media; it includes people and their attitudes, feeling, relationships, and skills. I know this seems a bit abstract and confusing, but just keep this in mind as we work our way through the communication process in this chapter.

THE CONCEPT OF COMMUNICATION

So, to begin with, why do we communicate? It seems like an obvious question, but it is important to consider before we start dissecting the communication process. There are many reasons why we communicate, but they can be boiled down to a few basic concepts. First, we communicate because we want to pass along information. We want to tell someone something. This is one of the most basic motivations for communication. We also communicate because we want someone to do something. We're trying to get a specific outcome or action. This is an important part of management communication. Following this idea, we communicate to persuade someone of our point of view. We feel we have a strong or important idea and we want others to understand why it is important, so we do what we can to communicate this to others. Finally, we communicate because we want others to have a certain perception of ourselves, such as a friendly person, a stoic listener, or a scary dictator. All of these perceptions are built in part from how an individual communicates.

Communication is one of those things that everyone has an idea of, and many ideas share similarities, but the basic definition of communication is hard to represent. It is the dissemination of information, and yet this is only part of it. It is both speaking and listening, but there is still more involved. It includes the mode of delivery, word choice, body language and facial expressions, and anything else that has an influence on how a message is sent and received. However, regardless of what is included, the first thing to recognize and accept is that communication is a process. It is much more than just a simple group of steps along a linear path, which makes it complex and complicated.

Despite communication being a complex concept, there is a plethora of models of communication. In an attempt to define communication, many scholars have put together such models. Although these models can be useful, they are often too simplistic. On the other hand, while I'm not sure it's possible to properly model the complexity of communication, having a visual can help build an understanding of the concept. Regardless of the theorist, the models of communication tend to have the same basic modules (as shown in Figure 7.1), each of which makes a significant contribution to the overall communication process:

1. *Sender and receiver*—These two concepts are grouped together because they work in tandem. The source of the message is the sender, the person or group that creates the message. On the other end is the receiver, the source that must understand or act on the message.
2. *Encoding and decoding*—Encoding is the process of formulating messages, choosing the content and symbols to convey meaning. Message encoding is determining what we want to be understood (content) and how we believe it can best be presented (choosing symbols). Decoding is the process of assigning meaning by the receiver to message symbols generated by the message source. Decoding is taking what we see and hear from others and deciding how it should be interpreted or understood.
3. *Message*—The message is the symbolic attempt to transfer meaning; it is the signal that serves as a stimulus for the receiver, which is subject to situational and cultural influences. In essence, the message is what is being communicated and what is understood.
4. *Channel*—The channel is the medium through which the message is transmitted. These include oral, written, electronic, and visual. There is an endless array of channels for communication. It is important to

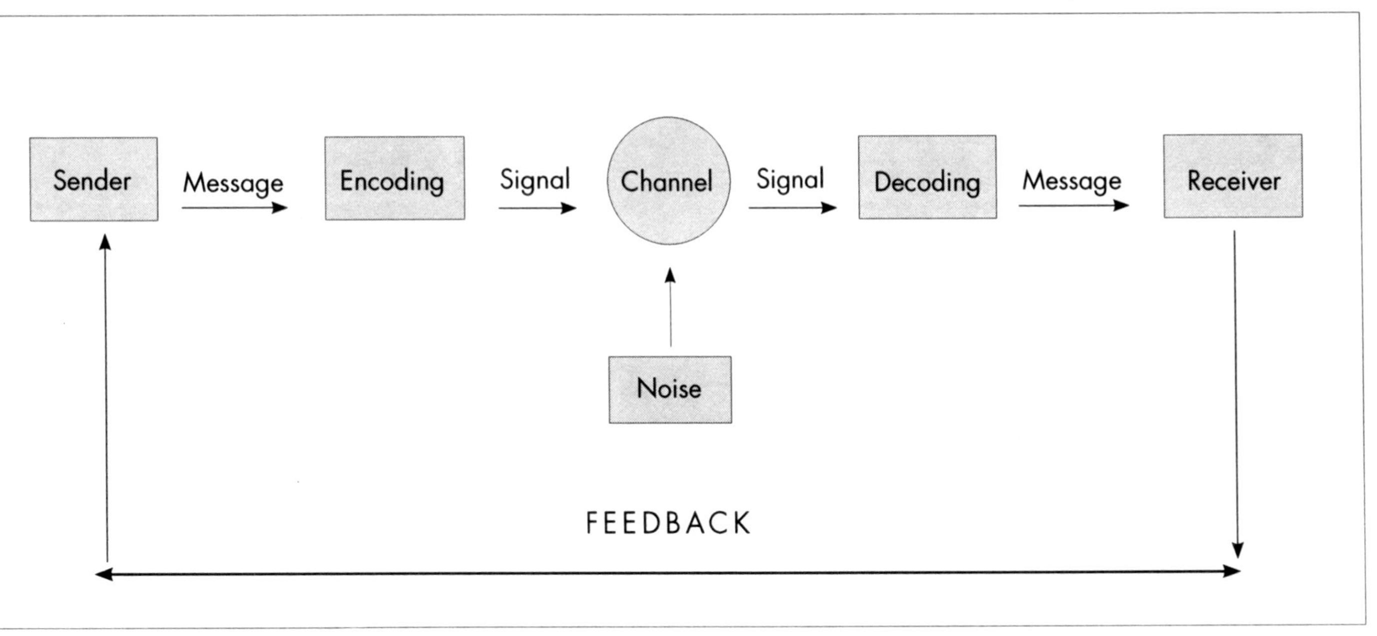

FIGURE 7.1 Model of Communication

note that channels can distort messages both technologically and in sensory reception. The selection of one channel over another may act as a message all its own.
5. *Noise*—Noise is the distortion or interference that contributes to discrepancies between the meaning intended by the sender and the meaning assigned by the receiver. It can be an auditory interference (static on a phone line, loud noises nearby, etc.), or it can be the result of a lack of understanding, multiple meanings for a single term, or the channel of delivery. All of these can shift or change the message from the original intent.
6. *Feedback*—Feedback is the back-and-forth between the sender and the receiver. Feedback can be as simple as a smile or a nod to acknowledge receipt and understanding, or more complex, such as answers, clarification questions, or actions based on the message. Feedback is very important to the communication process, as it allows the sender and receiver to build understanding. (Dyer, Hayden, & Lanctot, n.d.)

There are other important concepts to consider as part of the communication process, ones that are rarely included in models. One of the most important is the idea of competence. This includes one's knowledge, sensitivity, skills, and values, which are all used to both encode and decode messages. Competence is also influenced by experience and cultural background, both of which shape how an individual or group defines the norms of the communication process. The success of a communication heavily depends on the competence of the sender to construct a message and on the receiver's ability to decode the message.

Competence in communication depends on the skills of the parties involved. Essentially, effective communication can be broken down into a few key points. First, it is important to develop good listening skills. This goes well beyond just letting another person speak. Effective listening involves paying attention, keeping an open mind, and asking questions to ensure understanding—basically showing that you are engaged in the communication process. This not only allows the listener to actually hear what is being said, but it also encourages two-way communication.

When looking at communication, one must also consider the context and the environment in which the communication takes place. This helps to define the formality of the communication, as well as how it may be decoded or interpreted by the receiver. For example, a quick conversation in a hallway will be perceived differently from one in a meeting in a boss's office or in a closed-door meeting. Each of these settings provides a different context for the communication, and how it is interpreted often depends on the individual's or group's experience.

TYPES OF COMMUNICATION

Formal and Informal Communications

In all organizations, communication can be broken down into formal and informal communications. Formal communication is tied directly to the organization and is a matter of record. Official communications include information that is expected to be acted on and commitments that are to be honored. Most formal communication includes a written component as a record. It can also include oral conversations, particularly if the resulting information is to be measured in any way. There has to be a record of the expectations.

Informal communication is much more nebulous. It can range from a closed-door meeting to an off-the-record conversation to a conversation in the lunchroom. Informal communication can include daily feedback from managers about the work being performed without any formal record made of it. It also refers to gossip within an organization. Informal communication can also be the nonverbal component of any communication, such as body language or setting.

The use of both formal and informal means of communication may be intentional, with informal approaches providing additional information beyond the formal communication. However, there are two important points to consider regarding the formality of communication. Formal communication almost always includes some kind of record; it could be a written record or some form of digital record. Informal communication is rarely recorded and can easily be distorted as it spreads throughout an organization. Both heavily influence how the information is interpreted and used.

Interpersonal and Group Communications

Probably the most common type of communication is interpersonal communication. This ranges from a quick comment in passing to formal notifications such as memos and the employee handbook. Interpersonal communication is generally broken down into either oral or written, which can be formal or informal. Formal interpersonal communication includes personnel reviews, setting of individual expectations, and formal feedback on day-to-day work. Quick comments in passing, sharing information over lunch, or passing along gossip can be seen as informal interpersonal communication.

In addition to interpersonal communication, there is group or networked communication. This is the way in which information is transmitted on a broader scale across an organization and includes both oral and written communication. Group or networked communication reflects the flow of information within an organization usually based on the organizational chart, although it is not limited to just "official" lines of communication. Tracing how gossip is spread within an organization is an excellent example of informal networked communication.

There are various ways to model network or group (team) communication, but essentially the idea is to look at how information is communicated within an organization and to identify which individuals send and receive messages. Is all formal communication centralized and filtered through one office or individual? Is information passed down through the organization in a long delivery chain? Are employees encouraged to share information, or are there set offices through which information must pass before being passed on to others in the organization? Is there open communication across all departments and levels?

DIRECTION OF COMMUNICATION—VERTICAL AND HORIZONTAL

Looking at networked and team communication provides a nice lead into the direction of communication within an organization. Organizational communication can be divided into two basic directions: vertical and horizontal.

Vertical communication is split into two distinct directions: upward and downward. Upward communication is the passing of information from the lower levels of the organization upward, such as an employee reporting to a manager. Downward communication is any transfer of information from the top of the organization to the lower levels, such as a director announcing a new policy to be instituted by each department. These directions of communication are based on the organizational structure. One of the reasons for establishing the organizational structure is to define reporting relationships, which establish the formal lines of communication. The organizational chart provides a visual representation of the lines of communication. Vertical communication is the vehicle for most of the formal communication in an organization. Both upward and downward communications are the official channels of organizational communication.

One thing to note before we discuss the challenges of vertical communication is that in order to be successful, vertical communication needs to be two-way. In other words, regardless of the direction, feedback is an essential part of the vertical communication process. For example, a policy shouldn't just be passed downward; there should be an expectation of upward communication based on reaction, understanding, and implementation. Performance reviews shouldn't just be given. There should also be a chance for reaction and questions. Upward communication should be acknowledged, even if it is not acted on or relevant at the time. Employees need to know their messages have been received and understood as much as managers need employees to understand their orders and expectations of work.

Both upward and downward communication have challenges. Upward communication is often distorted or incomplete because of fear of reprisal. Even when encouraged, employees are guarded in how they will comment on organizational policies, management performance, or even their own performance. Rather than provide accurate information, employees will often communicate what they think management wants to know, leaving out details or problems that may reflect badly on an employee or a department.

Managers can counteract some of the challenges by listening to feedback and acting on suggestions or, if they cannot act, explaining why. If employees recognize that they are heard, they are more likely to continue to communicate. Managers should also make a point to check in with employees on a regular basis. This does not have to be a formal meeting, but by simply being present, asking questions, and listening, managers can create an atmosphere of more open communication.

The challenges with downward communication involve comprehension and consistency of the message. Comprehension can be a challenge as different departments have their own focus and responsibilities, both of which may not be understood by other departments. The same can be said about the various levels of a hierarchical organization. How a problem is discussed and understood varies depending on the level and on how close it is to the problem or to a specific aspect of the problem. Consistency of the message, on the other hand, has less to do with understanding than it has to do with the many channels and filters a message must pass through to get to each employee. Depending on the structure of the organization, there may be many levels of a hierarchy through which any downward communication must travel. At each level there is a potential for revision or reinterpretation of the message. By the time a message reaches the lowest levels of an organization it may no longer resemble the original message.

Asking for and encouraging feedback can help minimize some of the challenges of downward communication. When new policies or procedures are introduced, include time for employees to ask questions. Management should schedule regular meetings, such as every two weeks or once a month. Even if there is little news, meetings provide a forum for discussion. Employees should receive regular feedback on their work, as well as formal evaluations on a regular schedule. Regular feedback will allow managers and employees to build a common understanding of expectations and to create a space for discussion of changes and challenges.

Whereas vertical communication is the upward and downward communication in an organization, horizontal communication is the sharing of information across and among departments. Unlike vertical communication, horizontal communication is not encouraged or defined by the organizational structure. Connections or relationships among departments are generally not defined beyond assigning a department or position to a specific level of the organizational hierarchy. Horizontal communication is often informal communication, consisting of questions in hallways, conversations as part of social functions, or quick comments before meetings. It can also have a formal component, such as shared resources, project team assignments, and joint task force responsibilities. In these cases, the communication is generally part of a larger organizational message and will be recorded.

As with vertical communication, there are challenges to horizontal communication. First and foremost, if horizontal communication is not encouraged and supported, it probably will not happen, at least not in any formal capacity. Informal horizontal communication does tend to take place, at least in terms of social interactions, but even this may be limited if departments have little to no interaction. In rigid hierarchies, such as bureaucracies, there is little to no encouragement to communicate across departments. The focus of the structure, and hence the communication, is strictly on clear vertical lines of authority. Relationships among departments focus more on reporting relationships than on shared responsibilities or communication. As a result, horizontal communication is not part of the overall management expectations.

Horizontal communication is also hampered by a lack of understanding among departments. If department A and department B have different functions within the organization, they may not understand the other's contribution to the organization, or to their own goals, and see no reason to communicate with them. Other departments or individuals are reticent in sharing information for fear of losing power or influence. Knowledge is power, and some view sharing information as losing some of the power that results from being the one who knows.

There are ways to encourage horizontal communication. Managers can stress the importance of collaboration and attempt to minimize competition among departments. Project teams can be established, using individuals from a variety of departments. These teams compel employees to interact and to communicate, hopefully leading to some understanding of how each department contributes to the overall organization. Additionally, having departments located in close physical proximity can help to weaken some of the barriers to horizontal communication simply by creating a space for informal interactions and communication. It's harder to ignore someone who sits next to you than it is someone located across the building.

Understanding the challenges of organizational communications can only help to facilitate the process. Yet, this is not enough. Managers need to be aware of some key principles of organizational communications. Management must first fully understand and support the idea that communication is needed because it is central to the functioning of the organization. Managers must model this behavior by developing effective skills, such as listening, knowing when and how to speak, asking questions rather than assuming, and sharing feedback in a respectful manner. Employees should be responsible for asking for clarification when they don't understand or need more information. However, in order for employees to feel comfortable asking questions, managers must encourage the behavior. There should be a formal plan in place regarding formal communication within and outside the organization.

MODES OF COMMUNICATION

Now that we've defined the directions and types of communication, we should spend a few minutes considering the modes of communication. These can be as important to understanding the message as the message itself. A written memo has a different connotation than a quick phone call or an e-mail. The mode used is part of the decoding process and shapes the understanding and interpretation of the information.

As mentioned earlier, formal communications are recorded, usually in a written format. As a result, a written communication is usually a formal communication, although it can be informal. However, almost every written communication has a formal component, as it provides a record of the communication. Oral communication, on the other hand, is more often informal than formal. If an oral communication is a formal communication, it is documented in some way, such as a written record or witnesses to the communication.

Technology has introduced hybrid modes of communication. E-mail, instant messaging (IM), and texting are generally considered to be more informal than formal. The language often used, the tools for expressing emotion, and the ability to send off a quick note creates a very informal feel. It is important to note, however, that despite feeling informal, these methods of communication provide a record. E-mails are usually saved on a company server. If the text or IM is sent on the organization's computers or phones, there is an official record of the communication. Despite the very informal feel, these electronic forms of communication should be treated as formal communication.

MISUNDERSTOOD COMMUNICATIONS

One constant throughout this chapter is that understanding is central in communication. It is only through a shared understanding that individuals will communicate effectively. A discussion of communication would not be complete without mentioning the role of misunderstanding. In communication models, misunderstanding is noise because it prevents the receiver from interpreting the message as intended by the sender. However, misunderstanding has a much more significant role than just noise. Building a shared understanding or a shared reality relies as much on what is understood as what is not. It's not enough to focus on what is understood; a complete picture of the overall communication process also includes what isn't understood. By also looking at the misunderstanding—what was confusing or misinterpreted and why—one can identify issues with language, cultural differences, and the mode of communication. All members of an organization should be responsible for asking questions when they don't understand. If misunderstanding is not part of the communication process, this step is left out.

Tone and cadence are also important concepts to consider in the communication process, especially in relation to misunderstanding and miscommunication. The tone and cadence of a communication can have a strong influence on how it is received. For example, a sarcastic comment, a hurried speech, and a slow-paced explanation all provide a different framework for understanding. How the tone and cadence are understood often depends on the cultural background of the receiver. This is one of the most important reasons why the background of the intended recipient(s) should be considered in the construction of the message. Humor can be a strong communication tool but only if it is understood, as it is a cultural concept that does not always translate well. Word choice is another consideration in communication. Language and words are symbols but not necessarily universal symbols. The decision to use one term over another will alter the understanding of the message. That's not to say that the message won't be understood; rather, the choice of words and language will shape *how* it will be understood.

Attitude is also important in communication. How each party approaches the process influences the final outcome. In order for communication to take place, both the sender and the receiver must want to communicate. Both parties involved must be committed to communication, to creating a shared understanding. The sender must be flexible and willing to restate the message as needed, and the receiver must be willing to ask questions, get clarification, and provide feedback. Otherwise, there won't be real communication. All that will happen is the passing of information from one source to the next, with no guarantee of consistency or understanding.

CONCLUSION

Ultimately, it is up to management, those with authority and power, to model good communication. Managers and employees should be trained in good communication skills, such as effective listening, asking for and providing feedback, and being sensitive to others' backgrounds and levels of understanding. Management must encourage employees to communicate, provide opportunities for communication, and be willing to accept feedback on their own communication. While this will not provide the perfect communication system or plan, it will lay the foundation for creating an effective organizational communication process.

CASE STUDY

Change is in the air, or so it appears. The gossip mill is running at faster than full speed, and everyone has something to say. There is a rumor going around that someone is in trouble, but no one is sure who it is. As we know, there are two communication mediums in the workplace—official and unofficial. Right now the unofficial is running everyone at the library ragged.

No one is being fired, but there was a controversial board meeting where the performance of the director was mentioned in uncomplimentary terms because of the current economic downturn. It is time to work on damage control. How can the management team find a way to manage the communication situation that is going on in the library? How can this be done without saying anything concrete? Come up with a way to deal with this.

Next, the newspaper has caught wind of the rumor. Someone has told a friend, who told someone else, who told a buddy who works for the local newspaper. Now the reporter is calling the director for a statement about the potential firing of an employee at the library. The board needs to be brought into the damage control as the situation is spiraling out of control. From a management standpoint, there are a couple of challenges. What do you tell the newspaper? What do you tell the staff? How do you handle the board? What is the true situation, and how much of it do you disclose to everyone? Or do you just deny it because it is a made-up situation based on innuendo and drama?

It's your library, so it is your choice on how to deal with this before it blows even further out of proportion.

References

Dyer, A., Hayden, M., & Lanctot, D. (n.d.). The Shannon-Weaver model defined. Retrieved from www.uri.edu/artsci/lsc/Faculty/Carson/508/03Website/Hayden/ShanWeav.html

Searle, J. R. (1994). The construction of social reality. New York, NY: The Free Press.

Further Reading on Organizational Communication

D'Aprix, R. (2008). *The credible company*. San Francisco, CA: Jossey-Bass.

8

CHANGE MANAGEMENT AND ORGANIZATIONAL CULTURE

Diane L. Velasquez and Lisa K. Hussey

"Group life is never without change, merely differences in the amount and type of change exist."
—Kurt Lewin, 1951, p. 199

Change is often a scary concept for organizations. Change requires that we step outside of our comfort zones. In fact, change implies that comfort zones may be a thing of the past. Change can be small, large, or medium sized, but all of it scares most people because it infringes on "what we have always done," what we know how to do, and what we expect. Essentially, change alters the status quo, an area of comfort and predictability. The status quo may be boring, but it is safe. Safety is often valued over almost anything else, which acts as a barrier to change, even productive change. However, in our modern society, resisting change as our environments evolve will simply lead to failure. Hence, it is essential for libraries and library managers to understand the role of change and how to deal with its effects on both the organization and the employees.

A phrase that many of us hear when we begin work in a new place, no matter the type of organization, is "this is how it has always been done." However, just because something has always been done a particular way doesn't mean it is the best or only way it can or should be done. In fact, there may be many different ways a task can be done. Innovation is essential to organizational growth, and any process, no matter how successful, can be improved upon at some point.

There is a secret that is out there in the universe: change is really the only constant. This is true in society, and it is true in organizations. Organizations that refuse to change usually eventually stagnate and die. Even the most static organizations are always changing, even if it is something as simple as introducing new employees. The people within the organization must either accept change or move on. Yet, many stay at a particular organization and are unhappy for various reasons. Some stay out of fear of ending up in a worse situation; some are unable to leave because of other commitments; and others are simply waiting for retirement. Sometimes the idea of looking for another job and perhaps leaving never enters their mind because they have always been at this place or this was their dream job at one time. Many times dream jobs change because the other people on the job change, but the person within them doesn't change with the different facets of the job. Instead, the person remains in the position, unhappy, and spends most of the time focused on how much better it was when things were how they used to be. When this happens, the person should move to the next new dream job or opportunity, but this rarely occurs out of a fear of change, even if it might be a change for the better. Regardless of the reason, unhappy or stubborn employees are simply one of the potential barriers to change that managers must face and find ways to overcome. Otherwise, the organization itself is in danger of becoming static and irrelevant. However, before we address organizational change directly, we should spend a few minutes discussing the role of organizational culture.

ORGANIZATIONAL CULTURE

Organizational culture pretty much informs every aspect of organizational life. For lack of a better way to describe it, organizational culture is the atmosphere and feel of an organization. It is the "intangible phenomena, such as values, beliefs, assumptions, perceptions, behavioral norms, artifacts, and patterns of behavior. . . . Culture is to an organization what personality is to the individual—a hidden yet unifying theme that provides meaning, direction, and mobilization" (McNeal, 2009, p. 126). It develops over time as an organization copes with "problems of external adaptation and internal integration" (Stueart & Moran, 2007, p. 148). In other words, organizational culture results and develops from an organization's interactions with its environment and the interactions within the organization.

There are three main contributors to organizational culture: "the beliefs, assumptions, and values of the organization's founder, the learning experiences of group members as the organization evolves, and new beliefs, values, and assumptions brought in by new members and leaders" (Schein, 1980). As this shows, culture happens at all levels of an organization, and each level has the potential to contribute to and shapes the organizational culture. Obviously, as with communication, those in power do a lot to shape culture, but power is not the only thing that defines culture. Culture is also influenced by the day-to-day interactions of the employees, as well as their individual outlooks and cultural backgrounds, all of which evolve as employees leave and new ones are introduced. It is how these pieces fit together that creates the organizational culture.

How do you assess the culture of an organization? Well, basically you have to observe a lot, including management interactions with staff, interactions among staff, communication patterns, espoused values, practiced values, interactions with and expectations of the public, and leadership style. In addition to this, the values, outlooks, and personalities of the individuals who make up an organization also contribute. Even when acting as a "professional" or toning down one's normal behaviors, individuals do not stop being themselves just because they are at work. Their quirks and foibles are part of what can influence the overall organizational feel and atmosphere. Part of what builds culture is the tension that exists in organizations, which is created by the many unique and different characteristics of each individual employee. This tension is further increased by the idea that individuals must give up part of themselves to be part of the organization (Smith & Berg, 1997). As discussed in Chapter 14 on conflict, this tension is not necessarily a bad thing. How it is acknowledged and used is what contributes to the organizational culture.

One of the most prolific and influential theorists on organizational culture is Edgar Schein. In his book *Organizational Culture and Leadership* (2003), he looks at organizations from the standpoint of group members and culture. Because organizational theorists do not agree on one meaning for culture (Bolman & Deal, 2003; Cameron & Quinn, 1999; Schein, 1970, 1980, 1999a, 1999b, 2003), Schein's (2003) definition of organizational culture, which incorporates the ideas mentioned, is used in this chapter. Organizational culture is:

> a pattern of shared basic assumptions that was learned by a group as it solved its problems of external adaptation and internal integration,

> that has worked well enough to be considered valid and, therefore, to be taught to new members as the correct way to perceive, think, and feel in relation to those problems. (Schein, 2003, p. 17)

However, in addition to looking at individual contributions, he also describes three different levels of culture that determine the degree to which a phenomenon is visible to an observer (Schein, 2003), as follows:

> Artifacts are the first level of culture. Artifacts are everything that one can see, hear, or feel when encountering a new group with an unfamiliar culture. Artifacts can include technology, rituals, ceremonies, policies, procedures, and visible products of the group. In libraries, artifacts include books, computers, programming, services, and the buildings themselves. (p. 28)

The second level includes the espoused beliefs and values each member holds. In other words, this level is made up of the public statements of values, such as mission and vision statements, and the shared behaviors. Over time the group reflects original beliefs and values that become rooted as the bottom-line fundamental values (Schein, 2003, p. 28). These bottom-line values are deeply rooted and determine how the group forms and validates its beliefs, strategies, goals, and philosophies. Decisions and actions are often explained by referring back to these espoused beliefs and values.

The third level comprises the underlying unconscious beliefs that every member in the group holds. These are rarely, if ever, acknowledged or even recognized, as they are unconscious. They are the unquestioned acceptance of certain expectations and the unspoken code of conduct. It is simply the way things are done. In a social unit, basic assumptions have become so ingrained that one finds little variation among group members.

These basic premises tie to what Argyris calls "theories-in-use"—the implicit suppositions that actually guide behavior, that tell group members how to perceive, think, and feel (Argyris, 1993; Argyris & Schön, 1978, 1996). The third level is essentially invisible unless one is willing to spend a significant amount of time observing and asking difficult questions.

Each level of culture is influenced by the other levels. Artifacts are the physical reflection of the values and norms of the organizations. The espoused values are influenced by the underlying assumptions and implicit beliefs that drive organizational behaviors. As a manager, it is important to recognize these influences, as they are central to any attempt to alter or change the organizational culture. Simply changing the artifacts or restating the espoused values will not result in real change because the underlying assumptions have not been addressed. This is another reason why change is complicated and often difficult; assumptions are the hardest to change because they are usually unconscious. Assumptions are concepts or ideas that "just are." They can be deeply held beliefs that are never questioned, but they influence everything we do. They inform how we interact with others (always be polite), how we structure our lives (be successful at work no matter what), or select our careers (working to help others). Keep all of this in mind as we discuss organizational change.

CHANGE AS PROCESS

When discussing change, it is important to begin with the understanding that change is a process. Often change is modeled in a set of linear steps. Although these steps usually include each stage of change, they generally do not reflect the complexity or fluid nature of change. The process of change is complex. Managers and individuals should approach the process in a thoughtful and deliberate manner. With this in mind, let's review the steps involved in change. These steps are dynamic and interactive (Griffin, 2008):

1. Recognize that change is needed.
2. Discover/diagnose why the change is needed.
3. Set the goals for the change (planning).
4. Decide how to implement the change (method).
5. Implement the change.
6. Evaluate the process as it happens, and then evaluate the results.

The first stage is usually one of the most difficult. We don't often go looking for change, so we fail to recognize the need for change until a problem or a full-blown crisis occurs. Managers should try to be proactive and look for both opportunities and threats that may require change, but this is not always easy to do. Even the most proactive manager gets surprised sometimes. However, once the need for change is recognized—perhaps through proactive means or in reaction to an event—managers should take the time to consider the change and why it is needed. In other words, this is the time for managers to stop and consider why this is happening. The worst way to approach change is by simply reacting to solve a problem or deal with an opportunity. In either case, simply reacting almost always results in problems and does not address the original need for change. The diagnostic process can easily result in the discovery of other changes needed, which should be included as part of the change process.

The next step is planning and setting the goals for the change. This includes planning how to introduce the change, identifying who is involved in the process, and setting up the expectations. Communication and feedback are essential tools to both the planning stage and the overall change process. Change planning should be as thoughtful and thorough as any other planning process within an organization. There has to be flexibility in expectations and goals, but before any changes are implemented, there should be defined goals and a plan for how to implement each one.

Once the plan has been considered and formulated, the next step is to implement the plan. This may seem obvious, but it is easy to get caught up in planning for change but never actually implementing the change. Communication is central, as employees will need feedback on their contribution, identification of each stage, notification of any alterations to the process, and declarations of success or failure.

Evaluation of the change process is not limited to just whether it was a success or a failure. Each step and stage of change should be monitored and evaluated, as would be done in any planning process. As each step is introduced, managers should request feedback and provide guidance as the process progresses. When missteps and barriers hinder the process or a step is finished successfully, evaluation of the process provides insight into potential alterations or reinforces goals and expectations of the next step.

An important, yet often unrecognized aspect of the change process is mourning. "Humans cannot accept change without mourning what has been lost" (Volkan, 1997, p. 36). The loss of comfort and security is only a piece of the process, but members of the organization will experience the loss as they would any other type of loss. This is natural and should be expected. Part of the planning process is dealing with resistance but also allowing some space for mourning what was before moving onto what can be.

Each part of the change process provides the chance to identify opportunities, threats, and issues within or related to the organization. This is why it is a fluid process. Change is rarely limited to one minor aspect or a single department. Any change—major, minor, tiny, or seemingly insignificant—has the potential to radiate throughout the organization. Managers must be prepared to deal with the benefits and consequences of all types of change. This is why the concept of organizational change is so important in management.

ORGANIZATIONAL CHANGE

Many theorists have written about organizational change, but one of the most influential is Kurt Lewin. His work has had a profound impact on social psychology and on experiential learning, group dynamics, and action research (Lewin, 1952; Smith, 2001). Lewin looked at change from a group perspective. According to Lewin, "group behavior is shaped by an intricate field of symbolic interactions and forces that not only affect group structures, but also modify individual behavior" (Burnes, 2007, p. 219). In other words, how people interact and how they view interactions, both through their individual worldview and within the context of the group or organizational culture, are the keys to group or organizational change. For organizational change to be successful, these "fields of symbolic interactions and forces" must also change. The results of the change depend on "which forces increase and which diminish" (Burnes, 2007, p. 222).

To illustrate his idea of group change, Lewin created a deceptively simply model, yet one that incorporates the complexity and challenges of organizational change. According to Lewin (1951), there are three stages in the change process: unfreezing, change/transition, and refreezing. Each stage of Lewin's theory is a complex process. The first step, unfreezing, involves identifying the need for change, planning, setting goals, and implementing the change. Essentially, in unfreezing, you are acknowledging that the status quo will no longer be the status quo. It is the act of stepping out of the comfort zone with the knowledge there is no return to the comfort zone.

While unfreezing is a challenge, it is the change/transition stage that can be the most confusing and exhausting part, as this is when the change is actually happening. During the transition there is a heightened potential for conflict because there is more stress. There will be resistance, for many reasons. Some will feel lost or unstable because they are not in control, or at least they perceive that they do not have the same control as before. Questions of identity and value accompany change and add to the stress and tension. Some employees will fixate on "how it was" and glorify the previous process and procedures. Others will fight change because of bad experiences. Essentially, the change/transition process, even when well managed, has some sense of chaos. This is why it is important to monitor and evaluate while providing opportunities for communication and feedback in all directions.

Eventually, the chaos evolves into some kind of order and the refreezing step takes place. Once change is implemented, a new way of functioning is developed and adopted. Sometimes it reflects the goals and expectations, and sometimes it is completely different. Either outcome can be the result of a successful change. Regardless, once a new routine is developed, a new status quo is created, and the change is frozen, or adopted as "normal" functioning.

Lewin's ideas highlight the challenges and benefits of group change. His work has been widely adopted, and his ideas have been further developed and expanded. Chris Argyris, Peter Senge, Edgar Schein, Warren Bennis, and Rosabeth Moss Kanter have been influenced by Lewin's theories and applied them in different ways to their own research.

Chris Argyris (1993; Argyris & Schön, 1978, 1996) developed the theory of double-loop learning to turn a dysfunctional organization into one that learns and overcomes barriers to organizational change. Double-loop learning is a process that helps the organization "learn to learn . . . [a method] to increase capacity for learning" (Schein, 1999b, p. 19). Double-loop learning requires reflective, in-depth analysis beyond the current question or problem by "expanding the analytical frame to identify and then challenge the underlying assumptions, the first level of organizational culture" (Batista, 2008, para. 5). It is a strategy for building consensus among individuals in an organization. Double-loop learning uses the process of interviews to understand the dysfunctional behaviors and defensive routines that occur in the organization and assists individuals to improve their effectiveness. By identifying the underlying assumptions, the group can acknowledge and deal with these influences, which can help to remove barriers in the change process.

Peter Senge (1990) built upon Chris Argyris's (1980, 1982) ideas on theory in action to build a learning organization for his book *The Fifth Discipline.* The third discipline, mental models, states that in order to be open to learning, individuals need to be able to alter their own mental models. Senge (1990) defines individual mental models as "deeply ingrained assumptions, generalizations, or even pictures or images that influence how we understand the world and how we take action" (p. 8). This principle is as important to groups as it is to individuals. To introduce change, such as learning, the organization must first uncover the ingrained assumptions and established generalizations that influence the values and actions of the group.

In her book about corporate America and the Internet, Kanter (2001) analyzed the digital culture that would be emerging in the 21st century. Kanter (2001) commented that "life is now defined by where we stand with respect to the Internet" (p. 1). This is as true today as it was when Kanter wrote it. She revisited innovation in an article she wrote for the *Harvard Business Review* that looked at the history of innovation in corporate America from the 1970s to the present. The best lesson learned was that "companies that cultivate leadership skills are more likely to net successful innovations" (Kanter, 2006, p. 82).

Organizational change or change management usually comes about because of a change in leadership, a cut in the budget, or a decision by the board of the library or another governing body that it is time for change. Sometimes the change is more cosmetic, like a building being built or undergoing an expansion. Technological changes will create other changes as well. It could be an institutional change at the city, county, or university level that changes the organization in some way. According to the *Oxford English Dictionary* (2009), *change* is defined as "the fact or act of changing; substitution of one thing for another; succession of one thing in place for another." The definition of *change management* is "the management of change and development within a business or similar organization; especially the management of people adapting to new conditions" (*Oxford English Dictionary*, 2009).

Change is connected to the organizational culture that is part of the library or information center that we work in on a day-to-day basis. Having said that, what exactly is culture? To some it is just the environment of the job, but it is actually much more than that. I like using Edgar Schein's definition of culture: "Think of culture as the accumulated shared learning of a given group, covering behavioral, emotional, and cognitive elements of the group members' total psychological functioning" (Schein, 2003, p. 17). In every organization, there are structures that each group is divided into. For example, if looking at the organizational hierarchy of a public library there is one group that is the entire public library, but from there it is divided into subgroups such as departments within the public library, as illustrated in Figure 8.1.

Each of the departments of adult services, youth services, technical services, and IT has its distinct culture. The overall public library culture comes down from the top or from the director, and the same can be said for each department. The department heads can influence or even determine the environment or culture of their departments. One

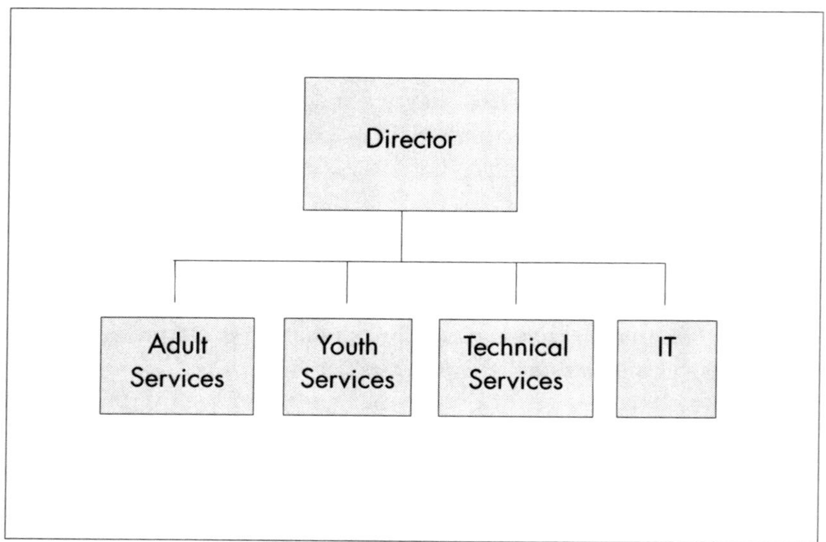

FIGURE 8.1 Sample Public Library Organizational Chart

truism of public libraries is that adult services and youth services do not usually work well if the departments are combined. The departments in essence have very different clientele. The adult services department works with patrons who are over 18 years old. The children and youth services department works with those who are ages 0 to 17 years old. The children's department is really a microcosm of the library—a mini library within the library because it has everything that the library has but caters to the children and youth of the community. The public library is an encapsulation of the individuals who work in the library, and the leaders in the library have imprinted to some extent their personality onto the groups.

The technical services department will have a different feel and flavor to it than the adult services department, and the groups of people who work in those library departments will work well together. When someone new comes into a department, the new hire will be indoctrinated into the methodologies of the group and in many ways will be, for lack of a better term, brainwashed into the group's everyday espoused values and beliefs that are embodied through strategies, goals, and philosophies (Schein, 2003, p. 25).

As can be seen from the chart presented in Figure 8.2, the organization of an academic library is much more complicated than that of a public library. The organizational chart shown is for a large university

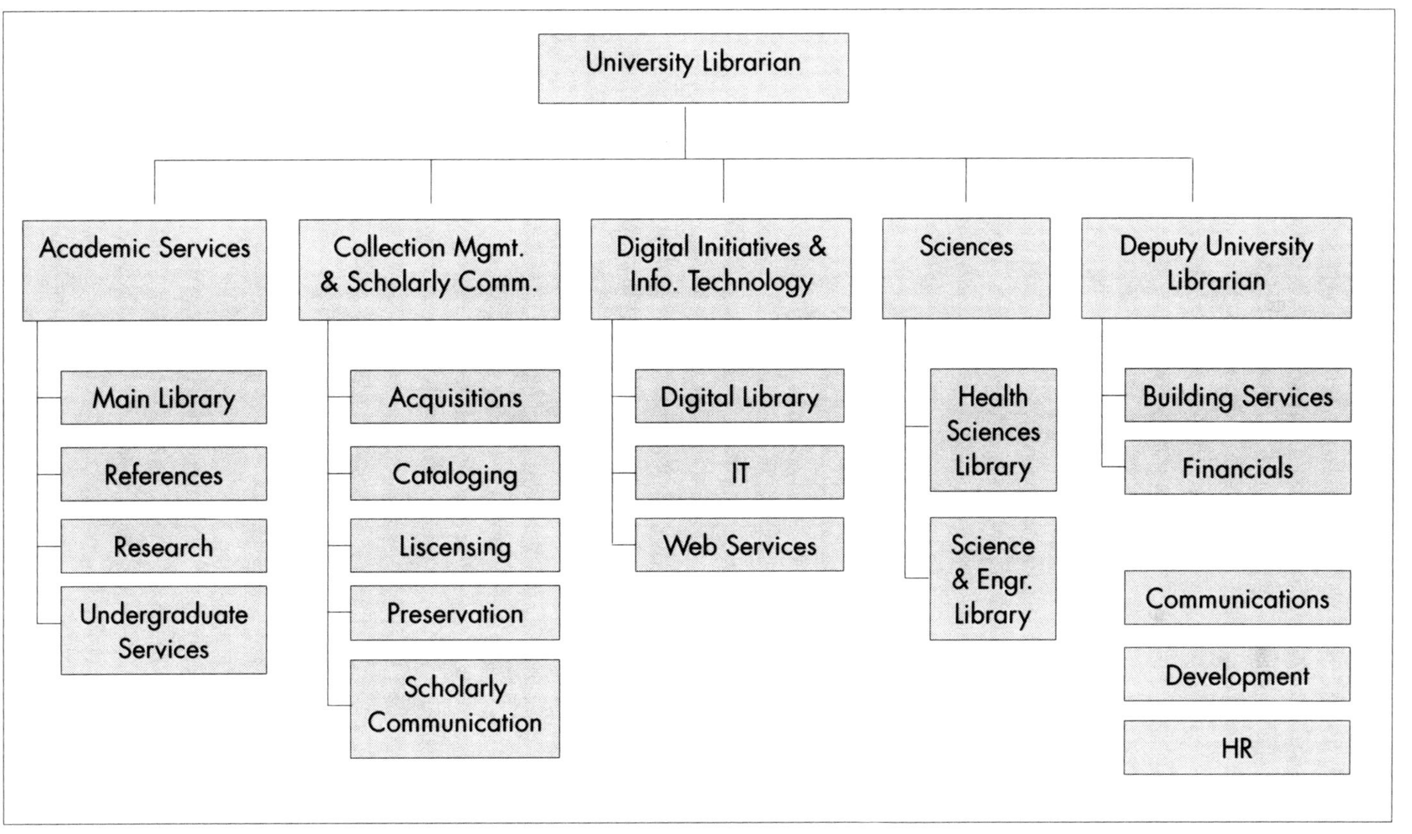

FIGURE 8.2 Sample Academic Organizational Chart

that caters to over 35,000 students and has both masters and doctoral students. The library also has multiple libraries within its purview. In this particular organization the health sciences library supports a medical school as well as a dental school. The undergraduate library is split between a social sciences and arts library and a science and engineering library. There may be many more libraries on any one campus. Depending on the specialties that the university has, there may be small libraries within different colleges and schools. Some universities may have as many as 10 to 15 different libraries, and whether or not they are under the university library management is up to university policy.

Changes in the structure or operation of an academic library, just as with a public library, can cause stress and problems. The biggest change within a library is usually when a new director or dean is hired, because each leader will have his or her own vision of where the library should go within the structure of the university or the community. Many within the library community may question and wonder whether the library structure will be better off once the changes have been completed. Change is never easy for those who are undergoing the changes.

The artifacts of the organization are the visible, tangible structures and processes that every group in existence tends to collect and organize (Schein, 2003, p. 25). Examples of artifacts are organizational charts, procedural manuals, employee handbooks, new-hire paperwork, processes that employees do on a day-to-day basis, and any other visible organizational structures that are apparent to everyone. Even the building the organization is housed in is considered an artifact.

The organization also has underlying assumptions that are the unconscious, taken-for-granted beliefs, perceptions, thoughts, and feelings that everyone in the group has been given by other members (Schein, 2003, p. 25). Consider if you will that when you go to a new place to start a job there is always someone who tells you that "this is how we do things here." No one knows why that is so or how it started; it is just the way it's always been done. This is the unconscious belief that it must be done this way. Sometimes a new leader will come in and change that unconscious belief, and there will be trauma attached to the change.

Schein (2003) makes the comment that "every group must learn how to become a group" (p. 133). In Velasquez's (2007) study the majority of the public libraries that were studied were cohesive, well functioning groups that worked well together. All of the libraries had visible organizational structures and processes (Velasquez, 2007). Some of the artifacts included budgets, meeting minutes, process documents, job descriptions, licensing agreements, and other documents (Velasquez, 2007). Included in library artifacts are the rituals that each library goes through when a new employee is hired, such as the tour the new employee is taken on and by whom. As the new person is introduced to everyone in the library, each role will be clearly delineated and explained. Even some visitors have this experience at the public library when working with the director. By indoctrinating the new employee in the rituals of the library, it demonstrates clearly the culture that is inherent within it and how it operates on a day-to-day basis. The indoctrination is subtle and on many levels unconscious, but in time new hires will have an innate ability to traverse the library culture and understand what the group norms are for their department and the organization as a whole.

STRUCTURAL CHANGE

The idea of changing the structure of the organization is always considered to be something to be feared by those at the bottom because the change will be different from what has been before. A good example of this is when an academic library incorporates a library commons into a portion of the physical structure. Currently, print reference collections are being weeded and shelved in the circulating collection because there are more reference tools that are available online in databases like, for example, Credo Reference or the Gale Reference Collection. There are also single-title reference volumes available electronically that replace the print versions. When a reference department is remodeled, the reference print collection is moved, and the majority of it is turned into an electronic collection; this is a big change from how reference was conducted before. The change raises the question about whether a reference desk is even needed for questions. Should there be roving reference librarians equipped with iPads or the equivalent to handle reference questions? What is the best way to handle the reference encounter? Will there also be chat, e-mail, telephone, and social media to consider for answering reference questions? This change is big for a university library, and serving the students in the best way is what the reference librarians need to do. How do you serve the clientele in the best way?

One way to address change is to look at what other universities of all sizes have done in the past. Consider the best practices and what your university can afford to do to best serve your students. Here are some questions to consider:

1. Are all your students on campus?
2. Do you have a distance program? How does the library serve those students?
3. What tools will the students need?
4. What tools will the librarians need?
5. What training will the students and librarians need?
6. What will the tools and training cost?

The questions are not hard, but they need to be asked and researched. Asking students to be part of the change is always good. Students know what they need and want. Students will be open to assisting the library with assessment if it needs to happen. Just remember to evaluate the change and to see how it is working. If necessary, adjust it to make it work better.

LEADERSHIP AND CHANGE

Rainey (2009) states that leadership is the capacity of someone to direct and energize people to achieve goals. Leadership is critical in an environment where change is a constant. Bennis (1999) comments, "Most organizations have a tough time finding the right people to lead in an environment of constant change" (p. 193). Cope and Waddell (2001) studied leadership styles in e-commerce. Their findings support those of Rainey and Bennis. According to Cope and Waddell (2001), "In an environment that is constantly changing, the role of the leader has become vital" (p. 523).

Bennis (1999) believes there is a crisis in finding leaders. The author makes a distinction between managers and leaders. Bennis paints a portrait of a leader. "First, they have a great deal of self-knowledge. Second, they have a strongly defined sense of purpose. Third, leaders have the capacity to generate and sustain trust. Fourth, leaders have a bias toward action" (Bennis, 1999, p. 163). This portrait of business leaders was based on a study undertaken with Bert Nanus in 1985 (Bennis & Nanus, 2003). Brooke Sheldon (1991) repeated the study, this time with library leaders, and found similar traits. Sheldon interviewed 60 library leaders and found them to be visionary. She also stated, "Our leaders have also learned that focusing on two or three relatively simple goals works better than attempting to follow a complicated agenda that is open to many interpretations" (Sheldon, 1991, p. 81).

Another aspect of leadership is the fact that success is hard. Change is part of the life of leaders. Successful leaders have peaks and valleys just like the rest of us mortals. In any organization, no matter what type, stuff happens. Kanter (2011) makes the point this way: "Complacency sets in, making people feel entitled to success rather than motivated to work for it" (p. 34). So once a leader has a successful library, eventually things will change. People leave for new positions, the budget changes because folks who have responsibility for it move on or decide not to run for reelection, or whatever scenario you can imagine plays out. Something can happen that will call on all the skills of the leader to change whatever is happening in the library. Kanter (2011) advises, "Build the cornerstones of confidence—accountability, collaboration, and initiative—when times are good and achievement comes easily. Maintain a culture of confidence as insurance against the inevitable downturns" (p. 34).

A good leader has the ability to be nimble when successful or not so successful. Tying everything back to mission and vision is especially important. The changes needed for the organization should be evident by looking at the mission and vision. If a public library's mission is one that emphasizes lifelong learning, whatever change is happening should emphasize that mission as well.

RESISTANCE TO CHANGE

When a change in the organization is considered, the leadership should be able to explain it in a way that gets everyone on board. In many organizations when change begins, everyone starts complaining and heads for the nearest sand pit to hide their head and hope they are not involved. For many, change is dreaded as much as death and taxes. Resistance to change is something that is almost a norm in organizations, especially if the change involves any type of technology. Some individuals in organizations have the perception that newly introduced technology will be more trouble than it is worth. Some people in an organization will embrace change, and some individuals will resist it.

Needham (2001) explores technology-related organizations and their ties to libraries. The author comments that librarians often resist technological change as well as the organizational leadership needed to introduce them. Needham (2001) states:

> One obstacle is the distrust of leadership that seems to manifest itself in librarians whenever someone asserts such a role. In several organizations . . . the attempt to provide leadership among librarians has been compared to herding cats. (p. 148)

While herding cats is not something anyone would want to do, handling resistance to change is another reality of organizational life. Some of us embrace change; others run in the other direction as fast as possible. In a seminal work written for *Harvard Business Review,* Paul Lawrence discusses how to deal with resistance to change. The article was written in 1969 and shows that while technology and our societal fabric have changed, resistance to change has not. Although the article is at times dated, the advice in it is not. Lawrence (1969) suggests that getting the employees involved in the change appears to be good but may lead to trouble. He goes on to say management and leadership must understand what the basis is underlying the resistance the change (Lawrence, 1969). Blind spots and tunnel vision are not uncommon human problems encountered when addressing change, because many times we cannot see the forest for the trees and we are preoccupied with our role, not with the organization. Lack of communication about what the organization is attempting to do by changing an employee's role can undermine the entire idea of the leadership.

In two articles John P. Kotter discusses change and the strategies needed to successfully do so. In both articles he emphasizes the need to communicate and educate the workforce (Kotter, 2007; Kotter & Schlesinger, 2008). Telling the staff what is going to be happening before it occurs can head off some of the resistance. Communicating the ideas and explaining the need for and the logic of the change help people understand the concept of why the organization is moving forward with it (Kotter & Schlesinger, 2008).

Some managers are taken aback by the level of the resistance to change. Experienced managers know there will be some but don't take time to assess how much there will be. Kotter and Schlesinger (2008) state:

> . . . using past experience as guidelines, managers all too often apply a simple set of beliefs—such as "engineers will probably resist the change because they are independent and suspicious of top management." This limited approach can create serious problems. Because of the many different ways individuals and groups can react to change, correct assessments are often not intuitively obvious and require careful thought. (p. 133)

Again, going back to how the change is related to the mission and vision has to be emphasized. What were the goals and objectives of the change that the library or organization decided to implement? The level of resistance to change can be surprising because sometimes the people who resist that change are not the ones we expect.

A good example of resistance to change in libraries is when cataloging was automated. When cataloging was automated, many catalogers chose to leave rather than learn a brand-new system. The idea of going through conversions of the catalog, taking it from a manual system to an automated system, was, for some people, too much to be considered. When automation and then public access computers were introduced to public libraries, there was a transformative change in the way libraries conducted business. Any time something new happens, there can be resistance to change. The turnover of staff occurred for many different reasons. Some of the staff left because they chose not to adapt to the new technology. For others it was just time to move on to new things.

With any organization, there need to be goals and objectives and the determination whether they are being met. If goals are not being met:

> It makes members of the organization uncomfortable and anxious—a state that we can think of as *survival anxiety,* in that it implies that *unless we change, something bad will happen to the individual, the group, and/or the organization.* (Schein, 2003, p. 322, emphasis in the original)

During the organizational change that had occurred when cataloging became automated, the everyday processes and tasks of the staff were modified. The change was enormous because now catalogers were using computers to process books instead of a typewriter. By far the bigger issue in libraries was the resistance to change that occurred. As mentioned in the literature, resistance to change is something all industries that employ humans encounter (Bennis, 1999; Bennis & Nanus, 2003; Carayon & Karsh, 2000; Schein, 1999a, 2003):

> The key to understanding resistance to change is to recognize that some behavior that has become dysfunctional for us may nevertheless be difficult to give up because this might make us lose group membership or may violate some aspect of our identity. (Schein, 2003, p. 321)

As the quote by Schein points out, resistance to change can make people react as dysfunctional beings. The group identity and membership with the library is important to the people who work there. The group membership within the subculture of the departments is also important. As mentioned earlier, changes need to be sold; there has to be buy-in by senior management, and the director and department heads have to agree the change needs to occur. The long tenure of the employees speaks to the desire to stay in a place of employment because they like being there or there is some long-term reason (e.g., retirement benefits) for staying.

CONCLUSION

This chapter has explored organizational culture and change management in academic and public libraries. People in libraries are members of an umbrella organization—the library in which they work. Additionally, the other group culture they are a part of is departmental. Each department in the library has a unique group environment that differentiates its members. When a change of any kind occurs, it upsets the status quo. As has been mentioned, that can create what Schein (2003) calls group members that become "dysfunctional beings" (p. 321). This dysfunction occurs because we are enmeshed in "unlearning, because what we have learned has become embedded in various routines and may have become part of our personal and group identity" (Schein, 2003, p. 321, emphasis in the original).

While change is not something on which to place a good or bad value judgment, it does impact the people in an organization. Sometimes substantial pain occurs while the change happens and creates havoc within the organizational culture as well as the subcultures. While those of us within these cultures live with it, some like it, and others do not.

All of our organizations are changing all of the time. As mentioned at the beginning of the chapter, change is a constant. We all need to get used to it, as we live in an ever-changing world.

CASE STUDY

The Owl Public Library board of trustees has hired a new director, Victoria Wellington. The board is very excited because she has become known as a change agent. She has turned around libraries that have become stagnant like the Owl Public Library. The staff is not as excited even though they were part of the hiring contingent.

Owl Public Library is in a city of 200,000 and has a central library with three branches. Each of the outlying branches has its own manager, and Victoria will manage the central library. Table 8.1 presents the

TABLE 8.1 OWL PUBLIC LIBRARY PERSONNEL BY BRANCH

Staff	Owl PL—Central Branch				Falcon Branch		Hawk Branch		Osprey Branch	
	Ref	*YA*	*Tech*	*IT*	*Ref/YA*	*Tech*	*Ref/YA*	*Tech*	*Ref/YA*	*Tech*
Managers	1	1	1	1	1	0	1	0	1	0
Librarians	4	2	2	1	2	1	2	1	2	1
Para Prof	4	2	4	1	2	2	2	2	2	2
Other	0	0	2	0	0	1	0	1	0	1
TOTAL	9	5	9	3	5	4	5	4	5	4

personnel breakdown, which doesn't include branch managers.

The total of staff is 53 plus three branch managers and one director. The budget is $5 million. The city is cutting the budget for the next fiscal year by 15% because much information is now on the Internet. The Falcon, Hawk, and Osprey Branches each have 15 Internet-connected PCs for the patrons, five OPAC computers, two black-and-white printers, and one color printer. There is one copier. Copies for black and white cost 10 cents (printer and copier), and color printer copies are 50 cents. Owl Public Library has 45 Internet-connected PCs for the patrons, 15 OPAC computers, five black-and-white printers, and two color printers. There are three copiers—one on each floor. The cost of copies is the same as at the branches. The director, branch managers, librarians, and paraprofessionals who have a desk also have PCs. The director and branch managers all have their own printers. The librarians and paraprofessionals in the back share printers at all the branch libraries. At the Owl Public Library, everyone has their own printer.

The library has in the past used approximately 60% of the budget for personnel and 25% for materials including licensing fees and databases; all other costs need to come out of the remainder of the budget. Interlibrary loan costs have been going up in the past year or two as patrons have increasingly wanted items from outside of the library system.

With the 15% decrease in the budget, determine what changes Victoria will need to make. The "other" personnel are part-time pages or circulation clerks. Determine the hours for all the libraries and what programming the library will be able to afford. The state library provides minimal databases. Go to the state library website for the state your library school is in and determine what sources it provides and at what cost before determining other costs. Also find out if there are state statutes indicating what percentage of materials needs to be provided if necessary.

References

Argyris, C. (1980). *The inner contradictions of rigorous research.* New York, NY: Academic Press.

Argyris, C. (1982). *Reasoning, learning, and action: Individual and organizational.* San Francisco, CA: Jossey-Bass.

Argyris, C. (1993). *Knowledge for action: A guide to overcoming barriers to organizational change.* San Francisco, CA: Jossey-Bass.

Argyris, C., & Schön, D. A. (1978). *Organizational learning: A theory of action perspective.* Reading, MA: Addison-Wesley.

Argyris, C., & Schön, D. A. (1996). *Organizational learning II: Theory, method, and practice.* Reading, MA: Addison-Wesley.

Batista, E. (2008, May 11). *Double-loop learning: Executive coaching and change management.* Retrieved from www.edbatista.com/2008/05/double-loop.html

Bennis, W. (1999). *Managing people is like herding cats.* Provo, UT: Executive Excellence Publishing.

Bennis, W., & Nanus, B. (2003). *Leaders: Strategies for taking charge* (2nd ed.). New York, NY: Harper Business Essentials.

Bolman, L. G., & Deal, T. E. (2003). *Reframing organizations: Artistry, choice, and leadership* (3rd ed.). San Francisco, CA: Jossey-Bass.

Burnes, B. (2007, June). Kurt Lewin and the Harwood studies: The foundations of OD. *The Journal of Applied Behavioral Science, 43*(2), 213–231.

Cameron, K. S., & Quinn, R. E. (1999). *Diagnosing and changing organizational culture: Based on the competing values framework.* Reading, MA: Addison-Wesley.

Carayon, P., & Karsh, B. T. (2000). Sociotechnical issues in the implementation of imaging technology. *Behaviour & Information Technology, 19*(4), 247–262.

Cope, O., & Waddell, D. (2001). An audit of leadership styles in e-commerce. *Managerial Auditing Journal, 16*(9), 523–529.

Griffin, R. (2008). *Fundamentals of management* (5th ed.). Mason, OH: South-Western, Cengage Learning.

Kanter, R. M. (2001). *Evolve! Succeeding in the digital culture of tomorrow.* Boston, MA: Harvard Business School Press.

Kanter, R. M. (2006, November). Innovation: The classic traps. *Harvard Business Review, 84*(11), 72–83.

Kanter, R. M. (2011, April). Cultivate a culture of confidence. *Harvard Business Review, 89*(4), 34.

Kotter, J. P. (2007, January). Leading change: Why transformation efforts fail. *Harvard Business Review, 85*(1), 96–103.

Kotter, J. P., & Schlesinger, L. A. (2008, July-August). Choosing strategies for change. *Harvard Business Review, 86*(7/8), 130–139.

Lawrence, P. R. (1969, January-February). How to deal with resistance to change. *Harvard Business Review, 47*(1), 4–12, 166–176.

Lewin, K. (1951). *Field theory in social science: Selected theoretical papers.* New York: Harper & Brothers Publishers.

Lewin, K. (1952). Group decision and social change. In G. E. Swanson, T. M. Newcomb, & E. L. Hartley (Eds.), *Readings in social psychology prepared for the committee on teaching of social psychology of the Society for the Psychology Study of Social Issues.* New York, NY: Henry Holt.

McNeal, G.S. (2009). Organizational culture, professional ethics, and Guantanamo. *Case Western Journal of International Law, 42*(125), 125–149.

Needham, G. (2001). The concept of leadership in technology-related organizations. Journal of *Library Administration, 32*(3/4), 133–144.

Oxford English Dictionary. (2009). Retrieved from www.oed.com.ezproxy.dom .edu/view/Entry/30467?rskey=smdSTM&result=1#eid

Rainey, H. (2009). *Understanding and managing public organizations* (4th ed.). San Francisco, CA: Jossey-Bass.

Schein, E. H. (1970). *Organizational psychology* (2nd ed.). Englewood Cliffs, NJ: Prentice-Hall, Inc.

Schein, E. H. (1980). *Organizational psychology* (3rd ed.). Englewood Cliffs, NJ: Prentice-Hall, Inc.

Schein, E. H. (1999a). *The corporate culture survival guide: Sense and nonsense about cultural change.* San Francisco, CA: Jossey-Bass.

Schein, E. H. (1999b). *Process consultation revisited: Building the helping relationship.* Reading, MA: Addison-Wesley.

Schein, E. H. (2003). *Organizational culture and leadership* (3rd ed.). San Francisco, CA: Jossey-Bass.

Senge, P. M. (1990). *The fifth discipline: The art & practice of the learning organization.* New York, NY: Doubleday.

Sheldon, B. E. (1991). *Leaders in libraries: Styles and strategies for success.* Chicago, IL: American Library Association.

Smith, K. K., & Berg, D. N. (1997). *Paradoxes of group life: Understanding conflict, paralysis, and movement in group dynamics.* San Francisco, CA: Jossey-Bass.

Smith, M. K. (2001). Kurt Lewin, groups, experiential learning and action research. *The Encyclopedia of Informal Education.* Retrieved from www.infed .org/thinkers/et-lewin.htm

Stueart, R. D., & Moran, B. B. (2007). *Library and information center management (7th ed.)*. Westport, CT: Libraries Unlimited.

Velasquez, D. L. (2007). *The impact of technology on organizational change in public libraries: A qualitative study (Doctoral dissertation)*. Retrieved from ProQuest Dissertation & Theses. (Accession No. 3349069.)

Volkan, V. (1997). *Blood lines: From ethnic pride to ethnic terrorism.* Boulder, CO: Westview Press.

Further Readings on Change Management and Organizational Culture

Bernfeld, B. A. (2004, Summer). Developing a team management structure in a public library. *Library Trends, 53*(1), 112–128.

Denhardt, R. B., Denhardt, J. V., & Aristigueta, M. P. (2008). *Managing human behavior in public and nonprofit organizations.* (2nd ed.). Thousand Oaks, CA: Sage.

Giesecke, J., & McNeil, B. (2004, Summer). Transitioning to the learning organization. *Library Trends, 53*(1), 54–67.

Holloway, K. (2004, Summer). The significance of organizational development in academic research libraries. *Library Trends, 53*(1), 5–16.

Ishii, K. (2004). Communication network use during organizational change: An examination of an integrated social information processing model. *Dissertation Abstracts International, 65*(12), 4401A.

Kaarst-Brown, M. L., Nicholson, S., von Dran, G. M., & Stanton, J. M. (2004, Summer). Organizational cultures of libraries as a strategic resource. *Library Trends, 53*(1), 33–53.

Lee, S. (2000). Organizational culture of an academic library. *Dissertation Abstracts International, 61*(08), 2968A.

Ostrow, R. L. (1998). Library culture in the electronic age: A case study of organizational change. *Dissertation Abstracts International, 59*(08), 2766A.

Phipps, S. E. (2004, Summer). The system design approach to organizational development: The University of Arizona model. *Library Trends, 53*(1), 68–111.

Schein, E. H. (1996, Fall). Three cultures of management: The key to organizational learning. *Sloan Management Review, 38*(1), 9–20.

Schein, E. H. (1999). *The corporate culture survival guide: Sense and nonsense about cultural change.* San Francisco, CA: Jossey-Bass.

Schneider, B., Brief, A. P., & Guzzo, R. A. (1996, Spring). Creating a climate and culture for sustainable organizational change. *Organizational Dynamics, 24*(4), 7–19.

Schwartz, C. A. (Ed.). (1997). *Restructuring academic libraries: Organizational development in the wake of technological change*. Chicago, IL: Association of College and Research Libraries.

Varner, C. H. (1996). An examination of an academic library culture using a competing values framework. *Dissertation Abstracts International, 58*(01), 0014A.

9
MARKETING

Diane L. Velasquez

Marketing is a tool that a great library uses to spread the word that the management of the library has produced some fantastic programming and services that their patrons would like to know about. The ability to use marketing is not something every library is adept at in today's world. In fact, many librarians see marketing in the same light as they view a used car salesman—it is slimy and corporations use it to sell their products. While a library does not sell its product per se, if the director and his or her staff do not have people coming in the door, the library will eventually lose its funding and have to close the door. According to the American Marketing Association (2007), the official definition of *marketing* is: "the activity, set of institutions, and processes for creating, communicating, delivering, and exchanging offerings that have value for customers, clients, partners, and society at large."

Most tax-supported libraries are governmentally run in one way or another. The public library, an academic library at a public university, a special library connected to the academic library, and a school library are just a few examples. Unless the library is 100% privately funded, it is governmentally funded to some extent through taxes. Nonprofit or not-for-profit libraries are funded through a foundation, religious order, donations, or some other way and are true nonprofits. A good example of this is a private university academic library that is funded through a religious order or organization. All of these types of libraries need to use marketing to get people through their doors to use their programs, services, books, databases, librarians, and whatever else they want to offer.

Marketing is a word that many librarians and directors hear and immediately say that they want nothing to do with it for their library.

Librarians associate marketing with poor salesmanship and telemarketers. This trait is really not the case. Marketing is "selling" the library to the community, stakeholders—internal and external—employees, and other organizations. Before looking at marketing in detail, the first thing to do is define some terms and jargon commonly used in marketing.

MARKETING MANAGEMENT

Marketing management focuses on exchanges of information between the organization and the consumers. Consumers in the case of libraries can be called patrons, customers, or students and faculty. The ultimate objective of marketing is to influence the behavior of the consumers in order to make choices. Marketing uses jingles and branding in order to achieve a marketing mind-set. The concept of marketing

1. doesn't educate,
2. doesn't change behavior or values, but
3. may influence behavior.

One of the tenets of marketing is the four Ps—price, product, promotion, and place. When marketing a nonprofit or government agency, price is not as critical as the rest. Schultz, Lauterborn, and Tannenbaum (1994) suggested that there are four corresponding Cs that apply to customer service (see Table 9.1).

Again as with price, customer product is not as important in a nonprofit or government agency. These two are negligible and should not be considered unless the library is giving something away that needs to be regarded as the cost of doing business for the marketing budget.

TABLE 9.1 FOUR Ps AND Cs

Four Ps	Four Cs
Products	Customer solutions
Price	Customer cost
Place	Convenience
Promotion	Communication

Note. Adapted from *Marketing Management (12th ed.)*, by P. Kotler and K. L. Keller, 2006 (New York, NY: Prentice Hall).

Adapting the four Ps to encompass the library and its services can produce the categories shown in Table 9.2.

Using both the four Ps and the Cs is considered a strategy based on an integrated marketing mix. When creating a marketing strategic plan it is important to consider both sets. In my mind, customer service is intricately linked to marketing. If the staff provides excellent customer service, the patrons will want to come back. Excellent customer service will bring back only those customers who are already patrons. To bring in those who are not, one needs marketing. Word of mouth is one way, but there are many others types of marketing.

Historically marketing is product oriented by selling radios, autos, electric lights, and so forth. Marketing and sales are connected in most corporate organizations. The sales mind-set is focused on products and services and how to obtain the most "bang for the buck" spent on the marketing dollar. Every dollar spent in marketing should coincide with sales. In a service organization (still talking about corporations) marketing should also increase sales of the service, whatever it might be—banking, brokerage, financial, and so forth.

The target audience mind-set starts with what the organization is and what it wants to offer. This is a backwards approach. Target audiences will decide what transactions will occur, not the marketer. The marketing planning must begin with the target audience, not with the organization. Organizations must study target audiences' needs, wants, perceptions, preferences, and satisfaction through surveys, focus groups, and other means.

For instance, when Apple introduced iPods there was no market really there, but the company created one. In time, Apple introduced other MP3 players with different memory levels that catered to differ-

TABLE 9.2 LIBRARY FOUR Ps

Four Ps	Library Four Ps
Products	Library Services and Programming
Price	Taxes
Place	Library Building and Website
Promotion	Promotion or General Selling of the Library Program and Services

Note. Based on notes from a marketing lecture for LIS 770 Management for Libraries and Information Centers, Dominican University, River Forest, IL, by D. L. Velasquez, 2011.

ent customers. All of them sold and sold well. This, in marketing and sales parlance, is called creating a market. Let me explain. Apple created a market where there was not one. Previously everyone used cassette tapes, CDs, minidisk players, and other types of bulky conveyances to listen to music. Apple created a new product that no other company ever considered. The company was ahead of the market, and no one knew that it would create a brand-new way of listening to music. The iPod caught everyone off guard, including the music industry. Now there are many different types of MP3 players, but by and large the most common ones are still in the iPod family, including the iPhone. As with the iPod, Apple took the cellphone to the next level with the iPhone. Now, Apple is taking the computer to the next level with the iPad.

When marketing products, most often marketing managers look at the features and benefits of the service or product and determine how best to emphasize those with their message. When looking at libraries the first thing to determine is what type of library it is? Is it academic, public, or special? Once that is determined, how is it funded? Is the library funded through taxes or private funding like a foundation, religious organization, or some other way?

If it is through tax monies, it is a government agency—this includes some public libraries and academic libraries. It can even include some special libraries that are quasigovernment organizations, such as the Smithsonian Institution that runs museums with special libraries. The Smithsonian receives a portion of its funding through the federal government's budget, and the rest of its budget comes from private donations through the Smithsonian's foundations. The Smithsonian runs all of the museums and zoos that the federal government owns or has an interest in.

If the funding is through a foundation, religious organization, or donations (this is not an all-inclusive list) it is a nonprofit. The last type of library is the corporate library, which is within a profit-driven company with a profit-and-loss statement; sometimes it even has stock, though there can be private companies. Corporate libraries are usually the ones at the most risk and have to justify their existence the most often. Why is this? Corporate libraries are for the internal use of the company and do not have external customers. A corporate library has no revenue flow and uses money that could potentially make the bottom line bigger. So the librarians who run the corporate libraries are constantly justifying their existence by proving that the service they provide helps the research and development group, marketing, or whomever. This case is one in which outreach and excellent customer service can help keep the library from being removed from existence.

In a public agency (think of a public or academic library that is being funded through tax dollars) the librarians need to have rapport with the agency or department head over them. For instance, in an academic institution the dean, director, or university librarian typically reports to the provost or assistant provost of a campus. In a public library, the director reports to a board of trustees or to the city manager or mayor. In each of these cases, it is imperative for the directors to build rapport with their supervisor.

In the academic library, if a director or dean has not done a good job of building rapport with the academic colleges and schools, it could create an atmosphere where the library may have a flat or decreasing budget. Why? The director has not convinced the provost that the materials and services the library provides have value. For instance, I had a department manager of a school once tell me that everything he needed for his scholarly work was on his computer through commercial databases. He thought he did not need the library. The problem with that type of thinking was that the commercial databases are purchased and made available by the academic library. No one had explained that piece of the puzzle to him. If the library went away, who would negotiate the contracts and licensing agreements that are necessary to have the commercial databases? What would happen if he needed a book and the library couldn't afford to purchase it or retrieve it through interlibrary loan because the budget had been cut too much? The dean of the library had done a poor job of explaining the library's role in the big picture of the university. The other part that most of the deans and department heads need to understand is that in order to get accreditation for the different schools, departments, and colleges there must be an up-to-date library.

In the public library world, the relationship between the director and the city management is just as important. The other relationship that is important is with the community. There have been directors who haven't believed how important this relationship is, and it has caused problems for their libraries. I won't get into all the different models of city governance here, but the relationships among the library directors and the city manager, mayor, city council, and library board are all very important. Each of these particular stakeholders needs to be kept informed of what is going on in the public library.

Public library directors should be marketing their library directly to all the stakeholders in the community. How can people come to a booktalk or a storytime if they do not know about it? Assuming everyone knows about the programming or that there is no digital divide in the town is asking for trouble. Putting it on the social media and the website is one way to get the information about programming out. What are some of the other ways? Local newspaper advertisements, flyers in the windows of local shops and supermarkets, talking it up at local service organizations, and staff discussing it wherever they go in town are some good ways. If each person in the library is not marketing the library, the library may eventually have its budget cut, and someone's job could be on the chopping block. It is everyone's job to market the library, even the pages.

An incident occurred in 2006 when the city of Salinas, California, had a multimillion-dollar budget shortfall. The city needed a referendum passed for a higher tax rate (sales tax), and the city warned the stakeholders that their public libraries, parks, and other "luxury" items the city paid for with taxes would be closed if it didn't pass. The citizens didn't believe this because the city had cried wolf too many times before. The library didn't take up the call and put together support to make sure the referendum was passed. When the referendum wasn't passed, all libraries and parks were closed. This caused an uproar, and the citizens were not happy; they had not believed the city manager. This is a good example of what happens when the director does not advocate to the stakeholders—in this case the community—what is going on with the budget. It took the City of Salinas with the help of the community over a year to get funding back in place for the libraries to reopen. By the time the Salinas libraries reopened, most of the staff had found new jobs.

MARKETING MIX

Many libraries need to market themselves to the community, schools, businesses, senior citizens, service organizations, and churches. By reaching out to the area, you can make everyone aware of the services that are available at the library no matter what kind it is. How you market makes a difference—this is called the marketing mix. With today's electronic media, it has become more complicated. There are many different ways to get to the public. Here is a list of some of the communications that can be developed:

1. Banner ad—side of a truck or bus
2. Blog
3. Brochure

4. Direct mail
5. E-mail
6. Magazine or newspaper advertisement
7. Poster (can include billboards, flyers)
8. Product container
9. Radio
10. RSS feed
11. Social media—Facebook, Twitter
12. Shopping bag logo
13. Television—cable or broadcast
14. Website (adapted from Andreasen & Kotler, 2008, pp. 288, 302)

Each of the different types of communications has pros and cons. Some are more impersonal than others. The level of penetration that each type of marketing communication will have to convince someone to come to the library, to go to a program, or to use a particular service will also be different. Each type of patron will have a different openness to the various means of marketing as well. The type of communication could be based on the ages of the patrons and what they are used to as far as how they communicate and receive information from the library regarding programs and services.

Target Market

Whom is the library attempting to reach with the advertising? People who already come to the library or someone who has never been to the library? New immigrants, people who have just moved to the community, or new students who have just enrolled at the university? Both the intention of the message and the group it is aimed at will determine how the message should be worded; that is, what the message should say, how to say it, when to say it, where to say it, and who should say it (Andreasen & Kotler, 2008, p. 304).

Services and Programming—How Do Users Know?

Another consideration in communicating with the users or patrons is to ask them what they need or want as far as programming and services. There is a small limitation to this approach. Asking patrons what they want will only get to users who are currently using the library and will not reach those who are not using the library. Still, if the users are asked and the library can afford to do what the users are suggesting, the idea needs to be marketed.

STRATEGIC MARKETING PLANS

Many times when an organization wants to implement a cohesive plan of marketing, it will write a strategic marketing plan. This type of plan has a similar look and feel to a strategic plan except that it is totally focused on the marketing aspect of the business.

The strategic marketing plan addresses just marketing the organization. Like a regular strategic plan, it starts with the mission statement of the organization. What is the mission statement? The mission statement should show that the organization has opportunities, competence, and commitment (Drucker, 1990). Enabling marketing of all three for a service organization is a must to prove there is an ultimate goal.

The marketing plan will contain the following elements:

1. Executive summary
2. Mission statement
3. Analysis of the macroenvironment
4. SWOT analysis
5. Portfolio analysis
6. Objectives
7. Proposed marketing strategies
8. Evaluation methods
9. Timetable
10. Budget (adapted from de Sáez, 2002)

Executive Summary

The executive summary is an overview of the entire report in just a couple of pages. The executive summary needs to give a good review of the situation where the library is marketing-wise, where the management team wants to go, and how the team plans to get there. It doesn't need to be an in-depth report of the history of the library. This is where the management team sells the board, the provost, or whomever they report to on the belief that marketing the library is what they need to do to move the library forward. The key issues of the marketing plan need to be presented, not a long, wordy, windy overview of everything.

Mission Statement

Include any part of the mission statement of the library that is relevant to the marketing of the library. Some libraries have succinct one- or two-line mission statements. Others are expressed in rather lengthy paragraphs. The marketing plan should tie back to the mission and vision of the library because that is what everyone in the library is working toward.

Environmental Analysis

The variables that make up the environmental analysis are typically those in the political, economic, social, technological, and legal spheres. In the library and information center of today, the technological and legal spheres are constantly changing, and these two should always be in view. The political, economic, and social may not have as much influence as the others. Economic downturns, however, can increase traffic the library and strain the technology within a public or academic environment. For instance, perhaps the PCs used for Internet access are seven years old and weren't planned to be replaced for another two, but increased traffic due to a recession has created such a demand for PCs that there are more outages than usual. This is actually a marketing issue because your patrons will tell other patrons that the computers often break down at your library. How the library management deals with it may need to be budgeted, planned for, and marketed to your patrons.

SWOT Analysis

A SWOT analysis sounds like the cops are at the doors with guns and will be running in. This is nothing further from the truth. A SWOT analysis monitors the following aspects of the internal and external marketing environments (Kotler & Keller, 2006):

Strengths
Weaknesses
Opportunities
Threats

Strengths: What are the organization's strengths? What does it do best? The marketing analysis needs to look internally and externally.

1. Perhaps the children's department at the public library undertaking a SWOT analysis is excellent. The storytime is always packed. Maybe there should be more than one a week, or maybe there should be one on the weekend and two during the week. Is there outreach to local preschools and elementary schools?
2. The academic liaison for the history department is excellent. Sally works so well she is always booked up with doctoral students to

> help with their research. She also works well with the professors on their undergraduate and graduate courses. Perhaps what she does well could be taught to other departmental liaisons so that everyone is excellent in their customer service.

Weaknesses: What are the things internally and externally the organization does poorly? What are the service items the organization could improve on? Perhaps the organization doesn't get the word out about programming. Maybe there needs to be better outreach to immigrant populations. There is always something an organization can do better.

Opportunities: What is the organization missing? Could the organization be doing something it is not? For a public library that has a large Spanish-speaking population, perhaps ESL classes. Another consideration for a public library is that staff could offer tutoring for folks who do not read well and need help improving their skills. An academic library might need better maintenance and administration of their printers. Any library might offer a class emphasizing that not everything can be found on the Internet.

Threats: Threats to a service organization that is funded through tax dollars may be a little harder to identify than its opportunities, but it is possible. Many public libraries feel threatened by Barnes & Noble and Amazon. People who purchase their own books, e-books, CDs, DVDs, and so forth do not need to go to a public library. What is another way to get that group into the library? At academic libraries, there is the same problem. Many of the faculty and students do not think they need to go to the library. Everything they need is online and on the Internet. (They wish.) What services the academic library can provide to counter the threat of everything being available on the Internet is something to consider. The following is a list of potential competitive threats to libraries:

1. Brick-and-mortar bookstores
2. College libraries
3. Internet
4. Internet bookstores
5. Other schools' libraries
6. Public libraries
7. Smartphones
8. University libraries

Once the organization has done a SWOT analysis it will know what kind of marketing needs to be done to get people in the front door. The

TABLE 9.3 TARGET AUDIENCES

Public Academic Library	Private Academic Library	Public Library
Administration	Administration	Children
Congress	Deans of schools/ colleges	City council
Deans of schools/ colleges	Donors	Community
Donors	Faculty	Congress
Faculty	Federal government	Donors
Federal governmentl	Funding organization	Friends of the Library
Friends of the Library	General public	Library board
General public	Library staff	Library staff
Legislature	Mass media	Mayor
Library staff	Staff	Patrons
Mass media	State government	P–12 schools
Staff	Students	General public
State government	Volunteers	State government
Students		Taxpayers
Taxpayers		Volunteers
Volunteers		

marketing message will be tailored to what the SWOT analysis indicates the organization lacks and excels in and will cater to the people in your community. First, the organization needs to know who its public, or target audience, is. Table 9.3 provides a list of target audiences for three entities, a publicly funded academic library, a privately funded academic library, and a public library. Once its public is known, the library can cater to it.

Portfolio Analysis

In any type of library (academic, public, or special) there are various pieces and parts called departments that offer different services and programming. These services and programming can be at different levels of product lifecycle (recall the earlier example about aging computers).

There may or may not be a competitor for the services that the library provides. In some rural areas, the public or academic library may be the only place in town to find that special book or computer connection.

In a public library, for example, does it make sense to cater to the small-business community special research services for an hourly rate? Can the library support personnel for something like that? Is this a pilot project or something for the long term? These are all things to think about when putting a plan together.

All different types of libraries, when considering a portfolio analysis, need to be aware that there may be other places that their services could be marketed. The hard questions need to be asked before making the plan public or putting it forward with the board or provost. Once they see a revenue-generating idea, the powers that be just may want to move forward with it. Are the funds available to support additional services? Are the personnel available? Can you hire more people to support each new service or program?

Objectives

Marketing objectives are precise statements that outline what is to be accomplished by the organization's marketing activities (McDonald & Payne, 1996, p. 119). Specific objectives are quantifiable and usually include what the organization wants to improve by a certain percentage. The chief aim is that it is measurable. A mission statement is usually pretty vague. An objective will answer a what, when, where, how, and who question and by how much. For instance, the children's programming wants to improve attendance to storytime by 10%. This is a measureable objective.

Another example: The undergraduate research services department wants to improve reference appointments by 20%. Reference questions at the reference desk need to be responded to within five minutes. Both of these objectives are measurable.

Solid objectives can be easily measured, collected, and achieved. An objective that is not achievable will just frustrate the staff and the people who have to manage the objectives.

Marketing Strategies

A marketing strategy describes how the marketing objective will be achieved (McDonald & Payne, 1996, p. 119). What are the means by which the organization is going to achieve the measurable objectives that have been set out by the management team? The marketing strategies are the general content of how the organization intends to go about informing the community about its programming and services. These can entail different items. In a government agency or nonprofit, sales is not the focus, but people coming in the door is what management wants to have happen.

As with any management process, there will be policies and procedures governing how the marketing will be organized, including the branding (if desired) of the programming and services. How will the community know these items are available? The management team will decide how to promote the events through the different types of media that were discussed earlier in the chapter.

Evaluation Methods

Whenever an organization follows a new plan, the management team should assess and evaluate whether or not it was effective. Were the results expected? Did the programs and services pull in the expected people, or did they not pull in enough to justify the costs associated with the program? For example, let's say a local author was brought in to promote a recent book, and only 10 people showed up. The cost for the author was $500. It essentially cost the organization $50 per person to bring in that author plus whatever other costs were incurred for advertising, promotion, refreshments, and personnel time. This is not a good or useful level of expenditure, but it would be more than worth the overall money spent if 200 people showed up. Based just on the money spent for the author, it would cost $2.50 per person, which is affordable.

Assessment and evaluation methods, like objectives, need to be measurable and quantifiable. Evaluation should also take into consideration what was done right and wrong. If something was not exactly perfect, what can be done in the future to make the event or a similar event better? The best way to find out this type of information is to ask the people who attended the event. If it is a children's or teen event, ask the target group. Kids, teens, and adults are willing to give feedback—just ask for it. Like the management team, the patrons who spend time giving feedback have the same goal to make events, programs, and services better for everyone.

Timetable

What is the timetable for the marketing plan? The typical plan will cover a year or two. If the plan covers more than a year, it will sometimes be estimated with the idea that it will be tweaked once the events occur in the first year and there is evaluation and assessment done on the initial events. As mentioned earlier, not all the events will be perfect. Some will fail and need to be replaced with new ones. Some programs and services will need to be tweaked. The summer reading program in public libraries is usually changed every summer with a new theme and prizes.

Proposed Budget

The marketing plan's budget will usually be informed by the financial situation in your city, county, school, college, university, or company. The budget may not be huge. It is amazing how easy it can be to stretch funds with a little imagination and the use of electronic media. Do not depend on electronic media for all of your marketing messages; not everyone uses it. Use the budget wisely, and spend most of your budget on your biggest programs and services. In a public library, the summer reading program can be huge, as it is the one reading program for adults. In an academic library, the beginning of the semester can be a time when special events get new or transfer undergraduate and graduate students into the library.

CASE STUDY

You are the director of a public library in a community that over the years has experienced a definite shift in the ethnic demographics. There is no question that the makeup includes many more immigrants than before. You have already been purchasing materials in other languages (depending on where your library is located, this could be Spanish, Chinese, Vietnamese, Polish, Korean, or some other language) and have created signage in the library in the new immigrants' language and in English. Still, you feel more could be done to attract the new immigrant community to the library. This is confirmed when you do an informal sampling of patron records and compare them to the census count for the area. While you want to build up usage by the immigrant population, you certainly don't want to do it at the expense of other groups.

You contact the head of the outreach division of the state library, asking if there might be grant funding for outreach activities at your library. Happily, the state library has just received a grant and will be looking for well-defined plans so that appropriate funds can be allocated for outreach activities at public libraries. You are told that there is a good chance that if your plans are viable, your library could receive as much as $10,000. While the money won't be yours until you submit your proposals and obtain approvals, you are very encouraged about the possibilities.

You call a meeting of your staff in order to discuss this issue. What can you do to bring in more of the immigrant population to the library? What would attract them? What could you offer to entice them to come in? How could you market your services to them?

You need to develop a cohesive plan to submit to the state library's outreach division in order to receive the funding. How would you go about putting together a marketing plan to target these new immigrants in your community? What services would be of value to them? Consider all programming and service possibilities when putting the plan together.

References

American Marketing Association. (2007). *Definition of marketing.* Retrieved from www.marketingpower.com/AboutAMA/Pages/DefinitionofMarketing.aspx

Andreasen, A. R., & Kotler, P. (2008). *Strategic marketing for nonprofit organizations* (7th ed.). Upper Saddle River, NJ: Pearson Prentice Hall.

De Sáez, E. E. (2002). *Marketing concepts for libraries and information services* (2nd ed.). London, UK: Facet Publishing.

Drucker, P. (1990). *Managing the non-profit organization: Principles and practices.* New York, NY: Harper Business.

Kotler, P., & Keller, K. L. (2006). *Marketing management* (12th ed.). New York, NY: Prentice Hall.

McDonald, M., & Payne, A. (1996). *Marketing planning for services.* Boston, MA: Butterworth Heinmann.

Schultz, D. E., Lauterborn, R. F., & Tannenbaum, S. I. (1994). *The new marketing paradigm: Integrated marketing communications.* Lincolnwood, IL: NTC Business Books.

Further Readings on Marketing

Aharony, N. (2009). Librarians' attitudes towards marketing library services. *Journal of Librarianship and Information Science, 41*(1), 39–50.

Bell, C. R., & Patterson, J. R. (2009). *Take their breath away: How imaginative service creates devoted customers.* Hoboken, NJ: John Wiley & Sons.

Bernard, E., Osmonbekov, T., & McKee, D. (2011). Customer learning orientation in public sector organizations. *Journal of Nonprofit & Public Sector Marketing, 23*(2), 158–180.

Dowd, N. (2011, January-June). Is mobile marketing right for your organization? *Reference Librarian, 52*(1/2), 166–177.

Drucker, P. (1990). *Managing the non-profit organization: Principles and practices.* New York, NY: Harper Business.

Duckor, A. S. (2009, January/February). From awareness to funding. *American Libraries, 40*(1/2), 45–47.

Jones, D. Y., McCandless, M., Kiblinger, K., Giles, K., & McGabe, J. (2011, April-June). Simple marketing techniques and space planning to increase circulation. *Collection Management, 36*(2), 107–118.

Kotler, P., & Levy, S. J. (1969, January). Broadening the concept of marketing. *Journal of Marketing, 88,* 10–15.

MacDonald, K. I., vanDuinkerken, W., & Stephens, J. (2008). It's all in the marketing: The impact of a virtual reference marketing campaign at Texas A&M University. *Reference & User Services Quarterly, 47*(4), 375–385.

Nunn, B., & Ruane, E. (2011, April). Marketing gets personal: Promoting reference staff to reach users. *Journal of Library Administration, 51*(3), 291–300.

Ratzek, W. (2011, June). The mutations of marketing and libraries. *IFLA Journal, 37*(2), 139–151.

Shontz, M. L., Parker, J. C., & Parker, R. (2004). What do librarians think about marketing? A survey of public librarians' attitudes toward the marketing of library services. *Library Quarterly, 76*(1), 63–84.

Sikowitz, J., & Weeks, A. C. (2009, March/April). Marketing the Mount Pleasant Public Library to transitory residents. *Public Libraries, 48*(2), 38–44.

Zauha, J. M. (2003, March/April). You can get there from here! A marketing and public relations program for Montana libraries. *Public Libraries, 42*(2), 117–121.

10
FINANCIAL MANAGEMENT

Diane L. Velasquez

Financial management, fiscal management, budgeting, paying the bills, and planning for the future—whatever we call it, it usually strikes fear in the hearts of librarians when they are told they have to manage money. Directors, deans, and department heads are promoted into positions involving finances without having been formally taught how to run a budget or having even taken an elementary accounting class that explains how credits and debits work. There has to be revenue (income) coming in to pay for the expenditures (expenses) that everyone needs to run the business of the library, whether it is a nonprofit, a for-profit, or a government agency. In order to pay the employees; buy the materials and other resources; put on the programs; and have lights, Internet connections, and computers, money has to come in and go out on at least a monthly basis.

Acquisitions or collection development librarians may manage a small budget for a particular collection that is their responsibility. In a public library, librarians may be responsible for all of the children's and young adult fiction and nonfiction collections that are purchased, no matter the format. In an academic library, a librarian may be responsible for just the business section, purchasing the materials and making suggestions regarding the serials to support that section. In a special library, depending on the type, librarians would support their particular collection specialty. All of this entails watching a budget, negotiating with a vendor, and making the best deals possible for your patrons and library. The best deal is coming in under budget or spending less than you have. The worst deal is coming in over budget or spending more than you had. Perfection is matching the revenue to the expenditures and spending every penny exactly.

Everyone has a personal budget and has encountered the same challenges, and maybe has had to hit a savings account or credit card to cover unexpected expenses like car repairs or medical bills. Unexpected expenses can happen at libraries as well. The server dies unexpectedly, or the elevator goes out. A computer server never gives notice like human employees when problems occur or gives the director or IT technician time to go out and buy a new server before dying. The server usually dies at the worse time possible—the peak of the tax season when everyone is running to the library to do their taxes on the computers and to e-file, or in the middle of an integrated library system (ILS) software upgrade—you get the idea. This chapter will give you insight into some of the quirks and nuances of running a budget for a library. There are different types of budgets, but no matter the type, hopefully it includes a small reserve for emergencies.

OPERATIONS BUDGETS

In this chapter, the main type of budget we will be discussing is the operations budget that runs the library on a day-to-day basis. Another type of budget is the capital budget, which is for capital improvements such as expanding the building, building a new facility, or doing some remodeling; it is called a capital budget because capital funds are expended and the budget is amortized over a 20–30 year time line.

Budgeting for day-to-day operations involves a rather straightforward examination of budgetary categories and reports that center on resources and accountability. An operations budget covers the resources needed to run the library on a daily, weekly, monthly, or quarterly basis. When the library doesn't have sufficient resources, the managers have to start thinking about what they will and will not be able to accomplish. In this way, budgeting is related to planning; the objectives of a library generally require resources in some form for their success. The key to good management of finances in a library is to tie the line items in the operations budget to the vision and mission statements. In the strategic planning stages when the mission and vision statements were being created, there should have been budget line items tied into those goals and objectives.

For instance, let's say the ABC Public Library has as its vision statement to improve lifelong learning and education for its community, and the overall mission is to improve lifelong learning. Hopefully in the goal statements there were SMART (specific, measurable, achievable, realistic, and timely) goals or objectives that would enable the library to do this (see Chapter 5 on strategic planning for more about SMART goals). For example, the library will hold four nonfiction author visits with one each focusing on space, do-it-yourself projects, cooking, and crafts for kids. The four authors will engage different patron groups, and all topics will be educational. If the authors are local, all the better, as the programs will probably be inexpensive, but if the authors live in the surrounding area they may be willing to donate their time in exchange for some good publicizing of their event in local newspapers, on the library's and the authors' websites, via the Internet, and around town. As long as the event is well attended and the programming is smooth sailing for everyone, this will be money well spent.

LINE ITEM BUDGETS

Most nonprofits or government agencies work on what is called a line item budget. Each line item—expense category—has a certain amount of money designated to it. For example, Table 10.1 presents a budget for the Utopian Library at Thomas More State University.

In the example the actual revenues were $500,000 less than expected in the Actual Year 2010–11. This caused the library dean to determine that the reserves to be set aside would cover the extra expenses. As can be seen, there were some unexpected increases in some of the line items. These cannot really be planned for. Having a 5% to 10% reserve in place for these kinds of situations is a feasible thing to do. It gives the library a safety net. Once the library realizes it is running short, it can put things on hold and wait until next year, or let positions that are unfilled because of retirements, terminations, or resignations remain unfilled until next year. Perhaps it can apply for additional grants to make the budget the next year. Another possibility is to increase a portion of the tuition or fees that the academic library receives in the next academic year.

Now let's look at a scenario for a public library budget and see what we think about the budget for the community. In my management course, I split the class into groups and have each run a library (the libraries can be academic, public, or special) over the length of a semester. Each group puts

TABLE 10.1 UTOPIAN LIBRARY BUDGET

	Proposed 2010–11	Actual 2010–11	% Change Prop. vs. Act.	Projected 2011–12	% Change 2010–11
REVENUE					
State Contribution	$4,000,000	$3,500,000	−13	$2,500,000	−29
Grants	15,000,000	15,000,000	0	15,000,000	0
Tuition	4,375,000	4,375,000	0	6,562,500	50
Total Revenue	**$23,375,000**	**$22,875,000**	**−2**	**$24,062,500**	**5**
OPERATING EXPENSES					
Salaries and Benefits					
Mgmt. Salaries	$2,000,000	$1,859,405	−7	$2,000,000	8
Prof. Salaries	3,500,000	3,598,423	3	3,600,000	0
Other Salaries and Wages	3,000,000	2,948,547	−2	3,000,000	2
Benefits	3,740,000	3,701,935	−1	3,790,000	2
Total	**$12,240,000**	**$12,108,310**	**−1**	**$12,380,000**	**2**
Materials					
Books	$1,500,000	$1,487,651	−1	$1,200,000	−19
Serials	250,000	200,489	−20	250,000	25
CDs	75,000	50,876	−32	75,000	47
DVDs	75,000	80,475	7	100,000	24
Microfiche	25,000	24,038	−4	25,000	4
Licensing Agreements	3,000,000	3,408,684	14	4,000,000	17
Internet Costs	272,500	270,000	−1	382,813	42
Total	**5,197,500**	**5,522,213**	**6**	**6,032,813**	**9**

TABLE 10.1 UTOPIAN LIBRARY BUDGET (continued)

	Proposed 2010–11	Actual 2010–11	% Change Prop. vs. Act.	Projected 2011–12	% Change 2010–11
IT Services					
Computer Maintenance	$250,000	57,592	–77	250,000	334
PC Costs—New	1,000,000	750,841	–25	1,000,000	33
Printers/Scanners/Other	250,000	250,786	0	250,000	0
Software Upgrades	250,000	152,975	–39	250,000	63
ILS Upgrades	100,000	100,894	1	100,000	–1
Total	**$1,850,000**	**$1,313,088**	**–29**	**$1,850,000**	**41**
Professional Development					
Professional Development	$175,313	$150,248	–14	$180,469	20
Travel Costs	58,437	41,872	–28	60,156	44
Total	**$233,750**	**$192,120**	**–18**	**$240,625**	**25**
Other					
Building Maintenance	$250,000	$305,815	22	325,000	6
Office Equipment Maintenance	500,000	485,015	–3	500,000	3
Projects	750,000	500,486	–33	750,000	50
Office Supplies	250,000	358,045	43	410,000	15
Total	**$1,750,000**	**$1,649,361**	**–6**	**$1,985,000**	**20**
Reserve	$2,337,500	$2,282,028	NA	1,804,688	NA
Total Expenses	**$23,375,000**	**$22,875,000**	**–2**	**$24,062,500**	**5**

together a budget based on a total of $600,000 with 10 employees. The only full-time employees required are a director and a reference librarian. Any other employees up to the remaining eight are at the whim of the group. In my case, I put two years of a budget together showing a total of $635,000 as a proposed budget in Fiscal Year 2010–11 and a 10% decrease in Fiscal Year 2011–12. Table 10.2 presents my Bluebird of Happiness Public Library budget.

The big difference between the academic and public library budget is where the revenues come from. The state university's money comes primarily from the state and from library fees built into the tuition as well as some grant money. In my case, I put quite a lot of money in grants, but that is utopian thinking. Depending on the size of the university, the number of holdings (tangible collections: books, serials, government documents, etc.), size of the student body, and whether it is a doctoral or a master's institution will determine how many librarians and paraprofessionals there will be on staff. Small private liberal arts colleges, unless the alumni are extremely generous with donations, tend to have a small staff in the library.

Public libraries are funded through a couple of ways—property taxes are the most common. Sometimes public libraries are funded through sales tax, as is the one in Oak Brook, Illinois. The property tax is called a *millage* because the library portion is a percentage or mill of the taxes levied. In some areas, the tax is on personal property as well as on property. In Missouri, for example, personal property is taxed for library and other purposes. It is not taxed at a high percentage rate, but it does accumulate enough taxes along with the property taxes to fund the libraries well. The percentage depends on the taxing authority of the library or municipality that the library is attached to. Some libraries are run by the county instead of the city. Other public libraries are fully independent of the city or county. In that case, if the library needs an increase in funding, the director and board have to take the requested tax increase before the voters. There is no certainty that the voters will approve a tax increase. Tax increases also depend on the reporting structures in the state where the library is. Some states have funding laws that determine that libraries of a certain size need to have collections funded at a certain percentage of the budget.

PERSONNEL BUDGETING

How are the numbers for personnel determined? Generally, personnel (salaries, wages, and benefits) accounts for 45% to 65% of a library

TABLE 10.2 BLUEBIRD OF HAPPINESS PUBLIC LIBRARY BUDGET

	Proposed 2010–11	Actual 2010–11	% Change Prop. vs. Act.	Projected 2011–12	% Change 2010–11
REVENUE					
Property Taxes	$500,000	$475,000	–5	$427,500	–10
State Aid	50,000	40,000	-20	10,000	-10
Grants	25,000	35,000	40	31,500	-10
Investment Income	10,000	12,000	20	10,800	-10
Contributions	30,000	40,000	33	36,000	-10
Copier Income	5,000	3,570	-29	3,213	-10
Other Income	15,000	17,000	13	15,300	-10
Total Revenue	**$635,000**	**$622,570**	**–2**	**$560,303**	**-10**
OPERATING EXPENSES					
Salaries and Benefits					
Salaries	$250,000	$230,000	–8	$213,750	-7
Benefits	62,500	57,500	–8	53,438	-7
Total	**$312,500**	**$287,500**	**–8**	**$267,188**	**-7**
Other					
Building Maintenance	$10,000	$15,000	50	$13,500	–10
Other Equip. Maintenance	5,000	7,500	50	6,750	-10
Projects	9,000	5,000	–44	4,500	-10
Office Supplies	10,000	12,500	25	11,250	-10
Total	**$34,000**	**$40,000**	**18**	**$36,000**	**-10**
Materials					
Books	$25,000	$20,000	–20	18,000	-10
Serials	10,000	8,000	–20	7,200	-10

TABLE 10.2 BLUEBIRD OF HAPPINESS PUBLIC LIBRARY BUDGET (continued)

	Proposed 2010–11	Actual 2010–11	% Change Prop. vs. Act.	Projected 2011–12	% Change 2010–11
CDs	5,000	7,500	50	6,750	-10
DVDs	5,000	7,500	50	6,750	-10
Licensing Agreements	35,000	40,000	14	36,000	-10
Internet Costs	30,000	30,000	0	35,000	17
Total	**$110,000**	**$113,000**	**3**	**$109,700**	**-3**
Professional Development					
Professional Development	$2,500	$0	-100	$1,500	100
Travel	5,000	2,000	-60	1,800	-10
Total	**$7,500**	**$2,000**	**-73**	**$3,300**	**65**
IT Services					
Computer Maintenance	$25,000	$30,000	20	$27,000	-10
PC Costs—New	15,000	20,000	33	18,000	-10
Printer/Scanners/Other	10,000	5,000	-50	4,500	-10
Software Upgrades	15,000	10,000	-33	9,000	-10
ILS Upgrades	50,000	45,000	-10	46,902	4
Total	**$115,000**	**$110,000**	**-4**	**$105,402**	**-4**
Reserve @ 10%	$63,500	$72,070	Reserve @ 7.5	$42,023	
Total Expenses	**$635,000-**	**$612,757**	**-4**	**$560,313**	**-9**

budget. Salaries and wages include everyone who works in the library from the highest level like the director or dean to the lowest levels including maintenance staff and pages. By law, everyone needs to be paid at least at the federal minimum wage level. What is included in benefits? Benefits for a full-time regular employee include Social Security payments by the employer that matches the amount the employee pays; this is called FICA, which stands for Federal Insurance Contribution Act. The employer matches the Social Security payment amount for Medicare as well. Some states require state disability insurance payments, called SDI. Employers also pay federal unemployment tax assessments (FUTA) on all employees. Other benefits include voluntary benefits that the employer chooses to provide, such as medical, dental, vision, long-term disability, and group life insurance.

The employer also may provide vacation and sick benefits. Some employers group this together into what is termed *paid time off* (PTO). When an employee accrues vacation and sick time or PTO, it is shown on the pay stub or calculated in the human resources (HR) office on a biweekly, semimonthly, or monthly basis. When PTO is provided, it

TABLE 10.3 CONVERSION OF DAYS PAID FOR ACCOUNTING

	Monthly	Semimonthly	Biweekly
Vacation Days			
10	0.83	0.42	0.38
15	1.25	0.63	0.58
20	1.67	0.83	0.77
25	2.08	1.04	0.96
Sick Days			
5	0.42	0.21	0.19
PTO			
18	1.50	0.75	0.69
23	1.92	0.96	0.88
28	2.23	1.17	1.08
33	2.75	1.38	1.27

usually includes a few more days and is meant to be all inclusive; any time taken off, whether for bereavement, illness, vacation, or anything else, all comes from the PTO time. No additional time is given. As an example to show how PTO is accrued, Table 10.3 illustrates what accounting would have to put aside each payday for vacation and sick time.

This would enable accounting to take an employee's hourly rate of $10.00 and multiply it by the number of vacation days once converted into hours. The hours that had accrued for January through June, which would be 40 if the employee is relatively new, would cost $400 to accrue vacation time for that employee for one week. Each employee would have an accrual, so there would be a cost for providing vacation for each employee and potential sick time. The policies the library has would determine how sick time is considered—whether it is paid out if the employee doesn't use it or the time would be lost. In PTO all time is available for the employee to use, as none of it is designated specifically for sick time, and the employee needs to use all of it by the end of the year.

Part-time employees' benefits include FICA, Medicare, and FUTA at the minimum. Depending on the number of hours part-time employees work, some employers allow them to prorate vacation and sick time. Other employers do not.

As can be seen, the personnel salary and wage numbers actually have some sense to them. The key to the number is how many employees there are in the library and how many are professional librarians (MLS/MLIS holding) and paraprofessionals. The last item that can influence the personnel budget is where in the United States a library is located.

TABLE 10.4 PUBLIC LIBRARY POSITIONS (ACTUAL)

Title	Salary
Director	$60,000
Reference Librarian	45,000
Children's Librarian	45,000
PT—Children's Librarian	25,000
PT—YA/Adult Librarian	25,000
PT—Circulation/Pages (3)	30,000
TOTAL	**$230,000**

The west and northeast regions tend to be the most expensive places to live, and the salaries follow suit somewhat. The south tends to be a less expensive place to live and salaries are not as high there. Table 10.4 shows the employees included in the salary line item at the Bluebird of Happiness Public Library.

MATERIALS COSTS

Materials costs vary according to the size of the library. In the past few years, overall budgets have dropped or stayed flat in academic and public libraries (Bosch, Henderson, & Klusendorf, 2011; Hoffert, 2011). When budgets drop, there is an ancillary drop in materials budgets. If a budget holds steady, this is still not good news for materials costs. Materials costs have gone up in recent years as well. The library dean or director and the staff will have to make difficult decisions about what to cut. Materials in public libraries are approximately 20% of the budget—this includes adult, children, and young adult materials in all formats. For the academic library it is approximately 30–35% (Nicholas, Rowland, Jubb, & Jamali, 2010).

In the budget given for the Utopian Library the materials cost is 25.1% of the budget; for the Bluebird of Happiness Public Library, it is around 20%. Both budgets are adequate at best and probably resemble some of the hard choices that libraries around the United States have to make. The choices of materials can be difficult because periodicals and electronic journals are expensive in the scientific fields for academic libraries. According to Bosch, Henderson, and Klusendorf (2011), many academic libraries are going to need to start to unbundle their consortium and electronic journal choices to bring down costs. Some library deans and directors may even go to a pay-per-view journal purchasing system if one becomes available. Publishers and librarians will be looking at a changed way of doing business in the near future.

In public libraries, directors are facing some of the same choices. Costs are going up and up, and budgets are being cut or staying flat. Any increase in the cost of materials will cause painful choices to be made by public librarians, and patrons will not be happy about them. The trend to e-journals may follow in public libraries as well. At this time, many magazines in public libraries still tend to be ordered and received in paper format.

Next, there are serials. This is a very different challenge for libraries because their prices have been going up for years. Concerns will differ across environments. In public and school libraries, the periodicals most frequently subscribed to tend to be relatively inexpensive (general interest and children's periodicals are usually at the bottom of the price list). In academic and many special libraries, the prices tend to be high and the price increases highest as well. This has presented a budgetary problem for many libraries for about two decades. Assume you have been getting budget increases over the most recent five years of 1% to 3% a year. Now assume that, even in a public library, the average price increase for periodicals has been 4% to 5% a year. You can see that it doesn't take very long for there to be a substantial impact on the total materials budget. For example, the University of Missouri Libraries budget has not changed in six years (0% growth). As you might expect, serials prices have continued to rise during those years. One effect has been the need to purchase fewer books. Another has been serials cancellations. Very quickly the nature of the library can change because of the external financial forces that have inevitable and profound effects on the library's budget. This can create an adversarial relationship between the departments whose serials are very expensive (hard sciences like chemistry, physics, and biology; some social sciences like economics, political science, and business) and the librarians who make the collection development decisions.

Book costs are also increasing. If the operating budget is flat or decreasing when book costs are increasing—as they have been—fewer books can be purchased. While libraries do get discounts, that still isn't enough to continue to purchase at the past rates when books were less expensive. Budget wisely and get suggestions from the faculty that is supported by the collection development staff. Checking book reviews and getting feedback on what is being used in courses to support the curriculum also makes sense.

There was a discussion on one of the electronic discussion lists recently about a specialized encyclopedia that is available in print and online for $3,000. The encyclopedia was written and edited by experts in the LIS field. The editors were surprised to find that many of the university libraries had not purchased it. The price of the encyclopedia for a three- or four-volume set is very expensive even if it is specialized. In a time of budgetary crisis, this is not the time to be spending a large amount of money on an encyclopedia when that money could purchase many more books in a cross section of disciplines. This can be a difficult choice, but $3,000 could be all the money one discipline has to spend in a small or medium-sized academic library for an entire academic year.

In a public library, depending on size, 20% to 25% appears to be approximately what is spent on book materials. The money will need to be allocated to the adult, children, and teen areas based on the community demographics. Do not shortchange one area for another. Children's books can be just as pricy as adult books. Replacing well-loved classics in all areas is important for a good collection. If books in the collection are not being checked out, weed them. Make sure all of the space in your library is well used and books are circulating so that the budget dollars are well spent.

Another major issue in public libraries is providing access to Internet-connected computers. The average number of public access computers in a public library is 16, and the majority of public libraries offer wireless Internet access (Hoffman, Bertot, Davis, & Clark, 2011, p. 24). The importance of having Internet-connected public access computers is discussed in depth in Chapter 17, the chapter about information technology.

ZERO-BASED BUDGETING

What exactly is a zero-based budget? Well, when the budget cycle begins, the director or dean begins with a totally clean slate. There is no thinking that last year's actual numbers are the place to start. Everyone starts with a clean spreadsheet or piece of paper, depending on how their budgeting is done. Then each line in the budget is filled in from where things currently stand, and each director or department head figures out what he or she plans on spending for the next year. The goal is to spend exactly to the penny every dollar and cent received. As in a line-item budget, the revenue should equal the expenses, but at the end of the year they must be at zero. This isn't terribly complicated; it just creates constant adjustments every month.

The hardest part of this is to predict tax revenues for a library whose income is based on property taxes. If housing values go down, so will the tax revenues. This is the same situation for library incomes based on sales tax. When spending is down, the sales tax revenues will be down, and the appropriate percentage will be down for the library. For libraries that get a percentage of the city budget based on a charter (e.g., the City of Los Angeles), again, if property taxes are in a decline, so is the revenue amount allocated. Forecasting and predicting are a tough business.

On the academic side, no one ever knows what state legislatures are going to do. In an economic downturn I can guess pretty well and say they will cut the percentage that is going to go to the university or college system. Then the university system will need to have some tuition or fee increases to make up for the lack of state contributions. As mentioned earlier, the best way to do this is to have a library or information commons fee set up that every student has to pay with their tuition every semester. This way the library is guaranteed an amount, and the only variable is the number of students. A further option is to make the library fee higher for graduate students than for undergraduates. Why? Because graduate students tend to spend more time using research materials and also will spend more time with complicated research questions that need interlibrary loan of books and articles. By building in the cost of graduate research, the library is anticipating the cost. In most universities and colleges, undergraduates outnumber graduate students, and this way graduate students pay for the costs of their research.

IN-CLASS GROUP EXERCISE

Part 1

Budgeting is the curse of libraries. As many directors will tell you, there is never enough money for what each group wants to do. Complete this exercise in class:

Good news—for the next fiscal year there will be a 10% across the board increase. This means that all parts of the budget will increase by 10%.

1. Put together a $600,000 budget for your library along with the 10% increase for the next fiscal year. Include the following categories:
   a. Salaries (minimum of two full-time employees—a director and a reference librarian)
      i. Full-time
      ii. Part-time
      iii. Hourly Wages
   b. Staff Benefits (use a percentage and know what you used; include the federally mandated percentages for FICA, Medicare, and FUTA and any state disability taxes or any other local taxes there may be where your library is located)
   c. Materials
      i. Print
      ii. Electronic
   d. Other

i. Utilities
ii. Office Supplies—include postage
iii. Travel
iv. Insurance
v. Computer Equipment
vi. Building Maintenance
vii. Office Equipment Maintenance
viii. Software Upgrades
ix. Other Equipment
x. Service Contracts
xi. Licensing
xii. Professional Development
xiii. Other

e. Total—this should be the $600,000 plus the 10%

2. Do you need to fundraise for the next fiscal year?
3. What grants may be available?
4. Is state aid a possibility, or is it economically unfeasible?
5. Will your library apply for an e-rate for Internet or a plain old telephone service (POTS) assistant? If so, do you have an Internet filter already, or is this something else that will need to be purchased?

Part 2

Recently, Arabella Simon, one of your patrons, passed away and left your library a $2 million bequest in her will. Your parent organization would like to have control of the money, but the library thinks that because she named the library in the will that it is the library's to do with as it pleases.

1. What is your take on this?
2. If you keep the money under the library's control, what would you do with it?
3. Who would be responsible for it?
4. How would you handle this situation with the minimum of fuss?
5. Could there be fallout that the library will have to deal with in the future? Consider all of the possibilities.

References

Bosch, S., Henderson, K., & Klusendorf, H. (2011, May 1). Under pressure, times are changing: Periodical price survey 2011. *Library Journal, 136*(8), 30–34.

Hoffert, B. (2011, February 15). Uphill battle: Book buying survey 2010. *Library Journal, 136*(3), 36–38.

Hoffman, J., Bertot, J. C., Davis, D. M., & Clark, L. (2011, June). *Libraries connect communities: Public library funding and technology access study 2010–2011.* American Libraries, digital supplement. Retrieved from http://viewer.zmags.com/publication/857ea9fd

Nicholas, D., Rowland, I., Jubb, M., & Jamali, H. R. (2010, September). The impact of the economic downturn on libraries: With special reference to university libraries. *The Journal of Academic Librarianship, 36*(5), 376–382.

Further Readings on Financial Management

American Library Association. (2011). *The state of America's libraries 2011.* Retrieved from www.ala.org/ala/newspresscenter/mediapresscenter/americaslibraries2011/state_of_americas_libraries_report_2011.pdf

Bullington, J. (2009). About ICOLC and the ICOLC statement. *Collaborative Librarianship, 1*(4), 156–161.

Germain, C. A. (2009). Don't take marketing for "grant"ed: Building marketing efforts into library grant initiatives. *Public Services Quarterly, 5,* 217–222.

Harvard Business Essentials. (2007). Budgeting and understanding financial statements. In *Manager's toolkit: The 13 skills managers need to succeed* (pp. 217–264). Boston, MA: Harvard Business School Press.

Internal Revenue Service. (2011). *Publication 15: Circular E, employer's tax guide.* Retrieved from www.irs.gov/pub/irs-pdf/p15.pdf

Katzen, J. (2009, July). Understanding and recognizing excellence in lean times. *Serials, 22*(2), 108–112.

Robbins, J. B., & Zweizig, D. L. (Eds.). (1992). *Keeping the book$: Public library financial practices.* Fort Atkinson, WI: Highsmith Press.

Stueart, R., & Moran, B. B. (2007). Fiscal responsibility and control. In *Library and information center management* (7th ed., pp. 437–460). Westport, CT: Libraries Unlimited.

Walters, W. H. (2008). Research in practice: A fund allocation formula based on demand, cost, and supply. *Library Quarterly, 78*(3), 303–314.

11
ASSESSMENT AND EVALUATION

Jennifer Campbell-Meier

Assessment and evaluation is part of library management, whether you like it or not. Often assessment and evaluation is required by the federal government, state libraries, and accrediting bodies. Rather than waiting until the end of the year and scrambling for metrics, adding assessment and evaluation to your planning initiatives will make life easier for the management team and provides the organization with information you need to tell the story of your library to stakeholders for support and for funding. Chapter 5, "Strategic Planning," briefly discusses assessment and evaluation in the strategic planning process; in addition to strategic planning, assessment and evaluation should be included in project management and in new initiatives.

During the assessment process, goals are defined, evidence about meeting the goals is gathered, and then the evidence is used for improvement. Once the director or dean has decided what you want to accomplish, identify the measures to gather the evidence. It is important to define our concepts before delving further into the topic.

Goals and objectives are similar in that they serve to direct the organization. They describe the intended purposes and expected results of activities and establish the foundation for assessment. *Goals,* used primarily in policy making and general program planning, are statements about general aims or purposes that are broad, long-range intended outcomes. *Objectives* are brief, clear statements that describe these desired outcomes. Attention is focused on the specific types of performances that are expected to demonstrate the outcomes attained. A *plan* is a blueprint, specifying the resource allocation, schedules, and other actions necessary for attaining the goals.

The goals and objectives in the plan need to be assessed and evaluated. While often paired, assessment and evaluation are complimentary and are used at different stages during a planning cycle. *Assessment* is the process or means of evaluating work. Data is collected in a formal process of evaluation and may be used to develop or assess a plan. *Evaluation* is the development of a judgment about the amount, number, or value of something. When a project is evaluated, a decision is made about whether it met the stated goals and objectives and whether the outcomes were successful. In other words, management collects qualitative and quantitative data about a library's services, programs, and collections to see if the library is meeting the needs of the community or organization it serves (see Figure 11.1).

Evaluation and assessment do not have to be complicated. Together, they provide the ground work for improvement and, depending on what is being assessed, may lead to better planning of library services. Assessment should happen at all levels in libraries, and most libraries, whether public, academic, or special, may have regular assessment activities. These activities may be required by a governing or accrediting agency. The Institute of Museum and Library Services (IMLS) provides federal support for libraries through grants and state library programs. Every

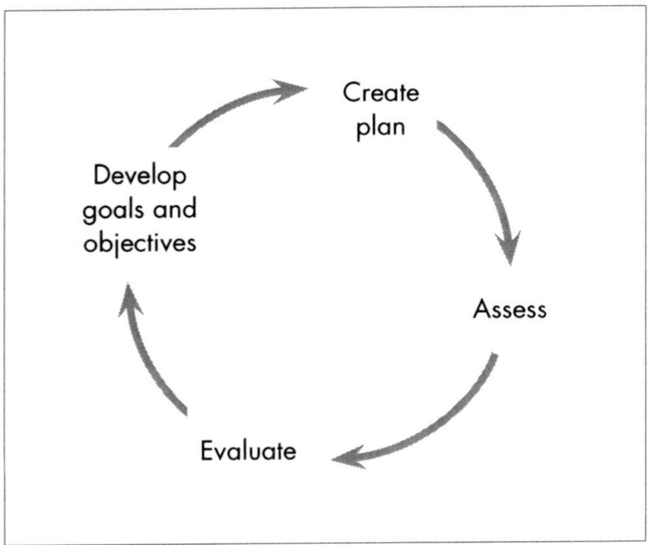

FIGURE 11.1 Iterative Evaluation Process

five years, state libraries have to develop a plan "to strengthen the efficiency, reach, and effectiveness of library services" (IMLS, n.d.b). A state library service identifies goals and initiatives to improve public library service. These goals are usually developed with input from public libraries and public library users throughout the state. Over the next five years, the state library service may ask public libraries for evidence that identifies how the goals and initiatives are being met at the public library level. For example, the Alabama Public Library Service (APLS) identified "Strengthen Youth and Family" as an area of need in its 2007 Five Year Plan (APLS, 2007). For each area of need, APLS developed associated goals and targets; for example:

> Strengthen youth and family by targeting library and information services to: (1) to youth (from birth through 17) in underserved urban and rural communities, including youth from families with incomes below the poverty line, and (2) to the parents and care-givers to improve their child-rearing knowledge and skills. (FY2008–2012) [as a goal associated with the need] (APLS, 2007)

Various outputs were developed to measure this goal; for example, the number of participants in the Statewide Summer Reading Program was to exceed 72,000 by 2011. In this case, local libraries would then collect information about the summer reading program and report the information to APLS.

MEASURES

Measures identify what the library is currently doing and what it needs to change for improvement. Choosing the right measures can help us make meaningful comparisons to standards, goals, objectives, or similar libraries. Both qualitative and quantitative measures are used to assess libraries. Qualitative measures frequently assess the quality of work or a program. Opinions and perceptions of service would fall into this category. A quantitative measure uses numbers and a unit of measure to provide meaning. Counts, ratios, and percentages are quantitative measures. Libraries use measures for inputs, processes, outputs, and outcomes to evaluate and improve systems and services. During the process, it is important to keep in mind what is being measured and what those measurements actually describe.

Input Measures

Input measures are descriptive statistics about the resources that support the library. This data is often reported to federal, state, and local officials, professional associations, researchers, and local practitioners for planning, evaluation, and policy (see Table 11.1). In addition, funding and accrediting agencies may require this data. Funding agencies like IMLS collect descriptive data about public libraries in the United

TABLE 11.1 EXAMPLES OF INPUT MEASURES (IMLS, PUBLIC)

Categories	Types of Measures
Organizational characteristics	Number of central libraries
	Number of branch libraries
	Population of service area
Staffing	Librarians with ALA-MLS
	Librarians without ALA-MLS
	Staff
Operating revenue	Federal revenue
	Local revenue
	State revenue per capita
Operating expenditures	Electronic materials
	Employee benefits
	Print materials
	Salaries and wages
Size of library collection	Current electronic serial subscriptions
	Current print serial subscriptions
	Electronic books
	Print materials
	Video material
Services	Circulation of children's materials
	Library visits
	Reference transactions
	Total circulation
	Total program attendance
	Users of public Internet computers

States to quantify how individual libraries are meeting the needs of local communities. The U.S. National Center for Education Statistics (NCES) collects the data for academic libraries for assessment. Input measures can be useful for comparing peer libraries. For example, a public library in a city of 30,000 people may use input measures like the total number of librarians to see how it compares to libraries in similarly sized cities. If the public library has four full-time librarians, and peer institutions have an average of six full-time librarians, the measure can be used to support the hire of two new full-time librarians to better serve the population. An academic library may be concerned about the space available for students in the building, especially if full-time equivalent (FTE) enrollment had increased. FTE is the total number of hours that both full-time and part-time students are registered for during the semester and divides all hours by the full-time undergraduate course load per semester, usually 12 hours. Database pricing structures for academic libraries are often based on FTE. The academic library can use input statistics to identify peer institutions based on FTE and then compare the number of seats, computers, or study rooms available in peer libraries. The statistics do not identify what is optimal but what other similar libraries have for benchmarking.

Process Measures

Process measures examine the efficiency of processes and procedures within the library. Libraries employ any number of procedures and processes throughout the day that use library resources, primarily staff time. It is important to review the processes to verify that the system in place is efficient and does not waste time or resources. Efficiency in the library will cost in both materials necessary and staff time, including benefits. Is it cost effective for a librarian to process books? Is it an efficient use of time for a librarian to print call number labels, or should that task be done by an hourly staff member? Productivity examines the time it takes from the start of a process to its completion. Perhaps a librarian is concerned that it is taking too long for a requested book to reach the shelf. By examining the step-by-step procedures involved in the process—in this case, acquisitions and cataloging—a librarian can identify processes that can be improved. Are orders placed daily? Once a week? Is there a cataloging backlog? Are books processed regularly? Are processed books waiting on a cart to be shelved? System reliability and downtime, as well as the availability of public workstations, are examined in information systems activity. If servers are down for several hours a week, users will be unable to access the materials and will turn to another source for information. Process measures focus on staff productivity and information systems and typically reveal how efficient a library is by focusing on the time and cost to perform an activity or a task.

Output Measures

Output measures describe how a library is used or utilized. These measures can examine the counts and use per capita of services, user satisfaction with a particular service or the library in general, the degree to which the collection is used, the use of online materials, and how a building is being used (see Table 11.2).

In addition to quantitative measures of a library, librarians are also interested in gathering qualitative data about user experiences and perceptions of quality. Satisfaction surveys determine the extent to which user needs were met and may also identify ways or places to improve service. Satisfaction measures identify the net satisfaction with a service or resource. Service quality, measured by tools like LibQUAL+, examines user satisfaction as well as gaps between service expectations and the service(s) received at the library. LibQUAL+ is a survey, developed by the Association of Research Libraries (ARL), designed to measure the service attitude of staff, access to information, and the library as a place. It focuses on the interaction between the user and the service provider using the gaps model of service quality. For example, LibQUAL+ participants identify their minimum level of acceptable service, their desired level of service, and the level of service received in the library. Library staff also participates in the survey, with individual staff members identifying their perceptions of the users' expectations (ARL, 2011). The data is used to quantify any gap that may exist between the perceived level of service and desired level of service and identifies areas for improvement.

Outcomes Assessment

Outcomes assessment involves gathering and evaluating qualitative and quantitative data that identify that an organization's objectives, goals, and outcomes not only correspond to its mission but also are being accomplished. According to IMLS, outcomes are "benefits to people: specifically, achievements or changes in skill, knowledge, attitude, behavior, condition, or life status for program participants" (IMLS, n.d.a). An outcome must be measurable or observable, manageable, and meaningful. Outcome-based evaluation (OBE) is the measurement of information about indicators that identify change and illustrate to what extent a program has met its outcomes. OBE is widely used in academic, school, and public library settings especially with funding

TABLE 11.2 OUTPUT MEASURES

Categories	Types of Measures
Services	Number of books cataloged
	Number of interlibrary loan requests
	Number of reference transactions
	Number of titles ordered
	Number of virtual reference transactions
Quality	User satisfaction
Collection use	Average circulation per volume
	Loans per visit
	Number of items charged
	Proportion of the collection borrowed
	Proportion of the collection unused
Electronic resource use	Number of database sessions
	Number of public access Internet users
	Number of searches
	Number of search sessions
	Web link statistics
Building activity	Attendance
	Program/instruction attendance
	Remote uses
	Seat occupancy rate
	Service point use
	Total number of uses

Note. Compiled from *Public Libraries Survey Definitions: Fiscal Year 2010 Data Element Definitions,* by the Institute of Museum and Library Services, n.d., retrieved from https://harvester.census.gov/imls/pdf/PLS_Defs_FY2010.pdf; *The Evaluation and Measurement of Library Services,* by J. R. Matthews, 2007 (Westport, CT: Libraries Unlimited); *Output Measures for Public Libraries: A Manual of Standardized Procedures* (2nd ed.), by N. A. Van House and D. Zweizig, 1987 (Chicago, IL: American Library Association).

and accreditation agencies as well as state and local governments. OBE provides libraries with performance measures for effective library services and service priorities designed to meet the needs of local users.

OBE may use output measures, like satisfaction surveys, to identify areas of improvement and provide baseline measurements during an evaluation period.

University students have some familiarity with outcome assessment. Courses have goals, objectives, and student learning outcomes. Student learning outcomes usually contain the following:

1. An action word that identifies the performance to be demonstrated
2. A learning statement that specifies what learning will be demonstrated in the performance
3. A broad statement of the criterion or standard for acceptable performance

Now, you may wonder, "Why do I care about learning outcomes? I want to be a librarian, not a teacher." If you are doing any kind of user instruction or information literacy instruction at a school, public, or academic library, learning outcomes need to be developed so the librarian will know what to do and if it was done well. The format can be adapted for student learning outcomes for use with a program or service in the library.

Learning outcomes contain action verbs, like those collected in Bloom's taxonomy of educational objectives. The outcomes are often formatted: "Students will (verb or action) in order to (result)." For example, "Students will develop a topic-relevant vocabulary in order to search databases effectively." According to Debra Gilchrist (2009), there are five questions for assessment design:

1. Develop outcomes—"What do you want students to be able to do?"
2. Develop curriculum—"What does the student need to know in order to do this well?"
3. Identify pedagogy—"What activity will facilitate learning?"
4. Identify assessment measures—"How will the student demonstrate the learning?"
5. Create criteria for success—"How will I know the student has done this well?"

The assessment design works for noninstruction library activities as well if the questions are revised (see Table 11.3):

1. Develop outcomes—"What do you want to be able to do?"
   Start by having a library staff meeting and brainstorm about what services may be developed or improved. What should an ideal library user know, understand, and be able to do? Consult the

website for your state library, accrediting agency, or professional/disciplinary organization; outcomes may already exist for services or programs at various levels. During this part of the process, consider inviting representatives from stakeholder groups like the library board, trustees, Friends of the Library, faculty, or students to this brainstorming session.

Develop consensus on a first draft of a list of outcomes. This is a draft of outcomes that may be revised several times during the strategic planning process. Outcomes should change over time to meet the needs of the community being served or to align with the outcomes of associated organizations, the state library for a public library, or the university for an academic library.

2. Develop a plan or a program—"What needs to happen in order to do this well?"
3. The outcomes can be used to develop a strategic plan or a specific program.
4. Identify the appropriate methodology—"What will facilitate this?"
5. Gather feedback from those who used a service or attended a program about how well they perceive that outcomes were addressed.
6. Identify assessment measures—"How will I know this happened?"
7. Assess services and programs using tools specifically geared to measure achievement of each of the outcomes.
8. Create criteria for success—"How will I know it was a success?" Use the data collected to evaluate services and programs at the end of the planning or reporting year. Revise outcomes and measures as needed for next year's plan.

Repeat these steps regularly and as needed to improve library services and programs.

Outcomes can be assessed by direct measures that identify what has happened or has been achieved or by indirect measures that infer a change has occurred and suggest what may be done to improve the process. The measures are complementary, so using both direct and indirect measures for assessment is useful (see Table 11.4).

Libraries are being held accountable to stakeholders and cannot rely on a single measure of assessment. With decreasing library budgets, libraries need to carefully examine input measures to verify that money is allocated appropriately. Process measures examine whether the funds are spent efficiently. Output measures identify user satisfaction with library programs. OBE measures the performance and value of the efforts at the local level. A holistic approach that gathers data about services, using multiple measures, provides a multidimensional image

TABLE 11.3 SAMPLES LIBRARY OUTCOMES AND MEASURES

Outcome	Measures
The library will conduct a LibQUAL+ survey and compare data to 2002 data to identify areas of success and of need.	• LibQUAL+ data
Keep library faculty and staff updated by distributing accurate phone information, include contacts and instructions on how to access voice mail off campus.	• Voice mail instructions • Distribution of contact list
The library will be a gathering place for the local community.	• Attendance at programs • Gate counts • Number of active community users • Number of community members with library cards • User survey
Access services will improve staff ability to provide IT service to patrons.	• Access services will maintain a log of • IT assistance opportunities and assess monthly for areas of training needs • Access services will report training opportunities and IT collaborations in monthly reports.
Public services will develop partnerships with three organizations during the 2012 fiscal year .	• Meetings with community groups • Meeting room usage
The reference department will develop one new program a month.	• The number of participants • The number of programs • Specific outcomes for programs

of the library within the community and among peer institutions. Measuring outcomes can tell stakeholders where the tax dollars are being spent and justify a library's existence and why it is important to the community, board, or board of regents.

ASSESSMENT TOOLS

The management team and librarians have a choice of many instruments for improvement. In order to choose the right tool for assessment, each organization has to first decide what measurements are

TABLE 11.4 METHODS FOR GATHERING EVIDENCE

	Direct Measures	Indirect Measures
Qualitative Methods	• Participant interviews • Think-aloud protocol	• External reviewers • Focus groups
Quantitative Methods	• Content analysis • Tests	• General surveys

Note. Adapted from *The Evaluation and Measurement of Library Services*, by J. R. Matthews, 2007 (Westport, CT: Libraries Unlimited).

going to be done with the tools; then the director or dean needs to identify where the library is in the process and, finally, decide if it is necessary to expand or focus the scope. It is helpful to think about the tools by how they are used. Remember that many of the tools used in assessment can be used at various stages in the process. Benchmarking, for example, compares your library's work practices to the best similar practices in other libraries. The comparison can provide new ideas or improvements and can be used as a process analysis tool or as a data collection and analysis tool. Let's look at a few tools we can use during the assessment process.

Project planning and implementation tools are used for managing and improving projects. Three examples of tools for planning and implementation are the balanced scorecard, stakeholder analysis, and storyboards. The balanced scorecard provides an overview of a library's performance by examining four perspectives: the customer, internal business, innovation and learning, and finance. Measures, indicating progress toward a goal, are developed for each perspective. Stakeholder analysis identifies the individuals or groups with an interest in an issue. The analysis can be used to improve an area based on stakeholder needs or develop an action that considers the perspectives of all interested parties. Successful projects include stakeholders in the planning process to verify that the appropriate needs are met. A storyboard is a visual display of a process, often used to think through how users will accomplish a specific activity. A web redesign team may use a storyboard to capture new pages and explain how a user would accomplish relevant activities, like searching for a book.

Process analysis tools are used when the organization wants to understand a work process or some part of a process. Flowcharts and work flow diagrams are just two examples of process analysis tools. A flowchart is a picture of the steps of a process in sequential order. Flowcharts can be used to show how a process is done or identify areas of improvement. A work flow diagram is an image that shows movement through a process.

Data collection and analysis tools are used to collect and analyze data. Sampling and surveys are frequently used to identify user needs. Sampling allows the librarian to select a few items or people out of a larger group in order to question, examine, or test the items and draw conclusions for the entire group. Surveys collect data from targeted groups of people or users about their opinions, behavior, or knowledge.

Case Example

During the decision-making process, it may be difficult to reach a consensus. The public services librarians at Smallville Public Library have been working on programs for the upcoming month. Unfortunately, there is only enough money to support one of the four programs that have been developed: story hour, nonfiction book club, fiction book club, and game night. Rather than selecting the best program, each librarian is voting to continue the project in which he or she feels invested due to time spent researching or developing the program. Rather than split six votes among four projects, the library director decides to try using paired comparisons. Instead of voting for one of four projects, the public services team chooses between pairs of options until all choices are compared. Given the option between story hour and a nonfiction book club, four people voted for story time and two people voted for the nonfiction book club (see Table 11.5). The voting continued until all options were compared. When tallied, story time received the most votes and thus will be developed further.

Table 11.5 Paired Comparison Example

	A vs. B	A vs. C	A vs. D	B vs. C	B vs. D	C vs. D	Total
Story Hour	4	5	3				12
Nonfiction Book Club	2			1			3
Fiction Book Club		2		3		4	10
Game Night			3		6	2	11

Cause analysis tools assist in the discovery of the cause of a problem or situation. Contingency diagrams and force field analysis are both used to identify potential problems that may occur during planning or programming. Contingency diagramming uses brainstorming and negative thinking to identify what could go wrong with a plan. Force field analysis identifies the positive forces that support an action and the negative forces that restrain it.

Evaluation and decision-making tools help narrow down a group of choices or evaluate how well the library has done something. The director, dean, or organization can use a decision matrix or paired comparisons to evaluate choices; the decision matrix evaluates and prioritizes options from a list of weighted criteria, and paired comparisons narrow a list of options to the most popular choice.

DEVELOPING AN EVALUATION PLAN

Evaluation must meet several basic requirements to be effective. First, too much information can be just as bad as too little information. The management team, director, or dean does not have to, nor should, collect every possible bit of data about what is being assessed in the hope that it may be potentially useful. Evaluation activities should be meaningful because they should relate specifically to a library's objectives. The evaluation should provide librarians with useful information about tasks over which they have control and influence. Table 11.6 provides a worksheet for planning evaluation activities.

There are several steps to follow in creating a new or improved evaluation plan:

1. Examine the objectives that have been outlined by the library for the service or program to be assessed (these should be taken directly from the strategic planning documents).
2. Identify those outcomes that will be assessed. Rather than attempting to assess all the outcomes associated with the goal or objective, choose those that seem most critical to the overall goals and that can be meaningfully measured.
3. Identify data sources that measure the goals. The sources may be circulation records or statistical information you already collect or a specific user population or group about which you would like to have more information.

4. Select your assessment tool(s)—methods or instruments for gathering evidence to show whether the outcomes have been achieved. Determine if there are existing data sources or tools that may be used or if new tools must be selected or developed. Select those tools that seem most appropriate to the objectives or the services being assessed.
5. Identify who will collect the data.
6. Identify when data will be collected. Consider choosing a typical week in the library schedule for data collection to provide a snapshot of library operations for the rest of the year.
7. Specify procedures for analyzing and interpreting the evidence gathered in assessment. Prior to administering assessments, create a scoring rubric or other method of evaluating results, and determine the library standard for performance expectations (e.g., success equals a 20% increase in the number of students participating in a summer reading program). Determine if the assessment will be episodic (a snapshot of a service at one point in time) or ongoing (a recurring, consistent, and comparative assessment of a service over time).
8. Determine how the information that results from assessment can be used for decision making, planning, service and program evaluation, and improvement. Develop means whereby involved library staff can review the data, make recommendations for change as appropriate, and incorporate such changes in the planning cycle.

CONCLUSION

Good evaluations rely on the development of a strategic plan that defines the organizational activities and resource allocations, as well as goals that define the outcomes that major divisions and departments must achieve. In addition to a strategic plan, libraries should also develop an assessment plan that identifies which outcomes and goals are most important to the library and how they will be assessed. Good information in the right hands is a lever for change. Assessment and evaluation lead to wiser planning and budgeting and improved library services.

CASE STUDY AND DISCUSSION QUESTIONS

Pat is the librarian for a departmental collection located within the business school of a state university. This is her second year in the library;

TABLE 11.6 SAMPLE ASSESMENT WORKSHEET

Objective	Outcome	Sources of Data (circulation records, users)	Assessment Tools (systems report, interviews, surveys)	Who Collects the Data	When Data Is Collected	Analysis Procedures	How Information Will Be Used

her first was spent reorganizing the collection and rearranging the space to make it more user friendly. She has been collecting circulation and reference statistics and gate counts by hour and has her appointment calendar noting any meetings with faculty and classes as well as student appointments. Pat also spent the year working with the administration and faculty members to identify the organizational goals and objectives of the school. She thought it was important to learn the organization so that she can develop a strategic plan for the business library.

Pat knows that she would like to develop outcomes for the library, but first she wants to see how her library compares to peer institutions. In addition to a peer review, Pat is interested in developing learning outcomes for library instruction within the business school. There is no formal instruction program, but the faculty and administration are interested, and the business school is required to collect measureable outcomes for instruction for accreditation. Discuss the following questions:

1. The dean would like to know what effect Pat's changes have had.
    a. What direct measures can she use to report the change?
    b. What indirect measures can she use?
    c. Are there any areas for improvement that the indirect measures may identify?
2. What kind of measures will Pat need to collect for a peer comparison?
3. How can the comparison data help Pat during the planning process?
4. How can Pat identify what the students and faculty need to develop an instruction program?

References

The Alabama Public Library Service. (2007). *The Alabama Public Library Service Services and Technology Act five year plan.* Retrieved from www.imls.gov/assets/1/AssetManager/Alabama%20Plan.pdf

Association of Research Libraries, Statistics and Assessment Program. (2011). *LibQUAL+ tools.* Retrieved from www.libqual.org/about/about_survey/tools

Gilchrist, D. (2009). A twenty year path: Learning about assessment; learning from assessment. *Communications in Information Literacy,* 3(2), 70–79.

Institute of Museum and Library Services. (n.d.a). *Outcome based evaluations.* Retrieved from www.imls.gov/applicants/basics.aspx

Institute of Museum and Library Services. (n.d.b). *State programs—5-year plans.* www.imls.gov/programs/5year_plans.aspx

Further Readings on Assessment and Evaluation

Anderson, L. W., Krathwohl, D. R., & Bloom, B. (2001). *A taxonomy for learning, teaching, and assessing: A revision of Bloom's taxonomy of educational objectives.* New York, NY: Longman.

Carter, E. W. (2002). "Doing the best you can with what you have": Lessons learned from outcomes assessment. *Journal of Academic Librarianship, 28*(1/2), 36.

Dudden, R. F. (2007). *Using benchmarking, needs assessment, quality improvement, outcome measurement, and library standards: A how-to-do-it manual.* New York, NY: Neal-Schuman.

Dugan, R. E., & Hernon, P. (2002). Outcomes assessment: Not synonymous with inputs and outputs. *Journal of Academic Librarianship, 28*(6), 376.

Heath, F. (2011). Library assessment: The way we have grown. *Library Quarterly, 81*(1), 7.

Hernon, P., & Dugan, R. E. (2002). *An action plan for outcomes assessment in your library.* Chicago, IL: American Library Association.

Kyrillidou, M. (2002). From input and output measures to quality and outcome measures, or, from the user in the life of the library to the library in the life of the user. *Journal of Academic Librarianship, 28*(1/2), 42.

Wallace, D. P., & Van Fleet, C. (2001). *Library evaluation: A casebook and can-do guide.* Englewood, CO: Libraries Unlimited.

Wright, S. P., & White, L. S. (2007). *Library assessment.* Washington, DC: Association of Research Libraries, Office of Leadership and Management Services.

12
INTERNAL AND EXTERNAL STAKEHOLDERS

Diane L. Velasquez

What exactly is a stakeholder? A stakeholder is someone with an interest in an organization. According to *Oxford English Dictionary* (2009), it is "a person, company, etc., with a concern or (esp. financial) interest in ensuring the success of an organization, business, system, etc." For a library, be it academic, public, or special, many different types of stakeholders, both internal and external, can have an interest in the success of the organization. Many times the director or dean will be accountable to one or more stakeholders and have some reporting relationship with them and others who use the facility and the organizational assets.

How the relationships with stakeholders are defined should again go back to the mission and vision of the library. Deans and directors interact with stakeholders as part of their job, and many in these positions sometimes forget that they must please stakeholders just as much as those who pay their salaries. Why? Many people will have something to say about what the library does or does not do for their community—a word that takes on different meanings for different libraries. For a public library, community means the people who live in the surrounding areas whom the employees of that organization serve. For an academic library, community is the scholarly world they inhabit, which includes students, faculty, and staff. The academic library that is publicly funded through taxes or has some responsibility to the public, such as being a part of the Federal Depository Library Program (FDLP), needs to serve the public at large, the geographic community, as well as its university community.

INTERNAL STAKEHOLDERS

This section discusses academic and public libraries separately because their communities of stakeholders can be different.

Academic Libraries

Academic libraries exist to support the curriculum of the university or college in question and the research of the faculty. These are the two primary reasons the academic library collects materials, and so two of the internal stakeholder groups are the students and the faculty members. The academic library will also support the staff and the administration of the university or college. If the library is part of a state university system it will also support any state structures that are put in place, such as a board of regents or other state governing system.

The staff and administration of the university or college are usually separate from the faculty. The staff is usually the administrative support personnel and sometimes the librarians. Librarians can be classified as faculty or staff, depending on the university or college where they are working. As a side note, if the librarians are considered faculty and have tenure attributed to them, they must traverse the "tenure track" just as faculty members do, with its associated publishing, service, and other requirements, though the publishing requirements are not usually as stiff for librarians as for normal teaching faculty.

In a private university, there could be a board of trustees, church authorities (Catholic, Lutheran, or other type), foundations, advisory boards, employees, unions, or a corporation that may oversee the organization in some manner. All of these different types of boards or foundations may have a say in what the library may or may not put in its collection. Just as faculty can have a say in the collections or databases in a library, so can the governing board of the university.

Academic libraries sometimes have Friends of the Library groups for the purpose of fundraising for the library. As for public libraries, volunteers run the Friends groups and organize fundraising events for the university community. Books or other tangible materials (records, CDs, DVDs, VHS tapes, etc.) that have been weeded from the collection are always good items to sell; the group may have a silent auction at some event when a notable person is coming in to give a lecture; or there could be other creative ideas the Friends group has for raising money. I know at one university I graduated from, people could donate money in the name of a person and have a gold leaf placed on a tree (fake, of course) that was inside the library on a wall.

Public Libraries

Public libraries have many internal stakeholders that can have a say in what the organization does. The governing boards of a public library are boards of trustees or boards of directors. Not all public libraries have boards that manage the library. Some libraries report directly to a municipal structure like a city, village, or county. In the case of a municipal structure, the library director is a department head and reports to a city manager or assistant city manager. In the case of a city manager, there is usually an advisory board of trustees that will advise the director when asked. The advisory board of trustees is consulted as needed, and the director takes the board's opinions under advisement only.

Friends of the Library groups (FOLs) and library foundations are two other internal stakeholders that can influence a public library. Both groups are charitable organizations under IRS rule 501(c)(3) and are tax exempt. The FOLs and foundations donate money to public libraries for their collections or other purposes. The library director is sometimes on the board of one or both as an ex officio officer. The FOLs will sometimes sell weeded books or other materials through a shop in the public library to raise funds. Some FOLs will assist when there are bond issues to raise money for the library. Many times FOLs will sell rare and older books on the Internet using eBay.

Employees are internal stakeholders with an interest in the public library. Some are unionized and others are not. There are no hard-and-fast rules about which libraries are unionized and which are not. For instance, Chicago Public Library is unionized, but many of the suburban libraries in the outskirts of Chicago are not. Unions have an interest in how the library is run because what happens influences how their members are treated by the management and municipal organization. The union contract that is negotiated between city management and the union determines how the library interacts with the employees in regards to pay, personnel matters, seniority, and most things related to the library and employment. Depending on point of view, a union contract can either simplify or complicate how one looks at the management of the personnel of the library.

Employees, whether unionized or not, should be treated with honesty, respect, and integrity. The library management team should work with and treat employees as management would like to be treated. The library staff is the backbone of the library, as these folks make sure the programs and services get done for the patrons. They serve the public no matter what type of library they are at, and management should go out of its way to show appreciation for the hard work that the staff in the library does.

The city, county, or village where the public library resides is an internal stakeholder. There are exceptions to this, but for the most part municipal or county structures have an interest in what happens at the library. The library budget is usually set by the city or county and influences what the library does with its money. The rare case where this is not true is when the library is independent of the city or county and is in its own taxing district. When these libraries want an increase, they are on their own and must go before the taxpayers to get a millage increase on property taxes. There are advantages and disadvantages to both types of library infrastructure connections; they depend on how the director would prefer to deal with stakeholders and the community. When the library is an independent taxing agency, the library management may determine there is a need for an increase in funding. The library director and the board would need to place a tax bond on the ballot for the voting public to determine.

EXTERNAL STAKEHOLDERS

The external stakeholders consist of the people outside of the internal workings of the academic and public libraries. The city, village, and county are considered part of the internal workings of the public library. The administration of the university is considered part of the internal workings of the academic library. It is interesting to see that some stakeholders are internal for one type of library but are external for another type of library, and thus this section discusses all categories of libraries together.

Businesses of all types can be patrons to either public or academic libraries. Small businesses use public libraries to access business information on their competitors and for general business purposes. Some businesses will contract with graduate business schools and have a particular class do some analysis for them, and the class will need to use the academic or public library to access information on the industry. The amount of information available through databases, the Internet, indexes, and directories on business is staggering if people know what they are looking for. There is less information available on private businesses, but some can be found; again, knowing what to look for and where to look for the information is the key to finding business information. Librarians are trained to find information of all kinds. Those who have taken a business information class will know about the many sources that can be tapped to find information for businesses of all sizes and shapes.

Nonprofit organizations like churches are great partners with libraries to get out information that the community needs to have. For instance, if there is a particular immigrant group that needs information on federal and state assistance, getting information to the church where they go will get it to the group. Socioeconomic information in particular is usually helpful to get to the church to help the needy. Also, the public library and the churches, synagogues, temples, and so forth can partner with one another to work on food drives, coat drives, and other types of activities over the holidays.

Other charitable organizations in the community, such as the Kiwanis, Lions, and Rotary clubs and Jaycees, can be stakeholders for the public library as well as the academic library. For public libraries, a member of the library's management team may be a member of a charitable organization so that the library is represented. It is not uncommon for the director to be a member of the Rotary, a department head the Kiwanis, the assistant director the Lions, and so on. This way the library has broad representation, and when the different charitable organizations have events, the library can be represented. Another aspect of having librarians represented in the different charitable organizations is that the other members will know what is going on with the library and can share that information with their families, business acquaintances, and friends. This is another way to market the library.

The general community is an external stakeholder for both academic and public libraries. Getting information out to the public about the different programming choices and services that the library has is important. If the public doesn't know about the programming and services, they cannot use them. Most parents know about storytimes, adult booktalks, and computer classes, but classes to help folks learn how to find jobs may not be as well publicized as programs for the children. The library management commonly believes that the community intuitively knows what is going on in the library. This is not true. Like any other type of organization or business, all libraries (academic, public, and special) need to market their events and programs. Even the summer reading program for children and youth needs to be marketed to the community, as there may be people who have just moved into the community prior to the program commencing and may not realize it is available.

Academic libraries also need to market their services and programs to their community, especially when the new school year begins in the fall. If the patrons are not aware of the events, programs, and services the library provides, how can they take advantage of them? As is mentioned in Chapter 9, marketing and advertising through more than one channel is necessary to reach all of the potential patrons.

Although the FOLs and foundations were covered as internal stakeholders, donors are external stakeholders that both academic and public libraries need to cultivate. Many people who have used libraries all of their life could decide to leave money from their estates to the local public library or their university library. One public library I visited was left $1.25 million from a community member. Cultivating donors is something every library dean and director should consider doing so that when money is short, there are other ways to pay for programming and services. People who leave money in their wills sometimes leave money for very specific purposes. It is always best if they don't, but if they do perhaps you have an idea about what they can leave their money for. Also, small donations on a year-to-year basis are not a bad idea either. The donations are tax deductible if given to an FOL or a foundation, and they can help the library in small ways. Libraries are not charities, and donations to them are not always tax deductible.

Faculty from both public and private K–12 schools may visit the public library to get books for their classes to supplement what is available in their school library. Sometimes the teachers check out fiction; at other times they need nonfiction books. The faculty may also give the children's librarians or the children's section a heads-up when there is a school project coming. It is helpful to know that a group of kids will be coming to the library for resources on a specific topic, such as information on the history and geography of Mexico or the United States, or for a science fair project. Prior notice can save the children's department from letting someone check out all the books on the subject. Also, assisting the teachers from the local schools can let other librarians know what's going on in the curriculum.

Another aspect of the K–12 curriculum is homeschooling. Parents who homeschool their kids will need assistance from the children's librarians about nonfiction and fiction to support what they are teaching. The parents may have very specific ideas about what they do and do not want, so be patient with them. The parents who homeschool are still patrons, albeit a very specialized group. They may request specific books and textbooks. If possible, the library should try to assist them.

The federal government is an external stakeholder for public libraries and for some academic libraries if they are in an area where there are no public libraries. How? The federal government has started to direct people to public libraries in order to get government forms off of federal websites. The patrons may or may not know exactly what they want. These patrons are not usually well versed in the computer or government information or the Internet (Velasquez, 2010). For instance, the IRS no longer mails tax forms to public libraries and expects the libraries to pull the 1040s off of its website for the public.

The Internet is an external stakeholder, because most public, special, and academic libraries have websites. Not only do libraries have websites but they also use Twitter, Facebook, and other Web 2.0 tools to access the Internet and the World Wide Web to publicize their events. With the advent of technology that has exploded in the past 20 years libraries have been increasingly using the Internet to get their message out. Their users also use the Internet to access the databases and catalogs when not in the library.

The mass media is an external stakeholder for all types of libraries. Anything that happens in a positive or negative vein at a public or academic library can end up in newspapers, journals, blogs, wikis, or other outlets. When budget cuts happen in public libraries, the news media usually covers it, and many newspapers now have blogs where their readers will join in and comment. This aspect of the media has a fairly immediate impact because the library will get not only the newspaper's take on what is happening but also the community's input via online comments.

Patrons are an external stakeholder because they come from outside the library or institution. For children, the first distinction for a public library is that it cannot act in loco parentis. A minor child in a library is a parent or guardian's responsibility, not the public library staff's. Some parents may see the library as a place to drop off the kids—the library staff are not babysitters. Having a policy in place regarding minor children in the public library is something that can alleviate this situation. Children having access to the Internet is another part of the stakeholder relationship that can be dicey. Make sure your library follows its state's laws about the Internet and children, as age requirements for access vary among states. In one state parents have to sign for children up to 19 years of age to access the Internet in libraries. Whether the computers in the children's area are connected to the Internet is up to each individual library, and filtering becomes the next issue if the computers are connected. If the computers are connected to the Internet with no filtering, does the public library have a policy that parents have to sign giving the child permission to be on an unfiltered computer? If the computers in the children's area are not connected to the Internet, filtering is not an issue. Just make sure the software on them is age appropriate.

Filtering of computers that adults use in the public library needs to be considered as well. If the computers are filtered, will the library remove the filters if asked to? Again, having a policy in place for the stakeholders will solve this situation in an easy way. The short answer is that all libraries that receive any federal funding must filter (see Chapter 13, "Ethics and Confidentiality," for further discussion of this). According to the Children's Internet Protection Act (CIPA), all computers in libraries that receive any federal funding (e.g., E-Rate, ESEA Title III, or LSTA), including staff's, must be filtered.

If no federal funding is received, then filtering may be a choice for the library. Some states also have filtering laws if state funds are used, so be aware if your state requires your library to filter based on state funding mandates, which are called Son of CIPA laws. When there is no requirement to filter, filtering becomes a choice for the library management. Whatever decision is made, make sure to have a policy that spells it out for the stakeholders. Also have a policy on what to do in the event pornography is watched in the library. According to the First Amendment, pornography is not against the law unless it is child pornography. It can get pretty ugly when the media decides to go into a library and see what everyone is looking at on their screens. Having a policy in place for Internet usage and other potential problem areas can help manage difficult situations. Make sure an attorney looks at your policies and says their wording is okay.

In academic libraries the majority of the patrons will be over 18; however, some who come in will be under 18. Some high school students may want to do their homework with more high-powered databases, or they were told to go to a college library for a particular resource. Be prepared to have some younger patrons (under 18 but probably in high school or middle school) in the academic library, and have a plan for how to serve minors.

A stakeholder group that is often overlooked is composed of those who don't go to the public library. Many times the members of this group actually support the library with their tax dollars but haven't been in a library since they were a kid. Perhaps they are too busy or they don't have a reason to go. This group is one that should be cultivated to come back to the library. It is a group we cannot afford to discount.

Private and public schools are users and thus stakeholders of public libraries. Their students will come in and do their homework, and public libraries provide homework help for K–12 students. It is important to have a liaison to all schools (private and public) in the area who knows what is going on during different times of the year. Another group of schools to cultivate is the preschools. Preschool classes often visit the library for storytimes, or librarians will provide storytimes at the preschool. Getting the younger kids involved in the library now can help keep them as library users as they get older.

People who go to senior citizens centers or live in assisted living facilities or rest homes comprise another group of stakeholders. Patrons who are over a certain age (usually 65) may have different needs than younger adult patrons (18–64) and the kids in our libraries. Senior citizens may need large-print books and may not be comfortable with technology. Large-print books are easy to provide—make sure to order some for your patrons. Technology is a little more difficult to deal with. Many senior citizens are not comfortable using the Online Public Access Catalog (OPAC) and wish for the days of the card catalog. Be patient with seniors and be willing to assist them in their searches of the catalogs and with using the other technologies that are now in the library.

The state legislature is a stakeholder of some public libraries and publicly funded academic libraries. The state legislature provides funding for libraries through budget appropriations. Some states do not appropriate any money for public libraries. The funds are paid to the state through income taxes in some states and through sales taxes in others. The state can cut the funding or increase it according to the budgetary environment of the day. The different houses of the state legislatures in 49 states and the unicameral house in Nebraska determine the funding levels and whether or not there is a climate for funding public libraries. The best advice is to build rapport with the local state representatives where the library is located.

Academic libraries, on the other hand, are typically funded as part of the overall budgetary line item of the state university or college it is attached to. For instance, in Missouri, the curators of the University of Missouri have all campus presidents turn in a budget, and the curators will ask for a certain amount from the legislature. The legislature will determine to fund the university campuses at a certain level, and the rest of the money comes from tuition and fees paid by the students. The university or college may also apply for grant money from different organizations and foundations to supplement the budget, but it is typically very specifically determined where the grant funding will go.

The federal government is a stakeholder, as it funds less than 1% of all libraries through Library Services and Technology Act (LSTA) grants, E-Rate, and Elementary and Secondary Education Act (ESEA) Title III monies. The LSTA grants are administered by the Institute of Museum and Library Services (IMLS) to state libraries and then down through public and academic libraries. ESEA Title III money is administered through the Department of Education to school libraries. E-Rate is applied for by individual public libraries to the Federal Communications Commission (FCC).

Taxpayers are stakeholders in the library no matter what type the library is. There will be members of the public who will not be pleased a specific piece of material has been purchased and will say that they are upset their tax dollars have been spent on it. The idea that their tax dollars have been spent in a tangible way that can be seen can sometimes make someone who is not really a supporter of the library into a "problem child." The best way to deal with someone like this is to turn it into a positive. There are thousands of materials in the library, and there must be something the person likes.

CUSTOMER SERVICE

Whether the stakeholders are internal or external, librarians must maintain excellent relations with them. This is done through customer service.

Librarianship is a customer-focused profession. This statement should cause no surprise. The majority of our patrons are served in face-to-face transactions with staff. The most common transaction is checking out books, but today this is being automated more and more through automatic checkout machines. Customer service is that personal service we provide our patrons when we work in the library. It can be through the reference desk in a face-to-face, computer-to-computer, or telephone transaction.

Excellent customer service is something many of us believe is in the past. This is not true. Excellent customer service should be something everyone strives to give to their patrons on a daily basis no matter how their day is going. Everyone has a story of that terrible customer service experience at XYZ Store that they have shared with all their friends. In the Internet age it is more difficult for an organization to recover from having a reputation for poor customer service than ever. Poor customer service stories go viral in a matter of hours. Someone posts a YouTube video that's a parody of the poor service they received; the company it is portraying has just had their reputation shredded. Everyone thinks it is funny except for the executive who has to take all those lemons and make lemonade out of the experience.

I have worked at companies where excellent customer service was the byword and when one experience got away from us, it was not pretty, but these stories are in the days before the Internet and You-

Tube. Now it is very easy to lambaste someone's reputation and the customer service department in one fell swoop by going on the Internet. Whatever is put out on the Internet is there forever. So be very careful about what you personally put out there.

How can you avoid the YouTube lambasting that happens so easily these days? By training your staff in excellent customer service, and, yes, I said training. Most staff have not had customer service training because everyone assumes that it is something people learn how to do through osmosis. This is one of the biggest fallacies about customer service out there. Being trained makes all the difference.

Did you know when you smile when you are talking on the phone the person on the other end can tell? If you are frowning, that is also easy to hear over the phone. I am not talking about Skype but the regular phone or cell phone. Smiling makes a big difference. Being pleasant makes a difference. So does saying "Hello," "Thank you," "You're welcome," and the other pleasantries we learned in kindergarten. The basic skill in customer service is listening. We have two ears and one mouth for a reason—the proportion of listening to talking should be 2:1.

None of this information is earth shattering, but it makes a big difference. So does following up with patrons. For instance, you had a reference interview with someone and got her started on her way. Check in with her to make sure she doesn't need anything else. She will be impressed that you did this, because most librarians start patrons their way and then forget about them. Following up is an easy skill to learn.

Helping people find the information they need for their project is fun. Even helping seven-year-old patrons check out books is fun because they have a very different outlook on what is important than we do. Smile and have fun. Provide excellent customer service, and your patrons will thank you for it.

CONCLUSION

The internal and external stakeholders of libraries are wide and varied groups. Many of them are just the normal patrons the librarians and staff see on a day-to-day basis and are a pleasure to work with and serve. Stakeholders are the folks who make it possible for the library to exist at all levels—financial, material, supervisory, administrative. Not all of them will be great to work with all the time. This is just like everything else. Smile and they will wonder what you are up to.

CASE STUDY

The community paper has been reporting that the local library is purchasing foreign language materials for the immigrants in the community who speak that language and allowing the materials to be checked out. As well as materials, programming has been marketed that targets this group. Certain members of your town are outraged that the public library is cultivating these foreigners and using taxpayers' money to do it. This is a small, rural community, and some people feel that this is a waste of money, that these foreigners should learn the language of the country they live in rather than be catered to by having materials in their language.

The director needs to cool down everyone's temper and to calm down the constituency. What are some ways this can be accomplished without getting members of the community more upset? Come up with a plan for a positive spin on what is going on at the library. How should this be handled?

References

Oxford English Dictionary. (2009). Stakeholder. Retrieved from www.oed.com .ezproxy.dom.edu/view/Entry/246856?redirectedFrom=stakeholder#eid

Velasquez, D. L. (2010, December). E-government and public access computers in public libraries. In A. Woodsworth (Ed.), *Advances in librarianship: Exploring the digital frontier* (Vol. 31, pp. 111–132). New York, NY: Emerald.

Further Readings on Internal and External Stakeholders

Alita, J. (2001, December). Creating an Internet policy by civic engagement. *American Libraries, 32*(11), 48–50.

Anderson, C. L. (2011). Moving the library agenda forward: Librarians collaborating with the chief library administrator to cultivate campus constituencies. *Journal of Library Administration, 51*(2), 242–254.

Bell, C. R., & Patterson, J. R. (2009). *Take their breath away: How imaginative service creates devoted customers.* Hoboken, NJ: John Wiley & Sons.

Blixrud, J. (2004, December). Balancing stakeholder interests in scholarship-friendly copyright practices. *ARL,* 237, 8.

Campbell, D. K., & Cook, R. G. (2010). An experiential market research analysis: A partnership between teaching and library faculty. *Journal of Business & Finance Librarianship, 15,* 171–178.

De Long, K., & Sivak, A. (2010, Summer/Fall). The blind man describes the elephant: The training gaps analysis for librarians and library technicians. *Library Trends, 59*(1–2), 336–379.

Fernandez, J. (2009, September/October). A SWOT analysis for social media in libraries. *Online, 33*(5), 35–37.

Harer, J. B., & Cole, B. R. (2005, March). The importance of the stakeholder in performance measurement: Critical processes and performance measures for assessing and improving academic library services and programs. *College & Research Libraries, 66*(2), 149–170.

Hill, S. (2008, December). The workplace: Survival strategies in a cost-cutting environment. *Information Outlook, 12*(12), 16–21.

Moran, B. B., Marshall, J. G., & Rathbun-Grubb, S. (2010, Summer/Fall). The academic library workforce: Past, present, and future. *Library Trends, 59*(1–2), 208–219.

Quinn, A. C., & Ramasubramanian, L. (2007). Information technologies and civic engagement: Perspectives from librarianship and planning. *Government Information Quarterly, 24*(3), 595–610.

Stratigos, A. (2003, March/April). Managing up: Stakeholder relationship imperatives. *Online, 27*(2), 69–71.

Urs, S. R. (2004). Copyright, academic research and libraries: Balancing the rights of stakeholders in the digital age. *Electric Library & Information Systems, 38*(3), 201–207.

Wand, P. A. (2011). Key library constituents in an international context. *Journal of Library Administration, 51*(2), 242–254.

Zhu, X., & Eschenfelder, K. R. (2010, November). Social construction of authorized users in the digital age. *College & Research Libraries, 71*(6), 548–568.

13
ETHICS AND CONFIDENTIALITY

Diane L. Velasquez

The idea that we even have to discuss ethics and confidentiality is sad. With the advent in corporate America in the past few years of Enron, WorldCom, and other businesses that decided ethics were flexible, talking about ethics is mandatory. Some graduate library and information science schools have an ethics course that students can take.

Imagine for a moment that you are holding a ruler in front of you in a vertical position; there are high marks on one side and low marks on the other that measure ethics. Everyone has a place where their ethics might be for sale. Some of us have extremely high ethics and will not compromise on what we consider our principles of what is right. Others have low ethics and would sell their mother for a quarter. The rest are somewhere in the middle. None of these is a bad position; this is just how the world works and how the world has worked for millennia.

Ethics are the basis of the governments, organizations, schools, and businesses that comprise the societal fabric of our everyday lives. Everyone has a different definition of what their personal ethics are as measured on a high to low scale. There are people with flexible ethics; that is, their ethics change as the situation they are involved in changes. Flexible ethics can thus be considered situational ethics. Depending on the standpoint, none of these different measures of ethics is good or bad; this all hinges on how the person viewing the situation sees the variables and the outcome.

CODES OF ETHICS AND LEGAL GUIDELINES

Code of Ethics of the American Library Association

In the library world, most codes of ethics are based on the American Library Association's (ALA) Code of Ethics (ALA, 2008; see Exhibit 13.1 at the end of the chapter for the full text of the code). The ALA Code of Ethics has been in use since 1939 and has been revised three times over the past 70-plus years. The ALA Code of Ethics is an optional doctrine that libraries can choose to adopt. Most libraries do choose to use it as a basis of how they will operate, as it discusses providing service to patrons, how librarians and staff will treat one another, privacy rights of patrons, intellectual property rights, and some other commonsense items. The first thing all of us have to understand is that not everyone has common sense. Setting out a basic code of ethics is a necessary first step to make sure we treat one another ethically and with integrity.

We also need to treat our patrons and coworkers well. Parking our personal opinions at the door is necessary to making sure we don't influence what happens in the workplace with our personal agendas. Everyone has an opinion about what is going on in the world. At work, we need to moderate that opinion, keep our mouths shut, and do our jobs. Discussing the current political situation in our country, our religious opinion, or anything else is just not appropriate fodder at the workplace even if someone asks us. If it is after hours and you are having drinks in a bar, have at it, and have a great discussion on what you feel the ills of the world are and how you think they can be fixed.

Other Library Association Codes of Ethics

The ALA is not the only library association that has a code of ethics. Many of the other specialized library groups do as well. The following groups have codes of ethics or ethical guidelines that are available on their websites:

- American Association of Law Libraries (1997)—aallnet.org
- Medical Librarian Association (2010)—mlanet.org
- Special Librarian Association (2010)—sla.org
- Society of American Archivists (2005)—archivists.org

See also Exhibit 13.1 at the end of this chapter for the full text of the first two codes.

Most of the codes of ethics are similar to the ALA code but incorporate issues that are specific to the particular group. For instance, law librarians have a statement regarding not practicing law. Again, the codes of ethics of the various special library associations are regarded by the librarians as something they want to work under, as their members know these are part and parcel of the association.

Children's Internet Protection Act (CIPA)

The Children's Internet Protection Act (CIPA) was passed and signed into law by President Clinton on December 21, 2000, as part of a spending package for fiscal year 2001. CIPA requires public schools and public libraries that receive discounted telecommunications services under the E-Rate plan or a service paid with funds under Title III of the Elementary and Secondary Education Act (ESEA) to block or filter Internet access to visual depictions that are obscene, contain child pornography, or are otherwise harmful to minors. CIPA requires libraries to provide reasonable public notice and to hold at least one public hearing or meeting to address Internet safety issues (Jaeger & Yan, 2009). In essence any library or school that receives federal monies under either program can lose its funding if it does not place filters on its computers. This also includes libraries that receive money under the Library and Services Technology Act (LSTA).

The filters may be disabled for adults who are conducting research when they ask library or school staff to do so. As far as libraries are concerned, not all libraries choose to filter computers, so they decide to go without the E-Rate monies. Some of the larger libraries, including San Francisco Public Library, Chicago Public Library, and New York Public Library, do not participate in the E-Rate program. For libraries that depend on the E-Rate monies, filtering is mandatory because the Supreme Court has upheld CIPA. For public libraries, which cater to both adult and children patrons, this can be a hassle. The way CIPA is interpreted by the Supreme Court justices is that librarians can easily disable the filter for adult patrons. I once interviewed a local library director for a class paper when I was in graduate school. The director stated that her library does not receive E-Rate funds, and the librarians did not want filters because it was not productive to have staff constantly installing and taking off filters. When talking about filters, it does include all staff and patron computers. Libraries can also choose not to disable the filters for adult patrons. It is the option of the library and may even be determined through a policy by the public library board.

E-Rate

- All E-Rate applications are handled through the FCC.
- Filtering is not needed for plain old telephone service (POTS) or other telecommunications infrastructure.
- Filtering is needed if it offsets Internet accessibility.

- Internet safety policies must include the monitoring of online activities of minors.
- As required by the Protecting Children in the 21st Century Act, minors must be educated about appropriate online behavior, including interacting with other individuals on social networking websites and in chat rooms, and cyberbullying awareness and response (FCC, n.d.).

Library Services and Technology Act (LSTA)

- LSTA is managed through the Institute of Museum Library Services (IMLS).
- State libraries request money for their state's programs
- State Programs: State Libraries (IMLS, n.d.): www.imls.gov/programs/state_libraries.aspx
- State Programs: State Allotments (IMLS, 2008–2012): www.imls.gov/programs/state_allotments.aspx
- Money is typically used to purchase or update computers but can be used for other things.
- Every single computer the library owns must be filtered—every computer and laptop in the library, whether used by staff or patrons.

Title III of the Elementary and Secondary Education Act (ESEA)

- ESEA affects schools from preschool to grade 12 (P–12).
- Any funds given through ESEA to P–12 or K–12 schools obligates the school to filter all computers even if adults use them.
- Most school districts filter as a matter of course.

CIPA was decided by the Third Circuit in the Eastern District of Pennsylvania and the U.S. Supreme Court in the case titled United States v. American Library Association. The three-judge panel held that "the library plaintiffs must prevail in their contention that CIPA requires them to violate the First Amendment rights of their patrons, and accordingly is facially invalid"; the three-judge panel sitting in the Eastern District of Pennsylvania ruled Sections 1712(a)(2) and 1721(b) of CIPA to be facially invalid under the First Amendment and permanently enjoined the government from enforcing those provisions. The Supreme Court justices agreed in a 6–3 decision.

Son of CIPA Laws

Some states, such as Georgia, have stricter laws than CIPA regarding filtering in their schools (K–12 and higher education) and public libraries that tie state funding to filtering Internet-connected public access computers. Son of CIPA laws, as these are called, can sometimes block benign information like health information. For example, let's say an assignment in class is to look up information regarding a health issue and a student chooses to look up breast cancer. This may be blocked because of the word *breast*. What is blocked is determined by the company that wrote the filter, and such companies do not to disclose how they write their code. The way the code is written is considered to be proprietary information. It is incumbent upon the library director and the IT staff to make sure they understand how the filtering software works or does not work.

USA PATRIOT ACT

Those who would give up essential Liberty, to purchase a little temporary Safety, deserve neither Liberty nor Safety.

—Benjamin Franklin, as cited in Platt, 1989, #1056

The United and Strengthening America by Providing Appropriate Tools Required to Intercept and Obstruct Terrorism Act of 2001 (USA PATRIOT Act; Public Law 107–56 §215), commonly known as the Patriot Act, was passed less than a month after the al-Qa'ida attacks on the World Trade Center in New York and the Pentagon in Washington, DC. This comprehensive law enforcement act was passed in order to deal with spiraling issues of terrorism occurring on American soil. The act, depending on one's viewpoint, changed our civil liberties as citizens and put into law certain intrusions that can now occur in our daily lives with little or no notice. The act was passed in the House of Representatives in a vote of 357–66 and in the Senate 98–1 (Essex, 2004, p. 333). None of the congresspeople who voted on the Patriot Act read the act (Mentre et al., 2007). Some provisions in Section 215 of the Patriot Act apply to libraries. These provisions give "federal investigators greater authority to examine all book and computer records at libraries—without demonstrating any suspicion that their targets are involved in espionage or terrorism" (Hamilton, 2004, p. 201).

What this means is that federal investigators can come into a library at any time, without a subpoena, and ask for records of what patrons have checked out or which computers they have used. Under Section 215 librarians who are asked for this information cannot speak about it to anyone or they will be in violation of the Patriot Act. This provision has been amended slightly as will be discussed later.

Many librarians are against enforcing the Patriot Act. After it was enacted, many libraries around the country decided to place signs and placards letting patrons know that there could be a risk involved in borrowing a book or signing up to use a computer. The Santa Cruz (CA) Public Library went even further by placing a shredder at the circulation desk so that all sign-up lists could be shredded daily. It should be noted that not all librarians are against it, and some feel it should be enforced vigorously. As with any political question before our country, there are people on both sides of the question.

What do librarians need to know? According to Section 215 of the USA PATRIOT Improvement and Reauthorization Act of 2005, the FBI and other law enforcement officials can get secret warrants to obtain business records, including records for libraries and databases. Another portion of the act allows for issuance of National Security Letters (NSLs). The change to the original Patriot Act is that the librarian, businessperson, or person involved in this situation can now seek the help of an attorney. Previously there was a gag order and those charged under the Patriot Act were not allowed to speak to anyone regarding the charges or even go to court to fight the charges. Section 215 of the USA PATRIOT Improvement and Reauthorization Act of 2005 has a sunset provision of June 1, 2015, which means the law was amended by the 112th Congress on May 26, 2011, by the PATRIOT Sunsets Extension Act of 2011. Warrants issued under Section 215 must be given out by the Foreign Intelligence Surveillance Court (FISC). The FISC is made up of seven federal justices who serve seven-year terms on a rotating basis. All actions from this court are kept secret. The warrants issued must be approved by the FBI director or his or her designee. One major change to the 2001 act is that if served you can consult an attorney and may file in the FISC to challenge the warrant.

Section 206 relates to roving wiretaps and the lone-wolf provision of the Patriot Act. The lone-wolf provision relates to those terrorists who act on their own. It can relate to libraries if the lone wolf uses a library to access information on its computers. It also has a sunset date of June 1, 2015. The rest of the act is now the law of the land.

How should a library deal with the Patriot Act?

- Have a policy in place regarding patron and employee information; make sure an attorney has looked at the policy and said that it complies with the law.
- Make sure that law enforcement officials have a subpoena or a warrant.
- Don't assume law enforcement is in the right.

- Understand that libraries have the right to disseminate information freely and confidentially.
- Make sure your ILS system deletes records entirely if your library system does not want to have to produce electronic records that would be cumbersome to procure.
- Be aware of our country's political environment.
- Attend conferences and informational sessions.
- Be aware of your state's confidentially laws.
- Prepare handouts for patrons.
- Discuss with your board, provost, and president as well as an attorney about how you will proceed if given a warrant.
- Train your staff.
- Have a current collection of political events books.
- Be ready for the press.

ALA Library Bill of Rights

The ALA Library Bill of Rights is a six-statement document that was adopted in January 1980 and reaffirmed with the inclusion of one word in January 1996 (ALA, 1996; see Exhibit 13.1 at the end of this chapter for the full text). Many public and academic libraries follow the strictures verbatim. Special libraries are a different case, as they can be within a corporate environment (meaning for profit), and blindly following ALA Library Bill of Rights may need to be approved by the board of directors or a vice president. In this section, the discussion will focus on public and academic libraries.

The ALA Library Bill of Rights works in tandem in many ways with the ALA Code of Ethics. The two documents are complementary, and when looking at them it is evident they should be used together. The Code of Ethics Statement III says: "We protect each library user's right to privacy and confidentiality with respect to information sought or received and resources consulted, borrowed, acquired, or transmitted" (ALA, 2008). This works directly with Statement V of the Library Bill of Rights: "A person's right to use a library should not be denied or abridged because of origin, age, background, or views" (ALA, 1996). In essence the two statements are saying that all users or patrons should have a right to privacy and confidentiality regardless of origin, age, background, or views.

I agree with these statements; however, it could be problematic for parents of minor children who want to know what their kids are checking out. As librarians we can inform them that we can't tell them because their children are entitled to the right to privacy just like everyone else. Preer discusses a way some libraries have tried to help parents ensure that their children do not go outside of preset lines:

> . . . some libraries offer family borrowing cards or, at the request of the parents, limit borrowing to certain portions of the collection. In essence, the parents have waived their children's right to privacy. The presumptive protection of privacy stays in place, while parents achieve the desired result for their own family. Thus, a policy that requires family borrowing cards or parental permission for children to access the entire collection is an inappropriate approach which dishonors the obligation to protect confidentiality. Requiring families to opt out of privacy protection, rather than asking them to opt in, is the ethical approach to confidentiality, service, and access. (Preer, 2008, p. 194)

Adopting a Library Bill of Rights is up to the director or dean and their board of trustees or other management oversight. The management team needs to make sure that everyone is able to live up to the strictures within it and to defend the Library Bill of Rights if necessary.

ETHICAL DECISION MAKING

The previous discussion focused on ideas that have been set out by the ALA; other associations like the Special Library Association, American Association of Law Libraries, and Medical Library Association; and Congress. Their codes of ethics or laws are prefaced upon the ideas about the values and integrity of an institution that someone or a group of people felt strongly about. Many times a manager, director, or dean will need to make a decision about something where there is no set policy.

A good example is some of the shenanigans that went on with Enron. Enron bought and sold electrical shares that created an artificial increase in the cost of electricity. Enron also bought and sold broadband bandwidth that did not exist—there were people in the company who created a market that did not exist. They were buying and selling something that didn't exist, and eventually the house of cards crashed. The people who worked at Enron had all of their pension funds in Enron stock, so when the market crashed, their pension funds were worth zero. This lesson is one many people working for a company learn the hard way—do not put all your financial eggs in one basket; diversify. The only people who got out from under were the people at the top of the company. Was this ethical? No, it is what the U.S. Securities and Exchange Commission (SEC) calls insider trading. The top-level people were selling off their stock before it dropped like a rock because they knew something was going to happen, but when asked in court under oath all of them denied it.

Warren Bennis (2003) discussed that "a major challenge that all leaders are now facing is an epidemic of corporate malfeasance" (p. 153). The idea that the short-term, bottom-line mentality of corporations would create leaders with integrity is false. With libraries and information centers, the bottom line is not so much about profit but whether or not the management teams have made their budgets without first going over the numbers assigned by the city, county, or university administrators. Libraries have not had the ethical crises that for-profit companies have had, but whenever someone is managing a budget there is always the potential for mismanagement or poor judgment about where the dollars are spent.

Bennis (2003) makes the rallying cry that "knowing oneself" (p. 47) is the key to being a leader of any type of company. Having integrity and believing that you can do the job ethically is important. When making decisions be sure you have all the information that is readily available. Sometimes decisions are made with less than you would like, but that is how the world happens sometimes. Do the best that can be done.

Running a for-profit business today is not easy. Running a library or information center is not easy. No matter the number of people reporting to the dean or director, 10% to 20% of your people will be problem children at any one time. Deal with them as you would like to be dealt with—with integrity and respect. I always think about this when something happens—what goes around, comes around. I have been around long enough to see it in action, that when someone does something mean-spirited to someone else, it always comes back to them. I may not be around to see it, but it always comes back. Don't talk behind peoples' backs and gossip—no good ever comes of it.

CENSORSHIP AND COLLECTION MANAGEMENT

Censorship of the library collection is really not a topic for a management textbook; however, many patrons will feel that management should address the content of books, DVDs, CDs, and other tangible items in the collection. Censorship is not the purview of the librarians in acquisitions. Choices about material for the library should be based on the collection management policy of the library. If there is not a collection management policy, there should be one. Make sure your library has a collection policy.

Another policy to have addresses what to do with books patrons donate. Make sure the book donation policy mandates that all books that come into the collection must follow the collection development policy. If the books don't follow the collection development policy, there should be caveats that the books can then be sold or donated to another organization. This way the donator knows you valued what you gave them but couldn't use it. Also put in the policy what you will not accept—magazines like *National Geographic* or anything else you don't need or want.

Finally, you should have a written policy on how to handle challenges that certain books, DVDs, and CDs are not appropriate. Have a form for people who challenge an item to fill out. Those who make a challenge should have read the book (or viewed it if it is a DVD); if not, the challenge is moot. How do they know what's in it if they haven't read, heard, or viewed the material? It is all hearsay. Challenges should receive a timely response. The best book on this subject is Jamie LaRue's (2007) *The New Inquisition: Understanding and Managing Intellectual Freedom Challenges.* LaRue sets out the issues a library director faces and how to handle them without getting off track.

CONFIDENTIALITY CONCERNS IN MANAGEMENT

There are many aspects to confidentiality in libraries. The main one is that patrons and their transactions are confidential. As was seen with the Patriot Act, changes have been made through federal legislation to what is and what is not private with regard to personal records that we all have that we consider confidential. The Patriot Act has made definite inroads into what can be breached without our knowledge, including our medical, financial, library, and other personal records, with minimal information by our government (Gorham-Oscilowski & Jaeger, 2008; Preer, 2008).

In this portion of the chapter, however, we will leave the Patriot Act behind and look at confidentiality from a management point of view. Being a director or dean of a library means being responsible for information that no one else in the library may know about or only one or two people in the library may have access to. I am talking about information in personnel files, financial information on donors, and general business information. Many times the library environment, depending on the size of the organization, feels family-like; and as in many families, there are secrets. Some information is just no one's business except for the director or dean and the employee in question. Let's explore this further.

Confidentiality and Human Resources

Employees come and go through an organization. The official term is *turnover.* Leaving an organization is not always a clean process; it can include iterations where someone is written up for something and put on a disciplinary program. This is a confidential process between the employee and the manager. The director or dean in most cases will know as well. Depending on the hierarchy of the organization, a department head and manager may also know what is going on. Keeping this information and the details of it confidential is necessary so that the employee has the ability to his or her job without everyone stirring up the gossip mill about "guess what happened to Sally Smith." To paraphrase a popular commercial, what happens with an employee and the manager regarding discipline stays with them in that office.

When I was working in corporate America about 15 years ago, I temped as an executive assistant to a president of a divisional office. He had a leak in his office because whenever there were human resources movements about to happen, they always got out. When his assistant went on maternity leave I took over for her, and the leaks stopped. The leaks were occurring through his assistant. People would find out somebody was being fired or let go, and this would spread like wildfire through the office. This is not information that anyone should be sharing, let alone the president's assistant. Needless to say, when she came back from maternity leave her job had changed drastically because of the leaks.

All personnel matters need to be confidential so that no one is aware of what is going on with the situation. Personnel information is the type of information that will get out through the gossip mills because it is juicy and usually about someone's life.

Business Transactions

Confidentiality of business transactions needs to be honored as well. No one needs to know who has donated money unless the donor chooses to let it be known. Many times people prefer to keep that information to themselves. If the library wants to advertise the information or market it in some way, ask first.

The other business transactions that need confidentiality are who is checking out what books, DVDs, CDs, and so forth. This information should stay confidential between the patron and the library. It is no one's business. As both the ALA Code of Ethics and the Library Bill of Rights state, everyone is entitled to privacy; and privacy shouldn't be denied because of "origin, background, age, or views" (ALA, 1996).

Payment of fines and any other financial transactions that patrons have with the library should be confidential. The ability to conduct business with the library should be treated fairly and with a right to privacy. Confidentiality of patrons' business matters is something we all expect when going about our daily errands.

Right to Be Left Alone

Patrons have a right to be left alone when in the library or any public space. Warren and Brandeis (1890) discussed this concept in relation to the advent of technology of the late 19th century and its creeping into daily life and the news. The technology Warren and Brandeis were discussing in 1890 was photography and the inclusion of images in newspapers. Now, in the early 21st century, a case could be made that with the Internet and the electronic plethora of smartphones, Web 2.0, Twitter, Facebook, and so forth it is harder to be left alone because technology is even more around us than ever before. Cameras all around us take pictures and record video of what is going on. News is instantaneous in the 24/7 world we live in today.

Warren and Brandeis (1890) felt at their time in history that "the press is overstepping in every direction the obvious bounds of propriety and of decency" (p. 196). What would they say about the overexposure of many of the celebrities of today? The ability to be left alone to do our work and know we are doing good work is something all of us at times want. It is not always something that is a reality or can actually occur.

We owe our patrons the respect to leave them alone if that is what they want when they are in the library.

CASE STUDY

The Heron Public Library has been notified that J. K. Rowling's books and movies about Harry Potter are being challenged because the plots involve witchcraft and magic. The patron, Rupert Loomis, is challenging the works because he feels that they promote non-Christian ethics and morals. He wants all seven books and eight movies to be removed from the library.

Rupert Loomis found that his eight-year-old son, Charles, was reading *Harry Potter and the Sorcerer's Stone.* When Mr. Loomis picked it up and started reading it, he was shocked to find out it was about magic and witchcraft and had evil events in it. As a born-again Christian, he felt the book did not conform to his morals, ethics, and values and should not be in a community library. Mr. Loomis plans to attend the next board of trustees meeting to bring this up.

As the director of Heron Public Library, how are you going to handle the book challenge that Mr. Loomis is presenting? What are the questions you have for Mr. Loomis? As a public library, should the organization be concerned about the community standards a patron has about the books that are in the collection? What about the movies on Harry Potter? Does it concern you that a widely popular book series and its associated movies are being challenged?

EXHIBIT 13.1
EXAMPLE LIBRARY ASSOCIATION CODES OF ETHICS

Code of Ethics of the American Library Association

As members of the American Library Association, we recognize the importance of codifying and making known to the profession and to the general public the ethical principles that guide the work of librarians, other professionals providing information services, library trustees, and library staffs.

Ethical dilemmas occur when values are in conflict. The American Library Association Code of Ethics states the values to which we are committed, and embodies the ethical responsibilities of the profession in this changing information environment.

We significantly influence or control the selection, organization, preservation, and dissemination of information. In a political system grounded in an informed citizenry, we are members of a profession explicitly committed to intellectual freedom and the freedom of access to information. We have a special obligation to ensure the free flow of information and ideas to present and future generations.

The principles of this Code are expressed in broad statements to guide ethical decision making. These statements provide a framework; they cannot and do not dictate conduct to cover particular situations.

I. We provide the highest level of service to all library users through appropriate and usefully organized resources; equitable service policies; equitable access; and accurate, unbiased, and courteous responses to all requests.

II. We uphold the principles of intellectual freedom and resist all efforts to censor library resources.

III. We protect each library user's right to privacy and confidentiality with respect to information sought or received and resources consulted, borrowed, acquired, or transmitted.

IV. We respect intellectual property rights and advocate balance between the interests of information users and rights holders.

V. We treat coworkers and other colleagues with respect, fairness, and good faith, and advocate conditions of employment that safeguard the rights and welfare of all employees of our institutions.

VI. We do not advance private interests at the expense of library users, colleagues, or our employing institutions.

VII. We distinguish between our personal convictions and professional duties and do not allow our personal beliefs to interfere with fair representation of the aims of our institutions or the provision of access to their information resources.

VIII. We strive for excellence in the profession by maintaining and enhancing our own knowledge and skills, by encouraging the professional development of coworkers, and by fostering the aspirations of potential members of the profession.

Adopted at the 1939 Midwinter Meeting by the ALA Council; amended June 30, 1981; June 28, 1995; and January 22, 2008.

Note. Used with permission from the ALA. American Library Association. (2008). *Code of ethics of the ALA*. Retrieved from http://www.ala.org/ala/issuesadvocacy/proethics/codeofethics/codeethics.cfm

American Association of Law Libraries Code of Ethics

The American Association of Law Libraries espouses the statement of professional ethics promulgated by the American Library Association, which states that:

A library

- Has a special responsibility to maintain the principles of the Library Bill of Rights.
- Should learn and faithfully execute the policies of the institution of which one is a part and should endeavor to change those which conflict with the spirit of the Library Bill of Rights.
- Must protect the essential confidential relationship which exists between a library user and the library.
- Must avoid any possibility of personal financial gain at the expense of the employing institution.
- Has an obligation to insure equality of opportunity and fair judgment of competence in actions dealing with staff appointments, retentions, and promotions.
- Has an obligation when making appraisal of the qualifications of any individual to report the facts clearly, accurately, and without prejudice, according to generally accepted guidelines concerning the disclosure of personal information.

In addition, the Association, in light of the special character and mission of its membership, espouses the principles that law librarians, while engaged in their professional work,

- Have a duty neither to engage in the unauthorized practice of law nor to solicit an attorney–client relationship.
- Have a duty to avoid any situations posing a possible undisclosed conflict of interest.
- Have a special duty, given the nature of their patron base, to treat confidentially any private information obtained through contact with library patrons and not to divulge any confidential information to persons representing adverse interests.
- Have a duty to exercise scrupulous care in avoiding any acts or even the appearance of misappropriating the work product of library patrons or professional colleagues to their own credit or profit.
- Have a duty to actively to promote free and effective access to legal information.
- Have a duty to society and the legal profession to work both individually and through their professional organizations toward improving the quality and minimizing the cost of the library component of the delivery of legal services.

Adopted, September 1978.
AALL Spectrum, November 1997, p. 15

Note. Used with permission of the American Association of Law Libraries. American Association of Law Libraries. (1997, November). *American Association of Law Libraries code of ethics*. Retrieved from http://www.aallnet.org/main-menu/Publications/spectrum/Archives/Vol-2/pub_sp9711/pub-sp9711-ethics.pdf

Code of Ethics for Health Sciences Librarianship

GOALS AND PRINCIPLES FOR ETHICAL CONDUCT

The health sciences librarian believes that knowledge is the sine qua non of informed decisions in health care, education, and research, and the health sciences librarian serves society, clients, and the institution by working to ensure that informed decisions can be made. The principles of this code are expressed in broad statements to guide ethical decision making. These statements provide a framework; they cannot and do not dictate conduct to cover particular situations.

Society

- The health sciences librarian promotes access to health information for all and creates and maintains conditions of freedom of inquiry, thought, and expression that facilitate informed health care decisions.

Clients

- The health sciences librarian works without prejudice to meet the client's information needs.
- The health sciences librarian respects the privacy of clients and protects the confidentiality of the client relationship.
- The health sciences librarian ensures that the best available information is provided to the client.

Institution

- The health sciences librarian provides leadership and expertise in the design, development, and ethical management of knowledge-based information systems that meet the information needs and obligations of the institution.

Profession

- The health sciences librarian advances and upholds the philosophy and ideals of the profession.
- The health sciences librarian advocates and advances the knowledge and standards of the profession.
- The health sciences librarian conducts all professional relationships with courtesy and respect.
- The health sciences librarian maintains high standards of professional integrity.

Self

- The health sciences librarian assumes personal responsibility for developing and maintaining professional excellence.

- The health sciences librarian shall be alert to and adhere to his or her institution's code of ethics and its conflict of interest, disclosure, and gift policies.

Note. Used with permission of the Medical Library Association. Medical Library Association. (2010). *Code of ethics for health sciences librarianship*. Retrieved from http://www.mlanet.org/about/ethics.html

Library Bill of Rights

The American Library Association affirms that all libraries are forums for information and ideas, and that the following basic policies should guide their services.

I. Books and other library resources should be provided for the interest, information, and enlightenment of all people of the community the library serves. Materials should not be excluded because of the origin, background, or views of those contributing to their creation.

II. Libraries should provide materials and information presenting all points of view on current and historical issues. Materials should not be proscribed or removed because of partisan or doctrinal disapproval.

III. Libraries should challenge censorship in the fulfillment of their responsibility to provide information and enlightenment.

IV. Libraries should cooperate with all persons and groups concerned with resisting abridgment of free expression and free access to ideas.

V. A person's right to use a library should not be denied or abridged because of origin, age, background, or views.

VI. Libraries that make exhibit spaces and meeting rooms available to the public they serve should make such facilities available on an equitable basis, regardless of the beliefs or affiliations of individuals or groups requesting their use.

Adopted June 19, 1939, by the ALA Council; amended October 14, 1944; June 18, 1948; February 2, 1961; June 27, 1967; January 23, 1980; inclusion of "age" reaffirmed January 23, 1996.

References

American Association of Law Libraries. (1997, November). *American Association of Law Libraries code of ethics.* Retrieved from www.aallnet.org/main-menu/Publications/spectrum/Archives/Vol-2/pub_sp9711/pub-sp9711-ethics.pdf

American Library Association. (1996). *Library bill of rights.* Retrieved from www.ala.org/ala/issuesadvocacy/intfreedom/librarybill/index.cfm

American Library Association. (2008). *Code of ethics of the ALA.* Retrieved from www.ala.org/ala/issuesadvocacy/proethics/codeofethics/codeethics.cfm

Bennis, W. (2003). *On becoming a leader* (Rev. ed.). New York, NY: Basic Books.

Essex, D. (2004, November/December). Opposing the USA PATRIOT Act: The best alternative for American librarians. *Public Libraries, 43*(6), 331–340.

Federal Communications Commission. (n.d.). *Children's Internet Protection Act.* Retrieved from www.fcc.gov/guides/childrens-internet-protection-act

Gorham-Oscilowski, U., & Jaeger, P. T. (2008, October). National Security Letter, the USA PATRIOT Act, and the Constitution: The tensions between national security and civil rights. *Government Information Quarterly, 25*(4), 624–644.

Hamilton, S. (2004). The war on terrorism: Consequences for freedom of expression and the integrity of library users. *IFLA Journal, 30*(3), 199–207.

Institute of Museum and Library Services. (2008–2012). *State programs: State allotments.* Retrieved from www.imls.gov/programs/state_allotments.aspx

Institute of Museum and Library Services. (n.d.). State programs: State libraries. Retrieved from www.imls.gov/programs/state_libraries.aspx

Jaeger, P. T., & Yan, Z. (2009, March). One law with two outcomes: Comparing the implementation of CIPA in public libraries and schools. *Information Technology and Libraries, 28*(1), 6–14.

LaRue, Jamie (2007). *The new inquisition: Understanding and managing intellectual freedom challenges.* Westport, CT: Libraries Unlimited.

Medical Library Association. (2010). *Code of ethics for health sciences librarianship.* Retrieved from www.mlanet.org/about/ethics.html

Mentre, A., Moore, A., Weinstein, B., Deal, C., Weinstein, H. (Producers), & Moore, M. (Director), (2007). *Fahrenheit 9/11* [Motion picture]. United States: Weinstein Co.

PATRIOT Sunsets Extension Act of 2011, Public Law 112–14, 125 Stat. 216 (2011).

Platt, S. (Ed.). (1989). *Respectfully quoted: A dictionary of quotations requested from the Congressional Research Service.* Washington, DC: Library of Congress.

Preer, J. (2008). *Library ethics.* Westport, CT: Library Unlimited.

Society for American Archivists. (2005, February). *Code of ethics for archivists.* Retrieved from www2.archivists.org/standards/code-of-ethics-for-archivists

Special Library Association. (2010, December). *SLA professional ethics guidelines.* Retrieved from www.sla.org/content/SLA/ethics_guidelines.cfm

Uniting and Strengthening America by Providing Appropriate Tools Required to Intercept and Obstruct Terrorism Act (USA PATRIOT Act). Public Law 107–56, 115 Stat. 272 (2001).

USA PATRIOT Act Improvement and Reauthorization Act of 2005, Public Law 109–177, Section 106, 120 Stat. 196 (2006).

Warren, S. D., & Brandeis, L. D. (1890, December 15). The right to privacy. *Harvard Law Review, 4*(5), 193–220.

Further Readings on Ethics and Confidentiality

Albitz, B. (2005, May). Dude, where are my civil rights? *Journal of Academic Librarianship, 31*(3), 284–286.

Doyle, T. (2001). A utilitarian case for intellectual freedom in libraries. *Library Quarterly, 71*(1), 44–71.

Frické, M., Mathiesen, K., & Fallis, D. (2000). The ethical presuppositions behind the Library Bill of Rights. *Library Quarterly, 70*(4), 468–491.

Reid, M. M. (2009, December). The USA PATRIOT Act and academic libraries: An overview. *College & Research Libraries News, 70*(11), 646–650.

Wengert, R. G. (2001, Winter). Some ethical aspects of being an information professional. *Library Trends, 49*(3), 486–509.

14
UNDERSTANDING AND RESOLVING CONFLICT

Lisa K. Hussey

Conflict is an inherent part of any organization. It is not a good or a bad thing; it simply is part of the human condition. As organizations are made up of people, conflict is a part of organizational life. The most common problem with conflict is not the failure to prevent it but rather the avoidance of or refusal to deal with it. Conflict emerges from any situation that increases tension, which can be as complicated as major changes or as simple as making a request. It is an irrational process—an important point to consider in conflict mediation and resolution, which will be discussed later in this chapter.

Conflict can be a creative force or a destructive force and, depending on the situation, can be both. Just consider that in order for something new to emerge, something old has to be removed or destroyed. This is part of change, but a part that most find uncomfortable or scary. Conflict results from the tension and fear of losing the old, even when the new is desirable. Good leaders and managers can take the energy from the tension and fear and channel it toward the potential change. Does this always happen, even with the best leaders? No, but the potential is there.

TENSION AND CONFLICT

So what causes conflict? To put it simply—tension. Within any organization, there are various levels of tension caused by differences.

Regardless of the organization, differences exist among employees' backgrounds, worldviews, expectations, and skill levels. These differences, while important to effective organizational functioning, create unease, an uncomfortable feeling that individuals get when faced with something they don't recognize or understand. This feeling manifests as tension within the organization. Before I go further, I want to mention that tension, like conflict, is neither good nor bad. It simply is. Tension is a part of organizational life. The more one tries to eliminate the tension, the more the tension will increase. What managers need to recognize is that it is how the tension manifests itself and how those manifestations are handled that are important.

Tension also emanates when individuals struggle to balance their self and group roles. Every employee in an organization deals with two identities: one as an individual and one as a member of the organization. When an individual commits to a group, such as an organization, she must surrender part of her individual identity in order to take on the group/organization's identity. In organizational speak, this is often referred to as loyalty or organizational commitment, or to what degree employees are expected to conform and how much individuality is encouraged. This balance between individual and group identity creates a tension within, which manifests in the relationship between employees. Take a moment and think about this idea on a personal level. Consider the various groups you are a part of and how that influences your own identity, what it took for you to feel comfortable as part of the group, and how you react when expectations are not met. What it all comes down to is maintaining a comfortable balance between how much one retains of oneself as an individual and how much one gives to the group. This is what creates tension (Smith & Berg, 1997).

It also helps to consider the simple concept that group life is paradoxical. As with individuals, groups have to maintain a balance between the cohesiveness of the group and the individuality of the members. Being a part of a group involves dealing with contradictory and opposing forces, emotions, and actions. These forces create tensions within the group, which can often lead to conflict. However, the paradox is not the existence of these opposites, it is that they stem from the same source and are needed to ensure the survival of a group. For example, diversity of skills and knowledge are important to organizations so they can be innovative and able to change within a dynamic social setting. Yet, the diversity or differences can create barriers to understanding and communication, which often leads to conflict. To minimize or resolve conflicts, the group must acknowledge the existence of the paradox and that the tensions are a part of everyday group life (Smith & Berg, 1997). Otherwise, the members will be stuck in a cycle of trying to relieve the tensions and creating more in the process.

Many groups or organizations are uncomfortable with the realities of conflict and tension. Rather than embrace both as potentially creative forces, the group or organization will try to reduce or eliminate the tension with the idea that this will prevent conflict. This doesn't work. In fact, it often leads to more conflict because problems will simmer. I am always cynical when an organization stresses how "happy" everyone is. I just don't believe it's possible, because people aren't that simple and tension is a part of life. With this in mind, if an organization can accept that tension is part of organizational life and that it has to function with it, the organization can be productive.

Group paradoxes exist because of the diversity of people. Groups need differences but often cannot find an effective way to work within the tension created by the differences. Paradoxes can come from many different sources. Often individual ambivalence and splitting into subgroups create paradoxes that lead to undermining the work of the group.

Individual ambivalence is when an individual struggles with the concept of being both an individual and a member of the group. At its most basic level, a group involves both the idea of belonging and the idea of being an individual. The group identity is both dependent on and unique from individual identity. An individual must define where he or she ends and the group begins. The paradox arises from dealing with the idea of being separate yet connected. The individual fights with the fear of losing one's self and being excluded at the same time. The individual struggle has an impact on the group as the group integrates the individual identity into its own identity; the group depends on a level of commitment from the individual. The group dynamic shifts as the individual deals with his or her ambivalence, which then increases the tension within the group.

Splitting can be both a productive process and a destructive process. Splitting involves the dividing of a group into subsets. These subgroups can work together toward a common goal or divide the group until it can no longer function. In most organizations, role specialization and subgroup formation are encouraged to improve efficiency. However, the same steps can also create factions and divisions within the organization. Role specialization can be a positive aspect, such as creating leaders, or a negative one, such as creating scapegoats. Splitting can be used in a positive way to foster the strengths of the subgroups. More often, however, it becomes a divisive and destructive pattern resulting from attempts to remove the tensions created from paradox.

So, to sum this all up quickly, people are uncomfortable with difference. Difference is needed for innovation and evolution, but it challenges the status quo, or what is known. As a result, difference creates tension among individuals, among subgroups, and within the organization. When tensions are ignored or repressed, they increase until they create conflict.

GROUP DEVELOPMENT

In any organization, tension begins as soon as two or more individuals have to work together. For this reason, it is important to understand the stages of group development and how they also contribute to conflict within an organization. Each stage represents a point when individuals are finding a way to balance their selves as individuals with their selves as group members. This process can be used to describe the formation of a small task force or the integration of new employees into an organization:

1. *Forming*—the initial stage where members of a group or an organization are getting to know one another, feeling out the situation, figuring out where each person fits, and finding acceptable common behaviors and standards. Conflict at this stage is mild, as most are trying to find ways to fit in. It is at this point that individuals try to get a sense of how much of themselves they should surrender to the larger group and how much they keep to themselves (Griffin, 2008; Smith & Berg, 1997).
2. *Storming*—this is when a lot of conflict happens as the members of a group start to set up roles for themselves and each other, but the members aren't quite sure of each other yet and haven't defined their expectations. An individual who began as friendly may suddenly become more reserved, or a cautious individual may begin to start participating more. This is probably the most difficult stage, because the members aren't comfortable yet. Although they do have more of a sense of each other, the roles and expectations are still unclear and acceptable behaviors are still being defined. Anxiety is especially high for the individual and the group (Griffin, 2008; Smith & Berg, 1997).
3. *Norming*—this is when it all starts to come together. Smith and Berg (1997) and Griffin (2008) say this is a period when individual anxiety is lowered, when roles and behaviors are better

defined, and the group begins to understand and function as a whole.

4. *Performing*—this is exactly what it sounds like. The roles and behaviors are defined, expectations are known, and individuals are able to address their roles because others have taken on their roles (Griffin, 2008).

The steps in group development highlight an important contributor to organizational culture and the potential of conflict—the behavioral norms of the group or organization. These norms are the standards of acceptable behaviors, which are introduced during early socialization into the group and are continually reinforced. Behavioral norms are not generalizable from one group to another or one organization to another. There will always be some variation in how the norms are enforced within the group, and there is a certain expectation of conformity. This may range from strict adherence to the behavioral norms to the acceptance of individual interpretation and application of norms. Regardless, some level of conformity will be expected, and those who do not conform are often treated as outsiders or become the scapegoat for bad situations.

So far I've spent quite a bit of time on some abstract and probably confusing ideas talking about identity and group formation. Why do these abstract and somewhat confusing concepts matter? They are central to understanding conflict, especially the very complex nature of conflict. It is only through understanding this complexity that a manager can effectively work toward resolving it.

TECHNIQUES FOR RESOLVING CONFLICT

There is another characteristic of conflict to discuss before we jump into the finer details of conflict mediation and resolution. It is essential that anyone trying to resolve conflict recognizes that each situation must be approached as a new conflict, even if it seems quite familiar. Just as each person is unique, each conflict is unique. It doesn't matter if the same people are involved or it sounds like the same situation is recurring. Chances are there's something new (or something unresolved) if a problem is happening again. Rather than providing a strict set of steps for dealing with conflict, discussions will focus on a few basic principles when dealing with conflict and how it might help improve the situation.

Conflict is not something that usually can be easily fixed. If it can, it probably really wasn't a conflict. Often when trying to solve a conflict, the manager will put a band-aid on a problem that needs stitches. Something to consider when dealing with conflict is that by the time an argument gets to management, it's not really about what both parties are claiming; rather, it is about something deeper, something that isn't going to be solved by finding what seems like an equitable solution or dividing up responsibility. Chances are the conflict will show up again in another form. For example, a manager might find that he or she is constantly dealing with issues between two teams, two branches, or two individuals. Every time a problem is solved, something new comes up. The immediate problem has been solved, but the actual conflict still exists because the real cause has never been addressed.

Conflict does not appear out of nowhere; it happens within a context. There is a history and a relationship between the conflicting parties that may not be evident to those not directly involved in the conflict, and understanding these factors is essential to successfully dealing with the issues. Without understanding the underlying origin of the conflict, the mediators will fail because they will be dealing with a manufactured cause, not the actual source of the problem.

You might be wondering about these underlying causes that aren't defined. They result from many things, such as a real or perceived slight, competition, jealously, misunderstandings—the list goes on. As resentment builds and is not expressed or dealt with, the conflict continues because none of the solutions address the real problem; they focus on the symptom of the problem, not the cause. To mediate a solution, a manager must understand that resentments can stem from many seemingly minor disagreements, small changes, or issues far removed from the current time frame. It is not enough just to look at the problem right in front of you. It is also necessary to look at the history between the conflicting parties, as well as the culture, setting, and context of the conflict.

If there is one guiding principle about conflict, it is that it is not rational and therefore cannot be fixed through simple, rational methods. Compromise, which always seems to be such a sensible way to deal with conflict, rarely results in a true resolution because it requires both sides to "give up" something, to settle for less than expected, even when presented as a fair and equitable option. To the rational participant—usually the mediator—compromise makes sense. However, to the parties involved in the conflict—those who are not thinking rationally about the problem—compromise represents a loss, not a solution.

When compromise doesn't work, the next step is often to force the conflicting parties to accept an imposed solution. Forcing a solution rarely works either, for many of the same reasons that compromise fails. When a solution is imposed on a conflict, the tension between the parties and now the mediator only increases. Forced solutions are even more of a loss than compromise because the conflicting parties had no say in what was surrendered. Coercion or force will only guarantee a revival of the conflict at some later time.

So, if compromise and coercion don't work, what should be done? One of the most effective steps is to use a mediator or a mediation process to uncover the underlying causes and work through the conflict. A mediator should be as neutral as possible—someone removed from the conflict. This can be a manager, an employee from another department, or someone from outside the organization. The important thing is that the mediator cannot be perceived as being biased toward one of the parties involved.

Mediators often divide conflict into two categories: resource based and identity based. Resource-based conflict is basically a disagreement over how much each party received of something, such as funding, materials, or employees. The resolution for resource-based conflict is to find a fair and equitable way to distribute the resources. However, conflict, regardless of how it is represented, is almost always rooted in identity issues, whether on an individual or a group level. Identity-based conflict is one of the abstract and confusing concepts mentioned earlier in the chapter. It is also important to recognize that identity-based conflict includes issues centered around the identity of the group as well as the identities of the individuals. We must consider how the group identity both influences and is influenced by the individuals who make up the group.

Most individuals do not recognize their group affiliations until the group is threatened. At this point, the group becomes an essential concern of the individual and helps to create psychological borders to separate the group from others—all of those who are not part of the group. When under stress or threat, groups regress to immature behavior. What this involves is returning to childlike behavior where the world is simple and can be divided into simple categories such as black and white, good and evil, us and them. The group members build psychological borders to separate themselves from all that is "bad." In other words, the group members identify all who are not within the group and create enemies out of them. It is at this point that mediators are often called in to help resolve the conflict.

TECHNIQUES FOR CONFLICT MEDIATION

How does a manager or mediator effectively deal with conflict? To begin with, dealing with conflict requires respect—respect for the people involved in the conflict, respect for their points of view, and respect for the potential of the situation. Issues or items important to the parties involved in the conflict should be treated as important. When managers or mediators relegate something as trivial, they dismiss it and disrespect those attached to it. At that point, do you really think those individuals are going to want to work with that person to solve a problem? On the other hand, if mediators or managers understand this is important to the parties involved, whatever it is, they may just get more cooperation because it shows respect for the parties and for what they see as important. Does this mean a manager should cave in and let anyone have what he or she wants? No, but she does need to acknowledge that just because it's not important to her doesn't mean it's not important to the parties.

There are many resources available on conflict mediation. Entire consulting agencies have been built on dealing with conflict. Every manager has some framework or idea as to how to solve problems in organizations. What works best often depends on the parties involved and on their willingness to work through the process. However, regardless of the theory or method, communication is an essential component of the process. A manager or mediator has to be able to open up communication between the conflicting parties before any solution can be developed.

Mediators and managers have to listen and be open about when they hear. In *Narrative Mediation,* John Winslade and Gerald Monk (2000) discuss how to start a dialogue between two individuals who are fighting. I will describe the process in more detail shortly, but I want to highlight a main point first. Mediators must provide a forum for listening to each side without interruption and without judgment. The idea is to allow each side to present reality as he or she sees it without having to defend the viewpoint. Also, notice I used the term *dialogue.* This means building a shared understanding of the conflict, not pursuing a he said/she said situation. Both parties get a chance to tell their story as they see it. Sometimes, just understanding the other's view of a conflict can be a strong first step to solving the conflict. Is this a simple or easy process? No! Does it always work? No again. However, if you can get those involved in a conflict to actually listen to each other, it's a pretty big step.

As mentioned, *Narrative Mediation* lays out a nicely defined set of steps to deal with conflict. I am presenting the narrative mediation method not because I think it is the best but because it illustrates the complexity of the mediation process and the importance of respect throughout it. Winslade and Monk (2000) break down conflict mediation into three steps:

1. Engagement
2. Deconstructing the conflict-soaked story
3. Constructing an alternative story

These steps are fashioned in order to work with both parties' points of view and representations of reality. Underlying the format and practice of narrative mediation is the concept of discursive formations and the nature of truth. Both are tied into an individual's or a group's subjective representation of history and reality. What is truth to one may not be truth to another.

It is important to understand the concept of discursive formation and how it influences representations of history and power. "Power does not so much adhere to structural positions in hierarchical arrangements as it operates in and through discourse" (Winslade & Monk, 2000, p. 50). Discursive formations provide the foundation for understanding the beliefs and the acceptance of "truth" by individuals and groups. It is how these ideas are articulated, communicated, and presented. Ideas support certain positions over others and bestow entitlements on certain individuals. From this point of view, there is no one universal truth but rather many subjective truths depending on the discursive formation from which it evolved. In the mediation process, there is no right side and wrong side. Everything depends on the discursive formation that the party is working from.

Winslade and Monk use this concept to explain how power structures, reality, and subjective truths all influence conflict. Each side has a unique view of how and why the conflict developed. This is why the first stage of the mediation, engagement, is the telling of stories by both parties involved in the conflict. "Rather than searching for one true story, the narrative mode of thinking welcomes the complexity of competing stories and numerous influential background stories" (Winslade & Monk, 2000, p. 53). It is from the stories that the solutions to the conflict will eventually emerge. In this first stage, the mediator must deal with engaging both parties while providing an area of safety and trust by allowing them to articulate their stories without interruption or judgment.

In the second step, deconstructing the conflict-laden story, the mediator uses naïve questions, as if acting through simple curiosity, to clarify each position. The questions are presented in a simplistic manner, sometimes by just reframing earlier statements. This way, the mediator does not make assumptions or influence the reconstruction of the story with his or her own discursive formation. Using the deconstructed pieces, the mediator helps to externalize the story, to remove it from the personal to a more objective perception of the conflict. This allows both parties to hear and discuss the issues creating the conflict by removing the personal hurt and anger attached to the problem. Blame is not assigned to either party. The conflict is responsible for the harsh emotions, not the parties involved. While deconstructing the story, the mediators use their questions to identify dominant discursive formations and the resulting assumptions of entitlement, as well as alternative discourses (the underlying issues). Issues of respect and entitlement are dealt with in order to move on to an open space where both parties can work together to reconstruct the conflict and build a new story.

The final step, creating an alternative story, is completed after the conflict-soaked story has been deconstructed and both parties begin to agree on common points and achieve a mutual understanding. Parts of the alternative story can come from ideas or thoughts that the conflict had prevented from being articulated previously.

Narrative mediation is a good process for getting two individuals to work through a conflict. The concepts of speaking and listening are the strengths of this approach. The process provides a strong neutral arena in which both parties can discuss the conflict without feeling intimidated. The mediator provides opportunities for everyone to contribute. The importance of discursive listening allows for alternative points of view to be considered. Two individuals can successfully work within this structure to resolve conflict.

There is a significant overall weakness with the narrative mediation process, however, which is the lack of responsibility. The conflicting parties are not expected to accept responsibility for their parts in the conflict. Instead, the conflict is always one step removed from the participants. The conflict, not the parties, is responsible for the problems. While constructing the alternative story is supposed to prevent a regression to earlier behaviors, if the parties are ultimately not responsible, there is no reason for them to change. In addition, narrative mediation does not appear to be appropriate for conflicts between groups larger than two or three individuals. While it seems like a good process for individuals or very small groups, it is difficult to see how it would work with larger groups. The approach and questions focus so much on the individual that it would be challenging to try to translate it into a large group setting.

However, this doesn't mean that narrative mediation does not have applicable ideas for larger group conflict. Communication is important, regardless of the size of the groups involved in the conflict. With larger groups, mediators also have to deal with long-standing problems and regression of the group to past traumas or triumphs. In these cases, rather than try to create a common story, the mediator must work with both sides to find common ground. What is there that both parties share? How can the interests and goals of both sides be integrated to find one common goal? The answers to these questions are never easy, but by identifying common ground, the mediator has uncovered a point of agreement, an area that both sides understand and share. In other words, the mediator identifies a base from which to build more communication, understanding, and eventually resolution.

Mediation is a complicated and highly fluid process. It is impossible to claim that there is one method that will successfully work with any conflict because of the diverse nature of the individuals and groups involved. When dealing with large groups, the mediator must be careful not to diminish or otherwise threaten the group identity. Regardless of the process employed to deal with conflict, to be effective it must provide steps that allow for flexibility and space for different identities so that those involved do not feel loss but rather accomplishment at the resolution.

CASE STUDY

Dawn has just been hired by Funtown Public Library as the new department head for technical services. The department has six staff members: two cataloging librarians, two circulation clerks, one full-time page, and one librarian who handles interlibrary loan (ILL) and other technical services responsibilities. Before being offered the position, Dawn was warned that the department had dealt with some troubles recently, particularly between the professional and paraprofessional staff, which culminated with the resignation of the previous department head. Rather than being scared off by this news, Dawn sees it as a challenge and happily accepts the job.

During Dawn's first month, everyone seems to be working together, although there is a bit of strained or stressed feelings. These feelings intensify after a seemingly minor disagreement between one of the cataloging librarians and one of the circulation clerks. At the time of the disagreement, Dawn approached both individuals with a simple and seemingly balanced solution, which they grudgingly accepted. Then the ILL librarian got upset when the circulation clerks were not turning in the ILL requests as she instructed. The requests were being turned in and filled, but the ILL librarian felt that the clerks should do it in a way that she viewed as more efficient. Again, Dawn came up with a solution that both sides agreed "might" work. However, tensions only got worse. Three months later, the tensions exploded as the ILL librarian chastised one of the circulation clerks in front of a patron. The clerk told the ILL librarian, very loudly, to shut up and leave.

Both employees have come to Dawn with a grievance. To make things worse, the patron has filed a complaint about the incident, feeling she was given poor service. Dawn's boss calls her into his office and tells her to fix the problem. If something like this happens in front of a patron again, Dawn will be looking at disciplinary action.

What is Dawn's next step?

References

Griffin, R. (2008). *Fundamentals of management* (5th ed.). Mason, OH: South-Western, Cengage Learning.

Smith K. K., & Berg, D. N. (1997). *Paradoxes of group life: Understanding conflict, paralysis, and movement in group dynamics.* San Francisco, CA: Jossey-Bass.

Winslade, J., & Monk, G. (2000). *Narrative mediation: A new approach to conflict resolution.* San Francisco, CA: Jossey-Bass.

Further Readings

Lubans, J. (2005, Winter). Disagreeing agreeably. *Library Administration & Management, 19*(1), 36–38.

Rothman, J. (1997). *Resolving identity based conflict: In nations, organizations, and communities.* San Francisco, CA: Jossey-Bass.

Volkan, V. (1997). *Blood lines: From ethnic pride to ethnic terrorism.* Boulder, CO: Westview Press.

Volkan, V. (2004). *Blind trust: Large groups and their leaders in times of crises and terror.* Charlottesville, VA: Pitchstone Publishing.

Volkema, R. J., Farquhar, K., & Bergmann, T. J. (1996). Third-party sensemaking in interpersonal conflicts at work: A theoretical framework. *Human Relations, 49*(11), 1437–1454.

15

DIVERSITY

Lisa K. Hussey

The United States is a diverse society. Depending on where one lives, an individual can access a variety of cultures within a small area. Even within these cultures, there are subcultures, which expand or restrict the values and norms of the prevailing culture. While this might seem overwhelming, this diversity of culture, of language, of experience, and of values is part of what makes the United States as successful as it is. Diversity has potential on both a large and a small scale. Within organizations, diversity can act as a stimulant for innovation and growth, as different ideas are shared and contrasting points of view are considered. In recent years, diversity has become an important idea in management, and there is a growing discussion of the significance of diversity for the continued growth and success of any organization. In manufacturing, diversity can help facilitate new ideas and methods of production. In service organizations, diversity provides a base for understanding the needs and wants of the various groups in a society such as the United States. In a profession such as library and information science (LIS), being able to recognize and provide solutions for these needs are essential for our continued existence.

LIS is both a social and a service profession. Although many things go into what we do, at its very center, LIS is all about providing services to our communities. An integral part of providing these services is understanding the diversity of the community and how that diversity influences needs and expectations. To offer services effectively, one must first be able to identify and recognize the need for such services. If there is only one prevailing view of what constitutes needs or services within a community, opportunities for building relationships and support are overlooked or missed. Essentially, if we cannot meet the needs of our communities, our communities will not support us. Hence, LIS as a profession requires a diversity of backgrounds, experiences, and worldviews to build truly inclusive services. However, while diversity is important and provides amazing potential for any organization, it is also complex and, as with anything worth doing, requires commitment and patience.

DEFINING DIVERSITY

Before discussing diversity in LIS, it's important to define the term *diversity.* The basic definition of diversity is difference—difference between and among various groups and individuals. Differences range from such minor things as reading preferences or hobbies all the way to fundamental differences in ethnic heritages, religious beliefs, and socioeconomic backgrounds. This wide range contributes to the complexity and confusion that often accompany diversity initiatives. When creating a diversity initiative, the expectations and intended outcomes are not always clear. Are we looking for diversity of ideas and thoughts? Are we trying to introduce new cultural norms and values into the organization? Or are we trying to change the look or appearance of the profession? In other words, what exactly are we looking for when we say we want diversity?

In LIS, as in many other disciplines, diversity is a nebulous concept. The term is widely used but usually without an explicit definition, as if there is a widely accepted meaning. The reality is that diversity tends to mean something unique to each person. However, the most common understanding has to do with ethnic background, specifically focused on the "four protected minority categories recognized by the U.S. Equal Opportunity Act: African American, Hispanic/Latino, Asian American, and Native American" (Adkins & Espinal, 2004, p. 53). Although well intentioned, this understanding has a tendency to limit the diversity discussion to a visual diversity, one in which the focus is on characteristics such as skin color and facial features. It is also an approach that tends to put individuals from very different backgrounds into large, all-encompassing groups. These groups (African American, Asian American, Native American, and Hispanic/Latino) condense rich and unique cultures to a minimal and bland common identification, one in which many of those classified find little with which to self-identify. The result is a simplification of diversity, one in which individuals are reduced to these characteristics and broad classifications. This view of diversity can be seen as an attempt to alter the image of a profession without questioning any of the underlying ideas and assumptions that create the values and norms. However, as this tends to be the currently accepted view of diversity in LIS, it's important to spend some time discussing diversity from this point of view.

For over two decades, diversity has been an important topic in LIS. Numerous articles have discussed the lack of diversity in the profession, and various initiatives at the local, state, and national levels were created to increase diversity. Yet, despite these efforts, diversity remains an elusive goal in most libraries, archives, and information centers. LIS tends to be a relatively ethnically homogenous profession. In 2010, the U.S. Bureau of Labor Statistics reported that 83.9% of librarians are white, whereas only 77.1% of the U.S. population is identified as white, according to the 2010 Census (Hixson, Hepler, & Kim, 2011). This is in stark contrast to other community service organizations, such as those based in social work, where 37.4% of professionals are from ethnically diverse backgrounds, and nursing, with 34.4% of practical and licensed professionals identified as ethnic minorities (U.S. Bureau of Labor Statistics, 2010). Unfortunately, despite scholarship and fellowship opportunities, current enrollments in LIS programs don't reflect the numbers needed to improve diversity. According to the 2010 Association for Library and Information Science Education (ALISE) statistics, of those schools reporting enrollment by ethnic origin, almost 82.7% of all students enrolled in an ALA-accredited master of library and information science (MLIS) program are identified as white (ALISE, 2010). Of the accredited MLIS degrees awarded, only 17.7% were to graduates of ethnic origin other than white (ALISE, 2010).

Why are these numbers significant? Well, they show that despite higher enrollments in LIS programs, there has been very little change in the diversity of student bodies or within the LIS professions. It is still a very ethnically white profession. This matters because libraries and archives do not serve only ethnically white communities. Services are more likely to be used if the users can understand their relevance to them, not to just any user, but to themselves. Use can sometimes be better encouraged if presented by professionals who "look like" the users in the community or by individuals as representatives of a culture or community group who can explain how the services are relevant. This is not the only way, or even the most successful way, to increase use in LIS organizations, but the limited representation of diverse ethnic groups creates an image of LIS institutions as white institutions. In other words, who represents the LIS profession does influence how it is perceived.

VISUAL DIVERSITY

The challenges of diversity in LIS are not limited to just solving the problem of improved representation. If the focus is on improving the numbers of only certain ethnic minority groups, the main result will be improved visual diversity. Visual diversity is pretty much exactly what it sounds like—the differences are easy to see. Because this type of diversity is focused almost exclusively on physical characteristics, it can easily evolve into tokenism. "Tokenism is a situation that handicaps members of racial/ethnic minority groups who find themselves working alone or nearly alone among members of another social category" (Niemann, 2003, p. 100). Professionals in this situation often feel alienated, not because they can't see their role in the organization, but because other professionals perceive that the ethnic minority professional was hired solely based on ethnic characteristics, not skills and abilities. There are expectations of additional work, such as participating in diversity committees and outreach programs. In addition, there is a belief that these "token" hires will solve the diversity problem just by being there, when in reality the issues connected with diversity go much deeper and are much more complex. It can result in overwhelming pressure on minorities to do more than white colleagues to prove themselves while at the same time being ostracized from these colleagues. The end result is often burnout and possibly a decision to leave the profession, which only exacerbates the lack of diversity.

It is important to acknowledge that visual diversity does exist in many libraries, particularly public libraries where clerical and assistant positions are filled by individuals from the community. While it is incredibly important to have members of the community working in libraries, it fails to address the issue of diversity in the LIS professions. Clerical and assistant positions rarely, if ever, require the same education as the professional positions. Those who have the MLIS degree are more likely to have the positions of power, to make the decisions about policy and procedure, to support programming choices, and to have the greatest influence on guiding principles, such as the mission and vision. Individuals with authority, such as professionals, supervisors, and managers, have strong sway on the values of the organization, the establishment of behavioral norms, and the overall organizational culture.

In other words, those in positions of authority often control, or heavily influence, what are considered important and legitimate services. Even if there is visual diversity within clerical and paraprofessional positions, homogeneity at the professional level can act as a counter to any influence or contribution from those without authority. Hence, visual diversity is only a minor aspect of the diversity issue.

LANGUAGE OF DIVERSITY

The language of diversity in LIS is another important piece of the overall issue. Without going into a lot of social theory, it is important to understand that what we say and how we say it have meaning, and the significance of that meaning is increased or decreased based on one's power and position, be it as an administrator, as a professional, or simply as a perceived expert. This is reflected in the commonly used definition of diversity that focuses on ethnic minority groups. There is an implied acceptance of these groups as "different" from the norm or as an identifiable "other." This implied difference is also relevant to other diverse groups, such as those based on sexual orientation, religious affiliation, or socioeconomic status. Yet, there is very little discussion or clarification as to what the norm actually is, which in the United States is white middle-class values. Discussions of diversity tend to focus solely on the "others," or those who are different from the norm, without including whites or white culture as part of the discussion. "When whiteness is accepted as an invisible norm . . . white people, their assumptions, and ways are empowered" (Grimes, 2002, p. 382). This practice creates an automatic assumption of what is "right" or "good" and privileges one group simply because of its race.

An example of this language can be seen in the titles and content of some graduate courses focused on diverse populations. Many LIS programs provide classes on diversity, such as "Services to Diverse Users" or "Underserved Populations." These are in fact very important classes. Some students have never considered the variety of services and programming needed to serve a diverse community. However, how the course is presented will provide a basis for serving diverse groups, and not one that is always positive. Although content will differ depending on the instructor, teaching location, and LIS program, the main focus in such courses is how to better serve "other" communities, those that are not part of the norm. The inherent implication is that they are "special," that these groups need help rather than being integrated as a valuable contribution to the collections and the profession. It is not looking at various underserved populations and asking "what can we learn from these groups," but rather making sure these underprivileged and underserved groups learn the "best" way to get information. While both courses can provide an important basis for understanding the wider population, neither really addresses the wider issue of institutional practices that ignore the influence and contribution of white culture. Diversity becomes a focus on "others" rather than on an inclusive concept of integrating differences to improve and grow within an organization.

WHITE PRIVILEGE

All of this underlies another issue in dealing with diversity—the concept of white privilege—which is not discussed often in LIS but is central to understanding barriers to diversity. One way to describe white privilege is as an "invisible package of unearned assets which [any white person] can count on cashing each day, but about which [they] are meant to remain oblivious" (McIntosh, 1988, p. 1). Given the influence of white culture on our society, members of the white race, like myself, often don't understand how much harder it is to succeed as an outsider to the prevailing hegemonic culture. There is little to no recognition of having any advantage because of being white.

White privilege can be seen in institutional practices. Policies and procedures are set up as if everyone is starting from a level playing field, as if everyone has the same opportunities if only they would take advantage of them. This point of view targets the individual, not the group, and is an integral part of white privilege and its view of diversity. "Overemphasizing individuality allows the importance of group issues to be ignored . . . such a focus implies that fairness to individuals is all that matters" (Grimes, 2002, p. 400). When minorities or outsiders succeed, it is because of their individual gifts. However, in failure, these same individuals are often treated as representatives of their specific group, and the failure becomes part of the outside group. Whites, on the other hand, rarely deal with the same level of scrutiny. Failures and successes are usually credited to the individual, and just the individual.

One thing to understand about white privilege is that it is rarely a conscious and overt process. It is the result of the prevailing culture and values in the United States, which reflect those of white culture. Individuals in this culture, despite the privilege, must still work, compete, and sometimes fail, which makes it hard to recognize or acknowledge that it may have been "easier" or that one began from a position of privilege. The strong focus on the individual provides distance from a group affiliation, a process that further downplays the role of race in a white person's success. In the end, hard work is hard work. Success is success, and failure is failure. It is important to remember how these are seen and judged and the assumptions and worldviews of those making the judgments.

There are other challenges to diversity, such as the approaches and attitudes of those who are presenting and/or implementing any diversity initiative or process. If diversity is presented as "something we have to do," then there is automatically a negative attitude attached to the process. However, if it is presented as an opportunity, as a way to build on successful programs, to improve services, and to help the organization evolve, it creates a much more positive starting point. Either way, however, diversity in any form is change, and that needs to be addressed as part of the process.

DIVERSITY INITIATIVES

While diversity initiatives are almost always presented as positive and important, they all are introducing change to an organization. This is not a bad thing, but as any manager will tell you, change is not easy, and even the most positive change creates a feeling of uneasiness and tension. Most people don't like change; it's uncomfortable, and it's easier to simply stick with the status quo. However, in order to stay relevant and to effectively serve diverse communities, there needs to be a diversity of understanding and mind-sets as part of an organization, and there needs to be evolution and change in how things are done. As mentioned in other chapters, change can often lead to conflict. Diversity by its very definition is change. Hence, introducing diversity should be approached with the same thoughtfulness and preparation as planning for and managing change. However, this is often not the case.

Most people would like their diversity initiatives to be viewed as proactive, as actions from an institution to address the needs of all communities before or as they are arriving. In other words, many of these initiatives present an image of a program that is working to construct plans for the improvement of diversity and to create the libraries or information centers of the future. Despite their intentions, the majority of diversity initiatives are actually reactive, as they are often responding to the lack of foresight and action related to a changing society and evolving social priorities. Even many of the most thoughtful and successful programs have in part been created in reaction to the lack of diversity rather than as an early recognition of the current state of and potential growth for diversity within society.

A plethora of articles and books provide suggestions and practices for implanting diversity within organizations. Most of these resources provide reliable, practical steps, ones that have been used in successful diversity projects. Some of the common suggestions are commitment from management, employee buy-in for the programs, diversity training, new recruitment programs, and conducting diversity audits to gain a perspective of the current diversity status of an organization. These suggestions recognize the complexity of introducing diversity and usually present diversity as a process rather than as simple steps. All of these practices have some level of documented success and should be considered in diversity plans. However, although the concept of change is discussed with regard to resources, there is very little (if any) discussion of conflict as part of change.

This is not to say that conflict is entirely ignored, but it is rarely directly addressed. Concepts such as discomfort, disagreements, tension, miscommunication, and related phenomena are often mentioned in place of conflict or dispute. There seems to be some unspoken idea that if you plan for conflict, you are planning for failure. In diversity initiatives, it may seem as if you are expecting racism issues or that anyone who disagrees is automatically prejudiced, which is very often not the case. More often than not, problems arise not from overt racism but rather from more subtle causes, such as misperception based on representations in popular culture, a lack of understanding of various cultural norms, or simply incomplete knowledge regarding the diversity process. However, just because it does not develop from malicious intent does not mean that the potential for conflict should be ignored. Just as with any other change process, when introducing diversity, a manager should allow for the same reactions that surface for any other type of change: tension, unease, and possible conflict.

Recall another aspect of diversity I mentioned earlier, the need for different views and ideas in order to encourage innovation and growth. This goes well beyond visual and ethnic diversity, as it includes concepts that create diversity within and among various groups, such as experience, education, religion, and sexual orientation, to name a few. One of the easiest ways for an organization to falter is to be comfortable with current success and miss opportunities for growth. When there are multiple points of view, there are also more questions regarding decisions, policies, and procedures. Individuals who don't share the same mental models are more likely to ask questions, such as "Why is it done this way?" or "Why don't we try this?" These different views and approaches, while often frustrating, also provide a catalyst for looking at new ideas. When there is homogeneity of thought or vision, the members of an organization won't look for new ideas, as the ideas already in place seem to work. Maintaining this point of view is a great way to lose relevance in our modern, dynamic society. There is always something new, and it's important to be able to critically analyze new things before dismissing them as irrelevant or not important to us.

Despite attempts by various LIS organization, there really is no one-size-fits-all solution for increasing diversity within the profession. Diversity is one of those ideas that needs to be well thought out and considered before implementing. Looking at both successes and failures can provide good insights into possibilities, but whatever process is planned, it must be done within the context of the community served by the library, archive, or information center. Additionally, as a manager, you have to understand how you present and support diversity. As an LIS professional, you also have to consider what you see as "normal" and why. What does this mean about how you will accept difference and change? This is essential to thoughtfully considering and introducing diversity. If those with power—managers, supervisors, and professionals—don't openly and honestly support diversity and model appropriate behaviors, few others will.

CONCLUSION

Let me end with a few basic thoughts. First, diversity is good. It is essential to encourage and develop diversity within organizations, particularly those that focus on service to the wider population. Integration of new ideas and views can help create richer and more relevant services. Diversity allows LIS to evolve and grow, but it also allows the profession to retain its own identity because part of the process is incorporating the past and the current into the new. As I mentioned earlier in this chapter, diversity has great potential. There is almost no limit to what a diverse and well-functioning organization can accomplish. Of course, it's also important to remember that great potential can result in an amazingly positive result or an incredibly horrible failure. Either way, the organization will learn about what is possible and hopefully move forward from there.

Second, diversity is complicated, but that's a big part of what makes it good. Anything that is easy is not as likely to be valued. The amount of this chapter spent discussing the issues should make the complexity of diversity clear. However, despite the fact that it is complex, with the right attitude, managers can make diversity an integral part of how an organization functions. Rather than focus on the "have to" aspect of diversity, managers will be better served by considering the "what we can do" that results from diversity.

Finally, diversity is not an individual thing. Diversity requires commitment from an entire organization, including stakeholders and the wider community. It is a process, one that will have both success and failure. When successful, the next step is to ask how we can build and/or improve on what we are doing. With failure, the organization must learn from mistakes, move on, and find ways to be successful. Ultimately, diversity is not easy. Simple, one-dimensional plans will not result in any real change. This is not to say that small steps are not useful (as they usually are). When all is said and done, it's important to remember that no diversity initiative will ever be perfect. However, any steps toward improving diversity—in every sense of the term—can be seen only as a positive step forward.

EXERCISE

You are the director of Smalltown Library. You are the only library in town, with 15 full-time-equivalent employees. This includes six professional librarians (including the director), five full-time paraprofessionals, and eight part-time clerks and pages. The city closest to you, Bigtown, has grown exponentially over the past decade and has spread its boundaries. As a result, Smalltown is now right on the edge of Bigtown, bordering one of the poorer neighborhoods in the city. In looking at the recent census data, you realize that your town's demographics have changed significantly. Ten years ago, Smalltown was a bedroom commuter town, made up of mostly middle-class families. Now it seems very different. There are still many middle-class families, but now there are also a lot of families classified as living under the poverty line. Two recent immigrant groups, one from South America and one from Sub-Saharan Africa, have settled in Smalltown. The previous census reported that 68% of the population over 18 had at least a bachelor's degree. The latest census shows that this has dropped to 46%. The ethnic breakdown has also changed, reflecting a much more diverse population. Looking over your own data from the past five years, you realize that during this same time, use of the library has dwindled. As the director, you realize that the library needs to diversify its services.

1. What is your first step?
2. What programs or initiatives do you want to introduce?
3. Who is involved in the process?
4. How will you measure the success or failure of your new programs?
5. How do you introduce these ideas to your staff?

References

Adkins, D., & Espinal, I. (2004, April 15). The diversity mandate. *Library Journal, 129*, 52–24.

Association for Library and Information Science Education (ALISE). (2010). *Library and information science statistical report*. Chicago, IL: Author.

Grimes, D. S. (2002). Challenging the status quo? Whiteness in the diversity management literature. *Management Communication Quarterly, 15*, 381–409.

Hixson, L., Hepler, B. B., & Kim, M. O. (2011). *The white population: 2010*. Washington, DC: U.S. Census Bureau. Retrieved from www.census.gov/prod/cen2010/briefs/c2010br-05.pdf

McIntosh, P. (1988). White privilege and male privilege: A personal account of coming to see correspondences through work in Women's Studies. *Center for Research on Women: Working Paper Series*, 189. Memphis, TN: University of Memphis.

Niemann, Y. F. (2003). The psychology of tokenism. In Guillermo Bernal, Joseph E. Trimble, A. Kathleen Burlew, & Frederick T. Leong (Eds.), *The handbook of racial and ethnic minority psychology* (pp. 110–118). Thousand Oaks, CA: Sage Publications.

U.S. Bureau of Labor Statistics. (2010). *Employed persons by detailed occupation, sex, race, and Hispanic or Latino ethnicity*. Retrieved from www.bls.gov/cps/cpsaat11.pdf

Further Readings on Diversity

Adkins, D., & Hussey, L. (2006). Perceptions of the library by Latino college students. *Library Quarterly, 76*(4), 456–480.

Gabriel, R. J. (2010). Diversity in the profession. *Law Library Journal, 102*(1), 147–153.

Gollop, C. J. (1999, July). Library and information science education: Preparing librarians for a multicultural society. *College & Research Libraries, 60*(4), 385–395.

Gomez, M. (2000). Who is most qualified to serve our ethnic-minority communities? *American Libraries, 31*(11), 39–41.

Hall, T. D., & Grady, J. (2006, July). Diversity, recruitment, and retention: Going from lip service to foot patrol. *Public Libraries, 45*, 39–46.

Hankins, R., Sanders, M., & Situ, P. (2003). Diversity initiative vs. residency programs: Agents of change? *College & Research Library News, 64*(5), 308–315.

Hussey, L. (2010, Fall-Winter). The diversity discussion: What are we saying? *Progressive Librarian, 34–35,* 3–10.

Jolivet, L. C., & Knowles, E. C. (1996) Rethinking the Eurocentric library workplace: A multi-faceted process. *Reference Librarian, 54,* 103–114.

Josey, E. J. (1999). Diversity: Political and societal barriers. *Journal of Library Administration, 27*(1/2), 191–202.

Kreitz, P. A. (2008). Best practices for managing organizational diversity. *Journal of Academic Librarianship, 34*(2), 101–120.

McCook, K. P., & Lippincott, K. (1997). Library schools and diversity: Who makes the grade? *Library Journal, 122,* 30–32.

Neely, T. Y. (1998). Diversity in conflict. *Law Library Journal, 90,* 587–601.

Neely, T. Y. (1999). Diversity initiatives and programs: The national approach. *Journal of Library Administration, 27*(1/2), 123–144.

Peterson, L. (1995, July). Multiculturalism: Affirmative or negative action? *Library Journal, 120,* 30–33.

Peterson, L. (1999). The definition of diversity: Two views. A more specific definition. *Journal of Library Administration, 27*(1/2), 17–26.

St. Lifer, E., & Nelson, C. (1997). Unequal opportunities: Race does matter. *Library Journal, 122,* 42–47.

Wiegand, W. (1999, January). Tunnel vision and blind spots: What the past century tells us about the present: Reflections of the twentieth-century history of American librarianship. *Library Quarterly, 69,* 1–19.

Winston, M. (2010, Summer). Managing diversity. *Library Leadership & Management, 24*(3), 58–63.

16

FACILITIES MANAGEMENT

Lenora Berendt

Over the past 20 years, libraries have evolved into facilities that provide and support a variety of services, materials, and programs designed to serve an ever-changing patron landscape. They also serve a multitude of functions, such as providing comfortable, attractive, well-designed public and employee spaces; providing access to electronic resources and broadband Internet; and being an important connection to lifelong learning in their communities. Given this scenario, today's library directors and managers must be adept at handling any number of facilities-related issues at a moment's notice. Unfortunately, such issues are seldom discussed during the course of one's graduate library and information science studies; so, for many librarians, experience becomes a hands-on teacher (Trotta & Trotta, 2001, p. xi).

Responsibilities for maintenance and repair of library buildings requires monitoring safety and sanitation provisions; heating, air-conditioning, plumbing, electrical systems, grounds, and roof maintenance; disaster preparedness; equipment, contracts, insurance, and ADA compliance requirements; and more. It can be a daunting task for any new library director, and being prepared before an emergency occurs is the best way to avoid serious problems. The key is to ensure that a current maintenance plan is in place (and updated regularly) that identifies and defines individuals' responsibilities for the facilities, provides a framework for reviewing and assessing the plan's strengths and weaknesses, and includes policies and procedures to monitor and measure progress (Trotta & Trotta, 2001, p. 3).

OPERATIONS MAINTENANCE

Establishing goals and objectives is of paramount importance to any library facility's maintenance plan. Standards must be identified, documented, and implemented in order for the facility to be prepared for any maintenance issues that may arise. If there is no custodial or janitorial staff, a cleaning service must be engaged to fulfill that need. There must be an agreement between both parties regarding the scope and specifics of the services to be provided as well as an indication of when the contract can legally be terminated by either party.

In addition, specific housekeeping expectations should be clearly identified for the purposes of quality control. This will include designating housekeeping space to contain the necessary equipment and supplies. General building areas as well as restrooms, floors, and mechanical areas should receive daily attention in terms of interior housekeeping (Trotta & Trotta, 2001, p. 14).

Interior Maintenance

Library buildings should be maintained through knowledge and implementation of basic facilities management principles in order to support the functions of the library. Among these functions are providing sanitation and safety, making repairs and renovations, and pursuing beautification projects. Developing a quality-control checklist of tasks is one way of staying on top of daily (and other) maintenance issues. Facility spaces and tasks that should receive daily attention include the following:

- Cleaning drinking fountains
- Cleaning glass entryway doors and windows
- Cleaning restrooms
- Clearing entryway and other walking areas of tripping hazards
- Dusting
- Emptying trash
- Ensuring that all lighting (including emergency lighting) is in working order
- Ensuring that sufficient soap and paper products are readily available
- Regularly removing food from staff kitchen/eating areas
- Sweeping floors and carpets

Among the challenges librarians face these days is the presence of food and drink in library facilities. When such conditions exist, it is imperative that proper refuse receptacles be plentiful and kept clean. Pest control services may be needed to keep insects, mice, and other vermin from finding their way into the library building. Staff must also contribute to maintaining cleanliness in their work areas as well as in any staff lounge and/or kitchen areas where food may be stored or discarded (Robertson, 2009, p. 204).

Seasonal outbreaks of illness, particularly during the winter months, can wreak havoc in libraries if they are not prepared; maintaining a high standard of cleanliness is particularly important during these periods. Provide tissue and hand sanitizer to library visitors, make sure restrooms are cleaned daily, and encourage staff and patrons to wash their hands frequently in order to reduce the spread of bacteria.

When a library contracts with a professional cleaning/janitorial service, it is best to clearly document the library's cleaning expectations. A request to clean the bathroom may be interpreted in a variety of ways, so be sure to clarify which tasks are expected in terms of specific cleaning duties. This can be done by creating a checklist that is shared with the cleaning service and monitoring the work on a regular basis. It's not uncommon that shortcuts are taken and specific tasks fall by the wayside. Keeping your library facility clean and safe for your patrons and staff is one of your most important responsibilities, so be sure that you regularly review the work of your cleaning crew and communicate your expectations clearly and firmly (Robertson, 2009, p. 205).

Exterior Maintenance

Exterior maintenance includes a variety of outdoor tasks, some of which may be necessary on a weekly or daily basis. Clearing stairs, walkways, and parking areas of litter, debris, ice, and snow is crucial for public safety, as is trimming overgrown shrubs, bushes, and low-hanging tree limbs. Lawn care should include mowing the grass as well as removing leaves in the autumn, fertilizing as needed, seeding bare spots on the lawn, weeding, and controlling insects. Maintaining trees may require the assistance of a professional arborist, and landscaping should be done by an experienced gardener or professional. It is also a good idea to be prepared for unexpected weather and keep necessary supplies and resources handy should that occur (Trotta & Trotta, 2001, p. 51).

Daily tasks include emptying trash receptacles, picking up litter, and checking for broken windows and water leaks. Exterior lighting should be checked on a daily basis, particularly in entryways and parking areas. Also be sure to check visibility of library signage and remove graffiti promptly.

Additional exterior maintenance includes roof and gutter repairs, HVAC (heating, ventilation, and air-conditioning) and masonry repairs, power washing (as needed), and asphalt or concrete repairs to sidewalks, entryways, and parking lots. Snow and ice removal and salting/sanding of parking lots and walkways during the winter months is critical to maintaining a safe environment and should be monitored daily.

Developing and maintaining a checklist of tasks to be done daily, weekly, monthly, or seasonally is a great way to monitor the library facility and thus avoid forgetting an important task or process that needs to be completed on a regular basis. Maintaining a list of essential contacts as part of the library's tool kit is an asset in any situation requiring response to a critical situation (Ames and Heid, 2011, p. 11).

General Maintenance

A whole host of responsibilities is required of library directors and facility managers in terms of general maintenance of the facility. Such maintenance tasks may or may not require seasonal attention, but they will most certainly crop up at some point. Once again, maintaining a checklist and a list of contacts for specific services will provide peace of mind in case of an emergency. Among the mechanical, electrical, and plumbing issues that require seasonal or annual inspection are the following (Trotta & Trotta, 2001, pp. 94–95):

- Boilers
- Computer equipment
- Fire alarms and extinguishers
- Heating and air-conditioning units
- Lighting
- Pest control
- Plumbing
- Roofing and gutters
- Sprinkler systems
- Water heaters

Preventive Maintenance

Regular inspections are an excellent way to monitor and plan for maintenance and major repairs and/or improvements. These can be organized into several general categories, as shown in Table 16.1.

As with all major repairs or improvements, it is best to obtain bids and quotes for projects to be done in your facility. Of particular importance is to clarify specific processes, materials used, time lines, and so

TABLE 16.1 PREVENTIVE MAINTENANCE INSPECTION CHECKLIST

Structures	Components
Mechanical systems	❑ Are there heating, cooling, or ventilation malfunctions? ❑ Is there excessive noise? ❑ Are repetitive repairs being made?
Surfaces	❑ Is there cracked/peeling paint? ❑ Are hardware and windows in good repair? ❑ Is there rust? ❑ Is there torn or soiled carpeting?
Electrical systems	❑ Are there adequate outlets? ❑ Is there sufficient lighting? ❑ Are circuit breakers up to date? ❑ Is Internet speed consistent? ❑ Are there flickering or dimming lights?
Buildings	❑ Do walls, foundation, ceilings, stairs, railings, or floors have cracks? ❑ Do roof surfaces, flashing, gutters, or downspouts need cleaning or repairs? ❑ Is there wood rot or deterioration near windows and doors? ❑ Is there evidence of flooding?
Plumbing	❑ Are there leaky/dripping fixtures and pipes? ❑ Is there adequate drainage? ❑ Do toilet fixtures need repair? ❑ Is water pressure adequate?

Note. Adapted from *The Librarian's Facility Management Handbook*, by C. J. Trotta and M. Trotta (New York, NY: Neal-Schuman), pp. 94–95.

forth. No two bids will look alike, so it is the facility manager's responsibility to research and understand the processes in general terms. Understand what is included in the company's guarantee and whether it includes labor, materials, or both.

Once you have garnered a list of reputable, reliable, reasonably priced service resources and providers, keep it updated, and maintain organized files on each for future reference. If you are not sure how to begin, check with other institutions to find out which companies and services they use for their maintenance and repairs.

ENERGY AND ENVIRONMENTAL SYSTEMS MANAGEMENT

Monitoring and maintaining electricity, plumbing, water, heating and cooling, ventilation, humidity, telecommunications and technology, and Internet and digital services is a huge responsibility for today's library director or facilities manager. In addition to providing information, services, programs, and materials, the library must be equipped to maintain a comfortable environment for both patrons and staff. Current policies and procedures should be in place as well as a go-to contact list of suppliers, resources, and other service providers that can be consulted during a crisis or emergency situation.

Electricity

Electricity is among the most important utilities in any facility. It affects energy and maintenance costs, lighting, heating and cooling, and telecommunications and technology, so it behooves the director to complete an energy audit at least once annually. Preventive maintenance is crucial and, because of the dangerous nature of electricity and wiring, should be done by a licensed, professional electrician in order to maintain safe conditions (Trotta & Trotta, 2001, pp. 20–21).

Library patrons expect the best equipment available and the fastest Internet access possible, so maintaining the library's technology and telecommunications equipment is vital to any library facility and must be continually monitored and maintained. Among the items that require attention are the following:

- Bandwidth
- Broadband Internet access (ISP provider)
- Computers, printers, networks
- Electrical outlets
- Fax machines
- Modems
- Phone and T1 lines
- Servers (including backups)
- Wi-Fi

Periodically check your broadband and bandwidth to make sure they are providing the best possible service to your users. The use of uninterrupted power sources (UPS) is also critical for the protection of electrical equipment from power surges and blackouts. Investing in a backup generator in the event all electricity is temporarily lost due to unforeseen circumstances is also good insurance.

Consult the Uniform Electric Code (UEC) for details regarding proper electrical wiring standards as well as information on current trends and developments (Trotta & Trotta, 2001, p. 28). A professional electrician can assist in determining if there is any faulty wiring in your library.

You can save energy on lighting by determining the correct source and amount of lighting needed for the various activities performed in your library. Depending on the amount of illumination needed, specific types of lights can make the most of your library space, and specific scheduled maintenance activities can reduce loss of light and save energy:

- Painting surfaces to ensure that reflective light is at a maximum
- Replacing lamps
- Cleaning lamps and fixtures

Incandescent lights are the most expensive and bulb life is the shortest, but they provide good, comfortable lighting for long periods of time. Fluorescent bulbs provide comfortable light and last much longer than incandescent lights. High-intensity discharge (HID) bulbs last twice as long as fluorescents but do not provide the best color rendition, and the ballasts can be quite noisy.

Finally, it is a good idea to install a backup generator in case all electricity is temporarily lost due to unforeseen circumstances.

Heating, Air-Conditioning, and Ventilation

Maintaining an environment that is temperate and comfortable can be a challenge in many public buildings. Occupational Safety and Health Administration (OSHA) studies indicate that air quality issues are generally due to poor ventilation or inadequate ventilation, so it is important for facility managers to carefully monitor their libraries' ventilation systems. Maintenance tasks for proper air quality include checking:

- Air ducts
- Fans
- Filters
- Humidifiers
- Insulation
- Pipes (for leakage)
- Storage areas

Radon is a naturally occurring radioactive gas that accumulates in small spaces, seeping into buildings through cracks in walls or floors, joints, and floor drains, and can become a serious problem in older structures. Environmental Protection Agency (EPA) recommendations include long-term testing (90+ days) in order to determine radon gas levels. A licensed, experienced contractor should perform this testing and, if needed, recommend measures to lower the radon rate in your building (Trotta & Trotta, 2001, p. 49).

Microclimates are common and make it difficult to maintain comfortable temperatures, even with specialized heating, cooling, and ventilation equipment, referred to as HVAC systems. Microclimates generally occur in cooling towers, cold and hot water and mechanical refrigeration systems, and boilers. One of the biggest issues is human intervention; that is, too many staff members adjusting thermostats too often. Because it is not possible to please everyone in the building, the solution is to designate only one or two people to make adjustments to the temperature in your library. Lock all thermostat units, if possible; clean and/or replace filters regularly; set thermostats automatically by time of day/night and season; and periodically check air ducts if some areas of the library are warmer or colder than the rest of the building (Ames & Heid, 2011; Trotta & Trotta, 2001).

Humidity and Mold Issues

It is not unusual to have materials returned to the library in poorer condition than when they were checked out, but if it appears that an item has been water damaged, it should immediately be deleted from the collection and removed from the facility as soon as possible. Mold spores are common and numerous, so the chances of one item spreading spores to its neighbors on the library shelves is extremely high.

High humidity levels in a library facility can pose serious problems for materials. Materials made with paper are highly susceptible to damage from high levels of humidity, so it is important that the heating and cooling systems control it. Year-round levels of 30% to 40% are the standard and can be maintained by closely monitoring humidity levels and installing a dehumidifier if necessary (Trotta & Trotta, 2001, p. 50).

Mold is a naturally occurring fungus, but its spores can cause and contribute to various health problems, including allergies and congestion as well as more serious health issues, once it has spread to indoor environments. Some molds are toxic, producing poisonous substances that can affect the human body. These substances can be ingested through food, inhaled through air, or absorbed by contact with the skin. Mold issues have become commonplace in today's homes and workplaces and must be dealt with quickly and efficiently. Working with a certified inspector to inspect and test for mold, to remove or abate it when needed, and to clean up mildew is critical to keeping mold under control.

Water

Safe drinking water is regulated by the EPA, and it is important to check water service lines for lead content and other poisonous substances (Trotta & Trotta, 2001, p. 30). Water service lines installed before 1930 contain high-lead content and should be replaced. To ensure that the library is providing safe drinking water, be sure to change filters regularly according to the manufacturer's recommendations, and make sure that all drinking fountains are cleaned and sanitized daily according to documented housekeeping standards (Trotta & Trotta, 2001, p. 49).

Any history of flooding requires monitoring of leaks, standing water, and so forth, which can lead to mold and mildew if left unabated. Consistent monitoring of water leakage is critical and must be done consistently. If necessary, consult with a moisture control specialist to make sure there is no lingering leakage, mold, or mildew (Robertson, 2005, p. 84).

Plumbing

Plumbing includes pipes, drains, valves, and fixtures and may be connected to the HVAC system, which regulates the flow of water, air, and natural gas or oil so that all components run smoothly and efficiently. The best way to handle the plumbing system is through regular, consistent monitoring and preventive maintenance. To keep drains open and functioning, pouring boiling water down them is preferred over using chemicals. In the event of serious clogging of a pipe, a professional plumber should be consulted to handle the situation. Replacing worn-out washers will prevent the loss of water from leaking plumbing fixtures (Trotta & Trotta, 2001, p. 31).

Given the amount of time and effort required to maintain a library facility, it is a good idea to develop a maintenance plan for seasonal and annual review and repair of electrical, mechanical, and plumbing issues that surface over the course of the year. Table 16.2 provides an example of one way to monitor general maintenance via a time line, starting at the beginning of the fiscal year (Trotta & Trotta, 2001, p. 5).

SAFETY AND SECURITY

Maintaining safety and security in the building is among the most important objectives of the facility management plan. Making sure that

TABLE 16.2 SAMPLE MAINTENANCE AND REPAIR CALENDAR

Month	Maintenance Required
July	Clean and repair windows
August	Repair or resurface walkways and parking areas
September	Check/replace heating filters; shampoo carpets
October	Check sewers, outside pipes, downspouts; check roofing and clean gutters
November	Install weather stripping if needed; complete landscape work
December	Inspect security and fire systems, including fire extinguishers
January	Perform indoor repairs/remodeling
February	Inspect plumbing and electrical systems
March	Clean interior and exterior windows
April	Shampoo carpets; check/repair air-conditioning
May	Perform roof repairs, including downspouts and flashing
June	Do interior painting

Note. Adapted from *The Librarian's Facility Management Handbook,* by C. J. Trotta and M. Trotta (New York, NY: Neal-Schuman), p. 5.

all staff understand safety and security policies and can act appropriately at a moment's notice is paramount should an emergency occur. Knowledge of OSHA and EPA rules and regulations and a clear understanding of how to respond to an emergency can save lives. Preparedness is the key, and all employees must be aware of and follow all basic safety procedures. These may include the following (Trotta & Trotta, 2001, p. 114):

- Keep valuables out of public visibility.
- Keep designated doors locked.
- Check the condition and placement of fire extinguishers.
- Do not allow staff to walk alone to their cars after hours.
- Be alert for odd or unusual behavior.
- Tape emergency information to phones.
- Be alert in isolated areas such as elevators, stairwells, and restrooms.

Check all door locks periodically to make sure that they are in good working condition. Have those that are not repaired by a professional locksmith immediately. Install a security alarm, and make sure it is armed when the facility is closed and is linked to the security company as well as the police. Make sure that codes for employees are changed periodically, and be sure that employees do not share this information with others.

Instances of inappropriate and/or violent behavior will occur. All staff members must know when and how to respond. Any behavior that makes a patron or employee uncomfortable need not be tolerated and should be reported immediately. A standard incident report form should be readily available to report and document such situations. Let your security staff and/or police department know that you are open to them walking through the library. This presence often works as a deterrent and may discourage someone from engaging in inappropriate behavior.

Staff should also have code words in place for signaling others in situations where there is the possibility of threat or injury. Speak to your staff about this, and have a plan in place in the event a patron becomes abusive, threatening, or violent. Some libraries install panic buttons that are wired directly to their local police department. Although these measures may seem extreme, they can reduce injury and provide a more secure workplace.

Disaster Planning = Emergency Preparedness

A disaster is basically an emergency situation that has gotten out of control, so putting in place a plan to deal with emergencies can help to stop them from becoming disasters. There are two types of disasters: natural disasters, such a hurricanes, tornadoes, floods, and earthquakes; and disasters that result from human negligence. Libraries are solely responsible for developing detailed, clear disaster plans, yet many do not monitor them on a regular basis. For such plans and manuals to be useful and effective, they must be shared with employees and integrated into the strategic planning process (Wong & Green, 2006, pp. 71–72).

Disaster planning and emergency preparedness are critical to all public facilities and therefore require development of and adherence to a carefully written disaster plan. Consisting of six stages, disaster planning is a circular process and includes the following:

1. Planning
2. Preparation and prevention
3. Response
4. Recovery

5. Preparedness plan
6. Training

An effective disaster manual should include carefully constructed plans, procedures, and processes that will take the library from initial response through recovery from any disaster or emergency. Libraries must also be prepared to respond to disasters that occur outside of the library facility. One example is Hurricane Katrina and the aftermath. Libraries were inundated with people requiring information on supplies and services, because libraries were among the first to provide access to computers (via electricity) in the New Orleans area (Payton & Shields, 2008, p. 188).

It is noteworthy that under its Public Assistance Program, the Federal Emergency Management Agency now includes libraries as eligible for temporary relocation during major emergencies and disasters. Such a decision confirmed what librarians have always known: that "libraries are essential community organizations" (Kay, 2011, p. 1).

Disaster planning is a lengthy process that leads to the ability to understand and practice disaster preparedness. Key elements of an effective disaster preparedness plan include a phone tree with contact names and phone numbers and the order in which they should be called; contact information for emergency departments, insurance companies, and service agencies; policies and procedures for disaster response; an inventory list of salvage supplies/equipment and priorities; and a current floor plan marking locations of fire extinguishers, emergency exits, and any other pertinent items (Payton & Shields, 2008; Wong & Green, 2006).

Specific emergencies can be divided into general categories such as fire, mechanical problems, toxic fumes, flooding, accidents/injuries, and unexpected weather events. No matter what the emergency, it is critical that all administrators and staff be well trained in order to respond quickly and appropriately, no matter what the situation. "Having an ongoing sense of disaster prevention and preparedness is the culminating experience in disaster planning" and should be "an integral part of library administration and management" (Wong & Green, 2006, p. 81). Detailed information on the topic of emergency and disaster preparedness is available on FEMA's website (www.fema.gov).

EPA and OSHA Guidelines

The Occupational Safety and Health Administration (OSHA) and the Environmental Protection Agency (EPA) are proactive organizations in terms of issuing warnings regarding health and safety concerns, enforcing guidelines, auditing for compliance, issuing fines, and ordering shutdowns in cases of extreme noncompliance.

OSHA standards, rules, and regulations and other relevant information must be posted in all high-visibility work areas where employees can readily see them. The Occupational Safety and Health Act of 1970 provides employees with specific rights, and it also states that employees have obligations regarding OSHA. For example, both employers and employees should read, understand, and fulfill their obligations as stipulated by OSHA. The facility manager should closely monitor these practices and make sure that they are implemented and followed by all (Trotta & Trotta, 2001, pp. 118–119).

Americans with Disabilities Act (ADA) Compliance

Another safety and legal issue to keep in mind is to be compliant with the Americans with Disabilities Act (ADA). It is important that all patrons are able to easily navigate the library, and it is up to facility managers to ensure that aisles and other areas are wide enough to accommodate wheelchairs, that any possible obstructions are removed, and that no other types of hazards exist (Association of Specialized and Cooperative Library Agencies [ASCLA], 2010a; Trotta & Trotta, 2001, p. 184–186).

Titles II and III of the Americans with Disabilities Act of 1990 were reviewed and updated in September 2010. The updated version, 2010 ADA Standards for Accessible Design, can be accessed at the U.S. Department of Justice's website (www.ada.gov/2010ADAstandards_index.htm). The ASCLA (2010b) updated its series of tip sheets, which are available on its webpage Library Accessibility—What You Need to Know (www.ala.org/ascla/asclaprotools/accessibilitytipsheets). The ASCLA's (2010a) webpage Important Issues (www.ala.org/ascla/asclaissues/issues) provides links to the following ADA-related resources:

- The ADA Library Kit: Sample ADA-Related Documents to Help You Implement the Law (ASCLA, 2011a)
- APA Style: Removing Bias in Language (Re: People with Disabilities) (American Psychological Association, 2004)
- Australian Library and Information Association: Statement on Library and Information Services for People with a Disability (Australian Library and Information Association, 2011)
- Library Services for People with Disabilities Policy (ASCLA, 2011b)
- Section 508 Home Page (U.S. Government, 2011)

- U.S. Department of Justice ADA Home Page (U.S. Department of Justice, 2011)
- U.S. Department of Labor's Office of Disability Employment Policy (U.S. Department of Labor, n.d.)

One more important resource I'd like to mention is the ALA's (n.d.) Accessibility Basics for Librarians webpage. It is "An Educational Service of the American Library Association's Office for Information Technology Policy (OITP) Prepared by Leslie Harris & Associates and OITP." It currently lists 25 links to explore for more information on the ADA.

FISCAL ORGANIZATION AND RESPONSIBILITY

Because building maintenance and repairs must be performed, monitored, and paid for, it goes without saying that maintaining a budget and being fiscally responsible are important parts of the facilities management process. Current economic conditions often determine how much buying power a library facility can count on, so it is wise to procure funding from alternative sources such as fundraising and grant writing. It is also wise to investigate other, possibly overlooked ways to save money, including monitoring duplication of materials; performing cost/analysis calculations for expensive, upcoming capital projects; ordering supplies and/or equipment in bulk; returning damaged or defective material shipments promptly; regularly reviewing and renegotiating contracts and subscription prices; and keeping theft to a minimum (Trotta & Trotta, 2001, pp. 64–65).

Monitoring the budget on a monthly basis and keeping costs down can have a substantial impact on any budget. The implementation of a strategic plan is another way to focus more closely on specific areas of the budget in order to establish and accomplish the library's priorities effectively.

CONCLUSION

Maintaining a library facility is one of the most important responsibilities of any library director, but with the proper information, planning, and tools, it need not be a daunting task. Developing and implementing clearly documented policies and procedures and working with qualified service professionals will ensure that your library facility is safe and comfortable for all who enter its doors.

CASE STUDY

Alice Cooper is the new director of a small library near a large metropolitan area in the Midwest. The library was without a director for over a year, and the board of trustees hired her with high expectations for improving the library and serving its community of users. Among the top priorities is the development of facilities management and emergency preparedness policies and procedures.

One afternoon after two months into the job, Alice hears a loud voice coming from the computer area of the library and leaves her office to investigate. A patron who has been troublesome in the past is shouting at a child sitting at one of the public computers. Alice tells the patron that he needs to lower his voice, to which he responds by yelling at her for "allowing anybody into the library to use the computers." After asking him again to lower his voice and inviting him to speak to her in private, he continues his tirade, so Alice signals to one of her staff to phone the local police.

After the patron has been escorted from the library, Alice asks the staff where the incident report forms are kept so that she can document the incident. The staff has never heard of such a thing, and, upon further questioning, she realizes that they are fairly unprepared to handle a number of emergency situations. What should her first step be in terms of training the staff? What role, if any, should the staff play in developing effective policies and procedures?

References

American Library Association. (n.d.). *Accessibility basics for librarians.* Retrieved from www.ala.org/ala/aboutala/offices/oitp/emailtutorials/accessibilitya/accessibility.cfm

American Psychology Association. (2004). *Guidelines for non-handicapping language in APA journals.* Retrieved from www.colby.edu/psychology/APA/Bias.pdf

Ames, K., & Heid, G. (2011). Building maintenance and emergency preparedness. *Georgia Library Quarterly, 48*(1), 10–13.

Association of Specialized and Cooperative Library Agencies (ASCLA). (2010a). *Important issues: Americans with Disabilities Act (ADA).* Chicago, IL: American Library Association. Retrieved from www.ala.org/ascla/asclaissues/issues

Association of Specialized and Cooperative Library Agencies (ASCLA). (2010b). *Library accessibility: What you need to know.* Chicago, IL: American Library

Association. Retrieved from www.ala.org/ascla/asclaprotools/accessibility-tipsheets

Association of Specialized and Cooperative Library Agencies (ASCLA). (2011a). *The ADA library kit: Sample ADA-related documents to help you implement the law.* Chicago, IL: American Library Association. Retrieved from www.ala.org/ascla/asclaissues/adalibrarykit

Association of Specialized and Cooperative Library Agencies (ASCLA). (2011b). *Library services for people with disability.* Chicago, IL: American Library Association. Retrieved from www.ala.org/ascla/asclaissues/libraryservices

Australian Library and Information Association. (2011). *Library and information services for people with a disability.* Retrieved from www.alia.org.au/policies/disabilities.html

Kay, M. (2011). *FEMA recognizes libraries as essential community organizations.* Chicago, IL: American Library Association.

Payton, A. M., & Shields, T. T. (2008). Insurance and library facilities. *Library & Archival Security, 21*(2), pp. 187–193.

Robertson, G. (2005). Water finds a way: Dealing with leaks and floods in your library. *Feliciter, 51*(2), 83–85.

Robertson, G. (2009). Not for the squeamish: The dirty truth about your library. *Feliciter, 55*(5), 203–206.

Trotta, C. J., & Trotta, M. (2001). *The librarian's facility management handbook.* New York, NY: Neal-Schuman.

U.S. Department of Justice. (2010). *2010 ADA standards for accessible design.* Retrieved from www.ada.gov/2010ADAstandards_index.htm

U.S. Department of Justice. (2011). ADA home page. Retrieved from www.ada.gov

U.S. Department of Labor. (n.d.). *Disability employment policy resources by topic.* Retrieved from www.dol.gov/odep

U.S. Government. (2011, October). *Section 508.* Retrieved from www.section508.gov

Wong, Y. L., & Green, R. (2006). Disaster planning in libraries. *Journal of Access Services, 4*(3/4), 71–82.

Further Readings on Facilities Management

Cotts, D. G., Roper, K. O., & Payant, R. P. (2009). *The facility management handbook (3rd ed.).* New York, NY: AMACOM.

Kahn, M. (2009). *The library security and safety plan.* Chicago, IL: American Library Association.

Kahn, M. (2012). *Disaster response and planning for libraries.* Chicago, IL: American Library Association.

Page, J. A. (1999). When disaster strikes: First steps in disaster preparedness. *Serials Librarian, 36*(3/4), 347–361.

17

INFORMATION TECHNOLOGY MANAGEMENT

Diane L. Velasquez

First, this has to be said: Technology is always changing. Technology is always in flux. So if you don't like change, then librarianship is the wrong profession for you. In the past 20 years there has been a revolution in libraries of all kinds. Computer technology has invaded. When the silicon chip was invented in the late 1960s, it was determined by one researcher that the capacity of those chips would double every two years—this is Moore's Law (Moore, 1965). There were some early adopters who had computers in their libraries in the early 1980s when the technology was considered prohibitively expensive. The 1980s was the time of the TRS-80, Commodore 64s, Vic 20, and IBM Jrs. Apple also had a small piece of the market with the Apple 2 and Apple 2e. Later the Macintosh was big on the scene as well. All of this predated the opening of the Internet and World Wide Web to the public.

Prior to 1995 the World Wide Web was something academic and Department of Defense researchers used. Even the government was a slight user of this new technology created by Tim Berners-Lee. Little did any of us know what it would be the start of. One thing that needs to be emphasized is that the Internet and the World Wide Web have not always been here; they are still relatively new inventions. The Internet is still being molded into something we can all use. The mass of information and the billions of pages available boggle the mind. Supposedly librarians are experts in finding information. The Internet Archive (n.d.)

says there are over 150 billion webpages. The growth projections are phenomenal. The typical HTML page is 5 KB. By way of contrast the average book is probably 500 KB. The Internet and World Wide Web are not organized in any manner that makes sense. This must also be said: everything is not on the Internet, despite the media's, politicians', and many people's suppositions to the contrary.

How can it be easier to search and find things in the Internet and the World Wide Web? This gets to the idea of metainformation or what is commonly called headings, indexing terms, or classification systems imposed to enhance information retrieval. It is information about information. In fact, the web has no metainformation structure beyond some crude attempts based on knowledge of how search engines work. There is no attempt at a controlled vocabulary, no notion of hierarchy, see references, see also, use for, broader terms (BT), and narrower terms (NT), and only the sketchiest beginnings of Boolean logic in a few of the search engines.

So when we bring public access computers connected to the Internet into our libraries, we have an innate need to understand and organize its content. That being said, we need to understand the technology first. How can we manage something if we don't understand what it is? All libraries have servers, computers, printers, and so on. A desktop computer has a CPU, a computer processing unit, attached to a screen, a keyboard, a mouse, maybe speakers, a printer, a scanner, and so forth. Inside the CPU is where all the power is located. The software makes the hardware run. Understanding how the software makes the hardware run is what this is all about. If the software fails, nothing works. For PC users, the terminology for failure is *blue screen of death;* most know what this means. The computer has locked up and died; it needs to be hard rebooted, and hopefully nothing else is wrong. Mac users at this point just laugh. (The world has been split into Mac users and PC users. Some of us are both. In this chapter, this is moot.)

PROMINENCE OF INFORMATION TECHNOLOGY IN LIBRARIES

In today's libraries, information technology is a large part of the services they provide to the patrons. Computers are part of the tools librarians provide to access information. What kinds of information do librarians provide access to via computers?

1. Ask a Librarian services via chat, e-mail, or instant messaging
2. Commercial databases

3. Digital library branches
4. Digital reference works
5. Educational software
6. E-mail accounts
7. Games
8. Government information—federal, state, local, international
9. Homework resources
10. Interlibrary loan software
11. The Internet
12. OPACs
13. Social networks
14. Software programs for word processing and spreadsheets
15. Technology training

This list is by no means complete; I'm sure all of us can come up with many other things we access electronically. There was a time when computers were in libraries, but only the librarians had access to them and could search the databases. Things have changed a lot in just 20 years.

Because of the prominence of the information technology–based services that libraries offer, the physical resources—software and hardware—that provide the services are a major concern for management. Computers and their paraphernalia take up space in a library, but software and databases in many ways save space. How? Physical reference collections are getting smaller as more and more virtual reference collections become available through multiple vendors, making the print versions obsolete (Garrison, 2011). Current government information is available online. Federal government information prior to 1994, however, is generally still in print. The biggest misconception the public has is that everything is on the Internet. This just isn't so. Many books and references are available only in print. Be careful not to get rid of something unless it truly is available 100% online and in a digital format.

Computer hardware lasts a while but is constantly being upgraded. With the reality of library budgets (academic, public, and special), it probably isn't surprising to hear that most libraries don't replace the hardware unless they have to. In a survey of public libraries, it was found that most don't have a replacement or addition schedule (Bertot, McClure, Wright, Jensen, & Thomas, 2009, p. 19). Those libraries that do upgrade and replace their computers do so on a four-year replacement cycle (Bertot et al., 2009, p. 19). When medium-sized libraries were surveyed in the summer of 2009, the replacement cycle for the majority was also four to five years (Velasquez, 2010).

Even though software and databases can help save space, most public libraries still suffer from lack of space and are unable to add any additional public access Internet-connected computers. Another factor in decisions about hardware is the building's infrastructure, such as locations of electrical outlets and telecommunications lines, and the ease—or not—with which it can be adapted for more technology.

ADAPTING FACILITIES FOR INFORMATION TECHNOLOGY

At some point in their careers, library directors and managers will oversee renovations and adaptations of the building to handle the ever-changing information technology. This role became clear during the interviews conducted for a project completed in 2007 (Velasquez, 2007). When dealing with information technology, the directors or deans had adapted the building in some way or built a new facility. The adaptation can include expanding the facility or just finding new ways to add electrical and telecommunications outlets. Many buildings that academic and public libraries inhabit were built between 1900 and 2000. Buildings built prior to 1995 were not adequately planned with technology and computers in mind.

As an example, that technological challenges are part of the landscape when dealing with older buildings was discovered at the Williamsburg (VA) Regional Library (Kurzeja & Charbeneau, 1999). The library needed to update the children's department and during the renovation devised temporary quarters housed in an old bookmobile (Kurzeja & Charbeneau, 1999, p. 20). Just getting power and telecommunications to the temporary location was something that needed the creative abilities of the staff, but they managed. The staff survived their time in the bookmobile parked in the middle of a retail shopping center parking lot and learned they were more flexible than they realized (Kurzeja & Charbeneau, 1999).

Thomas (2000) discusses how to redefine library space in academic libraries to accommodate both print resources and computers. Her advice is applicable to public libraries as well:

> Librarians sacrificed the esthetics of library spaces as staff turned previously unwired areas into computer rooms. Many retrofitted libraries from that period obscured formerly handsome buildings in a web of cables and surface mounted conduits, replacing visually pleasing rows of bound books on wooden shelves with computers and printers. (p. 409)

Basically the libraries were retrofitting buildings that were not built for technology. One of the best suggestions that Thomas (2000) makes is this:

> Wire new buildings and renovated spaces beyond what is currently required. Think ahead to at least the next renovation. Provide alternatives for bringing both power and data to tables through flat wire and wall mounted cable channels. Design grids of wiring in the floor. Use universal cable to carry voice, data, and local area networks (LAN) access. Power, lighting, and telecommunications are three of the most important elements to consider when planning a library space. (p. 411)

Arizona public libraries have struggled with remaining relevant while adapting their buildings for the Internet age. In an article in *The Arizona Republic* newspaper, Seftel (2007) discussed that adding new services to the public library, like Internet services, brought different groups into the library. Seftel goes on to explain that libraries are reaching out to groups and trying to market books like the bookstores do to increase traffic and circulation.

Seftel (2007) quotes Leslie Burger, a former president of the American Library Association (ALA): "Once we started offering public computing, that brought people back to libraries and attracted a lot of groups that wouldn't have fit our 'library profile' in the past." As the former president of ALA, Burger was commenting on a generalization of Internet public access computing in public libraries.

THE INTERNET IN THE PUBLIC LIBRARY

Computers and the Internet have changed the public library's role in the community and society. Public libraries have had to adapt to the technological revolution that has been ongoing in society and culture since the 1980s. Tables 17.1 and 17.2 illustrate that public libraries did not overwhelmingly embrace computers or the Internet until after 1997. In the tables, "connected to the Internet" refers to both staff and public access computers. The year 1997 coincides with the beginning of the Gates Foundation grants to public libraries for the acquisition of computers and software (Gordon, Gordon, Moore, & Heuertz, 2003). Based on 1994–1996 statistics (Bertot, McClure & Zweizig, 1996), it appears public libraries did not generally provide public access computers until 1997.

TABLE 17.1 PUBLIC LIBRARY USE OF INTERNET AND PUBLIC ACCESS COMPUTERS (1994–2000)

	1994	1996	1997	1998	2000
% Connected to the Internet	20.9*	44.6*	72.3*	83.6†	95.7†
% of Public Access Computers	12.7	27.8	60.4	73.3	94.5

Note. Compiled from various Public Libraries and the Internet surveys: Bertot et al., 1994, 1996; Bertot, McClure, & Fletcher, 1997; Bertot & McClure, 1999, 2000.
*library systems
†library outlets

TABLE 17.2 PUBLIC LIBRARY USE OF INTERNET AND PUBLIC ACCESS COMPUTERS (2002–2011)

	2002	2004	2006	2007	2008	2009	2010	2011
% Connected to the Internet	98.7†	99.6	98.9	99.7	99.7	99.7	99.0	99.3
% of Public Access Computers	95.3	98.4	98.4	99.1	98.9	98.9	—	—
% Wireless	—	17.9	37.0	54.2	65.9	76.4	82.2	85.7
Avg. No of Workstations	8.3	10.8	10.4	10.7	12.0	11.0	14.2	16.0

Note. Compiled from various *Public Libraries and the Internet surveys:* Bertot, McClure, & Thompson, 2002; Bertot, McClure, & Jaeger, 2005; Bertot, McClure, Jaeger, & Ryan, 2006; Bertot et al., 2007; Bertot, McClure, Wright, Jensen, & Thomas, 2008; Bertot et al., 2009; Bertot, Langa, Grimes, Sigler, & Simmons, 2010; Bertot et al., 2011.
†library outlets

Prior to 1997 (Bertot et al., 1996), data from the National Commission of Library and Information Science (NCLIS) indicates that libraries serving a population of over 100,000 were more likely to adopt Internet connectivity than libraries serving smaller populations. Bertot and colleagues (1996) identify two factors for this finding: (1) the vision of either the leadership or the library board and (2) the desire of the library community served. According to the authors, these factors were less important to libraries serving smaller populations because of limited funding for technological innovation (Bertot et al., 1996).

After 1997, the Internet and connecting to the Internet through public access computers were rapidly adopted in public libraries. As can be seen in Tables 17.1 and 17.2, public libraries had 12.7% public access computers in 1994 (Bertot, McClure, & Zweizig, 1994, p. 29); this jumped to 98.9% by 2008. In 2007, the level was the closest to 100% at 99.1% (Bertot, McClure, Thomas, Barton, & McGilvray, 2007). When looking at the data compiled by the many surveys over the years on public libraries by Bertot and his colleagues, it is evident that while public libraries have Internet connectivity and public access computers available for their patrons, some difficulties have started to occur.

Two of the difficulties that public and academic libraries need to deal with at this time are maintaining enough bandwidth and keeping up with the technologies used by PCs and Macs. Public libraries do not usually use Apple products, so the worry there is just keeping up with PC technology, which changes every 18 to 24 months.

In their surveys, Bertot and his associates have tracked wireless connectivity in public libraries since 2004. As can be seen in Table 17.2, wireless penetration rates were at 17.9% in 2004 and rose to 76.4% in 2009. With public libraries maxing out the available space to put in desktop PCs, many of them are putting in wireless connections and purchasing laptops to expand their capability when they have the money.

Another interesting piece of data recorded in Table 17.2 is the average number of computers per public library. This is for all types of libraries no matter where they are located—rural, suburban, or urban. According to the results of the surveys, suburban and urban tend to have more computers than the rural libraries. Again, given the financial standings of these libraries, this makes sense. As can be seen in Table 17.2, from 2008 to 2009 the number of computers decreased slightly from 12 to 11 per library.

HARDWARE AND SOFTWARE ISSUES

It is impossible to keep up to date with how fast technology changes. The best the library can do is to update the hardware every four to five years and the software as often as possible.

Software

When discussing PCs in public or academic libraries, the most important aspect of software is to have adequate virus protection to keep the computers bug free. Many different people will be on the public access computers every day, using files that came from who knows where. Good virus protection will go a long way toward protecting the network, the servers, and the PCs.

Whatever software is used is determined by management and the cost of the software. There are many choices, including open access. Some vendors will offer software at reduced prices to libraries, so make sure to check out all the options before purchasing anything.

Having Apple Macs in an academic environment usually receives a big thumbs-up from the student body. Undergraduates are familiar with Apple hardware and software from their K–12 experience, as Apple has donated equipment to schools nationally and worldwide. My advice on types of hardware and software is to accommodate everyone and don't have one type of computer or software at the expense of another.

One reason I bring this up is that while Microsoft has cornered the market on software, especially in the corporate and government worlds, there are other options, including open access, as mentioned earlier. As far as browsers are concerned, Internet Explorer is not the only option, and having open access options is always a wise idea. I use three different browsers because there are strengths and weaknesses that each one has depending on what I am using it for.

Bandwidth

Bandwidth determines how large a communications packet can be transmitted on the line (copper, coaxial cable, or fiber-optic). In the 1980s and 1990s, most of us were using dial-up, so we were stuck with modems that transmitted only small packets of 56 kb (kilobits) per second of information. This is pretty slow given today's capabilities. Many home Internet users have either DSL (digital subscriber lines) from their phone company or cable modems from their cable company; both methods have varying levels of speeds. DSL runs on a copper, coaxial, or fiber-optic T1 line at 1.544 Mbps (megabits per second). Cable modems, in both homes and businesses, can run on coaxial cable at 512 Kbps to 52 Mbps.

One way to think about bandwidth is to consider how quickly patrons would like instant access to the Internet and its contents. When a computer program is turned on, how fast the e-mail or webpage loads can be of concern to a patron or a staff member. The speed is a function of the bandwidth. Whether or not the library is using desktop personal computers, wireless laptops, or patrons' personal computing devices (smartphones or laptops), the speed with which the different Internet browsers respond is a direct correlation to the bandwidth available in the library. If every desktop PC for patrons and staff is full, and there is a full house on the laptops both library and patron owned, the computers are going to be slower because the traffic is higher. It is similar to traffic during rush hour. The more traffic on the freeway or interstate, the slower it moves. Add in an accident, and it is a snail's pace. If the traffic thins out because there are fewer users, the browsers will speed up. The speed will correlate to the number of users and the bandwidth the library has available connected to the servers and modems.

Servers

The servers in an academic or public library are where the library's programs reside. For instance, the integrated library system (ILS) usually has its own server because it is a large program and would include the catalog. The ILS is made up of modules for the catalog, circulation, acquisitions, serials, and so forth. Commercial databases from different vendors can reside on the same server and will sometimes be collocated with the ILS if there is room and the hard drive on it is partitioned. Being partitioned means that the hard drive has been divided into separate spaces that won't encroach into other areas.

A big problem with servers, as with other types of computers, is that at times they will die. Unfortunately, servers are more expensive than a PC, as their hard drives are larger and backups need to be done on a nightly basis. A battery backup should be running on the server so that if the community does lose electrical power the system will at least not power down suddenly, get overheated, and lose data. Computers are delicate despite how most of us treat them. At times, they need to be babied. So making sure a server is powered down correctly can save data and extend the life of the server.

Electricity

When many of the library buildings were built, the last thing the architects had in mind were computers and the resulting technologies that go along with them. Therefore, one thing that can be sparse is electricity and the corresponding outlets. Printers take more power than computers and scanners. Copiers also take more power. What does this mean? The power a printer or copier pulls from an electrical circuit is larger than what a computer pulls. This becomes a problem especially when an electrical panel has been placed that can handle only a certain number of computers, printers, copiers, and all the other technical paraphernalia that goes with having a library or academic library commons. It may become necessary to add another electrical panel eventually.

This can be expensive in the short run but in the long run is an investment in the library's future expansion plans as more and more computers, laptops, printers, and so forth are brought into the library.

WHAT DOES TECHNOLOGY HAVE TO DO WITH MANAGEMENT?

New deans and library directors have to be able to manage the technology that comes with the library. In the larger academic and urban libraries there is normally someone on the staff who is responsible for the technology. In medium-sized public libraries, there may be someone who has knowledge about information technology (IT) as well as responsibility for it. There is usually an IT department, and sometimes the IT department works in tandem with the library. Smaller libraries, both academic and public, may be responsible for their own technology even if there is no one on staff who knows anything about it. In these cases a consultant may come in for the big jobs, such as loading new software or installing new computers, but the day-to-day stuff is up to the librarians. Sometimes the director or dean becomes the ad hoc IT person because no one else has either the time or the desire.

To manage the technology, the dean or director has to understand what all the jargon means and how it applies to the library. What is our bandwidth? Do we have enough bandwidth for the number of computers, printers, wireless routers, and patrons we have? Can we afford more? Do we want more, and can we handle more with the staffing levels we have? What does all of this cost?

Managing technology is not easy. There are many hard questions, and some patrons always want "more." They don't understand why there are not more computers, databases, printers, and what have you. In addition, unfortunately, the word on the street is that everything patrons need is on the Internet. Our job is to make patrons understand that not only is this false, but many sites where they go for information are not authoritative or offer good information. Our job is to provide great customer service and to help patrons find authoritative sources with great information.

CASE STUDY

Managing information technology is no picnic, although the Friends of the Library have recently donated ten new personal computers and a black-and-white high-speed laser printer. This means the library needs to expand the public access computer space, but there is a roadblock. There is no place to run additional telecommunications cabling, and the electrical panel is full. Additionally, because the electrical panel is full, there are no outlets available out on the floor. Furthermore, there are no desks and chairs for the new computers. The electrician is extremely stressed, as is the director.

Come up with some way to temporarily run the cable to put in ten public access computers and a printer. This will involve solving the following problems:

1. Where will you get the money to pay for new desks and chairs for the computers?
2. How can electrical and Internet outlets be run in the building without totally disrupting normal service?
3. How can the electrical panel issue be dealt with? Is there a way to temporarily provide power while a new panel is put in?

References

Bertot, J. C., Langa, L. A., Grimes, J. M., Sigler, K., & Simmons, S. N. (2010). *2009–2010 public library funding and technical access survey: Survey findings and results.* College Park, MD: Center for Library & Information Innovation. Retrieved from http://ipac.umd.edu/sites/default/files/publications/PLF-TAS_Report_2009-10_Full.pdf

Bertot, J. C., & McClure, C. R. (1999). *Moving toward more effective public Internet access: The 1998 national survey of public library outlet Internet connectivity; a report based on research sponsored by the U.S. National Commission on Libraries and Information Science and the American Library Association.* Washington, DC: U.S. Government Printing Office. Retrieved from http://ipac.umd.edu/sites/default/files/publications/1998_plinternet.pdf

Bertot, J. C., & McClure, C. R. (2000). *Public libraries and the Internet 2000: Summary findings and data tables.* Tallahassee, FL: Information Use Management & Policy Institute, School of Information Studies, Florida State University. Retrieved from http://ipac.umd.edu/sites/default/files/publications/2000_plinternet.pdf

Bertot, J. C., McClure, C. R., & Fletcher, P. D. (1997). *The 1997 national survey of public libraries and the Internet: Final report.* Tallahassee, FL: College of Information, Information Use Management & Policy Institute, Florida State University. Retrieved from www.ii.fsu.edu/content/view/full/6062

Bertot, J. C., McClure, C. R., Thomas, S., Barton, K. M., & McGilvray, J. (2007). *Public libraries and the Internet 2007: Report to the American Library Association.*

Tallahassee, FL: College of Information, Information Use Management & Policy Institute, Florida State University. Retrieved from www.ii.fsu.edu/content/view/full/6062

Bertot, J. C., McClure, C. R., & Thompson, K. M. (2002). *Public libraries and the Internet 2002: Internet connectivity and networked services.* Tallahassee, FL: Information Use Management & Policy Institute, School of Information Studies, Florida State University. Retrieved from http://ipac.umd.edu/sites/default/files/publications/2002_plinternet.pdf

Bertot, J. C., McClure, C. R., Wright, C. B., Jensen, E., & Thomas, S. (2009). *Public libraries and the Internet 2009: Study results and findings.* Tallahassee, FL: College of Information, Information Use Management & Policy Institute, Florida State University. Retrieved from www.ii.fsu.edu/content/view/full/6062

Bertot, J. C., McClure, C. R., & Zweizig, D. L. (1994). *The 1994 national survey of public libraries and the Internet.* Tallahassee, FL: College of Information, Information Use Management & Policy Institute, Florida State University. Retrieved from www.ii.fsu.edu/content/view/full/6062

Bertot, J. C., McClure, C. R., & Zweizig, D. L. (1996). The 1996 national survey of public libraries and the Internet. Tallahassee, FL: College of Information, Information Use Management & Policy Institute, Florida State University. Retrieved from www.ii.fsu.edu/content/view/full/6062

Bertot, J. C., Sigler, K., DeCoster, E., McDermott, A., Katz, S. M., Langa, L. A., et al. (2011). *2010–2011 public library funding and technical access survey: Survey findings and results.* College Park, MD: Information Policy & Access Center. Retrieved from http://ipac.umd.edu/sites/default/files/publications/PLFTAS_Report2010-11_0.pdf

Garrison, J. (2011, Fall). What do we do now? A case for abandoning yesterday and making the future. *Reference & User Services Quarterly, 51*(1), 12–14.

Gordon, A. C., Gordon, M. T., Moore, E., & Heuertz, L. (2003, March 1). The Gates legacy. *Library Journal,* 44–48.

Internet Archive. (n.d.). Home page. Retrieved from www.archive.org/index.php

Kurzeja, K., & Charbeneau, B. (1999, April). Remote but not alone. *Computers in Libraries, 19*(4), 20–26.

Moore, G. E. (1965, April). Cramming more components onto integrated circuits. *Electronics, 38*(8). Retrieved from http://download.intel.com/museum/Moores_Law/Articles-Press_Releases/Gordon_Moore_1965_Article.pdf

Seftel, E. (2007, May 10). Libraries reaching beyond books to remain relevant in Internet age. *The Arizona Republic.* Retrieved from www.azcentral.com/arizonarepublic/arizonaliving/articles/051007.html

Thomas, M. A. (2000, November). Redefining library space: Managing the coexistence of books, computers, and readers. *The Journal of Academic Librarianship, 26*(6), 408–415.

Velasquez, D. L. (2007). *The impact of technology on organizational change in public libraries: A qualitative study.* (Doctoral dissertation). Retrieved from ProQuest Dissertations & Theses. (Accession number 3349069.)

Velasquez, D. L. (2010, December). E-government and public access computers in public libraries. In A. Woodsworth (Ed.), *Advances in librarianship: Exploring the digital frontier* (Vol. 31, pp. 111–132). New York, NY: Emerald.

Further Readings on Information Technology Management

Blowers, H. (2012, June). Benchmarking your technology edge. *Computers in Libraries, 32*(5), 26–28.

Burke, J. J. (2009). *Neal-Schuman library technology companion* (3rd ed.). New York, NY: Neal Schuman.

Cunningham, K. (2010, April). The hidden costs of keeping current: Technology and libraries. *Journal of Library Administration, 50*(3), 217–235.

Knox, K. (2011). *Implementing technology solutions in libraries:* Techniques, tools & tips from the trenches. New York, NY: Information Today.

McKendrick, J. (2012, July/August). The rise of the digital public library. *Computers in Libraries, 32*(6), 17–20.

Moore, A. C., & Wells, K. A. (2009, January). Connecting 24/5 to millennials: Providing academic support services from a learning commons. *The Journal of Academic Librarianship, 35*(1), 75–85.

Zeeman, D., Jones, R., & Dysart, J. (2011, June). Assessing innovation in corporate and government libraries. *Computers in Libraries, 31*(5), 6–15.

18

GRANTS AND THE GRANT WRITING PROCESS

Catherine Hakala-Ausperk

When it comes to money, all managers have two responsibilities. One is stability, and the other is growth. Make no mistake. If you think your only budgetary job will be to effectively tie your library's expenditures to its strategic goals and make sure that, in the end, the numbers balance, then you're not living in the real world. Today, with more and more limitations on and reductions in library funding, a good manager or director must step up and bring in alternative funding. In many cases, that means grants.

In this chapter, you'll learn how to find alternative funding through grants. Most important, you'll learn that you can get those grants! Anyone who is knowledgeable about the organization, dedicated to its success, and eager to advocate for both can be successful at grant writing. Before we get into too many of the details involved, let's agree that this skill is a critical one and get all the traditional excuses out of the way (see The Pros and Cons of Grant Writing).

Managers simply can't ignore this part of the job anymore and pretend there's a justification for doing so. Your library needs you. Your staff needs you. Most of all, your community, customers, and patrons need you to ensure that funding is available—beyond the traditional options—to keep your library on the cutting edge, offering strong programming and resources even in tough financial times. So, let's get some grants coming in so that you and your staff can get to work.

THE PROS AND CONS OF GRANT WRITING

The Cons (or Why Managers Don't Do It)

- I can't afford to hire a development person.
  Use volunteers or a part-time grant person, hire someone to tutor you and your staff, start an internal grant committee—use the staff you have.
- I don't have time.
  I repeat, you're not alone. Let others do it, too! Get volunteers involved.
- Nobody will give us money; we get tax support.
  On the contrary, one glance through materials shows that the services offered by libraries are just what funders are looking to support. Think about it—building job skills, supporting preliteracy activities, keeping teens productive, enhancing the lives of seniors . . .
- I'm a terrible writer.
  Grants come in parts—you can share the written sections with staff who can write. You do the budget part, the calendar, or the reporting. What's your strength?
- It's too complicated.
  Grant applications are like recipes; you just need to follow the directions. Most funders give explicit directions, even to the point of offering preapplication workshops or one-on-one reviews with consultants. Why? Because they want to give the money away! That's what they are there for!

The Pros (or Why You Can Do It)

- It can be learned.
- Funders are looking to support exactly what libraries do!
- Your library will benefit.
- It'll be easier the second time. (And the third . . .)

PREPARE FOR SUCCESS

Gather Your Resources

If you decided all of a sudden that you wanted to speak French, you'd probably take some lessons, right? You wouldn't just try to start doing it. Same if you wanted to play the piano, move closer to a professional goal, or update all of your library's financial forecasting models. An Excel class or piano lessons might be in your future, right? Well, the same can be said for grant writing. One of the primary reasons some attempts at getting grants fail is because the attempt isn't done right. Some library managers, sitting alone in their office, decide one day that the newest initiative is perfect for a grant. So, they write one right off the top of their head. Then, they look around a bit, find a foundation name and address, and send it in. Next comes the rejection. After that, unfortunately, comes the notion that they can't write grants, they can't afford to hire someone who can, or it never works anyway so isn't worth the trouble.

To do anything new successfully, you have to be ready. There are lots of ways to do that. Take a class. Or, better yet, take several classes. If the last time you thought about the details of grant writing was when you read about it while in library school, it's a pretty safe bet that you have a lot yet to learn. There are workshops, courses (some offered by the foundations themselves), support organizations, and—yes—books and articles that can help you prepare for success.

At a local community college in Ohio, a nonprofit support agency offers a series of lectures and classes repeatedly, and many of them feature presentations by actual funders or grant reviewers. Remember, grantors want to give their money away. The goal of any foundation or funding initiative is to give money away and then report back on how the goals of the organization were met. So, get smart and get ready to take on this new challenge. Then, look for help that can make your efforts a success.

Another way to position your library to land grants is to use the talents of people whose life work it is or was to do so. One library advertised a grant researcher volunteer position and was overwhelmed with more than a dozen applicants from the community who wanted to help. Some of these grant professionals were retired and just wanted to use their formidable talents to continue to do some good. Others were laid off or in between jobs and wanted to keep their skills (and résumé) strong. Doing so while also helping the local library they loved was a win-win situation! Still others were working in the field of philanthropy and just wanted to share their knowledge.

It's a good idea if you are going to use volunteers to focus them on researching for funders rather than on writing or presenting the grants themselves. As you'll learn later in this chapter, a large part of grant writing success stems from relationship building that is best accomplished by library leaders directly. One look at *The Foundation Directory* (Foundation Center, 2011) will show you that there are literally thousands of organizations out there with very specific funding goals in mind. That's where your researchers can help—by identifying for your library the perfect match between your needs and the funders' goals.

Again, consider utilizing the professional expertise of people who have studied and professionally succeeded at grant writing for at least part of the process, especially if you're involved in a complicated and technical process. The Foundation Center, for example, has offices throughout the country and does a lot of its work online; it can provide, for a fee, the skills of professionals to help you hone your application to perfection. Sometimes, the small amount of money you'll pay for this professional "tweaking" can be worth its weight in gold when your grant comes through!

Finally, don't forget your staff. Grant applications are puzzles with very specific and often intricate parts that all fit together at the end. One part, for example, might be a thorough financial history and future projection, which you might not be the best person to create. Involve your fiscal officer or someone else on staff with the analytical talent and interest to enhance your application. Often, a complex and rewarding assignment such as this can provide job enrichment, motivation, and a fresh perspective on the value of an employee's role in the organization. The potential transformational impact of the program for which you're seeking funding might be best described by librarians on your frontlines. They see how the library changes lives every day, and perhaps it would be their words that could most effectively convey the goals your program has set.

People, classes, books, and other support staff and resources can and should be part of your preparation for successful grant writing. With all of this behind you for support, you're ready.

IDENTIFY YOUR PROJECT AND YOUR APPROACH

Realizing that you need to grow the financial options for your library, you've prepared yourself to embark on grant writing, and you're almost ready to go. There are just a few more things you have to do before you begin your proposal. First and foremost, you need to know what you want to fund. You need to identify your project. Too many grant applications end up on the receiving end of a refusal letter because someone got the bright idea to "get some money" and then set about looking for someone who had some to give away. Sometimes, even the newsletters that fill your mailbox can lead you down the wrong road. Learning that a funding organization likes to support libraries is not reason enough to embark on a lengthy and often cumbersome process of grant writing without a clear purpose or need in mind.

Some managers try to fit their square peg into a round hole. If they identify a funder who is interested in supporting technology, they begin fervently designing a program to meet those qualifications. The problem, often, is that the program is not needed. Be assured, that fact will reveal itself fast enough.

Rather, to begin the grant quest on a positive note, start at the beginning. Managers, either alone or working with an ad hoc group for support, should begin with their organization's strategic plan and budget in hand. Look carefully too, in these early stages, at your environment and community or customer needs. Inevitably, you're going to recognize a need that your library is unable to meet because of financial restrictions, and you'll have a key requirement in the grant writing process fulfilled. With a clear project in mind, managers should work to fully define it. What is the activity, program, or service to be funded? Why is it needed? Find statistics, both empirical and ephemeral, to support your case as you begin to build it and tie it to the mission and vision statements. What will the objectives of the project be? How will you know—and measure—if you've met them? What kind of a timetable is involved?

Finally, and perhaps most important, with whom will your library partner in this enterprise? There can be no stronger element to any grant proposal than the demonstration of collaboration as part of the plan, at best bringing together many elements of the industry, community, or even other funders. A bit more detail on each of these critical elements is needed:

1. *Need*—The existing need for your project to take place should be carefully and statistically documented. If you're going to offer a workshop series on résumé writing, include proof that there is an unemployment problem in your community. If you want to build a preliteracy center for families, cite kindergarten readiness scores and school studies that prove a lack of readiness of new students to succeed in school.
2. *Objectives*—Use realistic, achievable, and measurable results as objectives of your program or service. Funders want to be confident that their money will be put to good use. Make sure the outcome will be transformational, not just statistically defendable. In other words, don't use "have 50 people attend" as an objective for that résumé writing series. Rather, state that through follow-up communication and evaluations, more than 50% of the attendees will report they were able to land a job as a result of their improved skills.

3. *Measurement and evaluation*—Any seamstress or construction worker will tell you: measure twice, cut once. Take care in describing your evaluative process to ensure you'll be collecting real data, honest feedback, and a meaningful reaction to your program. It's not enough to take a head count at the beginning of an event or offer a "Goldilocks'" survey at the end to measure "great, really great, or fabulous" reactions. Include descriptions of professional, verifiable measurements, and be clear about when and how often you'll take them and how you'll compile and share the feedback.
4. *Timetable*—Illustrate clearly the process you'll go through from beginning to end to achieve your program's objectives. Include all aspects of the event, from selecting and training staff to marketing, presenting, and evaluating the program. Note on your schedule the dates you'll be avoiding and why. Even if specific reporting schedules are not required, you should offer them anyway as proof of your dedication to managing the grant funds well.
5. *Partners*—Money does not have to exchange hands in order for a group, organization, or agency to be considered a partner in your grant. You can and should collect simple letters of support as well to demonstrate to your funder that you run a cooperative and involved organization that has a recognized stake in the community. If you can find funds from other sources, those types of "partners" are also evidence that more people than just you and your staff believe in the project and will be offering support.

Finally, be able to represent your project accurately in terms of dollars and cents. Create a budget to accompany your proposal that is clear, easy to follow, and based in reality (you might even want to include some specifics in an appendix, if that's allowed), and most important that isn't padded for the benefit of the library. You'll be relying heavily on this budget during your reporting stages if you're lucky enough to get the grant, so ground it in a reality that you can support. Look for efficiencies and savings wherever you can, and note that you've done so. Be honest and be clear, and double check to ensure all your figures are accurately calculated.

IDENTIFY AN APPROPRIATE FUNDER

You're now ready to begin looking for the perfect match between what your library wants to do and who or what organization wants to see it done. Now is the time to put all those research skills of your staff to good use. You need to begin researching funders.

First of all, identify all of the places where you want to look. Because you manage a library, your resources list should be endless and at your fingertips. Bibliographies listing even more are also available both online and as appendices to many of the better guides.

If you are starting with corporations, Waddy Thompson (2007), in *The Complete Idiot's Guide to Grant Writing*, suggests that "the business section of your local newspaper and business publications, such as *The Wall Street Journal, Crain's,* and *Fortune,* are important sources of information on corporations (whose stock is up, whose is down) and corporate officers (who's in, who's out)" (p. 87). Furthermore, and perhaps even more valuable, he offers the suggestion that if you "can't stand the thought of reading business publications every day . . . enlist a retired business person to volunteer to do this for you!" (p. 87). Once you've identified a company that appears to be a good match, do even more detailed financial digging by reviewing reports found in EDGAR, the home of official filings with the Securities and Exchange Commission (available online at www.sec.gov/edgar.shmtl). Thompson says that "if your prospect is a top corporate CEO and you have heard that he or she has just received a major stock package, you can get the details from EDGAR and then decide how much to ask for" (p. 87).

But don't stop at commercial enterprises. Some of the best-funded and most generous sources to consider are nonprofit organizations and foundations, most of which exist to fund projects within specific areas of interest. The best place to begin this part of your quest is inarguably the Foundation Center, which describes itself as "the leading source of information about philanthropy worldwide." The Foundation Center can help you "access national, state and metropolitan area data on U.S. Foundations and their grants. Find out the assets and giving of the nation's grantmaking foundations, learn how they distribute their grant dollars, and identify the top recipients of their gifts" (Foundation Center, 2012).

That last part could be the most important thing to discover: what did the funders support recently? Often, a family or organization will turn its focus to a specific cause in reaction to a specific societal need or even because of the whim of a board member. If that focus has recently turned to libraries or literacy or computer education, this might be just the right place for you to start. Do your homework. There's nothing more frustrating than spending your and your staff member's time and energies crafting a well-presented grant application only to find out the donor hasn't awarded money in 10 years or has switched its interest in the past decade to scientific research.

Most useful to you may be that access to the Foundation Center's resource material is no longer limited to only those living in the in the large cities where the Foundation Center's offices are located. In the past few years, in order to extend its services worldwide, the Foundation Center opened more than 400 Cooperating Collections that provide access to their valuable searching tools. Many of these special database collections can be accessed in public libraries, and all locations are available on the Center's website. Additionally, the Center employs skilled grant researchers and writers who, for a fee, will provide even more extensive help for your project.

As mentioned earlier, it's at this point in your grant writing process that you can most successfully utilize the contributions of the volunteers you may have enlisted to be grant researchers. Whether they are retired specialists with years of experience under their belts or newly graduated library students adding to their résumés while job searching, if you can turn them loose on the myriad of books, articles, and databases available in the world of philanthropy, you're more likely to find the perfect match for your program and for your library.

A word of caution, though: remember that many successful grant writers will tell you that the entire process is more about relationships than facts and figures. Limit your volunteers to research and help with grant writing; you, as the manager, or your director should be making personal connections with your potential funders and letting them get to know what you're all about. Make an appointment for an in-person visit to introduce yourself, share your program plans, and let them know that you will be submitting a request for financial support. Invite representatives to your library to see firsthand what you're already doing; then take them to lunch and explain, in layman's terms, what you want to do more of in the future. Follow-up phone calls, e-mails, and even handwritten letters can go a long way toward cementing a real, honest, long-term relationship that can pay off for your library many times over.

Finally, a word is needed about government money. A quick review of your library school course work (or a visit to the American Library Association's or the Public Library Association's website) will remind you that there is a lot of government support for the work of libraries. Specifically and most notably, the Institute of Museum and Library Services, a federal agency whose mission is to inspire and support museums and libraries, provides federal money for major impact projects and

EXPERT ADVICE

Karen Sayre, a donor relations officer for the Cleveland Foundation who has worked in the world of philanthropy for many years, has some advice to share when grant seeking.

What are your top three tips for grant seekers?

Here are my thoughts about what is important for a grant seeker to consider before submitting a proposal or request for funds to a foundation or corporation.

Overarching all the information is a plea for nonprofits to understand that not all foundations are alike and not all proposals can be funded, so to the extent that is possible, grant seekers should try not to take a rejection of the request personally but try to see each submission as an opportunity to introduce the work of the organization to funders and to begin to develop a relationship with them for future requests.

1. Research your funder before any contact is made or proposals sent, and pay close attention to the restrictions to funding.

Many funders have a geographic focus or concentrate dollars in specific interest areas or limit the amount of grants, so if your organization or idea doesn't fit into those guidelines, don't assume that you will be the exception. Guidelines are written for a reason and need to be followed even if they don't make sense. Grant seekers that ignore the guidelines could be eliminated from consideration before getting a reading. For example, if published information on the funder says no phone calls, don't try to call, even if you think you could get through. If you are asked to submit multiple copies of your letter of inquiry or proposal, don't just send the master copy and assume the funder will make the extras. Then if there is a space restriction, don't use smaller typeface just to get more information into the page limit. Having said that, if you think your idea or organization is a fit and there is a contact at the foundation, you might try to schedule a site visit with the foundation staff person—or just a coffee meeting—to introduce the foundation to the work of your organization before you submit a proposal. The relationships that you establish with foundations and corporations are very important to the process of grant seeking, so don't ignore opportunities to get to know potential supporters and let them see the great work your agency is doing.

2. Write a concise and clear proposal that follows the structure that is asked for in the Request for Proposals or in the guidelines.

It is important to understand that program officers and trustees of foundations have to review many submissions for grants, and so it is critical to lay out succinctly who you are, what the need is based on appropriate research, why your organization is qualified to address the need, what the request is for, how you will evaluate the project, and what the budget for the request is. Your proposal should follow the establishment of SMART goals principles. That is, the proposal information should be specific, measurable, achievable, realistic, timely (SMART).

Understand that an effective proposal writer is nothing more or less than a good writer who follows directions. Leave the jargon out of your proposal, and keep the request brief and to the point. Use research to help the reader understand why your agency is equipped to address the problem and how you will know that your approach is appropriate. Include an unambiguous budget, and include additional narrative information for any line items that need more explanation. And finally, once the proposal is complete (using spell-check and grammar-check), have someone else read what has been written and give you feedback on the flow and the clarity of the request. Review the proposal several times before sending it out to a potential funder. Be sure to submit before the deadline, because if you wait until the date due, you might be too late and your request may not be considered at the time of submission.

You may have a standard template for certain types of proposals, such as those for general operating support. The template should be used sparingly, but if you are using a standard format that was submitted to another funder, be sure that you have replaced all allusions to another foundation's name in the submission—that's what the "find" function is for.

3. Keep a calendar to review and update submission and follow-up deadlines and decision dates (if known).

This will help you to keep track of who you have applied to and when you might hear whether or not you were funded. If you don't hear back from the foundation or corporation within a reasonable period of time after the decision date, you might contact the program staff to see what the outcome was. When keeping a calendar, you need to pay close attention to submission deadline dates and allow for the time lag between submission and decision when constructing a well-planned year.

If your proposal was not funded and you have developed a relationship with the foundation or corporate staff, you may ask to review why the request was not funded—what the board liked/disliked—and solicit suggestions on how you might strengthen a future approach. Keep the conversation focused on improving the request in the future, and do not reference the short-sightedness of the funder. Remember, grant seeking and grant making is an ongoing process, and you are building a relationship. Even if the request wasn't funded, your agency and/or project is now known to the funder for future consideration when it might be a fit.

supplies cash to the states, which distribute it as LSTA (Library Services and Technology Act) grants via state libraries. This is a rich and specifically directed resource for libraries that should not be overlooked. Visit your state library's website to learn more about the structure of its LSTA programs, the cycle of giving calendar, and specific services or topics that are today's subjects of interest. Many state librarians offer workshops that are specific to their guidelines and can be a great supporter for managers new to the application process.

Whether your library is asking for $100 from the local department store or $10,000 from a national organization, the right match and a strong connection are paramount to success in grant writing. So search, find, and get to know your funder!

FOLLOW THE GRANT MAKER'S DIRECTIONS

With a blank sheet of paper in front of you and the contact information for the perfect funder in hand, you are ready to begin creating your grant proposal, correct? As a member of the State Library of Ohio's LSTA Advisory Council and a frequent grant reviewer, I can tell you that in many cases the answer to this question is "No!" Many an application I've reviewed has started out a bit left of center, veered widely to the right, and never quite circled back to the main point. In short, the application was all over the map, never came really close to the format required, and ended up leaving most of the pertinent information needed out entirely. Why? The grant writer didn't follow the directions.

While it may seem rather elementary at this stage of the game to say so, you must follow the directions. All grant applications have directions, and you must be familiar with them before you write a word. They are given for a purpose (so that apples can be compared to apples and fair decisions made). If one application comes in at 20 pages long and contains at least one paragraph that takes up the first six, and the next application comes in with a detailed, ten-page budget breakdown that leaves the reviewer wondering what the final point is, it's likely neither will be approved.

Take the preapplication workshop, if there is one. Print out the detailed instructions, if they exist, and follow them to the letter. In short, present what the funder wants to see in the format in which the funder wants to see it, and nothing more. Following directions can get you thousands of dollars, and not following them can end up being a big waste of everyone's time.

When I first applied for LSTA funds (and after taking an ALA course on the topic), I began by inserting into my blank document a copy of the exact requirements provided in the directions, right down to the headings. Then, as I filled in my proposal, I left the headings exactly as I'd copied them and simply inserted my appropriate paragraphs below them. What I ended up with was a grant application that exactly matched the requirements of the program. We got the grant! While I'm not sure that format was completely the reason why, it certainly helped. I have reviewed dozens of applications for worthwhile, pertinent projects that I ultimately had to recommend not funding because there were more missing pieces (and fluff) than valuable information, and, without that information, I simply couldn't evaluate the concept.

Remember, grant reviews follow a score sheet of sorts. If the instructions tell you to list three clear, measurable objectives of your program, for example, it's likely each of those objectives is worth a certain number of points. If you list only one, however descriptive, but never get around to mentioning two more, you've likely lost at least 66% of the potential score you could have earned.

EXPERT ADVICE

Missy Lodge, Ohio's Associate State Librarian for Development and the state's experienced point person for Ohio's LSTA program, answers some questions about constructing the application. You may be surprised at how simple these significant errors can be.

What are the three most common mistakes people make when writing grant proposals?

1. They fail to read instructions and follow funder guidelines/requirements.
Too often those applying for grants do not carefully read and follow grant guidelines and instructions. At the very least this can lead to points being deducted by grant reviewers and, in the worst-case scenario, could lead to the disqualification of the proposal. If a proposal guideline states "no more than four pages," make sure the proposal is no more than four pages. If proposal guidelines indicate they will not fund equipment, do not put equipment in the budget.

2. They fail to proofread the application.
The mistake of not reading and following grant guidelines is closely followed by the mistake of not proofreading the application before it is submitted. In a competitive grant program it is the little things that can sway the decision to fund

or not fund. Extensive typographical errors, not spelling out or explaining acronyms, and extension errors in the budget are huge mistakes that could easily be avoided. Have someone else read the application before it is submitted, not for content, but solely to seek out the typographical, grammatical, and budgetary errors. A clean, well-presented application indicates that you are detail oriented. Your proposal is a product. The look of your proposal, regardless of the content, is a reflection of your library and the writer. The presentation of your application infers that you will also be as conscientious and detail oriented when implementing your project. For me, one of the hardest things to do is to keep reading a proposal that refers to "LISTA" or "LTSA." If an applicant cannot correctly refer to the grant program, my gut reaction is to toss it on the reject pile without reading the entire proposal.

3. They don't understand of the difference between goals, objectives, and activities.

Goals are long-term visions. Objectives are measurable, time-targeted, and benchmarked statements. An objective is what you want to accomplish through the project, and the activities are the specific steps to be taken to address the objective. Too often applications do not include measurable objectives. Instead the stated "objectives" are, in reality, activities. Confusing objectives and activities makes it extremely difficult to develop a good evaluation statement or metric:

What are your top three tips for preparing the best possible application?

Correcting the mistakes just cited would, of course be one tip for getting a grant approved. Aside from that, these are my top three tips for preparing the best possible application.

1. Ask questions.

If applicants have questions about whether or not their proposal idea fits the funding requirements or if applicants have questions while writing the application, they should contact the funder and ask. Although some foundations state in the proposal guidelines they do not wish to be contacted, most funding organizations, including state libraries and the Institute of Museum and Library Services, do want to be contacted. Talking through ideas and questions benefits both the applicant and the funder by making sure that the proposal being submitted meets all requirements and is an idea that the funder feels will merit funding consideration. This saves both entities time and effort; if an idea does not meet funder criteria it is not an efficient use of the applicant's time to move forward, nor is it productive for the funder to review a proposal that does not meet its criteria. For the LSTA program in Ohio, about one-half to two-thirds of applicants each grant round contact state library staff with questions or to have drafts reviewed. Although not all of these projects are funded, they consistently receive higher scores than those applications that are submitted without having contacted state library staff at some point during the process.

2. Make sure your application is mission driven.
Funders want to provide dollars to assist people; they don't want to purchase things. A well-developed proposal is going to focus on a need of the library or within the community, be it for early childhood literacy programs, workforce development assistance, or preservation of a special collection. All items listed in the budget must be tools required to address that community need. Budget items (particularly equipment) should not be purchased just for the sake of acquiring new and/or better equipment or materials. Unfortunately in the LSTA program we too often see "equipment grabs" with no tie to community needs or to providing a program to a targeted population.

3. Have partners.
At the federal, state, and local levels we are hearing more and more about collaboration and partnerships. For grant applicants, having partners is always beneficial, whether partners are required by the funding agency or not. Having partners will strengthen a proposal because it illustrates that the library is not acting in a vacuum with the proposal, and partners show that there is community buy-in and support for the project. Both support partners (those that write letters of support) and active partners (those that are part of the project planning or implementation) benefit any application.

You've spent a lot of time developing the idea for a useful, needed program for your customers. You and perhaps others have done the research legwork needed and found some great potential matches, and you'll spend more quality time writing your actual application. Keep it simple. Follow directions. Submit something that stands a good chance of being read, understood, and approved.

THE FINAL REVIEW

Before sending your grant proposal off and crossing your fingers, have others read it. I knew of one director who felt so superior to the staff that to admit to needing an editor would be paramount to taking a pay cut. Don't let that be you. Remember, lots of library staff members are frustrated (or even former) English majors. Do yourself a favor; no matter how carefully you think you crafted your proposal and edited it yourself, share it before you send it. It's also possible that the funder to whom you're submitting it accepts drafts and will offer presubmission feedback. Ask your evaluators to address these questions, too:

1. Have I used action words? "Sustainability will be achieved," "Success in preliteracy will be measured," and "Employment opportunities will be seized" all sound a lot better than "we will try to help customers find jobs." Do you know how many applications most reviewers read a day? Don't let yours be the one that finally puts them to sleep!
2. Are there spelling errors? Misplaced page breaks? Extra spaces between sections? In short, how does my application look? From the cover page on, it should snap, intrigue, and, most importantly, motivate the reviewer to turn the next page.

Take advantage of any opportunity you can find to send off a polished gem, and it's more likely your grant proposal will end up a winner.

You also need to know when to stop editing. If you've followed the steps outlined in this chapter, your proposal is ready to go. While editing and reviewing is good, too much is just a delay. Stamp it, send it, and move on to the next one.

Once you have mastered the elements of this process, set an annual goal for yourself to send out as many proposals per year as you can. What's the next project you need to have funded? Don't let the work you put into learning this process go to waste. Keep trying!

DENIED?

An editor once wrote this in a letter of rejection: "The girl doesn't, it seems to me, have a special perception or feeling which would lift that book above the 'curiosity' level" (Susie Smith's Children's Stories, 2011). Unfortunately for that editor, the book referred to was *The Diary of Anne Frank.* Although your grant proposal might not be fairly compared to this ageless classic, take the message to heart. If your first, second, or third grant proposal is denied, keep trying. The best approach to take is to back up and review your process, step by step, and try again.

Is the program you're seeking to finance truly worthy? Was it pertinent in the past few years but maybe not so much in today's world? Could the audience it's to serve be broadened or refined? Maybe your program objectives (or, more frequently, measurements) could be more clear or on target. Maybe the funder you located has changed its support focus since your resource was published. Or maybe there's a new supporter out there whose interest is more current or emphatic. Review the application itself with an eye toward the requirements you were to meet and the "big picture" impact you had hoped to have. Can a rewrite help?

There are plenty of areas of need, lots of places with money, and no shortage of benefit to your library to find and secure grants. All that is needed is a manager like you with tenacity, a willingness to learn, and an endless supply of determination to get the job done. Start over. Start writing. Try again!

APPROVED!

You can forget about free time from now on—you've caught the bug! While you reflect on the sense of great accomplishment you'll have after your hard-earned efforts have been rewarded with a check you can bring to the next board meeting, remember that your work here is far from done.

Go back to the funder's instructions regarding implementation, financial and narrative reporting, deadlines to be met, and any other follow-through details that are mentioned and stick to them.

You're going to have a lot of writing and reporting in your future to make sure you use this first money wisely and, best of all, to ensure that you can ask for more in the future (many funders love to see projects they helped initiate grow). Start with writing a thank-you letter. Remember, the relationship you nourished to get you where you are today—holding that check—is something to be cherished and developed. Even if this particular source can't offer future financial support, it undoubtedly has other contacts in the grant arena that can come back to benefit you over and over. Stay in touch. Report fully, report often, and provide the exact measures of follow up that are required of your grant.

Hopefully, your project will succeed, your new financial friendships will multiply, and—here's the most important goal we all share—your library will continue to thrive.

ONE FINAL NOTE ABOUT THE WRITING PROCESS

Many grant applications, while designed to meet a specific organization's, foundation's, or government agency's individual goals and desires, contain similar sections or components. Don't reinvent the wheel with every application you write. Keep copies of the parts that won't change, such as your organization's description and history, your strategic goals, and your statistical performance records, and reuse them (when asked to) in future applications. Sometimes, as with the preparation of multiple résumés for different jobs, just a little tweaking of standardized information can help you match work already done to the specific requirements of a new grant proposal.

CASE STUDY AND DISCUSSION QUESTIONS

An announcement is made that grant money is available for libraries to support preliteracy programs that build reading readiness and help prepare students for success in school. The maximum award will be $25,000, and the library must match this amount. Programs must address a proven need, and the impacts, in both output and outcome, must be measurable. Goals and objectives of the program must match the long-time goals of the organization. Programs must build on existing, successful initiatives. Successful applications will include the involvement and support of several relevant partners. Staff involved in the project must be qualified and must have reasonable time to invest. Applications are due in three months, awards will be granted within 60 days of the deadline, and the entire project must be completed within one year of award. Financial and narrative reports are due quarterly, and an on-site visit must be scheduled with the grantor.

1. How will you form your grant application team? Who will be on it, and why?
2. What will your time line look like?
3. How will you present and justify the need?
4. What will your program entail, and what will its objectives be?
5. How will you measure objectives, output, and outcome?
6. How will your program be evaluated? When? By whom?
7. Who will your grant partners be, and what roles will they have in the application?
8. What will your budget look like?

9. On what existing, successful initiative will your new program be based?
10. Who will lead the grant team, and what will be her or his responsibilities?

Note: It would be ideal to have a group of students work on this case study together, as a good model for how to approach an opportunity like this in the real world. When a grant opportunity is announced, a staff team should form and the application work be shared. The leader can then assemble the various parts of the application, fine-tune them, and remain responsible for seeing that details are covered. Several portions of the application, such as a study of the organization's long-term goals, descriptions of the library's funding and budget, and so forth, can then be saved to be reused in future applications.

FIVE SIMPLE GRANT WRITING TIPS

1. Get to the point. When I write a grant proposal, I sometimes imagine myself explaining the organization and the project to a ten-year-old, my grandmother, a lawyer, and a politician, in the same room, at the same time.
2. KISS: Keep it simple, stupid. Print your proposal on plain white paper without graphic decorations or other distracting features. Use standard margins and fonts. Keep it easy to read.
3. But what is the point? Use the five Ws (and the H). The person reading your proposal needs to understand who, what, when, where, why, and how.
4. Be professional. Focus on your organization's positive qualities, and let your dignified manner show your organization is respectful and responsible.
5. Show that you can measure results. The funding body will be more likely to fund projects that have specific measures in place for both quantitative (based on numbers) and qualitative (based on people) feedback. If I were planning a family games day in the park, a quantitative measure would be the number of people who showed up and the number of people who participated in various games, while a qualitative measure could be based on a short survey handed out to participants.

Note. Adapted from 5 Simple Grant Writing Tips for Proposals That Get Funded, USAfundraising.com, n.d., retrieved from www.usafundraising.com/fundraising-tips/5-simple-grant-writing-tips-for-proposals-that-get-funded

References

Foundation Center. (2011). *The foundation directory.* New York, NY: Columbia University Press.

Foundation Center. (2012). Locate charitable funders for nonprofit organizations. Retrieved from http://foundationcenter.org/findfunders

Susie Smith's Children's Stories. (n.d.). Famous rejections. Retrieved from http://susiesmith13.tripod.com/id12.html

Thompson, W. (2007). *The complete idiot's guide to grant writing* (2nd ed.). Indianapolis, IN: Alpha.

Further Readings on Grants and the Grant Writing Process

Gajda, R., & Tulikangas, R. (2005). *Getting the grant: How educators can write winning proposals and manage successful projects.* Alexandria, VA: Association for Supervision and Curriculum.

Hall-Ellis, S. D., & Jerabek, A. (2003). *Grants for school libraries.* Westport, CT: Libraries Unlimited.

Karsh, E., & Arlen, S. F. (2009). *The only grant-writing book you'll ever need: Top grant writers and grant givers share their secrets.* New York, NY: Basic Books.

Kepler, A. (2011). *The ALA big book of library grant money.* Chicago, IL: ALA Editions.

Landau, H. B. (2010). *Winning library grants: A game plan.* Chicago, IL: ALA Editions.

MacKellar, P. H., & Gerding, S. K. (2010). *Winning grants: A how-to-do-it manual for librarians with multimedia tutorials and grant development tools.* New York, NY: Neal-Schuman.

Staines, G. M. (2010). *Go get that grant! A practical guide for libraries and nonprofit organizations.* Lanham, MD: Scarecrow Press.

19

OUTSOURCING

Heather L. Hill

This chapter differs significantly from the others in this book in that it covers a phenomenon that is not necessarily a strategy chosen by library management but one taken by the library's governing body that can have a significant effect on library management: the outsourcing of the management and staffing of the library—not just one or more services—to a private vendor, which I refer to as whole-library outsourcing. Some outsourcing is not a new phenomenon in libraries; it has been a long-used tool by library management, particularly in cataloging. Even widely used forms of outsourcing are not without controversy, but whole-library outsourcing brings extensive controversy in no small part because of its extent and the fact that the decision is made by the library's governing body, sometimes without consultation with library management. Whole-library outsourcing seems to be a result of the current focus in governance for an increasingly stronger market presence in the public sector. Government libraries were one of the first types to be outsourced in the United States and the United Kingdom, and shortly thereafter special libraries became a part of this trend. Now public libraries, which are the focus of much of this chapter, have come under the purview of outsourcing.

For simplicity's sake, the terms *outsourcing* and *contracting* will be used synonymously throughout this chapter. Another term associated with whole-library outsourcing is *privatization,* a term that seems to hold more controversy in the library community than outsourcing. Those who are opposed to the outsourcing of whole libraries often utilize the word *privatization* perhaps because the connection to the word *private* emphasizes its distinction from *public* and highlights concerns over possible oversight lapses, or perhaps because the concept of outsourcing has such a long history in libraries that there is a need to distinguish a long-used tool of libraries from a new approach to governance.

Determining whether the outsourcing of whole libraries is privatization or not is beyond the scope of this chapter. What needs to be taken into consideration, however, is that none of these terms has a specifically fixed meaning. The nuances of the definitions can change depending on the viewpoint and motivation of the speaker. What cannot be argued against is that market ideology is having a profound effect on how local governing bodies perceive public libraries, and the long-term ramifications of this influence are largely unknown.

HISTORY AND CURRENT STATE OF OUTSOURCING IN LIBRARIES

Used since at least the late 19th century, the earliest forms of outsourcing consisted of librarians providing specialized information to one another. In 1848, William Frederick Poole, future librarian of Boston's Mercantile Library Association, published a journal index that would later become *Poole's Index to Periodical Literature* (Wilson & Fiske, 1900). In 1896, Cleveland Public Librarian William Howard Brett published his *Cumulative Index* to the *Selected List of Periodicals,* which later developed into the *Reader's Guide to Periodical Literature* (Eastman, 1940). Along with indexing, cataloging was a focus for outsourcing. The Library of Congress began making copies of its cataloging cards available to other libraries in 1901 (Taylor, 2004). Throughout the 20th century the use of outsourcing continued to grow and diversify.

Today, outsourcing is often used without comment for those tasks designated as nonlibrary work. These required library tasks, such as cleaning, maintaining the lawn, providing food, preparing payroll, and bookkeeping, are often contracted to companies that specialize in providing such services.

When the scope shifts to traditional library work, outsourced tasks include cataloging and processing, information and communication technologies (ICTs), collection development, and reference. Traditionally, outsourcing has been used to reduce duplication of effort, to perform odd jobs for which it made little sense to stockpile experience, and to obtain necessary expertise and equipment that are beyond the scope of the library's means.

Along with cataloging and indexing, other tasks that are often outsourced include cataloging titles in unfamiliar languages, binding serials, and addressing cataloging backlogs. In addition, many public, academic, and school libraries acquire at least some of their materials shelf-ready, meaning that materials arrive from the vendor cataloged, processed, and ready to be placed on the shelf.

ICTs are among the most frequently outsourced areas in libraries. Outsourced tasks include computer systems and network management, data recovery, retrospective conversion, website design, and website hosting.

Even reference and collection development are not immune to outsourcing. Outsourcing plays an increasing role in the collection development process, as more libraries rely on vendor services such as approval plans, standing orders, and blanket orders. In-house reference is still operated by library staff, but digital reference and services like homework help are sometimes outsourced.

The examples noted here are only a few of the many ways library management uses outsourcing to save money, create solutions to temporary challenges, augment local expertise, and provide increased service hours. As outsourcing has been such a long-used tool in libraries, in many cases it is considered routine and noncontroversial, but occasionally outsourcing has created significant controversy.

In the business community, outsourcing is often seen as a way to shift the provision of peripheral, noncore tasks to contractors to enable the organization to focus more intensely on providing its core services. A significant point of contention in the library community concerns the idea of outsourcing core services. In libraries, core services can be said to consist of cataloging, reference, and collection development. As noted earlier, significant outsourcing occurs in all three. What seems to bring about the most controversy is the extent of the outsourcing as when an entire service is outsourced or when the whole library is outsourced.

OUTSOURCING COMPLETE SERVICES

In 1993, Wright State University Libraries (WSUL) outsourced all of its cataloging and technical services operations to OCLC (Bénaud & Bordeianu, 1999). This was one of the earliest outsourcings of a whole department and proved to be significantly controversial at the time. Originally outsourced because of unspecified "personnel problems" at WSUL (Bénaud & Bordeianu, 1999; Duranceau, 1994), the cataloging continues to be outsourced today. Although complete outsourcing of cataloging is not a frequent arrangement, WSUL is not alone in having made this shift.

In 1996, the Hawaii State Public Library System (HSPLS) outsourced the entirety of the system's collection development, purchasing, processing, and cataloging to one vendor. The decision to outsource these activities was controversial, and criticism increased as knowledge of the effects of the contract became known. The contract rendered Hawaiian librarians essentially powerless to address cataloging problems in their libraries. Materials unsuitable for Hawaiian communities as well as unwanted duplicates entered the system, but library staff no longer had the power to remedy the situation (Knuth & Bair-Mundy, 1998; Strickland, 1999). The contract did not allow for the return of unwanted materials, nor could library staff add local donations to the collection as they had little ability to process materials (Knuth & Bair-Mundy, 1998; Strickland, 1999). The ensuing furor led to the contract being canceled in less than a year. Many of the challenges stemming from the HSPLS experience resulted from the decision to work with only one contractor, the decision to not retain any collection development funds in house, and a final contract that provided no flexibility for local staff.

After the experience in Hawaii, outsourcing collection development to such a level was avoided for many years. It was not until 2004, when the Phoenix Public Library (PPL) outsourced the entirety of its collection development, that such an experiment was repeated. In an effort to avoid the same end result as in Hawaii, PPL uses more than one vendor and has a more flexible contract in place that means needed items are purchased and helps avoid unwanted titles (Hoffert, 2007). PPL continues to contract collection development through vendors, but no other libraries are known to have outsourced collection development to this extent.

These three libraries are not alone in their shift to outsourcing a unit of the library, but they are some of the better-known and more prominent cases that arose from differing circumstances. At WSUL, a mix of a significant cataloging backlog and the inability of staff to reduce it as well as keep up with incoming materials led to outsourcing the entire cataloging unit. In Hawaii, significant budget cuts at the state level led the state librarian to outsource collection development, acquisitions, processing, and cataloging in an effort to avoid laying off staff (Eberhardt, 1997). At PPL, the realization that much of their collection development was already done on approval plan made the shift seem logical (Hoffert, 2007). Misgivings or disagreements with staff, the desire to save money, and a realization that outsourcing was already a significant part of the operation were the catalysts in these scenarios, and there are echoes of these justifications present today in whole-library outsourcing.

OUTSOURCING WHOLE LIBRARIES

Of greatest controversy presently is the outsourcing of the entire management and staffing of public libraries. The type of outsourcing described here exists on a different level than what has been discussed. Up to this point, the discussion has centered on decisions made by library management to address challenges in their libraries. The outsourcing of an entire library's management and staff is a decision made at the level of the library's governing body. Public libraries have only recently turned to whole-library outsourcing, but outsourcing at this level is not new for other types of libraries.

Government Libraries

From the mid-1980s to the mid-1990s, significant efforts were made to outsource government libraries in the United States and the United Kingdom. These efforts were made to increase cost-effectiveness, reduce the size of the civil service, and withdraw public service from areas where a competitive market existed.

The U.S. Office of Management and Budget's (OMB) Circular A-76 (2003) describes the federal government's policy on the performance of commercial activity: "The longstanding policy of the federal government has been to rely on the private sector for needed commercial services. To ensure that the American people receive maximum value for their tax dollars, commercial activities should be subject to the forces of competition" (p. 1, section 4). In 1983, the circular was revised so that "library operations" were included in the examples of commercial activities. Libraries outsourced as a result of the revisions in Circular A-76 included those of the Environmental Protection Agency, the National Oceanic and Atmospheric Administration, the Department of Energy, the Department of Labor, the Bureau of the Census, and the Department of Housing and Urban Development (Kettle, 1993).

During the same time, a somewhat different situation occurred in the United Kingdom. Although there seemed to be an assumption that a contractor could provide service more cost-effectively than the public sector, no contractors willing to take over government library services were found (Burge, 1999). In the early 1990s, the idea of outsourcing government library functions was tested again. This time contractors were available, but most bids came from other public sector units or former public sector organizations (Burge, 1999).

Special Libraries

The outsourcing wave hit special libraries in the 1980s and 1990s. Corporate restructuring, an increased focus on cost-saving measures, and the absence of a library advocate among higher-ranking corporate officials led to the closure of many corporate libraries (Matarazzo, 1981; Portugal,

1997). In place of in-house libraries, many organizations contracted with external information agencies to provide assistance on an as-needed basis.

Public Libraries

Consideration of outsourcing public libraries began in Australia and the United Kingdom in the mid-1990s. Although these arrangements did not succeed in the way they were initially planned, they led to the realization that public libraries were not immune to the wave of public sector outsourcing that was occurring. Many of the challenges faced in attempting to outsource public libraries in the United Kingdom and Australia mirror those encountered in the United States. A particular difficulty faced when attempting to outsource public libraries has been the lack of a competitive market, an issue that surfaced in each of the following attempts at whole-library outsourcing.

In the mid-1990s, public libraries in the United Kingdom and Australia fell under the umbrella of government-mandated compulsory competitive tendering (CCT), where local authorities were required to seek out bids from the private sector for the provision of services heretofore provided in house (Anderson, 1996). In the United Kingdom, certain services, including public libraries, were tested for outsourcing feasibility. In Australia, the focus was not on particular services but on a percentage of the local authority's budget (Anderson, 1996).

Australia's 1994 Local Government Act made Victoria's libraries the first public library sector to be exposed to CCT (Rochester, 2001). During the CCT process the most significant issue became the dearth of bidders; the only entities that placed a bid on running the public libraries were other libraries, in-house bids by current management, and one from a library cooperative (Anderson, 1996). In the end all but one of the bids stayed in house, but because of the new contract system the governance structure of the libraries had to change (Rochester, 2001). The library directors formed regional library corporations and then became the providers of library services that contractually worked with their only "client," the regional library board (Rochester, 2001).

The situation was somewhat different in the United Kingdom. After testing the CCT process with public libraries and realizing there was no viable market, it was decided that public libraries be exempt from CCT (Rochester, 2001). Even with exemption from CCT, some public libraries were still outsourced. Since 1990, six public library systems have been outsourced in the United Kingdom, but only one to a private company. Library services for the Luton Borough Council, London Borough of Redbridge, Wigan Metropolitan Borough Council, and the Glasgow

City Council are delivered through charitable trust models, an arrangement meant to provide, among other benefits, more fundraising flexibility. The Slough Borough Council libraries are managed by another local government, the Essex County Council. The library system for the London Borough of Hounslow was run by a charitable trust from 1998 to 2008 (Ball, Barton, Earl, & Dunk, 2002), but as of 2008 it has been contracted to a private company (Vaizey, 2010).

In 1997, outsourcing came to U.S. public libraries when officials in Riverside County, California, outsourced the management and staffing of their public library system to a private contractor. In the ensuing years, 19 municipalities across the country followed Riverside County's lead, and four others outsourced the management but not the staffing of their public libraries. As of 2012, 18 library systems are still managed and staffed by a private company (see Table 19.1), Two library systems that were wholly outsourced as well as the four communities where only management was contracted have reverted back to public management. The outsourced libraries are a diverse mix of systems that vary in size from a large 34-branch system to single-building operations and are geographically dispersed in five states: California, Tennessee, Oregon, Texas, and Kansas. Similar to the situations in the United Kingdom and Australia, there is a significant lack of competition in the U.S. market to provide public library management and staffing. To date there is only one company providing this service in the United States. For the majority of communities, there have been only two proposals submitted, one from a private vendor and one from the current library staff.

The justifications for outsourcing the public libraries in these communities varied. In some cases there were disputes among local governments that had previously comanaged library services, dissatisfaction with previous library management, and, most significantly, budget shortfalls that made outsourcing seem a solution to new fiscal constraints (Hill, 2009; Ward, 2007; Ward & Carpenter, 2006). These libraries had specific challenges that made outsourcing seem a possible solution. Some sort of strain or contention has been the catalyst for the majority of public library outsourcing in the United States, but healthy communities are not immune. At least two communities have contemplated outsourcing their libraries with seemingly no significant trigger. In these communities the library systems were well supported and considered strong. In one case, a city council member's interest in outsourcing led to exploring the idea but did not result in a contract (Hill, 2009). In another community, interest in exploring outsourcing on the part of the local government did lead to a contract.

TABLE 19.1 U.S. COMMUNITIES THAT HAVE OUTSOURCED THEIR PUBLIC LIBRARIES

Communiity	Year Outsourced Management Began
Riverside County, California	1997
Calabasas, California	1998—no longer under contract 2007
Lancaster, Texas	2001—no longer under contract 2008
Finney County, Kansas	2003
Red Oak, Texas	2003
Collierville, Tennessee	2004
Germantown, Tennessee	2004
Millington, Tennessee	2005
Leander, Texas	2006
Arlington, Tennessee	2007
San Juan, Texas	2007
Jackson-Madison County, Tennessee	2007
Jackson County, Oregon	2007
Redding Shasta County, California	2007
Moorpark, California	2007
Camarillo, California	2010
Collegedale, Tennessee	2011
Santa Clarita, California	2011
Farmer's Branch, Texas	2011
Osceola County, Florida	2012

In libraries being outsourced, management and staff are either shifted to other positions within the local government or let go and advised to apply for a job with the contractor. The contractor hires all management and staff who are then employees of the contractor. Some staff who were public employees of the library do apply for and obtain positions with the contractor, while others do not. The contractor's staff then operates the library in its day-to-day activities over the contract period, generally three to five years. Libraries managed in this fashion are still overseen by a board of directors, and the contracts are written such that these libraries still qualify as public libraries in the states in which they operate. Of those libraries that have made the transition to private management and staffing, only two have reverted back to publicly managed institutions.

In Australia and the United Kingdom, federal government austerity mandates sparked the exploration of outsourcing of public libraries. In the United States, the impetus has come from individual municipalities and counties. Part of the difference here is the governance of libraries in the United States, which is mostly controlled through each state; the criteria for what constitutes a public library in each state varies significantly based on a combination of state laws and regulations laid out by each state library.

NEOLIBERALISM AND NEW PUBLIC MANAGEMENT

In three countries there are similar justifications for outsourcing libraries. These include a desire to save money, a shift in thinking that the public sector should compete with the private sector (as in Australia) or that the public sector should not be involved in services where there is a market provider (as in the United States), and a strong ideological belief that the private sector is intrinsically better than the public sector and will provide better, more innovative services for a reduced cost.

As discussed earlier, outsourcing has long been used in libraries, but current approaches to governance in the public sector have accelerated its use and increased the scope of outsourcing possibilities. A current trend in public service management is an approach called new public management (NPM). NPM is the public governance offshoot of *neoliberalism,* a term coined to describe a growing ideology focused on limiting social safety nets, a belief in the supremacy of the market, and a strong opposition to state intervention (Duménil & Lévy, 2005; Giroux, 2008; Jurik, 2004). The NPM approach includes a strong focus on private sector solutions to public sector challenges. Outsourcing is an integral tool for NPM, and a significant tenet is the need to adopt market and business ideology in the public sector. Increasingly, public services are pushed to adopt capitalist market strategies where community members are customers rather than citizens. NPM has become a "normative model, one signaling a profound shift in how we think about the role of public administrators" (Denhardt & Denhardt, 2007, p. 13). From this approach comes the belief that a reliance on the market and private interests are assumed to be the best path for governance, while state intervention is deemed slow and inefficient (Duménil & Lévy, 2005; Giroux, 2008; Harvey, 2005).

EFFICACY OF OUTSOURCING

Whether outsourcing public libraries leads to the types of solutions that local governments desire is questionable. Studies of outsourced public libraries show mixed results. In some communities, use of the libraries declined after they were outsourced, while in others use increased but with corresponding increases in operational costs (Ward, 2007; Ward & Carpenter, 2006). While the belief in market solutions to public challenges is strong, there is not a competitive market for whole-library outsourcing, as there is only one vendor that currently provides this service. Results have been similarly mixed in Australia, where CCT led libraries to focus more strongly on evaluating library service, but at the same time some of the measurable performance criteria for managing the contracts were found to be meaningless. For example, an early performance criterion for contracted Australian public libraries was to increase sign-ups for library cards; this led to an increase in library cardholders in the community but not to any significant increase in overall library use (Rochester, 2001).

Meaningless or immeasurable performance criteria also plague the contracts for U.S. libraries. Performance criteria include such things as providing reference service and an overall mandate to provide "prompt, friendly, and accurate service" (Jackson County, Oregon, 2007). While few would dismiss the importance of providing "prompt, friendly, and accurate service," how such a criterion can be measured and evaluated is unknown. In another city, the contractor is charged to "define core library performance measurements" (City of Redding, 2006, p. 3), which seems to put the contractor in charge of developing the criteria by which it will be evaluated.

LIBRARY MANAGEMENT REACTIONS TO OUTSOURCING

Library managers and directors in affected communities have taken one of two strategies when whole-library outsourcing became a potential reality: cooperation or competition. The success of the latter strategy has varied. Exact figures of how many library systems chose each strategy are unavailable, but a few key cases can help illustrate the different actions.

Library management and staff in smaller communities seem more likely to actively participate in the outsourcing process. Because of its size, the contractor does provide for certain economies of scale; having access to a broader network of resources can be especially appealing to smaller and rural libraries that often suffer the most from a lack of resources and sometimes have difficulties attracting candidates for positions. In these communities, library staff and management fully cooperated with the development of the outsourcing contract, knowing they would have to reapply for their jobs with the contractor.

At least one library system was completely unaware of the contracting process until the call for bids was released to the public. The library director and staff did then create their own bid for services but lost the contract to the private company. In other communities library management and staff have been put into the awkward position of assisting the local government with developing the contract criteria while also creating their own bid to provide services. In the majority of cases the library staff worked on its own to develop its bid, but in at least two communities the library staff received assistance from its union. Most, but not all, of these communities ended up signing a contract with the private vendor.

Those communities where the current library staff "won" the contract did not form regional library corporations like those in Australia. Rather, the winning bid was the basis for the future library budget. Although some of these libraries continued to be publicly managed, it was not necessarily through the strength of their bid that they remained public. The contractor has more than 15 years experience at creating bids for library services. In no case studied has the current library staff ever underbid the private contractor. In one community, outsourcing the libraries would have hypothetically saved the municipality $500,000 over three years, but the libraries were kept publicly managed because of the public sentiment surrounding the idea (American Library Association, 2007).

What sometimes makes the difference in some communities as to whether the local library is outsourced is not simply a lack of community support for the idea of outsourcing public libraries, but a strong, vocal objection to the idea. Public sentiment also seems to play a role in communities that never advance to the stage of asking for bids for library services. In these communities, citizens vocalize their displeasure at city council meetings, through signed petitions, and in the local media through letters to the editor and editorials. Public support, while a seemingly necessary criterion for the library to remain publicly managed, is not a sufficient criterion. In many communities where there was strong public objection to outsourcing the library, and in the case of Santa Clarita, California, where two lawsuits were filed, the local government outsourced the libraries anyway.

The three connected groups in this process are the library management and staff, the local government in charge of providing library operations, and the community. Anecdotally, there seems to be a correlation between the relationships among these three groups and the potential for outsourcing. In some specific cases, the breakdown of the relationship between local governance and the public library's management led to outsourcing the library. In other cases, attempts by local governance to pursue outsourcing despite significant public criticism perhaps shows an undercurrent of discord already present between local governance and the community at large. Although library managers have limited control over the relationship between the community and local governance, there is a strong incentive to ensure that the library has a strong relationship with local governance and with the community.

LEGISLATIVE EFFORTS TO ADDRESS OUTSOURCING

As mentioned earlier, public libraries in the United States are governed significantly at the state level, and each state has its own criteria for what constitutes a public library. Efforts at the state level have been made both to increase the oversight involved in the public library outsourcing process and to curb it altogether. Legislative changes in California and Florida were the first to address this phenomenon.

On October 8, 2011, California passed Assembly Bill No. 438, which alters the libraries section of the State of California Education Code to provide controls for how the course of outsourcing California public libraries proceeds and what kinds of contracts result. The amended code concerns actions necessary during the outsourcing consideration process and those necessary for the fulfillment of the contract. The entity responsible for public libraries (board of trustees, common council, or other legislative entity) in a community that intends to pursue outsourcing that service must do the following:

1. Publish notice of the proposed action providing meeting date, time, and location for discussing the move.
2. Demonstrate that the contract will result in overall cost sav-

ings. (Costs for monitoring and evaluating the contract are to be included in the calculations.)

3. Ensure that lower pay and benefits for staff are not the sole cause of cost savings.
4. Ensure that the contract does not cause existing library employees to lose their employment or suffer a reduction in wages or benefits.
5. Ensure that library management contracts are the result of public, competitive bidding. (State of California, 2011)

These guidelines attempt to address many of the critiques brought up in the literature, including that it seems many local governments had already decided to outsource before any public discussion could take place, that current contracts have inadequate evaluation criteria, that wages and benefits may be impacted by outsourcing, and that, in many cases, there was no competition for bidding (Hill, 2009; Ward, 2007). What remains to be seen is how this law will actually affect future efforts to outsource public libraries, particularly in light of the complete dearth of a competitive market of providers for such services.

In Florida, changes were made not to the state code but to the definition of what type of entity qualifies for the State Aid to Libraries Program that gives grants to public libraries. Public libraries are not required to work within the guidelines of the State Aid to Libraries Program, but it is in the best interests of many of them to do so. The program provided more than 21 million dollars in grant money to Florida public libraries in 2011 (State of Florida, 2011b).

Through 2010, libraries that qualified for the grant program needed to have a "single administrative head who is an employee of the single library administrative unit" (State of Florida, 2010b). The Florida Department of State, Division of Library & Information Services, proposed in 2010 to alter this sentence to read, "single administrative head must be employed *full-time* by either the cooperative's governing body or a participating local government" (emphasis added) (State of Florida, 2011a).

This seemingly small change provides a significant impediment to public library outsourcing in the state. As mentioned earlier, the process for outsourcing a public library to this point had included management as well as staff. If the administrative head of a library, in order to be eligible for the State Aid to Libraries Grants, must be a full-time employee of the governing body, then the possibility of outsourcing public libraries in Florida is somewhat dimmed.

In response to the initial proposed wording change, the private library management company filed an administrative challenge. It argued that the changes would preclude it from doing business in the state when it had already spent more than $600,000 between 2004 and 2010 in soliciting contracts and marketing (State of Florida, 2010a). The court dismissed the claim, finding that the company's interest was merely speculative because currently no Florida public libraries were under a management contract (State of Florida, 2010a).

The changes made to the State Aid to Libraries Program stalled public library outsourcing in the state until 2012 when Osceola County contracted with the vendor for whole-library outsourcing. Osceola County was able to contract with the vendor and still qualify for State Aide to Libraries Grants.

FUTURE OF OUTSOURCED LIBRARIES

Australian public libraries seem settled in their contractual agreements, but fiscal difficulties in the United Kingdom have led to a growing interest in the idea of outsourcing more public libraries. In September 2011, the Wandsworth Borough Council decided that there is a small, yet viable market for public library services management and has opened public libraries to competitive bids (Director of Leisure and Amenity Services, 2011). Other communities in the United Kingdom are exploring outsourcing as a potential cost-saving alternative to significantly reducing hours or closing libraries. In the United States there was a gap in 2008 and 2009 when no libraries were outsourced, but in 2011 there was a sudden spike as three systems were contracted (see Table 19.1).

Outsourcing of whole libraries is still a rare phenomenon when one considers the thousands of public libraries in existence, but there is no reason to doubt it will increase in the future. Outsourcing of management and staff seems a particularly attractive option in times of financial distress as local governments look to do more, or at least the same, with less. As local governments adopt the tenets of NPM, with its push for increased outsourcing and reliance on the market for the provision of services, and as they feel increased budget crunches, public library budgets may well be a target, and outsourcing the entire library may be an approach adopted by more municipalities. Of course the reality of money savings is still to be proved, but current public governance philosophy assumes a faith in the market that public management seems not to share, namely, that the private market, because of competition, is cheaper and more responsive than public management.

References

American Library Association. (2007). Bedford mayor nixes outsourcing. *American Libraries Online.* Retrieved from www.ala.org/ala/alonline/currentnews/newsarchive/2007/august2007/bedfordnixes.cfm

Anderson, C. (1996). Contracting out in public libraries: The DNH study. *APLIS, 9*(1), 57–62.

Ball, D., Barton, D., Earl, C., & Dunk, L. (2002). A study of outsourcing and externalization by libraries: With additional references to the museums and archives domains. *Bournemouth University Occasional Papers on Library & Information Services, 5.*

Bénaud, C., & Bordeianu, S. (1999). Outsourcing in academic libraries: A selective bibliography. *Reference Services Review, 27*(1), 78–89.

Boss, R. W., & White, H. S. (1998). Guide to outsourcing in libraries. *Library Technology Reports, 34*(5), 563.

Burge, S. (1999). Much pain, little gain: Privatization and UK government libraries. *Inspel, 33*(1), 10–19.

City of Redding. (2006). *Request for proposals for administration and operations of the Redding Municipal Library and Shasta County Library System* (schedule number 3926). Redding, CA: Author.

Denhardt, J., & Denhardt, R. (2007). *The new public service: Serving not steering.* Armonk, NY: M. E. Sharpe.

Director of Leisure and Amenity Services. (2011). *Environment, culture, and community safety overview and scrutiny committee—14th September 2011.* Wandsworth Borough Council, London, United Kingdom. Retrieved from http://ww3.wandsworth.gov.uk/moderngov/mgConvert2PDF.aspx?ID=14838

Duménil, G., & Lévy D. (2005). The neoliberal (counter-) revolution. In A. Saad-Filho & D. Johnston (Eds.), *Neoliberalism: A critical reader* (pp. 9–19). Ann Arbor, MI: Pluto.

Duranceau, E. (1994). Vendors and librarians speak on outsourcing, cataloging, and acquisitions. *Serials Review, 20*(3), 69–84.

Eastman, L. (1940). *Portrait of a librarian, William Howard Brett.* Chicago, IL: American Library Association.

Eberhardt, G. M. (1997). The outsourcing dilemma. *American Libraries, 28,* 54–56.

Giroux, H. (2008). *Against the terror of neoliberalism: Politics beyond the age of greed.* Boulder, CO: Paradigm.

Harvey, D. (2005). *A brief history of neoliberalism.* New York, NY: Oxford University Press.

Hill, H. L. (2009). *Outsourcing the public library: A critical discourse analysis* (Doctoral dissertation). Retrieved from https://mospace.umsystem.edu/xmlui/bitstream/handle/10355/6126/research.pdf?sequence=3

Hoffert, B. (2007, September 1). Who's selecting now? *Library Journal, 132*(14), 40–41.

Jackson County, Oregon. (2007). *Professional services agreement between Jackson County and Library Systems & Services, LLC.* Document number 10712014.3.

Jurik, N. C. (2004). Imagining justice: Challenging the privatization of public life. *Social Problems, 51*(1), 1–15.

Kettle, D. (1993). *Sharing power: Public governance and private markets.* Washington, DC: Brookings Institute.

Knuth, R., & Bair-Mundy, D. G. (1998). Revolt over outsourcing: Hawaii's librarians speak out about contracted selection. *Collection Management, 23*(1/2), 81–112.

Matarazzo, J. M. (1981). *Closing the corporate library: Case studies on the decision-making process.* New York, NY: Special Libraries Association.

Office of Management and Budget. (2003). *Circular No. A-76: Performance of commercial activities.* Washington, DC: Author. Retrieved from www.whitehouse.gov/omb/circulars_a076_a76_incl_tech_correction

Portugal, F. (1997). *Exploring outsourcing: Case studies of corporate libraries.* New York, NY: Special Libraries Association.

Rochester, R. (2001). No real competition: Compulsory competitive tendering in Victorian Regional Library Corporations. *APLIS, 14*(4), 121–136.

State of California. (2011, October 8). *County free libraries: Withdrawal: Use of private contractors* (AB 438, Ch. 611). California State Legislature. Retrieved from www.leginfo.ca.gov/pub/11-12/bill/asm/ab_0401-0450/ab_438_bill_20111008_chaptered.html

State of Florida. (2010a). *Final order of dismissal, Library Systems and Services, L.L.C., petitioner, vs. Department of State, Division of Library and Information Services, respondent, and the Florida Library Association, intervener.* Division of Administrative Hearings, Case no. 09–4289RP. Retrieved from www.doah.state.fl.us/docdoc/2009/004289/09004289DWH-012810-13052905.pdf

State of Florida. (2010b). *Operating grants. Florida Statute 257.17. Public lands and property, public libraries and state archives.* California State Legislature. Retrieved from www.leg.state.fl.us/Statutes/index.cfm?App_mode=Display_Statute&Search_String=&URL=0200-0299/0257/Sections/0257.17.html

State of Florida (2011a). *State aid to libraries grants* (Grant information fact sheet). Department of State, Division of Library & Information Services. Retrieved from http://dlis.dos.state.fl.us/bld/grants/StateAid/Stateaidinfo.pdf

State of Florida (2011b). *State aid to libraries grant: Guidelines & application.* Department of State, Division of Library & Information Services. Retrieved from http://dlis.dos.state.fl.us/bld/grants/grants_docs/2012-2013_StateAid_Packet.pdf

Strickland, S. (1999). Outsourcing: The Hawaii experience. *Journal of Library Administration, 29*(2), 63–72.

Taylor, A. G. (2004). *The organization of information* (2nd ed.). Westport, CT: Libraries Unlimited.

Vaizey, E. (2010, July). *Re-modeling partnerships to meet the challenges of 2010.* Re-modeling Library Services Conference, London. Retrieved from www.culture.gov.uk/news/ministers_speeches/7223.aspx

Ward, R. C. (2007). The outsourcing of public library management: An analysis of the application of new public management theories from the principal-agent perspective. *Administration & Society, 38,* 627–648.

Ward, R. C., & Carpenter, M. (2006). Contracting public library management to private vendors: The new public management model. *Advances in Library Administration, 23,* 141–172.

Wilson, J. G., & Fiske, J. (Eds.). (1900). *Appleton's cyclopaedia of American biography* (Vol. 5). New York, NY: D. Appleton.

Further Readings on Outsourcing

American Library Association. (n.d.). *ALA professional resources on outsourcing and privatization in libraries.* Retrieved from www.ala.org/ala/aboutala/offices/oif/iftoolkits/outsourcing/default.cfm#statements

American Library Association. (n.d.). *Professional tips: Outsourcing.* Retrieved from http://wikis.ala.org/professionaltips/index.php?title=Outsourcing

Jensen, P. H., & Stonecash, R. E. (2005). Incentives and the efficiency of public sector outsourcing. *Journal of Economic Surveys, 19*(5), 767–787.

Martin, R., Brown, S. L., Claes, J., Gray, C. A., Hardin, G., Judkins, T. K., et al. (2000). *The impact of outsourcing and privatization on library services and management. A study for the American Library Association.* Denton, TX: Texas Woman's University. Retrieved from www.ala.org/tools/sites/ala.org.tools/files/content/outsourcing/outsourcing_doc.pdf

20

FUTURE TRENDS

Lisa K. Hussey and Diane L. Velasquez

As we've discussed throughout this book, planning and forecasting for the future are essential parts of management. To do this, managers must not only think about the future and remember the past but also understand that change is an inherent part of an organization and of society. Managers must be able to work with the present while preparing for the future. Peter Drucker identified the ability to anticipate change and to recognize opportunity as a vital leadership characteristic (Drucker, 1990). However, looking for the important trends is also one of the most important responsibilities of any manager. So, to end this book, we thought it important to spend a few pages talking about some of the trends we've experienced and considering a few of the trends we think might be important in the future.

Library and information science (LIS) like any other industry has trends that ebb and flow with the passing of time. Over the past 20 years many changes have created differences in the ways libraries, no matter what kind, are perceived by patrons, by funders, and by society as a whole. The biggest change has been the introduction of computer technologies into the societal fabric of our world. Computers entered not just libraries and information centers but also all the realms where we live, work, and play. Technology has become omnipresent in American society. Consider for a moment that when the power goes out many of us don't know what to do with ourselves because none of the things that we use works. If it happens in our workplace we are even more stymied because so much of our day-to-day work is tied up in what we do in front of a computer screen.

Trends in library and information centers are tied not only to technology but also to how we use it as a tool. Many times we get ahead of ourselves and think that the computers will take over the world.

Well, someone has to operate the technology, and libraries are well positioned not only to provide access to technology but also to educate patrons on how to evaluate and effectively use technology. Libraries and librarians can also act as mediators between digital natives and older methods of accessing information. I remember watching a television crime show recently in which the power grid went off and none of the digital devices the folks used in the show worked. There was one guy who was totally prepared because he had lived in the world before computers. He could run the mimeograph machine that worked without electricity, he had Polaroid cameras that took instant pictures, and he set up a bulletin board in place of the plasma TV. He had no problem going back to the time before computers because he wasn't real comfortable with computers anyway. The basic strategy the crime team used to catch the bad guy did not change, but the tools they used were different. It's important in LIS to acknowledge that technology is more than just computers; it's also books, microfiche, and all the other tools we use to provide access to materials and information.

The ability to predict the future in LIS is not a stable art form. At best, forecasting is an educated guess about the future, but it is an important step nonetheless. As professionals and managers, librarians and information professionals need to pay attention to trends and to expectations in society. Many of the future trends come from the corporate world; this sector tends to be 10 years ahead of government and nonprofits because it has the money to spend on the latest and greatest technology and tools. Trends and issues in the for-profit world tend to trickle down into nonprofits and governmental agencies, so LIS professionals, particularly managers, should look beyond their organization to make decisions about and plan for the future. While far from comprehensive, the following discussion covers a few of the significant trends and changes LIS faces in the future.

ECONOMIC ISSUES

Economic issues will always exist for libraries, archives, and information centers. As these organizations are nonprofits or government agencies, the funding for the library or information center resides in a parent organization such as a city, town, village, or county. Even libraries and archives in for-profit organizations have no ability to generate revenue for the good of the institution and are often seen as a financial burden. Therefore, libraries and related organizations must depend on outside sources, such as property taxes, tuition dollars, government funding, donations, and revenue from other departments to cover their budgets. In times of prosperity, libraries often enjoy more donations and may not have to fight as hard for budget dollars. In harsh economic climates, however, libraries must scrape, pinch, and beg in order to maintain a working budget. Regardless of the larger economic status, libraries will always need to prove why they are important and why they are relevant in order to receive funding. This is how it has always been, and we don't see this ever changing. Rather than seeing this as a burden, librarians and information professionals should approach it as a challenge. How do we, as a profession and as an organization, make sure our community and funders understand why we are relevant and important?

There are many examples of economic issues in libraries, such as continual changes in the global markets and financial world, perceptions of technology being more important than libraries and thus leading to budget cuts, and shifting demographics that result in fluctuations in funding streams like property taxes and tuition dollars. During the Great Depression, libraries managed to maintain services even when they were unable to improve collections. In the prosperous 1950s, libraries were built as new communities emerged in the suburbs. During the harder economic times of the 1970s and 1980s, libraries began limiting hours and freezing new hires. Graduate LIS programs were shut down as their relevance to the larger university were questioned. In recent times, we've seen the real estate market crash, the Big Three automakers bailed out by the U.S. government, and the banking industry falter. The result has been a strain on finances at all levels, particularly for entities that depend on public funding, such as public libraries.

As is often the case with economic issues in the United States, the people who are hit the hardest are the middle and working classes. In 2008, the economic meltdown was caused by the real estate bubble bursting and devaluing housing prices and property values. There were multiple causes for this crash, including poor decision making and questionable business practices. Subprime mortgages were being offered to people who could not afford them. This caused housing foreclosures at a rate never seen before in U.S. history, which resulted in a rapid decrease in property values. In some real estate markets, the price of property has dropped anywhere from 10% to 50%. The net result was a correlating drop in real estate taxes, monies that cities and counties rely on to pay for their services and programs, such as the police department, fire department, libraries, and park services. When the taxes received began to decrease, city management had to make cuts in their budgets. In many cities and towns, libraries and parks and recreation departments are the first things that are cut. Libraries are asked to do more with less, often as use increases because of the economic hardship within the community. This is common for rural, suburban, and small urban areas, but as this book is being written it is hitting the larger urban areas as well. One of the first was Philadelphia, when the Free Library of Philadelphia was faced with cuts for the first time in its history. The trend spread into dense urban areas like Los Angeles, New York, Boston, and Chicago. Los Angeles and Boston both had very unique solutions (Hussey & Velasquez, 2011). The Boston Public Library (BPL) made the requested cuts very public and used the support of the community to advocate for continued funding. Although BPL did have to deal with cuts to its budget, the community support helped to build awareness and saved four branch libraries from closure (Hussey & Velasquez, 2011). During 2010, the Los Angeles Public Library (LAPL) cut 328 positions with a flat library budget, which led to cutting hours to only five days a week across the LAPL system. In March 2011, the City of Los Angeles voters approved a measure to increase the library department's funding out of the city's budget incrementally over four years from 1.75% to 3.0% (Hussey & Velasquez, 2011). Chicago has a new mayor who just cut staff by 30% and the budget by $8 million (Public Libraries, 2011; Spielman, 2011). More libraries will be affected as time goes on, the national unemployment rate stays above 8%, and foreclosures continue in some of these areas.

How the library deals with budget cuts is just as important as how the patron views these cuts. Losing hours of service, programs, and materials is hard on your patrons and can be made worse by a library director who does not first consider the community but rather focuses first on the library. When cuts must be made, how the community is affected should be the first thought; next is how the library can maintain the most essential services as seen by the community—not as seen by the library. By building rapport with the city, county, or university management, deans and directors can get their libraries on the list of things that are important to fund. The alternative is that patrons and users will live without the library—not a good option for any of us (White, 1996).

TECHNOLOGY

Technological changes over the past 10 to 12 years have occurred at a faster pace than before. Consider that at one time you could access the Internet and World Wide Web only through a computer that had an Ethernet connection. Now you can use laptops, smartphones, netbooks, and other types of computing hardware that have the appropriate software with Wi-Fi access. Wires are optional. The change from wired to wireless access is a huge change. In less than 20 years, the Internet has become a central place for information seeking, and the tools used to access the Internet have evolved from desktop computers to phones or tablets that can be carried in a pocket or a purse. We have moved from slow dial-up connections to speedy wireless connections since 1995. This is a very rapid change, and the trend seems to be a continually increasing pace of innovation and change in technology. We'll discuss a couple of the more recent trends in technology.

Hardware and Software

When dealing with technology, it is important for managers to remember the underlying mission of libraries and information centers: service. Sometimes we get too caught up in our artifacts, such as the books and magazines we provide, and forget the purpose of our organizations, which is to provide our communities with the services they need. Fifteen years ago, we provided services through card catalogs and reference desks. Now, we use databases, online reference, and e-mail to help our patrons locate information at a distance. Technology didn't change the need to provide good services; it simply changed the tools with which we do this.

Technology, computers, and all of the gadgets are simply tools. Computers and their peripherals are cool tools that can be fun, as we have discussed throughout the book. Technology changes quickly, as we have discussed throughout the book as well. There is always something new and interesting out there for us to try. As Moore's Law states that the computing power of computer chips doubles every 24 months or so (Moore, 1965), the idea that computers and all the devices that we currently play with will change every 18–24 months is something to consider as well.

Currently in academic and public libraries most computers are approximately four years old and are changed out on a four- to seven-year cycle (Bertot, McClure, Wright, Jensen, & Thomas, 2009; Velasquez, 2010). The software may be changed more frequently than that, depending on the software licensing agreement between the vendor and the institution. This being said, open access software has begun to make an appearance on campuses and in public libraries. Open source software is software that is available free or inexpensively in its source code, which allows for local changes and innovation. On campuses the push for open source software many times comes from faculty, not from the library, but it can benefit all involved. Open source software is a way to expose students to a type of software or experience that may not be possible without expensive site licenses that the university or library cannot afford. In library and information schools, some faculty will choose open access options for teaching online instead of using the course management software provided by the university. It is a matter of what the faculty member is used to using. Regardless, librarians need to be aware of the various types of software available and required by faculty throughout the academic institution. Although there is almost always a separate IT department in academic institutions, the library is often the only place that is open when students are struggling with their work and need to ask questions. Being aware and being able to help makes the library relevant and useful to both students and faculty.

Distance Education

The nature of education has changed with technology. Twenty years ago, distance education usually involved a correspondence course that might include video relay. Today, distance education relies heavily on online classrooms run on software and incorporates lectures, discussion boards, chat rooms, and e-mail, among other tools. In this new digital education world, libraries still need to provide the same high level of service to students who are now scattered across a large geographical area. The challenge is to provide the same service to students at a distance as those who can come into the physical library. This challenge is not limited to academic libraries, as public libraries often become the "home" library for distance education students. Technologies such as electronic databases and online reserves, and services such as interlibrary loan and online or e-mail reference allow libraries to continue to provide good service. However, as the opportunities for distance education continue to grow, librarians and information professionals need to consider what they can do to meet the needs of these students.

E-readers

Another technological change that has occurred rapidly, and one we envision will continue evolving, is the use of e-devices. In this case, we are talking about e-book devices. Today, when you want to read a book, you don't have to go to the library and check out a physical book. You can access the books in a number of difference formats—EPUB and AZW being among the most popular—downloaded into a Kindle, Nook, or other e-reading device or onto a computer, netbook, smartphone, or iPad. The ability to read or listen to a book in a number of different formats has opened up the publishing industry. Like the music industry when iPods were established, the publishing industry was not 100% open to the idea of the new formats because it meant having to deal with authors and their agents for royalties, copyright, and publishing rights for yet another format. Some authors go directly to e-publishing instead of first publishing something in print as a way to self-publish and make money directly. Readers benefit too because e-books can be less expensive than books mediated by a publisher; there are no middlemen (think of the publisher) or other costs to be factored in. Self-publishing also means that everything is done by the author, from writing the book through establishing the distribution methods, which can be tiring. Publishers do earn their money, because they handle all those little details that authors don't have to.

What do e-books mean for the library? Most librarians are familiar with OverDrive, the company that handles downloads to most of the e-readers, smartphones, computers, and tablets on the market. Library staff have to know how to use various e-readers so that they can troubleshoot if a patron has difficulty with a download of an e-book (Dunneback, 2011). The three most popular e-readers are Amazon's Kindle, Barnes and Noble's Nook, and Sony's Reader, and each one has various generations of hardware and versions of software. Then there are the apps that transform computers, tablets, and smartphones into e-readers. Another way a book can be downloaded is in Adobe as a PDF file.

Determining what books to purchase through OverDrive is another task for each library's genre experts. The majority of articles and experts suggest purchasing a small amount of books every week because the website that each library will have on OverDrive will show the 100 newest books purchased for that week (Orr, 2011). Purchasing in small quantities allows the library, whether purchasing as part of a consortium or on its own, to constantly purchase new books (Dunneback, 2011; Orr, 2011). Another thing to consider is that sales statistics for 2010 show that e-books are 6.4% of 2.57 billion books sold in all formats (Kelley, 2011). This is a large increase from 0.6% in 2008 (Kelley, 2011). Sales of e-readers have also gone up considerably. Now that libraries are able to check out e-books, the expectation is that the circulation of e-books will increase too.

E-books have been in libraries for over a decade (Breeding, 2011), and how e-book lending is managed should now become a larger part of the discussion. When record albums first came into libraries they were treated as "other." Then came CDs and VHS tapes, and the audiovisual department was founded. This department handled something "other" than books and was treated as the red-headed stepchild. No one wanted to manage it, and it was usually one of the smaller sections in the libraries.

Movies have transitioned from VHS tapes to DVDs, and Playaways are becoming part of library collections. Books on tape and CDs, like DVDs, are shelved away from the books and again managed separately. Many times the DVDs or the CDs are more expensive than the books they represent, especially the unabridged versions of the books on CD.

OverDrive is an online service available only through a library website. It is something that needs to be managed and marketed. According to OverDrive, more than 30% of its users rarely or never set foot in the library building (Orr, 2011, p. 36). This means that many users need to be marketed to through other venues—the website, Facebook, Twitter, print ads, billboards, or whatever works to get to them. With 6–7% of the collection development budget going to digital media and with circulation of digital materials increasing, there has to be a resultant marketing effort to get patrons to use OverDrive. The belief that the September 2011 rollout of Kindles to the OverDrive family will increase circulation is great; however, not all of the digital publishers are on board with allowing their products to be checked out (Orr, 2011).

How libraries manage the digital portion of their collection, from cataloging it through offering downloads, is important to the patrons' customer service experience. If the process is complex and difficult to traverse, what's the point of even downloading that first book to their e-reader or computer? The library management team, whether it is in a public, academic, or special library, needs to make it as transparent and easy as possible. Frequently asked question (FAQ) primers should be set up at every reader or computer, and someone should be available who can walk novices through the process. This service is as important to some patrons as storytelling is to the toddlers. If the parents and the child have a poor experience, do you think they will be back?

Another important consideration is the Digital Millennium Copyright Act (DMCA) and what it means to everything digitized. The DMCA restores copyright protection of preexisting works from World Intellectual Property Organization (WIPO) member countries that had fallen into public domain in the United States but not in their home countries (U.S. Copyright Office, 1998). DMCA also prevents the circumvention of technology on such manufactured items as DVD or CD players that would enable someone to manufacture copies of DVDs or CDs for distribution (U.S. Copyright Office, 1998). This statement is not an attempt to demonize publishers. They are for-profit companies, and their end goal is to make a profit, which means figuring out a good price for their product. In the past, publishers would sell books and other media to libraries without worrying about the amount of use. Once a book is in a library, it can be checked out and used until it is removed from the collection because it is no longer used or because it has been worn out. Tangible media (books, CDs, etc.) have the copyright transferred to the library through the right of first ownership. Books and media in digital formats do not have the same physically limited life span. The only way a digital book "wears out" is if the server crashes or the file is corrupted. Digital works have the potential for almost unlimited use. Publishers, recognizing this fact, have begun to negotiate with libraries about the number of uses a digital title can have before it expires. This negotiation is ongoing, as there is still a significant distance between what publishers and libraries consider an "acceptable" number of uses.

SOCIAL MEDIA

As the tools to access the Internet have increased, so have the ways for individuals to interact online. Early on, e-mail and discussion boards were the main methods of online communication. Over the past 10 years, social media such as Skype, Facebook, and Twitter have altered the way in which people communicate and keep in touch. Individuals and groups can now interact with friends, family, and the workplace without ever leaving the computer. Although libraries already provide access to these media on computers and through wireless connections, we also need to take advantage of these opportunities to present ourselves and our services to the community. How can we, as LIS professionals, use these technologies to our advantage? What might be introduced in the future that libraries can use to maintain a relationship with the community?

In essence, technology has begun to change the ways that library managers must consider the delivery of services, collection development, and relationships with vendors. The methods will continue to evolve as new technologies are introduced and the perceptions and expectations of information change within society. However, despite these changes, libraries will still have to provide traditional services as needed by their communities. Just focusing on technology, particularly computers and the digital world, is ignoring a significant part of the population, those who either do not have access to technology or have chosen to not use technology. Our "traditional" services may be diminishing, but they are not going away. Libraries will still need to help people face to face, provide physical materials—particularly those that are not digitized—and create a comfortable space for users. Good managers know that while they have to plan for future trends, they cannot simply ignore or abandon what they've done in the past. Both future expectations and past successes must be evaluated in order to make good, educated decisions about what works, what might work, and what you can do now.

DIVERSITY

The last topic we want to touch on is diversity. Although an entire chapter in this book discusses the importance of diversity to the future of libraries, it is a concept that needs to be mentioned one more time. Diversity in society seems to be constantly increasing. This is not because our society is becoming more diverse but because we as a people are recognizing the many unique characteristics among individuals in society. As a manager, this means that you need to understand the role of diversity in your words, your actions, and your plans. No matter how homogeneous a group of employees may be, there is something unique about each individual. This is not limited to employees but also applies to the larger community. Differences in outlooks and in expectations of libraries are caused by many things, including socioeconomic standing, cultural mores, generational grouping, religious affiliations, family life, social cliques, and educational attainment, to name a few. This is not something to be wary of but rather something to embrace. Diversity provides amazing opportunities. The important thing to remember is not that differences exist but that these unique attributes can help us be innovative, identify new ideas, and recognize opportunities.

This chapter is a quick and basic overview of some concepts to consider in the future. There is so much more out there that we haven't covered, because each community will have its own changes and trends. As a manager, it is your job to pay attention, look beyond your own organization, and question your own assumptions in order to identify trends in society and the expectations of your community.

References

Bertot, J. C., McClure, C. R., Wright, C. B., Jensen, E., & Thomas, S. (2009). *Public libraries and the Internet 2009: Study results and findings.* Tallahassee, FL:

College of Information, Information Use Management & Policy Institute, Florida State University. Retrieved from www.ii.fsu.edu/content/view/full/6062

Breeding, M. (2011, November). Ebook lending: Asserting the value of libraries as the future of books unfolds. *Computers in Libraries, 31*(9), 24–27.

Drucker, P. (1990). *Managing the non-profit organization: Principles and practices.* New York, NY: Harper Collins.

Dunneback, K. (2011, Summer). E-books and readers' advisory. *Reference and User Services Quarterly, 50*(4), 325–329.

Hussey, L. K., & Velasquez, D. L. (2011, December). Forced advocacy: How communities respond to library budget cuts. In A. Woodsworth (Ed.), *Advances in librarianship: Librarianship in times of crisis* (Vol. 33). New York, NY: Emerald.

Kelley, M. (2011, September 1). New book industry survey shows robust e-book sales. *Library Journal, 136*(14), 12, 14.

Moore, G. E. (1965, April). Cramming more components onto integrated circuits. *Electronics, 38*(8). Retrieved from http://download.intel.com/museum/Moores_Law/Articles-Press_Releases/Gordon_Moore_1965_Article.pdf

Orr, C. (2011, September 15). The digital shift: Secrets of e-book success. *Library Journal, 136*(15), 34–36.

Public Libraries. (2011, November 4). Rahm Emanuel reduces size of Chicago library cut. PublicLibraries.com. Retrieved from www.publiclibraries.com/blog/rahm-emanuel-reduces-size-of-chicago-library-cuts

Spielman, F. (2011, October 11). Emanuel to cut Chicago libraries' hours. *Chicago Sun-Times.* Retrieved from www.suntimes.com/news/metro/8156275–418/emanuel-to-cut-chicago-libraries-hours.html

U.S. Copyright Office. (1998, December). *The Digital Millennium Copyright Act of 1998: U.S. Copyright Office summary.* Retrieved from www.copyright.gov/legislation/dmca.pdf

Velasquez, D. L. (2010, December). E-government and public access computers in public libraries. In A. Woodsworth (Ed.), *Advances in librarianship: Exploring the digital frontier* (Vol. 31, pp. 111–132). New York, NY: Emerald.

White, H. S. (1996, February 15). Our strategy for saving libraries: Add water to the thin soup. *Library Journal, 121*(3), 126–127.

Further Reading on Future Trends

Blowers, H. (2012, September). Measuring social media and the greater digital landscape. *Computers in Libraries, 32*(7), 27–29.

Gall, D. (2012, August). Librarian like a rock star: Using your personal brand to promote your services and reach distant users. *Journal of Library Administration, 52*(6/7), 549–559.

Herther, N. K. (2011). The sizzling e-book marketplace, part one: E-reader devices. *Searcher, 19*(3), 44–47.

Mallet, E. (2010). A screen too far? Findings from an e-book reader pilot. *Serials, 23*(2), 140–144.

Moyer, J. E., & Thiele, J. (2012). E-books and readers in public libraries: Literature review and case study. *New Library World, 113*(5/6), 262–269.

Nazari, M., & Webber, S. (2012, June). Loss of faith in the origins of information literacy in e-environments: Proposal of a holistic approach. *Journal of Librarianship and Information Science, 44*(2), 99–107.

Pattuelli, M. C., & Rabina, D. (2010). Forms, effects, function: LIS students' attitudes towards portable e-book readers. *Aslib Proceedings, 62*(3), 228–244.

Stagg, A., & Kimmins, L. (2012). Research skills development through collaborative virtual learning environment. *Reference Services Review, 40*(1), 61–74.

GLOSSARY

Abilene paradox. A phenomenon associated with group dynamics, particularly group decision making, wherein groups are unable to make a solid decision or the decision made is weak and ineffective. This often results from individuals understanding the situation but failing to communicate their desires and beliefs for fear of appearing contrary and out of a desire to be part of the group. The end result is a bad decision, one that is often counterproductive, and the group's members end up frustrated and dissatisfied by the process. *See also* GROUPTHINK.

ADA. *See* AMERICANS WITH DISABILITIES ACT (ADA).

administrative management. A set of theories that emphasizes the manager and the functions of modern management, which are divided into planning and decision making, organizing, leading, and controlling. These theories stress the importance of clear lines of authority and communication, as well as limited span of control, or having supervisors and managers oversee fewer individuals in order to better control and direct work.

Age Discrimination Act of 1967. A federal act that prohibits employers from discriminating against persons over the age of 40 in decisions about hiring, promotion, termination, compensation of terms, conditions, or privileges of employment. Age discrimination is also regulated by the Equal Employment Opportunity Commission (EEOC).

Americans with Disabilities Act of 1990 (ADA). A federal act that prohibits employers with more than 15 employees to discriminate against qualified individuals based on a disability and requires that employers make "reasonable accommodations" for employees with disabilities.

assessment. The process or means of evaluating work using data collected through a formal process whereby goals are defined and evidence is gathered to be used to develop, assess, or improve a plan. *See also* EVALUATION.

background checks. Investigations into a potential employee's job qualifications that are initiated by employers prior to offering employment with the prospective employee's knowledge and permission, including a criminal background check to determine whether a person has a felony record, an educational background check to verify a person's educational degrees, and a financial background check to ensure that the person has never embezzled or had major problems with money.

balanced scorecard. A performance management tool used in planning and implementation that examines four perspectives—the customer, internal business, innovation and learning, and finances—with measures indicating progress grouped by perspective and linked to institutional goals. *See also* STAKEHOLDER ANALYSIS and STORYBOARD.

bandwidth. The carrying capacity of any given communications system through some type of cable, such as copper, coaxial, or fiber-optic cable.

behavioral norms. The accepted and expected actions, processes, and procedures within a group or organization that act as standards but are often not written or explicitly stated. The expectations associated with these norms are identified when one or more members of the group or organization do or say something that does not conform with them. The corrections may be explicitly pointed out and explained, or they may take the form of ostracizing behavior against those who violate the norms.

behavioral school of management. A set of management theories that focuses on the employee and how to increase employee productivity through psychological techniques rather than the rules and regulations posited by such theories as scientific management. The role of the social world and employee satisfaction are central to these theories.

brand/branding. The use of a name, term, sign, symbol, or design to identify the goods or services of one seller or a group of sellers, agencies, and nonprofits and to differentiate them for their competitors (e.g., the road sign used to signify that there is a library in a particular town).

bureaucratic management. A management theory based on the work of Max Weber that defines efficient and effective management through a strictly defined hierarchy governed by clearly defined regulations and lines of authority. The goal of bureaucracy is a predictable, systematic, impersonal organization wherein control is based on authority and expertise and the organization is broken down into clearly differentiated spheres of competency and control that are organized into a well-established hierarchy. This theory of management depends on a rational-legal authority in which all functions and offices are governed by well-defined and codified rules.

capital budget. A budget in which funds are expended for capital improvements such as building expansions, new facilities, or remodeling and the budget is amortized over a 20- to 30-year time line.

cause analysis tools. Assessment tools that assist in the discovery of the cause of or potential for a problem or situation during the planning and programming phase. Common tools include contingency diagrams, which utilize brainstorming to anticipate problems, and force field analysis, which identifies the positive and negative forces that will support or restrain an action.

cause-related marketing. Marketing efforts that link an agency's or nonprofit's contributions to a designated cause to customers' engaging directly or indirectly in revenue-producing transactions (e.g., a telethon raising funds for a particular disease).

CCT. *See* COMPULSORY COMPETITIVE TENDERING (CCT).

charismatic leadership theory. A leadership theory that revolves around the person in the position of leadership and his or her personal characteristics, which may help drive staff, patrons, and others to want to follow his or her goals for the organization. Seen as magnetic, exciting, and energizing, charismatic leaders are at the heart of the success of an organization. Although they have great potential for positive influence, charismatic leaders can also be very destructive through narcissistic tendencies and the ability to motivate followers to follow blindly based on a persuasive personality.

Children's Internet Protection Act (CIPA). Enacted by Congress in 2000, a federal act that requires filtering of computers in schools and libraries when receiving federal funding to protect against pornography. *See also* SON OF CIPA LAWS.

CIPA. *See* CHILDREN'S INTERNET PROTECTION ACT (CIPA).

Civil Rights Act of 1964. A federal act that, under Title VII—Equal Employment Opportunities, protects an employee from discrimination based on national origin, race, color, religion, and sex (gender), with enhancements and improvements being made following congressional and federal court actions. All rights under this act are regulated by the Equal Employment Opportunity Commission (EEOC).

closed system. A system, such as an organization, that is self-contained and separate from its environment, with strong boundaries existing between the organization and the environment. Most closed systems do not rely on their environment for functioning because it has no influence on how the system functions; the environment cannot introduce anything into the system and thus the system can be picked up and moved to any location. *See also* OPEN SYSTEM.

COBRA. *See* CONSOLIDATED OMNIBUS BUDGET RECONCILIATION ACT (COBRA)

communication models. Attempts by theorists to provide visualizations of the communication process, most of which include the concepts of sender, receiver, message, channel, noise, and feedback as the basic elements of communication.

community. The people whom an organization serves, be they the inhabitants of the geographic area (e.g., in public libraries) or the specialized groups who belong to specific institutions (e.g., in academic libraries); also, the city, village, town, or county in which an organization is located.

compulsory competitive tendering (CCT). A cost-saving effort in place in the 1980s and 1990s in the United Kingdom and Australia that required some public services be offered up for bid to the private sector.

confidentiality. A principle of discretion employed in many professions to protect the content of personal and work-related communications and transactions from intrusion by outside agencies.

Consolidated Omnibus Budget Reconciliation Act (COBRA). A federal act that gives workers and their families who lose their health benefits the right to choose to continue their group health coverage with their group provider for 18 months under certain circumstances, such as voluntary or involuntary job loss, reduction in hours worked, transition between jobs, death, divorce, and other life events. Qualified individuals are required to pay the entire premium for coverage up to 102 percent of the cost of the plan.

contingency theory. A theory of management and leadership which states that there is no one best way to manage and that, instead, leaders need to look at each situation individually and fit their leadership style to suit the circumstances. The theory developed from the work of Mary Parker Follett and Joan Woodward, both of whom recognized that there was no one best way to structure or manage an organization and that managers and leaders must consider characteristics such as organization size, technology used, location, and environment.

contracting. *See* OUTSOURCING.

core services. Those services deemed to be essential to an organization, for example, cataloging, reference, and collection development in libraries.

data collection and analysis tools. Assessment tools that are used to collect and analyze data, such as surveys and sampling to identify users' needs; understand users' opinions, behavior, and knowledge; and measure reactions to products and services.

Digital Millennium Copyright Act of 1998 (DMCA). A federal act passed to close some holes in the Copyright Act of 1976, bringing the United States up-to-date with the World Intellectual Property Organization (WIPO) Copyright and Performances and Phonograms Treaties Implementation Act of 1998 that placed some works once in the U.S. public domain back under copyright coverage. The DMCA also addresses DVD and CD players by prohibiting tampering with the technology for the purposes of copying DVDs and CDs for distribution. A miscellaneous section of the act covers distance education, exemptions for nonprofit libraries, webcasting of sound recordings on the Internet, and vessel hull design protection.

diversity. Difference between and among various groups and individuals that can range from something as minor as reading preferences or hobbies all the way to fundamental differences in ethnic heritage, religious beliefs, and socioeconomic background. This wide range of possible definitions contributes to the complexity and confusion that often accompanies diversity initiatives.

divine right. One of the original theories of leadership which stated that people are born into leadership, that their position of power in society is ordained, a theory used to justify the rule and power of the monarchy.

DMCA. *See* DIGITAL MILLENNIUM COPYRIGHT ACT OF 1998 (DMCA).

effective listening. The practice of listening and paying attention when others are speaking that includes not only hearing others but also attending to facial expressions and body language as well as asking questions or restating comments to ensure a shared understanding of the message being conveyed.

Elementary and Secondary Education Act (ESEA). A federal law that, under Title III—Supplemental Educational Centers and Services, allows grants to schools that can be used for technology in the form of computers and peripherals.

e-marketing. Efforts to inform customers as well as communicate, promote, and sell products and services via the Internet and related technology.

ESEA. *See* ELEMENTARY AND SECONDARY EDUCATION ACT (ESEA).

ethics. Related to morals and moral philosophy, a system of delineating the principles of right and wrong behavior for members of groups to follow.

evaluation. The process of developing a judgment about the amount, number, or value of something in order to decide whether stated goals and objectives have been met and whether the outcomes were successful. The typical approach is to collect qualitative and quantitative data about an organization's services, programs, and products to see if they are meeting the needs of users. *See also* ASSESSMENT.

evaluation and decision-making tools. Assessment tools that help narrow down a group of choices or evaluate how well an organization has done something. Common tools are the decision matrix, which evaluates and prioritizes options using weighted criteria, and the paired comparison, which narrows a list of options to the most popular choice.

exempt (employees). Term used to describe certain employees who are exempt from overtime pay provisions and minimum wage according to the Federal Labor Standards Act. *See also* NONEXEMPT (EMPLOYEES).

Family and Medical Leave Act (FMLA). A federal act that allows employees with one year or more of service with an employer to take up to 12 weeks of unpaid leave for certain medical and family situations (e.g., adoption, caring for a parent), with coverage extending to either the employee or a member of the covered and eligible employee's immediate family. However, in many instances, paid leave may be substituted for unpaid FMLA leave.

Federal Depository Library Program (FDLP). Established by Congress to ensure that the American public has access to its government's information by providing depository libraries to safeguard the public's right to know and collecting, organizing, maintaining, preserving, and assisting users with information from the federal government. The FDLP provides government information at no cost to designated depository libraries throughout the country and territories, which in turn provide local, professional, impartial, and no-fee access to government information.

flowchart. A process analysis tool that presents a picture of the steps in a process in sequential order to show how a process is done or to identify areas of improvement.

FMLA. *See* FAMILY AND MEDICAL LEAVE ACT (FMLA).

focus group. A panel of six to ten people who are carefully selected and brought together to discuss various topics of interests. Many libraries that are considering an expansion will hold a focus group of community members to determine whether the expansion would be considered in a positive or negative light for the overall area.

Foundation Center. An online-based organization that provides the means to research grant programs and fundraising opportunities through access to national, state, and metropolitan area data about U.S. foundations and their grants, including information on the assets available, how grant dollars are distributed, and the top grant recipients.

Gantt chart. Created by scientific management theorist Henry Gantt, a chart used to track worker productivity versus expectations. Originally used to tie worker productivity to management's or supervisors' bonuses, the chart is now used in project management to illustrate project start and end dates, usually separating out each step and showing dependent relationships among the tasks.

Genetic Information Nondiscrimination Act of 2008 (GINA). A federal law that prohibits discrimination in health coverage and employment based on genetic information and provides a baseline level of protection against genetic discrimination for all Americans. Some states already have laws that protect against genetic discrimination in health insurance and employment situations, but the degrees of protection provided vary widely. All entities that are subject to GINA must, at a minimum, comply with all applicable GINA requirements and may also need to comply with more restrictive state laws.

GINA. *See* GENETIC INFORMATION NONDISCRIMINATION ACT OF 2008 (GINA).

goals. Statements about general aims or purposes that are broad, long-range intended outcomes or long-term visions, used primarily in policy making and general program planning.

groupthink. A phenomenon associated with group dynamics, particularly group decision making, wherein the group or team is dominated by an idea or expectation, and the members of the group end up agreeing with plans or policies even though these are shown to be ineffective. Any contrary view is dismissed, often disparagingly, and the focus remains firmly on the group's agreed-upon choice. *See also* ABILENE PARADOX.

Hawthorne experiments. A set of experiments carried out by Elton Mayo, Fritz Roethlisberger, W. J. Dickson, and W. Lloyd Warner at the Hawthorne Works in Cicero, Illinois, in order to assess the impacts of environmental conditions, rest periods, and other factors on the productivity of employees. These experiments identified the influence of social concepts, such as cliques and peer pressure, in the workplace.

Health Insurance Portability and Accountability Act (HIPAA). A federal act that provides rights and protections for participants and beneficiaries in group health plans, including protections for coverage under group health plans to limit exclusions for preexisting conditions, prohibiting discrimination against employees and their dependents based on their health status, and allowing a special opportunity for individuals to enroll in a new plan under certain circumstances.

HIPAA. *See* HEALTH INSURANCE PORTABILITY AND ACCOUNTABILITY ACT (HIPAA).

horizontal communication. Organizational communication that happens between and among departments at the same level in an organizational hierarchy, including collaboration between departments and project teams, meetings with other individuals in similar positions in other departments, and supervisor or manager meetings. *See also* VERTICAL COMMUNICATION.

HRM. *See* HUMAN RESOURCES MANAGEMENT (HRM).

human resources management (HRM). A type of management that involves everything related to hiring, retaining, disciplining, losing, and firing staff.

IMLS. *See* INSTITUTE OF MUSEUM AND LIBRARY SERVICES (IMLS).

in loco parentis. The legal doctrine under which an individual assumes parental rights, duties, and obligations without going through the formalities of legal adoption; most commonly used in relation to teachers and students.

individual ambivalence. The process an individual experiences as he or she balances his or her individual identity with his or her identity as a member of a group, a team, or an organization. Individuals must deal with the conflicting forces of maintaining individual identity while at the same time surrendering part of their identity to the larger group, team, or organizational identity.

input measures. Descriptive statistics about an organization's resources that are often reported to outside agencies and officials, governmental and otherwise, for use in planning, evaluation, policy making, and funding decisions. *See also* OUTPUT MEASURES.

Institute of Museum and Library Services (IMLS). A U.S. federal agency whose mission is to inspire and support museums and libraries through providing federal money for major impact projects and supplying cash to states to distribute as LSTA (Library Services and Technology Act) grants via state libraries.

integrity. Related to ethics, the concept of consistency in thought, word, and deed leading to development of an honest and consistent character.

job description. A formal description of an available position that includes job title, pay grade or schedule, identification of job, educational requirements, summary of job duties, activities and procedures, relationship of job to the institution, and job requirements; often also includes the line "any other duties as assigned" as a safeguard against any omissions in the description.

LibQUAL+. A survey developed by the Association of Research Libraries (ARL) to define and measure library service quality across institutions by examining the service attitude of staff, access to information, and the library as place, with a focus on the interaction between the user and the service provider using the baps model of service quality.

Library Services and Technology Act (LSTA). A federal act signed into law in 1996 by President Bill Clinton that provides for grants to public libraries that are managed through the state libraries.

line item budget. A budget in which each line item—expense category—has a certain amount of money designated to it.

LSTA. *See* LIBRARY SERVICES AND TECHNOLOGY ACT (LSTA).

management by objectives (MBO). A management strategy in which managers and employees agree on a set of objects for the organization and the employees work with managers to define individual goals within these objectives.

marketing. Activities and processes undertaken to communicate the value of an organization's products and services to the client base, stakeholders, and the community at large.

MBO. *See* MANAGEMENT BY OBJECTIVES (MBO).

mental models. The ways in which individuals perceive and understand the world around them, often formed from deeply ingrained, unspoken, or unconscious assumptions that are shaped by individuals' experience, cultural background, education, and position within an organization.

metainformation. Information about information, commonly composed of headings, indexing terms, or classification systems imposed to enhance information retrieval.

millage. The amount per $1,000 that is used to calculate taxes on property. The library portion of property tax is usually a percentage or mill of the taxes levied.

mission statement. A brief statement about an organization's purpose or reason for existing that guides the organization's activities that should demonstrate the organization's opportunities, competence, and commitment.

narrative mediation. A form of conflict resolution that requires the conflicting parties to participate in an open dialogue with a mediator, during which the conflicting parties are allowed to tell the story of the conflict from their point of view without interruption from the opposing side or sides. The individual stories are not labeled right or wrong but accepted as each side's perceived reality, and the mediator then breaks down each story to identify the common pieces and characteristics across the stories. Using these commonalities, the mediator works with the conflicting parties to create a common story and understanding of the conflict, which then acts as a basis for building a solution that is accepted by all parties involved in the conflict.

neoliberalism. An economic term describing a focus on deregulation, the privatization of public sectors and agencies, the limiting of social safety nets, and a belief in the supremacy of a laissez-faire approach to markets.

new public management (NPM). A component of neoliberalism focused on public policy that emphasizes managing government services like private businesses, with an additional focus on contracting for services that have historically been provided through public agencies. Proponents perceive government structures as large and cumbersome and government workers as lacking incentive to perform at a high level of efficiency.

nonexempt (employees). A term used to describe employees who are eligible for overtime and minimum wage payments according to the Federal Labor Standards Act. *See also* EXEMPT (EMPLOYEES).

NPM. *See* NEW PUBLIC MANAGEMENT (NPM).

objectives. Brief, clear statements that describe desired outcomes, with attention focused on the specific types of performances that are expected to demonstrate that these outcomes were attained; also, measurable, time-targeted, and benchmarked statements that define what is to be accomplished through a specific project and the activities necessary to achieve the outcomes.

Occupational Safety and Health Act (OSHA). A federal act that entitles all employees to safe work environments free from workplace hazards, with guidelines and procedures for what employees can do in the event of violations as well as different rules and regulations for employers, from fines to closing down the work site, to ensure that identified work hazards are dealt with properly.

open access software. Also known by the name *open source software,* software that is not owned by any corporation but is freely available on the web for anyone to use. Open source software is written by a consortium of programmers who work on it for free and keep the software up-to-date.

open system. A system that has a reciprocal relationship with its environment through limited, permeable boundaries that allow direct interaction with the environment so that influences can be both proactive and reactive. Such direct interaction with the environment provides the system with opportunities for feedback and the potential for innovation and growth. *See also* CLOSED SYSTEM.

operations budget. A budget that covers the resources needed to run the library on a daily, weekly, monthly, or quarterly basis.

organizational change. The process of introducing new ideas, new policies, new routines, and/or new individuals into an existing organization and thereby causing a shift or alteration to the existing accepted processes and procedures. Change can be both incremental and radical.

organizational change model. Based on Kurt Lewin's three-stage change process: the first step, unfreezing, involves identifying the need for change, planning, setting goals, and implementing the change; in the next step, change/transition, the organization goes through the process of incorporating the change, relearning routines, and making corrections or alterations as implementation continues; the last step, refreezing, takes place as this chaos evolves into some kind of order once the change is fully implemented and a new way of functioning is developed and adopted as part of the status quo.

organizational culture. The atmosphere and feel of an organization, its accumulated shared learning as well as its organizational structures and environment.

OSHA. *See* OCCUPATIONAL SAFETY AND HEALTH ACT (OSHA).

output measures. Statistics or measures that describe how an institution is used or utilized by examining such things as counts and use per capita of services, user satisfaction, and the degree to which products and services are used. *See also* INPUT MEASURES.

outsourcing. The contracting of any service an organization normally performs in house with its own staff and resources to an outside service provider that is often a for-profit business.

plan. A blueprint that specifies the resource allocation, schedules, and other actions necessary for attaining goals.

POSDCORB. An administrative management theory developed by Luther Gulick, this acronym defines the functions of management as planning, organizing, staffing, directing, coordinating, reporting, and budgeting.

power theory. Based on the work of Machiavelli and his book *The Prince*, a theory which states that a leader is a leader because of the successful utilization of power from any power base. The use of power not only will propel the person into a position as a leader but will also serve to sustain the person in that position. The role of the leader is to maintain and preserve the state (or the organization), which requires the leader to work outside of society's expectations for morality and behavior, and, thus, the leader is not judged by the same norms and morals as others.

privatization. Similar to outsourcing, the contracting out of services to the private market for service provision, generally used in reference to government services but applicable to other organizations as well, under an agreement that transfers control over policy decisions and management to an external, often for-profit agency.

process. A series of actions or steps taken to achieve an objective.

process analysis tools. Assessment tools used when an organization wants to understand an overall work process or some part of this process. Common tools include flowcharts, which use pictures of the process steps in sequential order, and work flow diagrams, which illustrate movement through a process.

process consultation. As a psychodynamic analysis of an organization, a process that looks beyond just the policy, structure, and artifacts of an organization to consider the motivations of leadership and employees and how these work together to form the organization.

progressive discipline. A disciplinary system that follows a set pattern of steps in the event of a discipline problem in the workplace: first, a verbal warning from the supervisor to the employee that is documented by the supervisor, dated, and put in the employee's file with a 45- to 60-day limit on fixing the problem; next, a written warning to the employee that has been completed and typically signed by the supervisor's boss with a 60- to 90-day limit on resolving the problem along with a notice that the issuing of a final warning could mean termination; finally, the final warning to the employee with a time limit of 30 days to solve the problem along with notice that failure to do so will lead to extreme consequences, up to and including termination.

project planning and implementation tools. Assessment tools used for managing and improving projects. Common tools are the balanced scorecard, stakeholder analysis, and storyboards. See also BALANCED SCORECARD, STAKEHOLDER ANALYSIS, and STORYBOARD.

qualitative research. Research that entails using nonnumeric data or measures such as observations, focus groups, or interviews.

quantitative research. Research that entails using numeric data or measures such as surveys, mathematical modeling, or variable designs.

resource-based conflict. A type of conflict that focuses on disagreements regarding available resources wherein the conflicting sides have differing perceptions of how much each party deserves and/or should receive of the resources.

scalar chain of authority. Straight chain of command from the top to the bottom of an organization that clearly defines lines of authority and communication from administration to the lowest levels of the organization.

scientific management. A management theory that defines management as a science and focuses on efficiency, with the goal of breaking down the work process to find One Best Way to complete the work. Workers receive training in the best way to increase productivity and are expected to be motivated by the ability to increase their productivity and thereby receive a monetary reward. This theory is generally considered the first of the modern management theories.

server. Hardware used to serve information to computers that are connected to it, allowing users to access programs, files, and other information stored on the server. Common servers are web servers, mail servers, and local area network (LAN) servers.

situational ethics. Decision making based upon the circumstances of a particular situation, and not upon fixed rules or regulations.

situational leadership theory. The theory that leadership is dependent on the situation, that different circumstances require different types of leadership, and that the level of leadership provided depends on the task at hand and the maturity of the followers. Thus, leaders must tailor their approach based on the skills required and the maturity of the employees being supervised within the organization.

SMART. An acronym used in goal setting to help focus goals and make them useful, the letters of which stand for *specific, measurable, achievable, realistic,* and *timely.*

Son of CIPA laws. In different states and cities, the more stringent filtering laws passed for public schools and public libraries regarding pornography and other information that are tied to funding and thereby force entities receiving money to place filters (sometimes the filter type mandated by the funder) on computers. *See also* CHILDREN'S INTERNET PROTECTION ACT (CIPA).

stages of group development. The four stages that each group or team goes through as the members transition from a collection of individuals into a cohesive and functioning unit, known as forming, storming, norming, and performing.

stakeholder. Someone with an interest, often financial, in ensuring the success of an organization.

stakeholder analysis. A project management tool used in planning and implementation that identifies groups or individuals with an interest in an issue to improve areas based on stakeholder needs and the perspectives of all parties. *See also* BALANCED SCORECARD and STORYBOARD.

storyboard. A project management tool used in planning and implementation that employs a series of sketches or scenes representing specific activities that are arranged in sequence to outline proposed actions. *See also* BALANCED SCORECARD and STAKEHOLDER ANALYSIS.

strategic planning. The process of looking into the future, figuring out where to go, and deciding how to get there; usually a multiyear plan that potentially looks five years into the future.

SWOT analysis. An analysis that assesses the current state of your library by examining the following aspects of the internal and external environments: strengths, weaknesses, opportunities, and threats.

synergy. The idea that the whole is more than just the sum of its parts; a concept used in systems theory. *See also* SYSTEMS THEORY.

systems theory. A theory that considers organizations or processes in terms of their parts and the relationships among those parts. The theory takes an overall, big-picture view of organizations as complex and multidimensional entities that incorporate individual pieces, with a focus on the shared functions and relationships among the pieces as well as the avenues for communication and feedback. *See also* SYNERGY.

total quality management (TQM). A management theory that focuses on continual quality improvement by building quality in the workplace through understanding and defining quality, reviewing and revising procedures through analysis and assessment, indentifying new ways to introduce quality, and ensuring that quality is achieved at each stage of the organization.

TQM. *See* TOTAL QUALITY MANAGEMENT (TQM).

trait theory. An early leadership theory that tries to identify the common traits of leaders so that relevant traits for good leaders could be defined and people having those traits could be identified as leaders.

transactional leadership theory. A theory that defines leadership as more of a give-and-take situation between leaders and followers, with followers giving their obedience to leaders and following directions based on expected rewards from the leader—a "tit for tat" system of motivation and reward. Rather than being leadership, this theory is more often related to management.

transformational leadership theory. A theory which posits that the leader's focus should be on developing relationships with followers in order to help motivate, empower, and positively transform them. A motivational leadership style is one that involves presenting a clear organizational vision and inspiring employees to work toward this vision through establishing connections with employees, understanding employees' needs, and helping employees reach their potential. Transformational leaders are often seen as highly ethical and moral individuals as they must model the behaviors they hope to inspire in others. The transformational leader's focus is external from the self, concentrating on others and how to help others.

USA PATRIOT Act. A law passed in 2001 following the September 11, 2001, terrorist attacks that reduced restrictions on law enforcement's ability to gather information in the name of national security, thereby restricting the concept of confidentiality for such businesses as libraries, bookstores, and financial institutions.

value. Related to ethics, the concept of something being of quality; in other words, worthy, important, and useful.

vertical communication. Organizational communication that travels along vertical lines within an organizational hierarchy, including communications both from the top of the organizational hierarchy downward to lower levels of the organization and from the lower levels of the organization upward to the higher levels of the hierarchy. *See also* HORIZONTAL COMMUNICATION.

vision statement. A positive, aspirational statement that describes what an organization does and what its service focus is for the community

visual diversity. Diversity achieved through hiring individuals with easily identifiable racial or ethnic characteristics, such as skin color, facial features, body type, or other easily observed differences, that differ from the majority within an organization or society. Visual diversity can also be seen as the process of tokenism, hiring or including individuals solely on the basis of their race, ethnicity, or other unique characteristic.

Wi-Fi. Short for *wireless fidelity,* a wireless networking technology that allows computers and other devices to communicate using a wireless signal.

WIPO. *See* WORLD INTELLECTUAL PROPERTY ORGANIZATION (WIPO).

wireless connection. Transmission of data via a wireless card to a wireless router that is based on the Wi-Fi standard, with the wireless routers being connected to a network, cable modem, or DSL modem to provide Internet access to anyone connected to the wireless network.

World Intellectual Property Organization (WIPO). A UN organization with a mandate from its member states to promote the protection of intellectual property throughout the world through cooperation among states and in collaboration with other international organizations.

zero-based budget. A budget based on a yearly cycle that begins with a totally clean slate, rather than working off of last year's actual numbers, with each budget line filled in with current numbers and each director or department head figuring out what he or she plans to spend for the next year. The goal is to spend to the penny every dollar and cent received with revenue equal to expenses and a balance of zero at the end of the year.

CONTRIBUTORS

Lenora Berendt is director of the Berkeley Public Library in Berkeley, Illinois, and an adjunct instructor in the Graduate School of Library and Information Science at Dominican University in River Forest, Illinois. She teaches reference, Internet fundamentals, user instruction, and collection management. Her research interests focus on user education, emerging technologies, and library marketing. Ms. Berendt received her MLIS from Brigham Young University and a BS in anthropology from the University of Utah.

Jennifer Campbell-Meier is assistant professor at the University of Alabama's School of Library and Information Studies, teaching in the areas of information services, management, and information technologies. Her research focuses on stakeholder groups involved in project planning and project management, recently concentrating on the development of institutional repositories. Dr. Campbell-Meier has published and presented on the topics of institutional repositories, information literacy, and information services. Over the past dozen years she has been active in community, scholarly, and professional services, including library board membership, leadership on campus committees, and involvement in state library programs and library associations.

Catherine Hakala-Ausperk is a library administrator, advocate, speaker and trainer who believes the future of our libraries depends on strong library leadership. She is currently executive director of the Northeast Ohio Regional Library System (NEO-RLS). A frequent speaker at national and state conferences, staff days, and workshops, she is a 27-year public library veteran and an adjunct faculty member of Kent State University's School of Library and Information Science. Hakala-Ausperk has been a contributor and guest editor for ALA-APA's *Library Worklife*; her book, *Be a Great Boss: One Year to Success,* was published in 2011 by ALA Editions. She is proud to be an Ohio Certified Public Librarian and an American Library Association Certified Public Library Administrator (CPLA). You can reach the author via her website, http://librariesthrive.com, or via e-mail at chakalaausperk@gmail.com.

Heather Hill is assistant professor at the University of Western Ontario, in London, Ontario, Canada. Her interests focus on the concept of *public* and what that means in a commodified society. A particular phenomenon of interest is public libraries: the place they hold in their communities, their relationships with the broader local governance structure, and the effects changing legislation have on them. Her other interests center around alternative licensing through Creative Commons attribution and large-scale public digitization projects such as the Internet Archive and Project Gutenberg.

Lisa K. Hussey is assistant professor at the Graduate School of Library and Information Science at Simmons College in Boston, Massachusetts, where she has taught management for libraries and information centers, reference, project management, and ethics. Her research interests include all aspects of management, including budgeting, collaboration, and change. She has also conducted research regarding diversity in LIS. Dr. Hussey has a PhD in LIS from the University of Missouri, an MA in Information Resources and Library Science from the University of Arizona, and a BA from the University of Miami, all of which, in addition to a good education, resulted in an obsession with college sports (Go Canes! Go Wildcats! Go Tigers!). She is a lifelong baseball fan, being obsessed with the Boston Red Sox, although she is also incredibly fond of the Arizona Diamondbacks. Dr. Hussey has used her interest in sports in her teaching of management, highlighting how a sports team can be seen as a microcosm of management.

Mary Wilkins Jordan is assistant professor at Simmons College. Her teaching and research areas revolve around effective administration of libraries. Prior to entering academia she worked as a public library director and administrator and was an attorney.

INDEX

A

P

You may also be interested in

Everyday HR

A Human Resources Handbook for Academic Library Staff

GAIL MUNDE

Readers will find Munde's handbook an effective atlas of the most traveled regions of the HR terrain.

ISBN: 978-1-55570-798-9

MANAGEMENT BASICS FOR INFORMATION PROFESSIONALS, 3rd Ed.

G. Edward Evans and Camila Alire

ISBN: 978-1-55570-909-9

LIBRARY AS SAFE HAVEN

Deborah D. Halsted, Shari C. Clifton, and Daniel T. Wilson

ISBN: 978-1-55570-913-6

LEAN LIBRARY MANAGEMENT

John J. Huber

ISBN: 978-1-55570-732-3

LIBRARY MANAGEMENT TIPS THAT WORK

Edited by Carol Smallwood

ISBN: 978-0-8389-1121-1

DEFUSING THE ANGRY PATRON, 2nd Ed.

Rhea Joyce Rubin

ISBN: 978-1-55570-731-6

MANAGING LIBRARY VOLUNTEERS, 2nd Ed.

Preston Driggers and Eileen Dumas

ISBN: 978-0-8389-1064-1

CPSIA information can be obtained at www.ICGtesting.com
Printed in the USA
BVOW04s1955270714

360569BV00009BB/155/P